CONTEMPORARY POLITICAL IDEOLOGIES

CONTEMPORARY POLITICAL IDEOLOGIES

Movements and Regimes

FIFTH EDITION

ROY C. MACRIDIS

Brandeis University

HarperCollins*Publishers*

Sponsoring Editor: Lauren Silverman
Project Editor: Bob Cooper
Design Supervisor: Lucy Krikorian
Text Design: North 7 Atelier Ltd
Cover Design: Jan Kessner
Cover Illustration/Photo: Morgan Russell. *Four Part Synchromy, Number 7.* 1914–15. Four sections, overall: 15¾ × 11½ inches. Collection of Whitney Museum of American Art. Gift of the artist in memory of Gertrude V. Whitney 51.33

Photo Researcher: Mira Schachne
Production Manager/Assistant: Willie Lane/Sunaina Sehwani
Compositor: BookMasters, Inc.
Printer and Binder: R. R. Donnelley & Sons Company
Cover Printer: Lehigh Press Lithographers

Photo credits
Page 31: The Bettman Archive; pg 33: The Bettman Archive; pg 35: Radio Times Hulton Picture Library; pg 39: The Bettman Archive; pg 58: The Bettman Archive; pg 63: UPI/Bettman; pg 102: Historical Pictures Service, Inc.; pg 114: Brown Brothers; pg 118: Brown Brothers; pg 133 AP/Wide World Photos; pg 157 Wide World Photos; pg 181: UPI; pg 197: The Bettman Archive; pg 210: UPI/Bettman; pg 213: Reuters/Bettman; pg 225: National Catholic News Service; pg 226: National Catholic News Service; pg 231: Reuters/Bettman; pg 237: Kristof/NYT Pictures; pg 249: Bettman/BBC Hulton; pg 252: Schlesinger Library, Radcliffe College; pg 274: © Davis, Photo Researchers; pg 277 Johnson/NYT Pictures; pg 292: Wide World Photos; pg 307: UPI/Bettman

Contemporary Political Ideologies, Fifth Edition

Library of Congress Cataloging-in-Publication Data
Macridis, Roy C.
    Contemporary political ideologies : movements and regimes / Roy C. Macridis. — 5th ed.
        p.   cm.
    Includes bibliographical references and index.
    ISBN 0–673–52165–6
    1. Political science—History.   2. Comparative government.
I. Title.
JA81.M316   1992
320.5′09—dc20   91-19607
                                                 CIP

92 93 94 9 8 7 6 5 4 3 2

*This book is dedicated to the memory of
my late son, Peter.*

One person with a belief is a social power
equal to ninety-nine who have only interests.
JOHN STUART MILL

Contents

Preface

The fifth edition of this book, the first appeared in 1979, is an indication of the vitality of political ideologies and the interest they hold for students. Without ideology, we are almost without a conscience, without law and order, without an anchor and a port. Without ideology, we can have no vision of other worlds we want to sail to. Ideologies fashion our motivations, our attitudes, and the political regimes under which we live. They not only shape and consolidate values; they also command change and movement.

This new edition is prompted by recent ideological changes that seem to be profoundly affecting the political landscape of our world. I have expanded my discussion of economic liberalism, capitalism if you will, and at the same time have tried to discuss as objectively as possible the demise of communism both as an ideology and a system of governance. In discussing what I call the "religious impulse," I have added a section on religious fundamentalism, Muslim and Evangelical. I have also greatly expanded my discussion of nationalism and nationalist movements. It is something of an irony that two of the most common ideological staples, religion and nationalism, are regaining militancy and prominence. I expanded my chapter on feminism (is it an ideology?) and added a new chapter on environmentalism (is it likely to become one?). In my conclusion, I raise the question that has been put forth time and again: Are ideologies on the decline? Have we reached a stage at which the basic ideological precepts of democratic liberalism, freedom, equality, and brotherhood, have been realized? Have we reached a stage at which basic rights on which there is a broad consensus can be implemented and safeguarded through social legislation? I do not think ideologies are on the decline; they are very much alive, providing a vision and demanding redress of grievances. As in previous editions, I try to present various points of view as objectively as one can and, as in the previous editions, I try with each and every topic to focus on central questions that will challenge the students.

So many colleagues commented on the previous editions that the list is as long as my debt to all of them is great. For this last edition, special thanks are due to three colleagues who commented extensively on the outline of this edition. Professor David Syfert, Professor Bertil Hanson, and Professor Merlin Gustafson provided me with extensive comments on the manuscript, and I thank both warmly. Professor David Schmitt of Northeastern University again gave me his detailed comments on this edition, as he did for all previous ones, and merits special thanks. Many thanks also to Professor Jonathan Sarna of the Department of Near Eastern and Judaic Studies at Brandeis University for his helpful suggestions. Lastly, my colleague Donald Hindley was of constant help with suggestions and advice, invariably drawing my attention to errors of commission and omission.

Professor Brian Weinstein of Howard University wrote to me about my section on black separatism, giving me the reaction of his students and his own critical evaluation. Kevin L. Parker, one of the students, and some of his classmates wrote me directly and gave me the benefit of their own reactions. I thank them all and, of course, more particularly the students who took the trouble to write to me.

As in the past, I was helped by a number of graduate students. Elizabeth Wingrove, who is now completing her doctoral thesis, helped me again with the chapter on feminism; Alan Minsk, who is now completing his law degree at Georgetown, continued to send me data on the Evangelicals and on the American conservatives. Amy Higer and Michael Gumpert provided me with data and materials, the first on nationalist movements and the second on environmentalism. And again, as in the past, my warmest thanks go to Geraldyn Spaulding for typing and retyping and putting the manuscript in a readable form. Finally, I want to thank Lauren Silverman, the political science editor of HarperCollins, and her assistant Richard Smith for their help and support. Special thanks also to Robert Cooper of HarperCollins for overseeing the production of the manuscript and to Joan Bossert for the excellent copy-editing.

This book is dedicated to my late son, Peter, who turned out to have been the only "ideologue" in the family. He drowned in the Columbia River on March 11, 1978, while trying to realize a youthful dream with his friend, Tim Black, crossing the United States from West to East by canoe.

Roy C. Macridis

Chapter
1

Political Ideologies

Introduction

Olympian bards who sung
Divine ideas . . .
Which always find us young
And always keep us so

Ralph Waldo Emerson
The Poet

Whether we know it or not, all of us have an ideology, even those who claim openly that they do not. We all believe in certain things. We all value something—property, friends, the law, freedom, or authority. We all have prejudices, even those who claim to be free of them. We all look at the world in one way or another—we have "ideas" about it—and we try to make sense out of what is going on in it. Quite a few of us are unhappy, discontented, critical of what we see around us as compared to what we would like to see. Some become alienated—rejecting the society and its values, sulking into their separate and private tents but ready to spring forth into action.

People with the same ideas about the world, our society, and its values band together. We are attracted by those with similar values and ideas, who like the same things we do, who have prejudices similar to ours, and who, in general, view the world in the same way we do. We talk of "like-minded" people, individuals who share certain beliefs and tend to congregate—in clubs, churches, political parties, movements, various associations, and so on. No matter how independent we claim to be, we all are influenced by ideas. We are sensitive to appeals made to us—to our honor, patriotism, family, religion, pocketbook, race, or class—and we can all be manipulated and aroused. We are creators and creatures of ideas, of ideologies, and through them we manipulate others or are ourselves manipulated.

Ideologies are very much a part of our lives; they are not dead and they are not on the decline anywhere, as some authors have argued.

Ah, but a man's reach should exceed his grasp,
Or what's a Heaven for?

wrote Browning in 1885. Almost a century later, a strong upsurge in ideological and utopian movements made powerful governments totter as many sought their own vision of heaven on earth. "Be rational; think of the impossible" was one of the slogans of intellectuals and students in the late 1960s.

Not only are ideologies surviving, their all-embracing importance is again being recognized. "Neo-Marxists" now agree that a drastic revolutionary overhaul of the society, if there is to be one, must be above all a moral and intellectual revolution: a revolution in the *ideology* of society. It must create its own "counterconsciousness," its own "counterculture"—a new set of beliefs and values and a new style of life that will eat, like a worm, into the core of prevailing liberal–capitalist orthodoxy. Only with its ideological core gone can the old society be changed and replaced.

But "ideologies" are resilient; they persist. The core is far more resistant to change than most people had thought. Established ideas and values cannot be pulled out like a rotten tooth. They have deep roots in the soil in which they grew. While there has been so much emphasis and discussion on ideologies that either brought about change or command change, little attention has been given to the complex of values, habits, and practices that resist change—to the phenomenon that may be called *ideological conservation*. The family, the church, attachment to property and nationalisms continued to defy, as we have seen recently in the break up of Communist regimes, the Communist-revealed and imposed truths. Ideological "formation" has been continuously in conflict with ideological "preservation."

WHAT IS AN IDEOLOGY?

Ideology has been defined as "a set of closely related beliefs, or ideas, or even attitudes, characteristic of a group or community."[1] Similarly, a *political* ideology is "a set of ideas and beliefs" that people hold about their political regime and its institutions and about their own position and role in it. Political ideology accordingly appears synonymous with "political culture" or "political tradition." The British or the Americans or the French or the Russians pattern their political life on the basis of different sets of interrelated ideas, beliefs, and attitudes.

Various groups, however, within one and the same political community may, and often do, at given times and under given conditions, challenge the prevailing ideology. Interests, classes, and various political and religious associations may develop a "counter-ideology" that questions the status quo and attempts to modify it. They advocate change rather than order; they criticize or reject the political regime and the existing social and economic arrangements;

---

[1]John Plamenatz, *Ideology*, p. 15.

they advance schemes for the restructuring and reordering of the society; and they spawn political movements in order to gain enough power to bring about the changes they advocate. In this sense, a political ideology moves people into action. It motivates them to demand changes in their way of life and to modify the existing political, social, and economic relations, or it mobilizes them on how to preserve what they value. In discussing ideologies—all ideologies—we must always bear in mind these two all-important characteristics: a given political ideology rationalizes the status quo, whereas other, competing ideologies and movements challenge it.

Philosophy, Theory, and Ideology

A distinction should be made between philosophy or theory on the one hand, and ideology on the other. *Philosophy* literally means love of wisdom—the detached and often solitary contemplation and search for truth. In the strictest meaning of the terms, *theory* is the formulation of propositions that causally link variables to account for or explain a phenomenon, and such linkages should be empirically verifiable. This is, of course, true for natural scientists. They operate within a clearly defined framework of rules accepted by them all. However, in the social sciences there is not as yet an accepted framework of rules, and it is very difficult to come up with empirical verifications.

What separates theory or philosophy from ideology is that, while the first two involve contemplation, organization of ideas, and whenever possible, demonstration, ideology shapes beliefs that incite people into action. Men and women organize to *impose* certain philosophies or theories and to realize them in a given society. Ideology thus involves action and collective effort. Even when they originate (as they often do) in philosophy or theory, ideologies are inevitably highly simplified, and even distorted, versions of the original doctrines. It is always interesting to know the philosophy or the theory from which an ideology originates. But it is just as important to understand ideology as a distinct and separate entity to be studied in terms of its own logic and dynamics rather than in terms of the theory from which it stems or of how closely it resembles that theory.

It is difficult to understand when and under what circumstances a theory or a philosophy becomes transformed into an ideology—that is, into an action-oriented movement. Important theories and philosophic doctrines remain unnoticed and untouched for generations before they are "discovered." The well-known German sociologist Max Weber makes the point by indicating that theories or philosophies are "selected" to become transformed into ideologies without, however, explaining precisely how, when, and why. History may be compared to a freezer where ideas and theories are stored for use at a later time. Different works of Plato, for example, have been at various times the origin of different ideological movements. Similarly, whereas a powerful ideological movement developed from the major works of Karl Marx, it is his early works—the "early Marx" or the "young Marx"—that have been adapted to suit some contemporary movements and tastes. The same is the case with powerful religious or nationalist movements that pick and choose from different parts of the Bible or the Koran. There is a dialectic between ideas, as such, and social needs; both are indispensable in order to have an ideology. Heartfelt demands arising from the social body may fail for the lack of ideas; and ideas may go begging for a long time for the lack of relevance to social needs.

POLITICAL IDEOLOGY: THE BUILDING BLOCKS

The debt most political ideologies owe to political speculation and philosophy is quite obvious when we look at some of the major themes that political ideologies address: (1) the role and the nature of the individual (human nature); (2) the nature of truth and how it can be discovered; (3) the relationship between the individual and the group, be it the tribe, the small city–state, or the contemporary state as we know it; (4) the characteristics of political authority—its source and its limits, if any; (5) the goals and the mechanics of economic organization and the much-debated issue of material and economic equality as it relates to individual freedom. Normative judgments about each of these themes and many more are the very "stuff" of contemporary political ideologies. Some have been hotly debated over many centuries and will continue to be debated.

The Individual

Political ideologies are addressed to each one of us; they all begin with one preconception or another about us—about human nature. Some believe that we are the creatures of history and the environment, that our nature and characteristics are interwoven with the material conditions of life and ultimately shaped by them. Human nature is plastic and ever-changing and with the proper "social engineering"—another term for education—it can be shaped into a pattern. Many ideologies assume that, with the proper changes in our environment and the proper inculcation of new values, "new" men and women can be created. There is nothing sacrosanct, therefore, in our present institutions and values; on the contrary, some of them are downright bad.

On the other hand, many well-known philosophers, especially those in the period of the Enlightenment and in the nineteenth century, have presented a different notion of human nature. People have some innate characteristics: we are born with traits of sociability, goodness, and rationality. We are also endowed with rights, such as life, liberty, and property. Institutions are but a reflection of these human traits and rights, and a political organization must respect them; indeed, it must provide the best means for protecting them. Therefore, the state that protects these rights cannot invade them—the state is limited. Finally, other political philosophers have argued that human nature is "greedy," "selfish," and "bellicose" and that it is the duty of the state to curb our ignoble drives. Political power and coercion are what make social life possible and safe.

Plato (c. 427–347 B.C.)

The Greek philosopher Plato was a disciple of Socrates and the founder of philosophic idealism, according to which ideas exist in themselves and by themselves, forming a perfect and harmonious universe. As a political philosopher, Plato wrote *The Republic,* a work describing an ideal state with a strict class structure ruled by philosopher–kings who divested themselves of property and family ties in order to rule for the common good.

Of particular interest are psychological theories of individual motivation, generally associated with economic liberalism, which we examine in Chapter 2. Rejecting the notion of natural rights, British philosophers and economists postulated an individual driven by desire who seeks only the gratification of pleasure. Each and all of us are motivated by the pursuit of pleasure and the only constraints are external—the pleasures and drives of others. Competition in a free market provides such constraints. Similar notions about the "political man," thirsty for power and glory, led to the formulation of theories of checks and balances—each power checking the other to provide for a balance that preserved the freedom of all. It was because of the depravity of human nature that James Madison, one of the authors of The Federalist Papers and our fourth president, considered government to be necessary.

The Nature of Truth

Is there one truth? Or is truth progressively discovered as many ideas and points of view compete with each other—every generation adding something to it? The notion that there is one truth revealed only to some or perceived authoritatively by them requires us to submit to it. We must hew as closely as possible to what is given, and obey those who speak for it. Human beings are thus deprived of the freedom to seek truth, to experiment with new ideas, to confront each other with different points of view, and to live in a system that tolerates different ways.

On the other hand, there are those for whom a constant exploration of the universe by human beings and a constant inquiry into the foundations and conditions of life are the only ways to discover truth. "Such is the nature of the understanding that it cannot be compelled to the belief of anything by outside force," wrote John Locke. People who hold this view favor competition of ideas, advocate tolerance for all points of view, and want to assure the conditions of freedom that are indispensable for ongoing inquiry. This is what we call *pluralism*. If one Absolute Truth did exist, pluralists would have none of it for fear that it would deprive human beings of the challenge of discovering it!

The Individual and Society

For some social scientists there is no such entity as an "individual." The individuals are perceived as part of a herd or a group whose protection and survival require cooperation. The individual is considered helpless outside the group or the state. The group or the state then makes the rules of conduct and establishes the relationship between rulers and ruled. The individual is a "social being"—first and last!

The other point of view stresses the opposite—the primacy of individuals. They are perceived as having originally lived in the state of nature and endowed with reason and natural rights. To protect themselves and their belongings, these individuals contrive to create a political society that protects their lives and their property. The political system—the state—is made up of individuals, by the individuals, and for the individuals. It is the result of a contract—freely entered upon.

As with theories about human nature, our view of the relationship between the individual and the society often determines our political ideology. Those who give primacy to the group show an inclination to emphasize the "organic" nature of society and the political system: it is a whole, like our body, and the individuals are like the cells of our organism. They are only parts that fit into the whole; they have no freedoms and rights. The "organic" theory puts the accent on the whole and the close interdependence of the parts that is required to make it function. This theory leaves little room for change, unless it is very gradual. Sudden change shifts the balance of existing relationships among the parts and hence endangers the whole—the society. The "organic" theory also is totalitarian in the name of society's overriding purpose to which all parts and individuals remain subservient.

Those who assume the primacy of the individual reach diametrically opposite conclusions. *The individual is what counts most.* Individuals *make* the political society in which they live, and they can change it. Political life is an act of will and political authority is based on consent. The society consists of a maze of overlapping, cooperating, or conflicting wills and units—both individuals and groups—participating in the political system. Change, reform, experimentation, and even revolution must spring from the will and the consent and the common effort and action of the individuals. If, as Thomas Jefferson did, revolution is to be envisaged, it must stem from the will of the majority of the people.

Political Authority

Basic divisions on the nature and organization of political authority derive from theories about the nature of truth and about the relationship between the individual and the group. Belief in one overriding truth leads almost always to an authoritarian position. It is *elitist.* It assumes that a small group "knows" and is capable of governing on the basis of certain qualities. For Plato these qualities were *intellectual:* the philosopher–king; for some they are *prescriptive:* based on inheritance. The qualities deemed necessary for governing could also be *charismatic:* appeal and personality, or *class*—either the property owners or the working class—having a historical mission of ruling or transforming the society.

On the other hand, those who postulate that political authority derives from the will of individuals favor limiting political authority in order to allow for participation and open deliberation. They advocate freedom of thought and expression, respect for individual freedoms, and freedom for associations, political parties, and all other organizations. *No claims to rule based on birth, heredity, wealth, intellectual superiority, or prescriptive titles are accepted.* No "monopoly of truth" is conceded—to anybody.

Equality and Property

Many of the most important political ideologies can be distinguished in terms of the answers they try to provide to the following questions: *Who produces and who decides what is produced? Who gets what and how much?* The answers are complex, and all the more so since the very concepts and questions, let alone the answers, are laden with emotions and values; they are steeped in ideology.

The central issue remains that of equality. For the early liberals, equality was interpreted narrowly to mean equality before the law, or equality of all to vote and participate in the choice of political leaders. Yet, unless people have equal access to education and material living standards (even if minimal), equality before the law is a fiction. Throughout the twentieth century, as we will see, those who advocated political or legal equality above all clashed with the proponents of material equality. There is a constant tension between material and economic equality on the one hand and formal legal and political equality on the other.

Property and the right of individual property have been the subject of intense ideological conflicts, as we will see. Few theorists and philosophers have given to individual property their unqualified blessing. Whenever they did, as it was the case with Aristotle and John Locke, among others, property was considered in physical terms—that which individuals managed by their labor to bring under their direct control. From Plato, who would have none of it, through the Christian fathers, down to many Utopian Socialists, and of course including Marxists, property was viewed, especially when unevenly distributed, as something disruptive of the community and social life. Property set one against another. It was not a natural right, but the result of forceful exploitation—the source of and the reason for inequality that accounts for social strife.

Liberal democracies have emphasized property rights—even when they have been forced to qualify them for the sake of greater material equality. Socialism and communism, on the other hand, have favored the socialization of property. Throughout the twentieth century, virtually all political regimes and all political ideologies have come to terms with the need for providing greater material opportunities and equality. Even when individual property is accepted, its uneven distribution has been a source of profound concern and a reason for reconsideration of property rights. How does a political system avoid excessive differences and inequalities? Taxation—in many cases steep progressive income taxes—has been used and the monies procured have been redistributed to the poor and the needy in the form of services and outright grants. This is the essence of the welfare state that became the political formula of all liberal democracies, until very recently.

Property is no longer defined only in terms of land or the real estate one owns or even in terms of liquid wealth and high salaries, although they are still important. For many people in most societies, "property" has now become "public" in the sense that it consists of claims against the state that individuals have for service and benefits to which they are entitled. Education, health, housing, transportation, old age pensions, unemployment benefits, and special assistance programs have become rights—"entitlements"—and they are just as important as property rights. Whatever the justification or the adequacy of such entitlements, they have significantly changed the distribution of material benefits and the nature of property in most all societies. For many people, such services and benefits have provided a cushion just as important as ownership.

Notions about human nature, truth, political authority, freedom, property and equality, and the production and distribution of goods and services outlined here are present in each and every ideology we will study in this book. They are the major building blocks of all contemporary ideologies and movements. Men and women organize behind their respective visions of a just and better world or barricade themselves to defend their own visions of justice. Political philosophy gives us all a chance to contemplate these notions in a detached and objective way; political ideologies and movements often transform them into a battle cry.

THE USES OF POLITICAL IDEOLOGY

An *ideology*, then, is a set of ideas and beliefs held by a number of people. It spells out what is valued and what is not, what must be maintained and what must be changed, and it shapes the attitudes of those who share it accordingly. In contrast to philosophy and theory, which are concerned with knowledge and understanding, ideologies relate to social and political behavior and action. They incite people to political action and provide the basic framework for such action. They infuse passion and call for sacrifice.

Legitimization

As pointed out earlier, one of the most important functions of a political ideology is to give value to a political regime and its institutions. It shapes the operative ideas that make a political regime work. It provides the basic categories by which the people know the political regime, abide by the rules, and participate in it. To perform this all-important role, a political ideology must have a *coherent set of rules* and must set them forth as clearly as possible. Although a constitution is a political document that embodies these rules, it cannot function well unless it is valued by the people. A political ideology shapes these values and beliefs about the constitution and lets the people know of their roles, positions, and rights within their own political regime.

Solidarity and Mobilization

A common sharing of ideas integrates individuals into the community, a group, a party, or a movement. Commonly held ideas define the things that are acceptable and the tasks to be accomplished, excluding all others. Ideologies play the same role that totems and taboos play in primitive tribes, defining what is common to the members and what is alien. The Soviet Communist ideology purported to unify those who adhered to it by branding the outside world of capitalism as the enemy. The same is increasingly so with Islamic fundamentalism. All ideologies perform this function of unifying, integrating, and giving a sense of identity to those who share it, but they do so with varying degrees of success. Nationalism as an ideology, for instance, has provided the unifying and integrating force that has made it possible for nation–states to emerge and retain their positions. The greater the integration sought and the stronger the solidarity to be maintained, the greater the emphasis on unifying symbolisms.

Leadership and Manipulation

Although ideologies incite people to action, what kind of action and for what purpose depend very much on the content and substance of an ideology. Manipulation of ideas, a special case, often involves the conscious and deliberate formulation of propositions that incite people to action for ends that are clearly perceived only by those in power or attempting to get political power. They may promise peace in order to make war, freedom in order to establish an authoritarian system, socialism in order to consolidate the position and privileges of the property holders, and so on.

Ideology can often be used as a powerful instrument of manipulation. Usually in times of social distress and anxiety, or when society seems divided into warring groups and frustration warps daily life, simple propositions and promises on how to remove the evils besetting society fall upon receptive ears and minds. Ideologies are great simplifiers. For instance, "Islam is the solution" is the cure-all slogan of Islamic fundamentalists. The demagogue, the leader, the self-professed savior is lurking somewhere in all societies at such times to spread his or her message and to manipulate those who seem to have nowhere else to turn.

Communication

A coherent set of ideas—an ideology—shared by a given number of people makes communication among them much easier. It provides a *common, highly simplified, special language*, like shorthand. Words have special meaning— "the Reds," "the bleeding-heart liberals," "the pigs," "the Establishment," "fat cats," "the power elite," "the chosen people," or "Communist conspiracy." These are terms easily understood by those who belong to a given group, and they help others to place them within a given ideological family. They are, of course, very crude terms, and ideologies usually provide more sophisticated ones. "The last stage of capitalism," "neocolonialism," "avant-garde of the working class," "democratic centralism," "democratic pluralism," "human rights," and "gradual change" are commonly understood by those who use them in their own respective political group or party. These terms can help the outsider to identify the ideological family to which the speaker belongs. A common ideology simplifies communication and makes common effort easier for all those who accept it.

Communication is also made easier because people with a common ideology look upon the outside world with the same preconceptions. They all have the same binoculars! People receive messages from the world outside and have to put these messages into some kind of order—into concepts. These concepts, in terms of which messages for the outside world are sorted out, depend on ideology. For some, the condition of the poor calls for study and concern; for others, it is a bore—the situation of the poor is attributed to innate laziness. This, however, is an extreme case. More frequent are cases of interpretation or evaluation, where the same event is seen from a different viewpoint—a different ideological perspective. The assassination of a political leader is applauded by some and mourned by others. Any Soviet move anywhere in the world is an indication of Communist aggression for some; for others, it is an inevitable reaction to American provocation! People may also reject messages because of their ideology. A mystic is blind to the world outside; for a scientist, the world is a constant source of wonder to be studied and explained.

Emotional Fulfillment

Some have argued that the primary function of an ideology is to rationalize and protect material interests or to provide for a powerful medium for their satisfaction. Thus, liberal democracy has been viewed as the rationalization of the interests of the rich and the relatively well-to-do, while socialism is an instrument for the satisfaction of the demands of those without property, the workers, and the poor. But it is not only interest that spawns an ideology. Emotional drives and personality traits are expressed through different ideologies. Not only do ideas simplify, they also tap emotions and often arouse the public into a frenzy. Nationalism and religious fundamentalism, Islamic or other, are but two illustrations among many. In recent years, the fight for or against abortion in the United States has reached a level of emotional crescendo that brooks no rational discourse and no easy compromise.

There also may be some correlation between ideology and personality types. There may be, for instance, an "authoritarian personality" that finds expression and fulfillment through being subject to rank and authority. An ideology can provide a form of expression to people with similar personality traits. Animal rights activists, environmentalists, proponents or opponents of the Equal Rights Amendment, as well as Democrats, Communists, and Fascists, all may give vent to their emotions through a particular ideology that fits their personality.

Ideology, then, provides for emotional fulfillment. People who share it are closely knit together; they share the same ambitions, interests and goals and work together to bring them about. A person who has an ideology that is shared with a group of people is likely to be happy and secure: basking in the togetherness of a common endeavor. Identifying with it, he or she is never alone.

Criticism, Utopia, and Conservation

Ideologies often embody social criticism. Critical examination of social and political beliefs has played an important role in the development of new ideologies and the rejection of others. Many beliefs have yielded to it, to be replaced by others. Institutions like slavery, property, hereditary monarchy, bureaucratic centralization, and many others have been critically challenged and accordingly abandoned or qualified.

In certain instances, criticism may be pushed to extremes. Certain ideologies are like a *dream*, an impossible and unrealizable quest: world government, perfect equality, abundance for all, elimination of force, and abolition of war. Many political ideologies have something of this quality, but those that have it in an exaggerated form are called *utopias*, a word derived from the Greek for "nowhere." If we give this particular meaning to the term, we are implying that an "ideologue" is either naive or dangerous or a little bit crazy, ignoring Shakespeare's pithy remark that dreams are the stuff that life is made of! The opposite of an individual who dreams of utopia is one who accepts the existing state of affairs—the conservation of the status quo—of the values and ideas that we inherited.

The noted German sociologist Karl Mannheim made the distinction between "ideology," the set of values and beliefs we share about our society, and "utopia," the critical exposition of new ideas for its restructuring. It is hard—except in the extreme cases—to know when we deal with an "ideology" or a "utopia." While ideas constantly emerge to criticize existing values and beliefs, there are also ideologies dedicated to the preservation of values. Conservatives and fundamentalists extol with passion the past and romanticize it. In so doing, however, they, too, often verge on utopia, since a return to past traditions, values, and beliefs is cast in terms of a critical evaluation and rejection of the existing ideology. Most all ideologies, even conservative and preservative ones, include elements of criticism of the present. Moreover, most all utopias share elements of the prevailing truths and values, even if they propose to recast them. The kingdom of God or of the Prophet is part of the values and beliefs of many, but few would like to sacrifice themselves to bring it about; the greed and selfishness of human nature are acknowledged by most, but few would call for a revolution to transform it.

Ideology and Political Action

Above all, ideology *moves* people into concerted action. Sometimes it moves a whole nation; sometimes it is a group, a class, or a political party that unites people behind certain principles to express their interests, demands, and beliefs. In France, socialism is still for many the vindication of a long-standing quest for equality—material equality. In the United States, on the other hand, it is political and economic liberalism—the freedom to produce, consume, think, and worship—that seems to be the major rallying point for many political movements. An example of a single-issue organization motivated by ideology to take political action is the environmentalist group Greenpeace, which both in the United States and elsewhere seeks to put an end to the despoliation of our physical environment; it shares many of the same objectives as the various "No Nuke" organizations. Other powerful single groups want to reintroduce religious teaching and prayers in the schools, while still others mount a fierce campaign against abortion. "Welfare liberals" continue to reconcile freedoms with state intervention and welfare legislation to mitigate the harshness of economic competition. Communism—whether adopted by a nation, a movement, or a party that challenges the existing political order—is an ideology that projects a vision of abundance, equality, and peace. Most of the Communist movements have viewed the Soviet Union as the legitimate advocate of a new social order that would replace the existing one. With the weakening of communism, many are searching now for a substitute.

The dynamics of politics, therefore, lie in the ideas people develop. But the same is true with political institutions, movements, social groups, and political parties. We have to focus on the ideologies they represent, and the beliefs they propagate and legitimize. The same is true for political attitudes. They, too, are fashioned by political ideologies. It is in terms of different constellations of attitudes that major political movements and ideologies can be identified and described. Liberals share common attitudes with regard to race relations, economic policy, prayers in the school, the United Nations, taxes, the draft, nuclear weapons, food stamps, social security, and so on. Conservatives can be identified in terms of a set of different attitudes with regard to some of the same issues; so can Socialists or Communists.

In studying political ideologies, we are also studying the dynamics of political systems—the type of political regime, its constitution, and institutions—the degree to which the regime is accepted, the existing conflicts within the regime, and the manner in which conflicts can be resolved. Compatibility of ideological outlooks makes for stability and acceptance; incompatibility always presages conflict, instability and possibly revolution.

THE INTELLECTUALS

Most ideologies have been shaped by "intellectuals"—the clergy, lawyers, professors, writers. The American historian R. R. Palmer in his book *Twelve Who Ruled*, which discusses the "Committee of Public Safety" that was responsible for the terror and the use of the guillotine against opponents in the last year of the French Revolution, finds that all twelve members of the committee had one thing in common—they were intellectuals. They came from different classes and had different professions, had different careers and lifestyles. Those who engineered the Bolshevik Revolution were also intellectuals, versed in philosophy, economics, and history, conversant in three or four languages. The only exception was Stalin, who survived them all after disposing of them all! The road to both the American and French revolutions had been paved by intense literary and philosophic work, with the writing of Benjamin Franklin, Thomas Paine, and Thomas Jefferson, and in France by the remarkable body of literature produced by a new school of intellectuals—the Encyclopedists.

Who are the intellectuals, and why do they play such an important role in the creation of ideas associated with the formulation of a new political ideology? There are no easy answers. But if we assume that most ideologies reflect interest, class, or status and rationalize given positions in the society, then ideas are directly linked with them. Rarely can ideologies rise above such positions or be dissociated from the interests with which they are linked—be they material or spiritual ones. The intellectuals, however, represent a group of people with no such positions and no such linkages or attachments to interests. They float somehow between, among, and above them. In this sense they have more freedom than all others to criticize and dream. They can use the word, written and spoken, the typewriter, the radio, the press, and the TV better than others— that is why they are intellectuals—and can therefore direct new messages where they wish. For example, it was a group of intellectuals in Britain who at the end of the nineteenth century introduced socialism.

Intellectuals criticize and manage to elevate their criticism to new ideological heights that transcend the existing formulations. In the same way that inventors or talented managers may renovate the state of the art in a trade or industry, intellectuals attempt to renovate society, its life, and its values, but with a far wider impact. The intellectuals influence profoundly and reshape our views and perceptions, and one of the reasons they do not dominate the society—except in some extreme cases—is that they are not a coherent group with common ideas, like a party. In fact, they are constantly at odds with each other. Another reason is that their messages are resisted by those to whom they are addressed—people don't like change. For instance, there has been a shared distrust between left-wing intellectuals and workers in liberal democracies. Workers feared that the ideology of intellectuals was but a device for them to gain power without necessarily providing to the workers the benefits they had promised. Workers feared that the Marxists intellectuals would become a "new class."[2] There has been little love lost, too, between the British Socialist intellectuals and the British trade unions. Similarly, during the uprisings against the "Establishment" in many liberal democracies in the late 1960s, which were spearheaded by intellectuals and students, the workers were reluctant to join in the protests. When they did, it was to improve their wages and conditions of

---

[2]Daniel Bell, *The End of Ideology,* pp. 355–357. Djilas, *New Class, An Analysis of the Communist System.*

work, not to change the society. As for the intellectuals in liberal capitalist regimes that purport to be democratic, they never made their peace with property and the free-market economy and more generally with the materialistic ethics of capitalism. For many of them, Marxism became the major weapon of criticism. It became a passionate commitment to save us all by creating a new society. It became in the words of another intellectual, Raymond Aron, an opium—intoxicating the intellectuals and opiating the people.[3]

Whether they dispense lifesaving drugs or opium pills, it is the function of intellectuals to stir up our thinking and our ideas about the world. They are a thorn in the flesh of every established order and prevailing ideology. Socrates was the first of many thousands to pay the price with his life. Scratch each and all of the intellectuals and you will find an ideologue. But by and large, they remain divided and therefore harmless. Only those among them who begin to develop a common set of beliefs geared to a common goal and who are in search of a new order may play an important role. They become "organic" intellectuals, assembling and synthesizing existing beliefs, compromising among many, rejecting others, and suggesting new ones until they form a "bloc."[4]

By and large, intellectuals perform a critical and innovative role that all societies need. They criticize the old and constantly open up new horizons of thought and social endeavor. As long as they exist, the formation of ideology will flourish.

TYPES OF POLITICAL IDEOLOGIES

Political ideologies address themselves to values: the quality of life, the distribution of goods and services, freedom and equality. If there were agreement on each of these values, there would be a single ideology shared by all. But there is no agreement within any society nor, needless to say, among the various political societies of the world. People hold different views; nations project different values and beliefs.

It is precisely here that we see the role of political ideologies: they mobilize men and women into action in favor of one point of view or another, and in favor of one movement or party or another. Their aim is invariably either the preservation of a given point of view or the overhaul of the existing state of things, including the political system itself. British squires who defended their privilege and property; the workers who formed trade unions or parties to defend their interests; the American conservatives—all have had a common set of ideas that united them into a common posture. The same is true for the small terrorist bands who seize planes. They want to destroy what they despise most—

---

[3]Raymond Aron, *The Opium of the Intellectuals.*

[4]The terms were used by the Italian Communist intellectual Antonio Gramsci.

the complacency of an orderly society interested in material satisfaction.

We can divide political ideologies into three broad categories.

1. Those that defend and rationalize the existing economic, social, and political order at any given time in any given society, which we call *status quo* ideologies.
2. Ideologies that advocate far-reaching changes in the existing social, economic, and political order, which we call *radical* or *revolutionary* ideologies.
3. In between there is, of course, a large gray area favoring change. We may call these the *reformist* ideologies.

One way to state the difference between *status quo, reformist,* and *revolutionary* ideologies is to think of maps and mapmaking. Someone who diligently learns to read a map and to travel by following given routes and signals may be considered to represent a status quo mentality or ideology: he or she simply follows the rules and the signs and is guided by them. On the other hand, a person who attempts to trace his or her own route and to change the signals, but not the destination, is a reformist. There is an agreement that the means must change, not the end. *But a revolutionary changes both the map and the destination.*

This classification is merely a formal one because ideologies shift and change not only in content but also in the particular functions and roles they perform. A revolutionary ideology, for instance, may become transformed into one of status quo when it succeeds in imposing its own values and beliefs. Similarly, the same ideology may be a status quo ideology, protecting the existing order of things in a given place at a given time, and a revolutionary one in a different place or at a different time. Communism in the Soviet Union is a status quo political ideology, while in other countries communism is considered to be a revolutionary one. While workers in the nineteenth century were protesting in the name of socialism against Western European liberalism, which had become a status quo ideology, liberalism was very much a revolutionary ideology in the eyes of many in Central Europe and Russia.

Status quo, reformist, and revolutionary ideologies can also be distinguished by the tactics used to realize goals. These include persuasion, organization, and force. Few, if any, ideologies rely exclusively on any one to the exclusion of others. Most use, in different proportions, all these tactics. The more fundamental and comprehensive the goals are and the more an ideology challenges the status quo, the greater the chances that it will be translated into a political movement that will resort to organized force, without, of course, neglecting organization and persuasion. A political ideology, on the other hand, that has limited and incremental goals, as is the case with reformist ideologies, is more likely to resort to political organization and persuasion.

In general, political ideologies and movements that challenge the status quo are more likely to use force at the time when they confront it. This was the case with liberalism before it overthrew the aristocratic and monarchical regimes in the eighteenth century and after, and with the Communist and other revolutionary movements first in Russia and later in other countries. Yet, when such political ideologies succeed—when they have been transformed into political regimes and have implemented their major goals and consolidated their position—persuasion and organization are likely to take the place of force.

There is one qualification to these generalizations. According to some analysts, there are some political ideologies for which force is a necessary and permanent characteristic. And there are others for which persuasion and political organization, rather than force, are inherent characteristics. Some authoritarian systems—and Communist regimes are included—institutionalize the use of force in order to bring about and maintain compliance. On the other hand, liberal and democratic regimes, committed to political competition and pluralism, eschew the use of force. If it is to be used, it is only as a last resort.

THE MAJOR POLITICAL IDEOLOGIES

Criteria of Choice

If we look at the spread of contemporary political ideological movements, we have a rich choice of subjects: liberalism, capitalism, democratic socialism, socialism, communism, national communism, consociationalism, corporatism, Eurocommunism, anarchism, Gaullism, Stalinism and post-Stalinism, communalism, self-determination in industry, Titoism, Maoism, welfarism, to say nothing of variations that come from the Third World under various labels. Which ones do we discuss, and why? We obviously need some criteria to help, and I suggest four: *coherence, pervasiveness, extensiveness,* and *intensiveness.*

Coherence   By coherence I have in mind the overall scope of an ideology, along with its internal logic and structure. Is it complete? Does it clearly spell out a set of goals and the means to bring them about? Do its various propositions about social, economic, and political life hang together? Is there an organization—a movement or a party—to promote the means of action envisaged?

Pervasiveness   Pervasiveness refers to the length of time that an ideology has been "operative." Some ideologies may be in decline over a period, only to reappear. Others have been operative over a long period, despite variations and qualifications. Whatever the case, the basic test is the length of time during which an ideology has been shared by people, affected their lives, and shaped their attitudes and actions.

Extensiveness   The criterion of extensiveness refers simply to a crude numerical test. How many people share a given ideology? One can draw a crude "ideological map" showing the number of people sharing common political ideologies. The larger the "population space" of a given ideology, the greater its extensiveness. How many people are influenced today by communism? By liberalism? By socialism? By anarchism? By religious fundamentalism? An estimate of numbers will answer the question of extensiveness.

Intensiveness   Finally, by intensiveness I mean the degree and the intensity of the appeal of an ideology—irrespective of whether it satisfies any of the other three criteria. Does it evoke a spirit of total loyalty and action? "Interest is sluggish," wrote John Stuart Mill. Ideas are not! They are like weapons, which in the hands of even a small minority may have a far greater impact on society than widely shared interests. Intensiveness implies emotional commitment, total loyalty, and unequivocal determination to act even at the risk of one's life. It was this kind of intensiveness that Lenin managed to impart to his Bolsheviks and to the Communist party.

Ideally, we should choose among various ideologies only those that satisfy *all* the criteria set forth here—coherence, pervasiveness, extensiveness, and intensiveness. However, this would fail to do justice to some ideologies that have played or are playing an important role in our political life, even though they may satisfy only one or two of these criteria, and so I intend to take several such movements into account. (See Table 1.1 for a sampling of ideologies and how they fare according to these four criteria.)

For each ideology discussed, I begin by examining the basic theoretical formulations to which it owes a major debt and describe its transformation into a political movement and, in some cases, into a political regime. We should never lose sight of the fact that we are dealing with ideas that become political movements and lead people to political action; and the fact that their "influence" can be assessed in terms of the strength of the movements and parties through which ideas become readied and armed for a struggle for supremacy. Ideologies are not disembodied entities; they are not abstractions. They exist because men and women share them and adopt them as part of their own lives. Ideologies are weapons when men and women make them so; but they are also havens that produce companionship, cooperation, and fufillment.

Value Judgment   One last remark is in order. If there are so many ideologies, and if all of us share different ideologies to help us "know" the outside world and to prompt us to act in one way or another, which one of them is "correct"? If all ideologies provide us with different views and perceptions of the world, how do we know what the world is really like? How can we describe the landscape if we use different binoculars? This is the nagging question throughout the book—the question of the validity of a given ideology. When it comes to political ideologies, there is really no authoritative test to produce definitive proof of validity. We can only present the various political ideologies in terms of their internal logic, their coherence, their relevance to the outside world, and the passion and intensity for action they infuse.

This book does not ask, therefore, which ideologies are "true" and which are "false." Instead, our approach will be expository: Where does an ideology come from? What does it posit? What does it purport to achieve? What have been its accomplishments or failures?

Table 1.1   THE POLITICAL IDEOLOGIES DISCUSSED

	Coherence	Pervasiveness	Extensiveness	Intensiveness
Democratic liberalism	Strong	Long	Wide	Weak
Democratic socialism	Weak	Long	Wide	Mediocre
Utopian socialism	Weak	Sporadic	Limited	High
Communism	Strong, but rapidly weakening	Long, but in the process of being questioned	Wide, but in the process of being regionalized	High, but increasingly weakening
Conservatism	Weak	Long	Wide	Weak
Fascism/nazism	Weak	Sporadic	Uncertain	High
Nationalism	Weak	Long	Wide	High
Anarchism	Weak	Sporadic	Limited	High
Religious fundamentalism	Strong	Sporadic	Selective, regional	Very high
Feminism	Weak	Gaining	Progressively widening	Uncertain
Environmentalism	Weak	Recent	Widening	Mediocre, but increasing

BIBLIOGRAPHY

Abercrombie, N., et al. *The Dominant Ideology.* London: Allen and Unwin, 1980.

Apter, David (ed.). *Ideology and Its Discontents.* Englewood Cliffs, N.J.: Prentice-Hall, 1964.

Aristotle. *Politics.* Translated by Ernest Barker. New York: Oxford University Press, 1962.

Aron, Raymond. *The Opium of the Intellectuals.* New York: Norton, 1962.

Bailyn, Bernard. *The Ideological Origins of the American Revolution.* Cambridge, Mass.: Harvard University Press, 1967.

Bell, Daniel. *The End of Ideology,* rev. ed. New York: Free Press, 1965.

Benda, Julien. *The Betrayal of the Intellectuals.* Beacon Press Boston, 1955 (Transl. by Richard Aldington).

Bluhm, William T. *Ideologies and Attitudes: Modern Political Culture.* Englewood Cliffs, N.J.: Prentice-Hall, 1974.

Bracher, Karl D. *The Age of Ideologies: A History of Political Thought in the Twentieth Century.* London: Weindenfeld and Nicolson, 1982.

Brown, L. B. *Ideology.* New York: Penguin, 1973.

Cox, Richard H. *Ideology, Politics and Political Theory.* Belmont, Calif.: Wadsworth, 1968.

Djilas, Milovan. *The New Class: An Analysis of the Communist System.* New York: Holt, 1957.

Feuer, L. *Ideology and the Ideologists.* Oxford: Basil Blackwell, 1975.

Gramsci, Antonio. *Selections from the Prison Notebooks*, edited and translated by Quintin Hoare and Geoffrey N. Smith, Lawrence and Wishart, London, 1971

—— *Selections from Political Writings*. edited and translated by Quintin Hoare and Geoffrey N. Smith, Lawrence and Wishart, London, 1977.

Grimes, Alan, and Robert Horowitz (eds.). *Modern Political Ideologies*. New York: Oxford University Press, 1959.

Habermas, J. *Legitimation Crisis*. London: Heinemann, 1976.

Hartz, Louis. *The Liberal Tradition in America*. New York: Harcourt, 1955.

Hill, Christopher. *The World Turned Upside Down: Radical Ideas During the English Revolution*. London, England: Penguin, 1975.

Jenkins, Thomas. *The Study of Political Theory*. New York: Random House, 1955.

Kramnick, I., and Frederick Watkins. *The Age of Ideology—Political Thought 1950 to the Present*. Englewood Cliffs, N.J.: Prentice-Hall, 1964.

Lefebre, Georges. *The Coming of the French Revolution*. Princeton, N.J.: Princeton University Press, 1967.

Lerner, Max. *Ideas Are Weapons: The History and Uses of Ideas*. New York: Viking, 1939.

Lichtheim, George. *The Concept of Ideology and Other Essays*. New York: Random House, 1967.

Mannheim, Karl. *Ideology and Utopia*. New York: Harcourt, 1955.

Marx, Karl. *Theses on Feuerbach*. In Robert C. Tucker: The Marx-Endels Reader, 2nd Ed. W. W. Norton, New York, 1978, pp. 143–146

McLellan, D. *Marxism after Marx*. London: Macmillan, 1980.

——. *Ideology*. Minneapolis: University of Minnesota Press, 1986.

Oakeshott, Michael. *The Social and Political Doctrines of Contemporary Europe*. New York: Cambridge University Press, 1942.

Palmer, R. R. *Twelve Who Ruled*. Princton, N.J.: Princeton University Press, 1961.

Plamenatz, John. *Ideology*. New York: Praeger, 1970.

Rude, George. *Ideology and Popular Protest*. London: Lawrence and Wishart, 1980.

Schumpter, Joseph. *Capitalism, Socialism and Democracy*, 3rd ed. New York: Harper & Row, 1950.

Shklar, Judith N. *Political Theory and Ideology*. New York: Macmillan, 1966.

Thompson, J. *Studies in the Theory of Ideology*. Cambridge University Press, Cambridge, England, 1984.

Trigg, Roger. *Ideas of Human Nature: An Historical Introduction*. Cambridge, Mass.: Basil Blackwell, 1988.

Watkins, Frederick. *The Age of Ideology: Political Thought from 1750 to the Present*. Englewood Cliffs, N.J.: Prentice-Hall, 1964.

Wolin, Sheldon. *Politics and Vision*. Boston: Little, Brown, 1960.

PART
One

DEMOCRACY: MANY ROOTS AND FAMILIES

Our constitution is called a democracy because power is in the hands not of the few but of the many.

Thucydides
Funeral Oration of Pericles

Democracy literally means "the government of the people." It comes from the Greek words *demos*, people, and *kratos*, government or power. The concept developed first in the small Greek city–states, the Athenian democracy (roughly between 450 B.C. and 350 B.C.) is what we usually point to as the principal early example. Pericles, the great Athenian statesman, speaking in 431 B.C., defined democracy in the following terms:

> Our constitution is named a democracy, because it is in the hands not of the few but of the many. But our laws secure equal justice for all in their private disputes and our public opinion welcomes and honors talent in every branch of achievement . . . on grounds of excellence alone. . . . Our citizens attend both to public and private duties and do not allow absorption in their various affairs to interfere with their knowledge of the city's. . . . We decide or debate, carefully and in person, all matters of policy, holding . . . that acts are foredoomed to failure when undertaken undiscussed.[1]

In this classic formulation, Pericles identifies the following characteristics of a democracy:

---

[1]Thucydides, *The History of the Peloponnesian War*. Edited and translated by Sir Richard Livingston. New York: Oxford University Press, 1951, pp. 111–113.

1. Government by the people with the full and direct participation of the people.
2. Equality before the law.
3. Pluralism—that is, respect for all talents, pursuits, and viewpoints.
4. Respect for a separate and private (as opposed to public) domain for fulfillment and expression of an individual's personality.

Participation, equality before the law, pluralism, and individualism for everyone (except for women and also the many slaves)—these were the cornerstones of early democracy, before it disappeared from Greece and the then known world after a relatively short revival in Rome.

CONTEMPORARY DEMOCRACY: MAJOR PHASES

Contemporary democratic thought can be traced back to the sixteenth century and earlier. It has many roots: feudal practices and institutions, theories about natural law and natural rights, the religious wars and the demand for toleration, the assertion of property rights and freedom to pursue individual economic ventures, the notion of limitations upon political authority—to name the most important of them. The basic landmark is provided by the English philosopher John Locke who, writing in the latter part of the seventeenth century, developed in some detail four of the cardinal concepts of democracy: *equality, individual rights and freedoms, including property, government based upon consent of the governed,* and *limitations upon the state.* Locke's theories led to the development of representative and parliamentary government.

The second historical landmark—the emergence of economic liberalism—came with the works of Adam Smith, especially his *Wealth of Nations* (1776), and of a new school of radical philosophers known as the *utilitarians.* In the first half of the nineteenth century, they developed the theory of the "economic man" who is driven by twin impulses: to satisfy pleasure and avoid pain. In line with Adam Smith, they constructed a theoretically limited state that would allow individuals freedom to pursue their own interests. The utilitarians became the exponents of economic individualism—that is, capitalism.

Throughout the nineteenth century, Locke's theory of consent and representative government was broadened, but economic liberalism and economic individualism came constantly under scrutiny and criticism. The works of the French philosopher Jean-Jacques Rousseau, especially his *Social Contract* (1762), were used to broaden the theory of participation so as to include everybody. The role of the state was reassessed to favor more intervention in economic and social matters for the better protection of the poor, the unemployed, the old, the young, and many disadvantaged groups. For the first time the notion of a *positive state*—one that acts to provide social services and to guarantee economic rights—appeared. Finally, beginning in the twentieth century and extending well into the present, socialists and a growing number of democrats have begun to broaden the notion of a positive state. They ask for sweeping reforms of the economic system so that the state assumes the obligation of providing an ever-increasing number of services. This has come to be known as the *welfare state*.

Socialists question economic individualism and want to replace it with a system in which the major productive resources are owned and managed by the state itself. The economy is to be run by the state, no longer for the purpose of profit, but to further social and community needs. Many of the Socialist parties were committed to this position until very recently, representing a synthesis that combined democratic political and individual rights with massive state intervention in the economy and socialization of some of the major units of production. In this part we do not include, of course, Marxism and the Communist regimes since they rejected democratic political practices and committed themselves to the socialization and management by the state of every branch of the economy—including trade, agriculture, and services.

In discussing democracy as an ideology, we are dealing therefore with a very rich and comprehensive body of thought and action—one that has undergone shifts and changes in the past three centuries and has produced a great variety of political movements. We will look at the liberal phase of democracy, its political and economic doctrine and institutions, its welfarist, socialist, or collectivist phase, and again the most recent reassertion of economic liberalism—capitalism.

Chapter
2

Democracy and Liberalism

Give me the liberty to know, to utter, and to argue freely according to conscience.

John Milton
AREOPAGITICA

Laissez-faire, laissez-passer.

*T*he individual—his or her experiences and interests—is the basic concept associated with the origin and growth of liberalism and liberal societies. Knowledge and truth are derived from the judgment of the individual, which in turn is formed by the associations his or her senses make of the outside world—from experience. There is no established truth, nor any transcendental values. Individual experience becomes the supreme value in itself, and the joining of many individual experiences in deliberation is the best possible way for a community to make decisions.

In its earliest phase, individualism is cast in terms of natural rights—freedom and equality. It is steeped in moral and religious thought, but already the first signs of a psychology appear that considers material interests and their satisfaction to be important in the motivation of the individual. In its second phase, it is based on a psychological theory according to which the realization of interest is the major force that motivates individuals. In its third phase, it becomes "economic liberalism"—generally referred to as capitalism.

Interest, in turn, is related to satisfaction of pleasure. Liberalism is anchored on this simple proposition: men and women strive to maximize pleasure and minimize pain. But it is not up to the collectivity to impose pleasure or pain; it is not up to a philosopher or a political party to determine it. On the contrary, it is up to individuals to pursue it and in so doing fulfill themselves. Knowledge that stems from experience and education will presumably set limits beyond which the maximization of pleasure will not be pushed; similarly, competition in an open market will set limits to individual enrichment.

The propositions of early liberalism were directed against eighteenth-century absolutism and the many feudal practices that lingered on. Absolutism, supported by a landed aristocracy, stifled human activity while maintaining the feudal privileges of the nobility at a time when the growth of manufacturing and commerce (even if ever so gradual) had begun to open up new vistas of individual effort, exploration, wealth, and change. National communities were divided internally into many jurisdictions with different laws, different standards, different tariffs, different regulations, and different weights and measures, all of which impeded communication, trade, and individual freedoms. The famous expression *laissez-faire, laissez-passer* was the battle cry of the burghers, the tradesmen, the money-lenders, the small manufacturers. "Let us do, let us pass" was the motto of the new middle classes. This liberalism was a challenge to the existing order, because laissez-faire capitalism, as we still call it, was the ideology that expressed the interests of the middle class; it stood against absolutism, and especially against political and economic constraints.

Liberals proclaimed individualism and individual freedoms—especially freedom of movement and trade; they borrowed from the past to develop what gradually became a comprehensive theory of individual rights to challenge and to limit absolute political power; they appealed to and represented the new rising classes and the new forms of wealth that began to appear in Western Europe. They also received the support of the peasants, against the landed aristocracy, and the workingmen, who became attracted by the promise of freedoms and equality. As a political ideology, liberalism appealed to large sectors of the society, while being opposed by the monarchy, the landed aristocracy, and the church.

THE THREE CORES OF LIBERALISM

Liberalism consists of three cores. One is moral, the second is political, and the third is economic. The *moral* core contains an affirmation of basic values and rights attributable to the "nature" of a human being—freedom, dignity, and life—subordinating everything else to their implementation. The *political* core includes primarily political rights—the right to vote, to participate, to decide what kind of government to elect, and what kind of policies to follow. It is associated with representative democracy. The *economic* core has to do with economic and property rights. It is still referred to as "economic individualism," the "free enterprise system," or "capitalism," and pertains to the rights and freedoms of individuals to produce and to consume, to enter into contractual relations, to buy and sell through a market economy, to satisfy their wants in their own way, and to dispose of their own property and labor as they decide. Its cornerstones have been private property and a market economy that is free from state controls and regulations.

The Moral Core

Long before Christianity, the notion had developed that the individual human being has innate qualities and potentialities commanding the highest respect. Because each individual is imparted with a spark of divine will or reason, each should be protected, respected, and given freedom to seek fulfillment.

The Stoics and the Epicureans put individuals—their freedom, their detachment, their personal life—above all considerations of social utility or political expediency. Early Christians went a step further to proclaim that all individuals are the children of God, that we are all brothers and sisters, that our first duty is to God, and that salvation is the ultimate fulfillment. Temporal powers cannot impinge on this, but even if they did (in order, for example, to collect taxes or to maintain order), there were still many things that belonged *only* to God.

A number of inferences stem from this notion of the moral and rational nature of the individual. Many of them have been institutionalized in the practice of liberalism and continue to be essential to it. Recent proclamations supporting human rights in the United Nations and elsewhere represent one of the oldest battle cries of liberalism.

Personal Liberty   Personal liberty consists of all those rights guaranteeing the individual protection against government. It is the requirement that men and women live under a known law with known procedures. Locke wrote: "Freedom is . . . to have a standing rule to live by, common to everyone of that society and made by the legislative power erected in it."[1] Such a law protects all and restrains the rulers. It corresponds to individual "freedoms"—freedom to think, talk, and worship. No police officer will enter one's home at night without due authority; no individual, even the poorest or lowest, will be thrown into prison without a chance to hear the charges and argue before a judge; no citizen will have to discover one Sunday morning that his or her church is closed, or that a son or daughter has disappeared, and so forth. To American students such freedoms appear self-evident and naturally due. Unfortunately, this is not quite so; in fact, they are in constant jeopardy everywhere.

Civil Liberty   While personal liberties in general define a set of protections, civil liberties indicate the free and positive channels and areas of human activity and participation. In liberal ideology and practice, they are equally valued. Basic to the liberal faith is the concept of freedom of thought. The only way to define this positively is to state it as the right of individuals to think their own thoughts and learn in their own ways from experience, with no one impeding the process. Freedom of thought is closely associated with freedom of expression, freedom of speech, freedom to write, freedom to publish and disseminate one's thoughts, freedom to discuss things with others, and freedom to associate

---

[1]John Locke, *Second Treatise on Civil Government*, chap. 4.

with others in the peaceful expression of ideas. We find these freedoms enshrined in the First Amendment to the U.S. Constitution, and also in many solemn documents in British and European political history—the Bill of Rights, the Petition of Rights, the Declaration of the Rights of Man, and so on.

The achievement and implementation of full civil liberties in the societies of Western Europe and the United States took time. Until the end of the nineteenth century, there were countries where people were excluded from political participation because of their ideas, religion, or race. Censoring the books, pamphlets, and the press was a common practice long after Milton wrote his famous pamphlet against censorship, *The Areopagitica*, in 1644. Freedom of the press had a particularly shaky existence until the end of the nineteenth century, and freedom of association—to form clubs, groups of like-minded people, political parties, trade unions, and religious sects—was hedged and qualified until almost the same time.

What is more, at no time could civil liberties be taken for granted. There were and still are constant exceptions and setbacks. There is always an inclination on the part of certain groups to deny to others what they do not like, and there is a pervasive suspicion on the part of political authorities of nonconformist and dissenting groups.

Social Liberty Freedom of thought and expression and protections against government in the form of personal and civil rights have little value if individuals are not given proper recognition so that they can work and live in accordance with their talents and capabilities. Social liberty corresponds to what we refer to today as opportunities for advancement or social mobility. It is the right of all individuals, irrespective of race and creed and irrespective of the position of their parents, to be given every opportunity to attain a position in society commensurate with their capabilities. Personal liberties may become empty or purely formal prescriptions otherwise. There is little hope in the lives of disadvantaged Mexicans, blacks, or the poor if they know that they and their children will always remain tied to the same occupation, status, education, and income. Only when equal opportunities are provided for all can there be freedom for all.

The Economic Core

As already pointed out, liberalism was the ideology of the middle classes, which rose to replace the old landed aristocracy. Their purpose was to liberate individual economic activity, to establish large trading areas that expanded to the nation–state and if possible the world, and to do away with all obstacles to the transport and trade of goods. It was their aim to reorganize the economy, to introduce new methods (the market), and to invest capital in factories and machines.

Economic liberties, and in general the economic core of liberalism, assumed at least as great an importance as what we have called the moral core. The right to property, the right of inheritance, the right to accumulate wealth and capital, freedom to produce, sell, and buy—all contractual freedoms—became an essential part of the new social order. Emphasis was put on the voluntary character of the relations between various economic factors, whether the employer, the worker, the lender, the producer, or the consumer. Freedom of contract was more valued than freedom of speech. A pattern of social life in which people were born and belonged in certain social categories or groups was shattered, and the individuals became free to shape their own situation by voluntary acts and contractual relations with others. One great British historian, Sir Henry Maine, claimed that the essence of liberalism lay precisely in this transition from "status" (fixed group relations) to "contract" (individual self-determination).

The meeting point of various individual wills, where contractual relations are made, is the market. Here the individual—the famous "economic man"—propelled by self-interest, buys and sells, hires laborers, borrows or loans money, invests in joint-stock companies or maritime ventures, and finds employment. The market reflects the supply and demand for goods, and this in turn determines their prices. The market is the best barometer to register economic activity, because demand obviously pushes prices up, and hence incites production until the demand is met and prices begin to level off. Since the market does not sanction the incompetent and the inefficient, goods produced that do not meet a demand or are not widely desirable fall in price, until the producer is driven out of business, and replaced by a shrewder one.

Thousands of individual entrepreneurs face not only millions of consumers, who compare quality and prices, but also each other. If a given product sells well and fast, other manufacturers will produce it, increasing the supply and thus bringing prices down. The system is supposed to be both sensitive to consumer demand as well as entirely open, allowing for the entry of new competitors and the exit of unsuccessful ones. Prices faithfully register the volume of demand and supply adjusted to it.

It is a system that at least in theory favors the consumer: prices cannot be fixed, the volume of production cannot be controlled, competition makes monopolies or cartels impossible. But the gains for the producers are also great; they can take advantage of the same law of supply and demand in hiring or dismissing workers, in settling on the wages to be paid, and in setting the prices of new products. It is a system that provides the best mechanism both for production and the satisfaction of wants, and its classic formulation was provided by Adam Smith.

Adam Smith and *The Wealth of Nations*   The bible of liberal economic theory was, and still remains, Adam Smith's *The Wealth of Nations*. Smith's purpose was to open the channels of free individual economic effort and to defend the free-market economy as the best instrument for the growth of wealth—individual, national, and worldwide. Each person, he assumed, is the best judge of his or her actions and interests. If people are allowed a free hand to pursue these interests they will, and by so doing will improve the wealth of the society and the nation as a whole. What counts above all is to give free rein to individual action. Adam Smith was what we would call today a moral and com-

Adam Smith (1723–1790)

Adam Smith, a social philosopher and political economist, is best known for his major work, *An Inquiry into the Nature and Causes of the Wealth of Nations* (1776), in which he developed his theories of economic liberalism, competition, and free trade. His major plea was to release human activity from all state administrative and economic controls, allowing the individuals to seek individual profit and the satisfaction of wants. Adam Smith claimed that there were fundamental economic laws, such as the law of supply and demand, that provided for the self-regulation of the economy. He is the father of economic liberalism.

passionate man. He was not particularly happy with the notions of greed and self-enrichment associated with the materialistic ethic that was emerging. But he believed, nonetheless, that self-interest—the profit motive—was the best vehicle for economic growth and the well-being of society as a whole. The cure to self-interest, even to greed, was to make it available to all through the market and competition! Let businessmen raise prices with an eye to high profits, others will be attracted to manufacture the same goods, and the supply will increase and as the prices fall. High prices, in general, attract producers and lead to competition that will bring about lower prices and increase efficiency in production by reducing costs. In this way, private property and profit in a free market benefit all. This is the famous "paradox": private gain becomes translated into public good.

Adam Smith favored a limited state. The government, he argued, should limit itself to three major tasks: defense, internal order and justice, and "certain public works or certain public institutions, which can never be for the interest of any individual, or small number of individuals, to erect and maintain." This last task looks like a big hole in the wall between the state and the economy that he erects, and we return to it later. But it is safe to say that what he had primarily in mind for the government was education, roads, a postal service, control of certain natural monopolies (i.e., water), and a program of public assistance for the poor. He was adamantly opposed to government interference in the market. The market alone would determine prices. He was against price-fixing, direct and indirect subsidies, protectionist devices, and outright grants and preferences for some industries and goods, as opposed to others.

Adam Smith was also the staunchest advocate of a worldwide free trade. It could provide for competition and, hence, efficiency and lower prices that ultimately would mean wealth for those across borders. In a famous passage, he pointed out that wine could be grown in Scotland instead of importing it from France. Special soil could be brought in, hothouses could be built, special moisture mechanisms developed. And the wine produced might even taste the same as the French versions—but the cost would be thirty times higher than French imports! His arguments are still heard today in meetings of the GATT (General Agreement on Trade and Tariffs), in which about a hundred nations are represented, as they try to promote free trade.

Though Adam Smith spoke of the "Divine Hand of Providence" bringing order and wealth out of the myriads of individual wills and interests that compete with each other in trying to satisfy their respective interests, his faith was not in divine providence. Rather, he believed that a social and economic harmony would result from the free competition and interplay of economic interests and forces. In his words, natural order would be promoted in every country by the natural inclinations of the individuals if political institutions had never thwarted those natural inclinations. If all systems of restraint were completely taken away, natural liberty would establish itself. Or as one of Smith's followers put the matter even more succinctly:

> As soon as a need becomes the object of public service the individual loses part of his freedom, becomes less progressive and less man. He becomes prone to moral inertia which spreads out to all citizens.[2]

---

[2]Cited by Harold Laski, *The Rise of European Liberalism*, p. 203.

Jeremy Bentham (1748–1831)

Jeremy Bentham was the founder of the Utilitarian School, which proposed that people maximize pleasure and minimize pain (the so-called *felicific calculus*), and that these impulses were the source of human motivation. His various works, such as *Fragment on Government* and *Defense of Usury*, and most particularly his *Introduction to the Principles of Morals and Legislation*, expounded the theories of individualism and economic freedom. Benthamite liberals were extremely influential through the nineteenth century in England in pushing for administrative, criminal law, taxation, and economic reforms.

Jeremy Bentham and Utilitarianism   But the real father of liberalism was Jeremy Bentham. His philosophy, followed also by James Mill and John Stuart Mill, is known as *utilitarianism*, from the term utility. Its basic elements can be summarized as follows:

1. Every object has a utility—that is, every object can satisfy a want.
2. Utility, as the attribute of an object, is subjective. It is what we like or do not like. It is amenable only to some crude quantifiable criteria that

relate to the duration, the intensity, and the proximity of the pleasure that a given object can provide. There are no qualitative criteria that can be established by anybody but the user. For some, a poem has a greater "utility" than a hot dog. For others, the hot dog comes first. The market ultimately registers utility as a reflection of the volume of goods in demand.

3. The purpose of our lives is to increase pleasure (that is, to use goods that have utility for each one of us) and to avoid pain. This is the *hedonistic* or the *felicific calculus* that applies not just in economic life but also in any other aspect of an individual's existence.

In order to work, this utilitarian model must be allowed to operate freely. If every man and woman were free to maximize pleasure and avoid pain, "the greatest happiness for the greatest number" would result. More people would be happy than unhappy!

The concept of utility and the utilitarian ethic are not restricted to the economy. It applies to everything. Social institutions, artistic works, education, philosophy—all must meet the test of utility and provide pleasure, in varying degrees, to some, or conversely result in pain if they are absent. *Utility* as a criterion of social, political, and economic life replaces moral and natural *rights*.

Thus, millions of individuals armed with small calculators, so to speak, constantly measure the pleasurable and the painful helping us to maximize the first and to minimize the second. The calculations are always directly related to self-interest, but they are not necessarily simple. The individual will have to balance a number of requirements—for example, the immediate utility an object may have compared to the far greater utility it may represent in five or ten years; the possibility of suffering deprivation and even pain *now* in order to enjoy pleasure later on; the pain that may be suffered in order to derive pleasure from protecting loved ones; the intensity of a given pleasure as opposed to its duration; and finally, overall considerations of peace and tranquility at home and national defense against outside enemies. The latter, too, represent a utility, no matter what the immediate pain of providing for them may be.

These considerations show that, while self-interest and the pleasure-maximizing calculations are the motivating force for all of us, a point comes when considerations other than the pure and immediate satisfaction of interest enter into the equation of social, political, and economic life. Self-interest gives way to *enlightened* self-interest.

John Stuart Mill and Enlightened Self-interest   Enlightened self-interest becomes an important criterion to guide the individual. For instance, someone who forgoes an immediate pleasure in order to derive a greater one later on shows enlightenment. Enjoying smaller pleasures in order to maintain a *fairly* pleasurable existence, rather than insisting on the maximum pleasure possible and in the process risking the loss of everything, also shows enlightenment. The same criteria apply to groups or classes of people. If they act in terms of enlightened self-interest, they may consider concessions to other social groups or classes rather than risk the loss of all they have.

John Stuart Mill (1806–1873)

John Stuart Mill was an English philosopher, who had studied under the strict tutelage of his father, a foremost utilitarian, James Mill. John Stuart Mill considerably modified utilitarian thought to abandon the simple pleasure-maximizing, pain-avoiding formula and to seek qualitative and "objective" criteria instead. In his essay *On Liberty* (1859) he developed the theory of moral (as opposed simply to economic) individualism and linked it to requirements of education and enlightenment. He was forced to introduce collective and social considerations and thus had to allow, contrary to what he seemed to profess, for state intervention. Many consider Mill, because of this to be one of the precursors of socialism; however, he is most well known as a strong advocate of individualism.

John Stuart Mill came to grips with this problem by redefining utility. He introduces qualitative standards and establishes a hierarchy of pleasures on the basis of criteria that are *not* subjective. Some pleasures are better than others because of their intrinsic quality, not because of the particular pleasure they give to an individual. A poem has more utility than a hot dog!

There is therefore a necessary gradation in the utility of different goods. Some have a higher value even if they give pleasure to only few; others may, in the long run, prove to be painful even if they give pleasure to many. What then? Should we introduce a dictator or a philosopher–king who will impose his hierarchy of pleasures upon society and make it produce goods and services that correspond to it? Or should we expect individuals to make the right choice?

The last question is not speculative. It is right before us. Driving a car is pleasurable, but by depleting our energy resources American drivers weaken the country to the point where it may be unable to defend many of the values that are equally pleasurable to us—our freedoms, for instance. A comprehensive scheme of public transportation would be preferable to private ownership of cars. But how can the people be led to make the right decision?

The utilitarians, and particularly John Stuart Mill, put their hopes in education, and in the wisdom and self-restraint of the middle classes. It was the obligation of the state to establish education, and it was the function of education to *enlighten* self-interest in terms of collective, group, social, and national interests and considerations. Education would transform an essentially hedonistic society into a body of civic-minded individuals—who in the last analysis would choose public transportation! They would put the general good above their own particular pleasure.

The Political Core

Four basic principles make up the political core of liberalism: *individual consent representation and representative government, constitutionalism*, and *popular sovereignty*.

Individual Consent   As we noted, beginning with the seventeenth century, there was a shift from the notion of 'status' to that of "contract." Contractual theories became the basis of political authority as men and women consented to bind themselves in a political system and to accept its decisions. The Mayflower Compact of 1629—the Pilgrims' "constitution"—is the best illustration.

It was John Locke who developed the theory of consent in detail. Men and women, he pointed out, live in the state of nature with certain natural rights: life, liberty, and property. At a given time, they discover that it is difficult to safeguard these rights without a common authority committed to them and to their protection. They agree to set up a political society consisting of a common legislature, a common judge, and a common executive. The first will interpret and safeguard the natural rights, the second will adjudicate conflicts about these rights, and the third will provide for enforcement. The contract is made by all individuals, and those who do not agree are not bound by it. They can leave! *The source of political authority and of the powers of state over those who stay is the people's consent.* The purpose of the state is the better preservation of the natural rights of life, liberty, and property.

John Locke (1632–1704)

John Locke was an English philosopher generally considered one of the founders of empiricism. His principal works include *Letters on Toleration* (1689–1692), *Essay Concerning Human Understanding* (1690), and *Thoughts on Education* (1693). As a political philosopher, Locke developed in his *Two Treatises on Government* (1690) the contract theory of the state, according to which the state is the custodian of natural rights and is founded upon the consent of the government in order to protect these rights—specifically, the rights of life, liberty, and property. Contract theory led to the elaboration of institutions of limited state and a limited government.

Representation   But who can make decisions within this system? According to Locke, it is the legislature elected by the people (at the time, to be sure, on a very limited franchise). However, the legislature must accept certain restraints, all of them implicit or explicit in the original contract setting up the political system. It cannot deprive individuals of their natural rights, cannot abolish their freedom, and cannot do away with their lives or take away their property. The political authority—the legislature—is restrained by the very nature of the compact that originally established it.

Locke's idea of representative government, then, is based on the notion that political authority derives from the people. But moral, civil, economic, or property rights cannot be transgressed. The majority and its elected representatives can make all and any decisions, but the original contract and the good sense of the people who made it, as well as of their representatives, restrain it from violating the people's natural rights. Thus, the British tradition establishes parliamentary sovereignty and majority rule rather than checks and balances and judicial review, as in the United States.

It should be noted, however, that while Locke gave to the legislature the right to make decisions without any limitations, his theory of representation and representative government applied only to a small number—those who held property. They represented the middle classes and the landed aristocracy. It was only much later, when the franchise was expanded to most citizens (and ultimately to all), that the problem of how to limit the majority—which might decide to take away the property of the few—assumed particular importance.

Theories of representation and representative government also stemmed directly from utilitarian premises that led ultimately to the "one man, one vote" principle. At first the utilitarians attacked the vested interests, the aristocracy, the landowners, the church, and the well-to-do, and discarded the notion that these groups, more than others, had a special stake in the country and hence had a special right to represent the community and govern it. John Stuart Mill argued that the best individual protection was to allow each and all to select their representatives. "Human beings," he pointed out, "are only secure from evil at the hands of others in proportion to their ability to protect themselves,"[3] and he believed that representation was the best protection.

However, Mill did not quite accept the notion of the supremacy of the representatives—the legislature—and with it the right of the majority to govern. He and many other liberals feared that, if all the people were given the right to vote and to elect their own representatives, and if decisions in the representative assembly were to be made by majority vote, then the poor would use their numerical strength to take care of *their* interests at the expense of the middle classes and all others. There were, therefore, a number of direct and indirect restraints. One was the proposition that representative government could function well only when the educational level of the voters had improved. Citizens

---

[3]J. S. Mill, "Considerations on Representative Government," in *Utilitarianism*, chap. 3, p. 43.

should learn to think of the "general prosperity and the general good" rather than their own immediate interest; in other words, the system could work well only when people as a whole acted according to their enlightened interest. Mill wrote:

> The positive evils and dangers of representative government can be reduced to two: general ignorance and incapacity, and the danger of its being under the influence of interests not identical with the general welfare of the community.[4]

He mentioned specifically the "body of unskilled laborers" who were ignorant and likely to act at the expense of the general welfare.

Mill also had an aversion to the development of large national political parties that could mobilize the vote and capture a majority through the organization and discipline of its members. Moreover, he was in favor of property and age qualifications. He favored these at least for the candidates for election, who in this way would come from the middle classes and would have the proper level of maturity and moderation. He also favored giving a great weight—more votes—to people with education. Finally, he was in favor of a second chamber, the House of Lords, representing "personal merit" and acting as a "moral center of resistance" against the decisions of a popularly elected assembly—that is, against the majority.

Despite their insistence on representation and elections, the liberals hedged and hemmed at the power of the legislature and the right of the majority to decide. They did not have enough confidence in the people. Yet, notwithstanding their fears of the poor, the ignorant, and "the many," the utilitarian premises led gradually to universal suffrage. Representation and representative government gradually spread, and with it majoritarianism, the right of the majority to form a government and make decisions for all, gained legitimacy.

Constitutionalism   The notion of restraints on political authority, as proposed by Locke, influenced the framers of the U.S. Constitution. They feared arbitrary and absolute power so much that they rejected a concentration of power in the hands of any one body, whether it be the legislature, or even the majority of the people. While stressing the idea of natural rights, individual freedoms, and the derivation of authority from the people, they wanted to find a way to make it impossible for any single organ or government to become truly sovereign and overwhelm the others. Their emphasis was more on how to restrain political power, even when it was based on the will of the people, than on how to make it effective.

The answer was a written Constitution that limits power, sets explicit restraints (including the ten amendments) on the national government and the individual states, and institutionalizes the separation of powers in such a manner that one power checks another. At no time would it be possible for one

---

[4]J. S. Mill, "Considerations on Representative Government," in *Utilitarianism*, chap. 6, p. 86.

branch—executive, legislative, or judicial—to overwhelm and subordinate the others. Having accepted the idea of fully representative government through periodic elections, the founders of the American Constitution put heavy restraints upon it.

This is essentially what we mean by constitutionalism. Constitutionalism provides solid guarantees for the individual by explicitly limiting government; it also provides clear procedures for the implementation of the government's functions. In many cases it establishes a watchdog, in the form of a judicial body, to safeguard the Constitution and all the restraints written into it. In addition, it provides procedures through which the responsibility of the governors to the governed is maintained by periodic elections. The government is both *limited* and *responsible*. But the idea of limitations is far more important than that of popular sovereignty. The U.S. Constitution established a republic, not a democracy.

Popular Sovereignty It was Jean-Jacques Rousseau who set up the model of a popular democracy before the French Revolution of 1789. He too found the source of political authority in the people. They were sovereign, and their sovereignty was "inalienable, infallible, and indestructible."[5] In contrast to those who favored representation and representative government, Rousseau believed in direct government by the people. There were to be no restraints on the popular will. He called it "the general will" and claimed that under certain conditions it was always right and that representation would only distort it. In the last analysis, he argued, nobody could really represent anybody else. Something like town meetings in small communities would be the only appropriate instruments for the expression of the general will.

Rousseau's affirmation of the absolute power of the general will, that many interpreted to be the will of the people, had revolutionary implications. It pitted an extreme doctrine of popular sovereignty against absolutism, which was current in France and many other continental countries in the eighteenth century. But it also antagonized liberals who believed in representative government with restraints and who were particularly reluctant to see all the people participate directly or indirectly in decisions.

Consent, representation, popular sovereignty leading to majority rule, and constitutional restraints on the state and its government (even on a majority) obviously emphasize different forms of liberal thought and put the accent on different values. They inevitably lead to different political institutions. Emphasis on constitutional restraints and the protection of individual and minority rights—economic rights at first—led to the type of liberalism, still very much in evidence in the United States, that restricts the majority and allows the judiciary to act as the supreme umpire. On the other hand, emphasis on the Rousseauian idea of popular sovereignty leads to unrestricted majority rule,

---

[5]Jean-Jacques Rousseau, *The Social Contract*, book 2.

Jean-Jacques Rousseau (1712–1778)

Jean-Jacques Rousseau was a French philosopher who, in contrast to the rationalism of the French eighteenth-century philosophers (the Encyclopedists), stressed the role of sentiments and emotions, thus becoming the precursor of many nineteenth-century romantics. He wrote widely on a number of subjects, but his two most important works are on education (*Emile*, 1762) and on politics (*The Social Contract*, 1762). In the latter he argued for the sovereignty of the people, claiming that the "general will" emanating from them is absolute and infallible. It was the combination of this theory of general will and his emphasis on feeling and emotion that led him to glorify nationalism as an all-embracing myth that creates unity and solidarity among a people. The best exposition of his theory of nationalism can be found in his *Considerations on the Government of Poland*, written in 1770.

either directly by the people or by their representatives. In between these two extremes, liberals and liberal institutions attempted, not always successfully, to find a solution that reconciled the idea of majoritarianism with the notion of restraints. Limitation on representative assemblies, various voting qualifications, a bicameral legislature in which one chamber is not directly elected by the people but represents wealth or birth or some other attribute of "moderation," and the veto of the monarch or a president were the devices most often used to deny a numerical majority the power to make decisions.

Throughout the nineteenth century, the main stresses within the political core of liberalism lay in the conflict between those who, in line with Locke and some of the utilitarians, advocated restraints on the legislature and the majority, and those who, in line with Rousseau's theory of popular sovereignty, pressed for uninhibited majority rule.

THE STATE AND THE INDIVIDUAL

Liberalism was an antistate philosophy and remains one in the sense that, all other things being more or less equal, it values the individual and his or her initiative more than the state and its intervention. Nowhere has this position been better set forth than in John Stuart Mill's essay *On Liberty*, published in 1859. To approach it, let us set forth two models, the totalitarian and the liberal. According to the first, the individual and the civil society (i.e., the family, economic organizations, school and universities, and so on) are controlled by the state. It is therefore the state that shapes the social institutions on the basis of a predetermined scheme of values. The state exacts conformity and obedience.

The liberal model presents an entirely different order of things. Individuals and their social institutions are separate from the state. Strictly speaking, they constitute two different spheres of life and action. But when the two spheres do intersect, the intersection should cover only a limited and recognized area. Spontaneity, creativity, experimentation, and the search for truth are within the domain of individuals and their social institutions. It is at best and at most the function of the state to maintain order, to see that nobody in his or her relations with others uses force, to protect civil liberties and personal freedom, and at the same time to maintain the economic freedom of the individual. In other words, the role of the state is to protect the individual.

In his essay *On Liberty* Mill summarizes this by asserting:

1. That every restraint imposed by the state is bad.
2. That even if the individual cannot do certain things well, the state should not do them for fear that it might undermine the individual's independence and initiative.
3. That any increase in the powers of state is automatically bad and prejudicial to individual freedoms: it decreases individual freedom.

Thus Mill views the state on the one hand, and society and the individual on the other, in a mechanical and antithetical kind of relationship. The increase

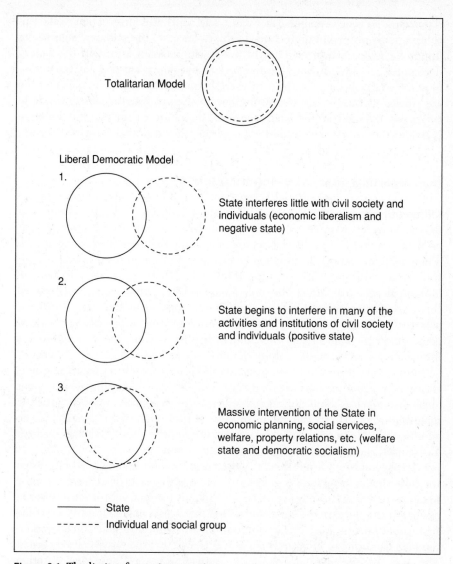

Figure 2.1 The limits of state intervention.

of powers of the state necessarily involves the decrease of powers of the individual; correspondingly, people must be extremely vigilant not to allow an increase in the power of state.

The most crucial problem for liberal thought has been the identification of exactly where the lines separating the state, on the one hand, and society and individuals, on the other, intersect. One might develop an elastic concept, allowing a fairly wide area within the intersecting lines, in which the state can intervene (numbers 2 and 3 in Figure 2.1). Or, in line with the thinking of early liberals, one might allow for the minimum area of intersection in which the state can intervene (number 1 in Figure 2.1). Here the intersection would encompass only order and protection. In this latter case, the state becomes something of a police officer or a "night watchman," making sure that the factory does not burn down and no thieves break in but otherwise allowing full autonomy within the factory, the university, the home, or the school. The smaller the area included within the intersecting lines of Figure 2.1, the closer we are to laissez-faire liberalism; the larger the area, the more we move in the direction of the *positive state* or the *welfare state*, perhaps even getting close to socialism.

Self-regarding and Other-regarding Acts

Different periods in the history of liberalism tell us where the lines have been drawn. War, for example, necessitates state intervention. But this was considered an exception, since there is an understanding that with the passing of such a national emergency the situation would revert to the original liberal model. John Stuart Mill provided us with a criterion for drawing the lines. To Mill, all individual acts that affect the individual—*self-regarding acts*, as he called them—are acts that cannot be controlled or regulated by the state. However, acts that concern and affect others—*other-regarding acts*—can and should come under the control and regulation of the state. Thus, the area within our intersecting circles should include the other-regarding acts.

But "affect" provides no clean standard. Is smoking self-regarding or other-regarding? Is the use of drugs self-regarding or other-regarding? What about alcoholism? What about pornographic literature? Violence on television? The manufacture of drugs? The administration and the high cost of hospitals? The additives put in our foods? Ownership and use of private cars? Nuclear energy? These are just the first questions that come to mind.

The second set of questions is more complex, and relates to exactly *when* the state should bring into its purview other-regarding acts (if we have managed to define exactly what they are). Can it do so only *after* an act is *shown* to affect others, or can the state exercise control because an act *might* affect others? The first would provide a very strict and limiting criterion. The state could regulate the manufacturing of drugs only when it is shown that they have caused cancer. The second interpretation, however, provides a very generous criterion whereby the state can intervene. It would do so every time there is some doubt about the consequences certain drugs can have upon individuals. Drugs that *might* cause cancer should be taken off the market. Whenever certain acts or goods *might* affect others, they should be regulated and controlled.

Mill did not have to answer these questions explicitly, because of the way he defined self-regarding and other-regarding acts. *All individual acts, he claimed, are self-regarding except those that cause harm to others. The criterion in terms of which other-regarding acts are defined is that of harm. Only if harm is done can the state intervene.* Commerce, production, consumption are self-regarding.[6] The state should not intervene. But so, of course, are freedom of thought and expression and freedom of association. The state should not intervene here either. So, in the last analysis, the individual has the right to get drunk and to use drugs. However, your actions become other-regarding, and hence invite state intervention, when they cause harm to others. You can stay in your attic drinking beer as long as you want; you are free to indulge in this self-regarding act. But if you start throwing the empty cans out of a window and you endanger passersby, then the act becomes other-regarding.

But the moment we give a more relaxed definition of what is other-regarding, and introduce the concept of *effect* or *influence* rather than *harm*, we move in the opposite direction to favor state intervention and regulation. The police officer may try to save you from too much beer or drugs, even if you have not harmed anybody! The question should be raised at this point about apparently self-regarding acts that nonetheless "affect" the society as a whole. Costs of production concern the entrepreneurs and come within their discretion. Suppose, however, people and whole communities are affected by the manner in which production is carried out. Streams may become polluted, the water supply becomes unhealthy, pollutants spread into the air. Undoubtedly, people will then say that these actions are other-regarding and must be controlled. But who will pay the *social cost* involved—the harm caused to others. We discuss this in Chapter 12 on environmentalism.

Pluralism   The liberal ethic and the liberal ideology are intensely individualistic. However, liberalism is used also to refer to the rights and freedoms not only of individuals but also of groups and associations. Replace the individual with the group or an association to which he or she belongs and you have pluralism. Groups demand and expect the same treatment in regard to tolerance, representation, and participation that the individuals have. With the breakdown of rigid class and religious or ethnic solidarities in many modern systems, thousands of groups have mushroomed. Groups organize; they make their demands. Public policy, it is expected, will then be made in response to their demands. As David Apter writes, "The notion of individual competitions is replaced [under pluralism] by a network of organizational competition, influence, accountability and information in which groups can organize and, by exercising rights, realize interests to affect policy outcomes."[7]

But groups may make claims that go beyond the mere satisfaction of interest. They may claim the same autonomy that the individuals claim. These are claims for ethnic, racial, local, functional, occupational, and economic auton-

---

[6]J. S. Mill, "Of the Limits of the Authority of Society over the Individual," in his essay *On Liberty*, ch. 4 in *Utilitarianism*.

[7]David Apter, *Introduction to Political Analysis*, pp. 314–315.

omy. Their implementation requires a great deal of decentralization of the democratic state. Very often demands on the part of certain groups even go beyond decentralization to assert separation and independence from the state. Sometimes pluralism is used to justify economic democracy—that is, the rights of certain groups and organizations to decide by themselves on the economic activities in which they are engaged without any intervention from the state.

As long as there is a basic agreement in the political society on the rules that determine political competition, pluralism and liberalism can coexist. But the moment a group or a combination of groups subordinate others, they will dominate the society and coerce the individual. This may clearly be the case with industrial corporations, trade unions, other economic groups, ethnic groups, and even religious sects. The early liberal theorists feared group dominance and tried in one way or another to make it difficult for groups to develop and to supplant the individuals. They argued that a group is not a moral entity like the individual. It overshadows the individuals and subordinates them to the imperative of group solidarity. As a result, groups pose the danger of subverting individual freedoms.

ACHIEVEMENTS: THE EXPANSION OF LIBERALISM

If we take a fairly thick brush and paint onto the canvas of the nineteenth century all the liberal achievements in the realm of economic rights, civil liberties, and political rights, the picture that emerges is breathtaking. The liberals and the liberal movements and parties changed the economic, social, and political structure of Europe, and drastically modified the international community as well. Some of the major achievements are listed here.

Slavery was outlawed. In the United States it continued until the Civil War, but the importation of slaves after 1808 had been declared illegal. In England the slave trade was banned in 1807, and slavery was abolished in the British Empire in 1833. France followed in 1848; the Netherlands in 1869; Argentina in 1853; Portugal in 1858; Brazil in 1888. Serfdom was abolished in Russia in 1861.

Gradually *religious disabilities* against holding political or other offices were abandoned virtually everywhere. Catholics, Protestants, Jews, Quakers, and nonconformist religious minorities were allowed full participation by the end of the nineteenth century.

After bitter controversies, *toleration* was granted, and church and state separated in many countries. Religious affiliation and worship became personal rights.

Freedom of press, speech, and *association* were granted. By the end of the nineteenth century, in Western Europe, Britain and its dominions, and the United States, rare were the cases where people could not express their views or were penalized for the views they did express, no matter how heretical or subversive.

The state began to provide *education* and to require children to attend school up to the age of ten, twelve, or fourteen.

The vote was gradually extended to all males first, and to women only after World War I. There was universal male suffrage in England by 1884; in France in 1848; in Italy by the end of the century; in Russia in 1905 (but not for long); and in Germany and the Scandinavian countries in varying degrees by the end of the century. In the United States, male universal suffrage (limited to whites) was established in the 1820s. Property qualifications for voters and candidates were eliminated, but some other qualifications—literacy, age, or residence—remained. All in all, the prediction of Lord Macaulay that "universal suffrage is utterly incompatible with the existence of civilization" proved quite wrong!

Nothing illustrates the force of liberalism better than the reforms undertaken in France after the revolution of 1830. The second chamber was changed from a hereditary one to one in which members sat for life; the electorate was broadened by lowering the age qualifications to twenty-five instead of thirty; property qualifications were reduced from three hundred francs to two hundred. Candidates for office were to be thirty years old instead of forty, censorship was abolished, extraordinary tribunals were eliminated, schools were set up in every commune by the state, and the control of church over the schools was put to an end. These reforms were modest; indeed, they stopped far short of what democrats wanted to accomplish. But they were moving in the direction of democracy. It took, for example, just eighteen years (after another revolution) before universal suffrage was introduced to France, in 1848.

Similarly, the liberal Reform Act of 1832 in England provided for a property qualification of ten pounds a year, thus excluding the poor and the workers from voting but allowing the middle classes to do so. The act increased the electorate to about 750,000 out of a total population of about 13.5 million. Further extensions in 1867 and 1884 followed, bringing the workers into the political system.

Constitutions, constitution-making, and *constitutionalism* were everywhere in the air. Even where a constitution had only symbolic character it still echoed the aspirations of citizens to limit government and establish the rules that made the holders of power responsible to the people or their representatives.

In Russia, a movement for a constitution which would limit the powers of the czar emerged in 1824; in Greece, liberal constitutions were promulgated in 1827 and again in 1843; in Germany, a liberal constitution was prepared by a convention that met in Frankfurt in 1848; in France, liberal constitutions were promulgated (after the failure of the ones established during the French Revolution) in 1830, 1848, and 1871. In Spain, Portugal, Italy, and in many Latin American republics, constitutional documents came into force by the end of the nineteenth century and often earlier. Even Poland, the Austro-Hungarian Empire, and the Ottoman Empire experienced liberal reforms that were embodied in constitutional documents or charters.

These reforms were not granted easily; occasionally, they were granted only to be withdrawn. Frequently liberal political movements were repressed, but the overall impact was the same—broadening and safeguarding civil liberties and extending political participation to an ever-growing number of people in every political system. Above all, they imposed responsibility and restraints, no matter how fragile and temporary, upon the holders of political power. This in itself helped to erode the claims of absolutism.

Representative government became increasingly accepted throughout Europe and in the English-speaking countries. With the exception of Russia (with a notable interval between 1905 and 1914), there was hardly a political system in the nineteenth century that did not introduce representative assemblies and did not give them some (often considerable) power over decisions. In many cases, the assembly was given the power to censure the government and force it out of office. Representative assemblies participated in the formulation of laws and decided on taxation and expenditures. Within limits (and sometimes without any restriction) debate was free and representatives were not liable for their words and actions in the legislature.

As the suffrage expanded to new groups, *political parties* began to emerge, seeking the vote in order to govern on the basis of pledges they offered to the electorate. They became transmission belts between the people and the government, making the latter increasingly responsive to popular demands and aspirations and helping translate demands and wants into policy and action. Parties emerged, at first in the United States where male universal suffrage was introduced as early as 1824, with platforms, leadership, organization, and ideological loyalties. In England, they gradually evolved from factions and cliques, manipulated and controlled by the king and the landed gentry, into national organizations representing the new towns and the middle classes. The Liberals and Conservatives, the two large parties, established national headquarters, designated candidates, prepared their platforms, solicited membership, and vied for office against each other after the middle of the nineteenth century. The Conservatives followed the logic of liberalism and enacted legislation enfranchising new groups by lowering property qualifications. Their leader, Benjamin Disraeli, spoke of the union between "the cottage and the throne," an expression that symbolized the reconciliation of the aristocracy with the principles of democracy and the needs of the common man.

In France, the nobility continued to influence the vote, and political parties were numerous, badly organized, regional rather than national, and without clearcut platforms. Until 1880 their differences were about the political regime: some favoring the republic, others a return to the monarchy, and still others aspiring to Bonapartism. It was only by the very end of the nineteenth century that the Socialists became unified into one party; the centrist groups— republican, anticlerical, and liberal—formed the Radical-Socialist party.

In Germany, the powerful Social Democratic party had the best organization and the largest membership and became revisionist and reformist rather than a revolutionary party. It was opposed by the Center party (liberal but appealing to Catholic groups), the Liberals (a middle-class party), and the Conservatives.

Almost everywhere the development of political parties strengthened liberal democratic principles and institutions. Parties allowed the people to opt directly for candidates and policies and brought the governments that emerged from elections closer to their control.

Liberalism had, of course, a profound impact on *economic life*. Freedom of movement (a simple right in our eyes) became a reality for the first time. Journeymen, merchants, manufacturers, and farmers could move not only their produce and goods but themselves without any prior permission or restraint. They could dispose of their property and do as they pleased with it. Individuals became free to change professions just as easily as they could change their domiciles; they could enter into partnership or agree to provide their services on the basis of mutually binding agreements. Not only their home but also their property became a "castle" against intervention, regulation, and confiscation by an arbitrary ruler.

There was (though not everywhere) a *trend against all forms of tariffs* and all indirect restrictions on the movement of goods—first felt against internal tariffs that allowed cities, municipalities, or regional authorities to tax goods at the point of their entry or exit. But beyond these internal tariffs, a great movement was under way, spearheaded by British industrial and trading groups, to reduce and even to eliminate all external tariffs that taxed goods coming into or moving out of a state. It favored worldwide free trade. As Richard Cobden, one of Adam Smith's disciples, stated in 1846:

> There is no human event that has happened in the world more calculated to promote the enduring interests of humanity than the establishment of the principle of free trade.[8]

Despite their aversion to state intervention in social and economic matters, liberals were forced to consider *limited interventions*. "Poor laws" were introduced to keep the destitute from starvation. As unemployment assumed menacing proportions in the 1840s, public workshops were established in France, and at one time they employed as many as a quarter of a million people. Child labor legislation gradually began to prohibit the employment of children under certain ages and required them to go to school. A ten-hour working day was decreed in England in 1846, and factory laws began to provide for the safety of workers. Now workers were to receive compensation for accidents caused by their work. By the end of the century, many of these measures had been expanded to provide added protection, including the first steps in the direction of health insurance.

In the name of liberalism, a vast movement in favor of *national self-determination* and national independence spread over Europe. It culminated in the Wilsonian principles of self-determination. Throughout the nineteenth century, dynasties disintegrated and new nations came into being. Greece (1827), Norway (1830), and Belgium (1830) became independent. In Poland, a liberal national uprising in favor of independence took place in 1831. Italy became a unified national state in 1870, and Germany followed in 1871. The Ottoman Empire, encompassing the Balkans, Turkey, and the Middle East, cracked wide

---

[8]Cited by Donald Read, *Cobden and Bright*, p. 65.

open, allowing for the emergence of a number of independent states, some late in the nineteenth century and the beginning of the twentieth. Bulgaria, Romania, part of Yugoslavia, and Alabania became new national states. The Austro-Hungarian Empire evolved into Hungary, Serbia, and ultimately Czechoslovakia. Powerful liberal independence movements manifested themselves within the Czarist Empire. Most of these new states undertook constitutional reforms, providing for individual rights, election and popular participation, and restraints on the government.

CONCLUSION

In overall terms, nineteenth-century liberalism shows a remarkable record in bringing forth and institutionalizing civil rights, political rights, and economic freedoms. It was equally potent in causing a profound reconsideration of the position of the aristocracy, the church, and many unreconstructed traditionalists. But the century was also remarkable for the growth and the unprecedented development of technology and production. This, despite the many miseries that continued to afflict the workers, gave credence to some of the assertions of Adam Smith and the utilitarians. Economies grew; world population began a rapid climb; water and rail communications were established, bringing people closer together in their national community as well as in the world; new cities developed rapidly while many old ones were literally torn apart and rebuilt; currency in gold or paper money and new banking practices facilitated exchange; and savings were channeled into new investments. Nations mushroomed in the name of self-determination. The best eulogy on the spirit of the innovation and the modernity that bourgeois liberalism exemplified was given by its greatest critic, Karl Marx, in the *Communist Manifesto*.

> Constant revolutionizing of production, uninterrupted disturbance of all social relations, everlasting uncertainty and agitation, distinguish the bourgeois epoch from all earlier times. All fixed, fast-frozen relationships, with their train of venerable ideas and opinions, are swept away, all new-formed ones become obsolete before they can ossify. All that is solid melts into air, all that is holy is profaned.

By the end of the century, a new factor was injected into the liberal philosophy—social justice. It was needed to support individuals in one form or another when their self-reliance and initiative could no longer provide them with protection, or when the market did not show the flexibility or the sensitivity it was supposed to show in satisfying basic wants. A new spirit of mutual aid, cooperation, and service began to develop. It became stronger with the coming of the twentieth century.

BIBLIOGRAPHY

Apter, David. *Introduction to Political Analysis*. Cambridge, Mass.: Winthrop, 1978.

Bentham, Jeremy. *An Introduction to the Principles of Morals and Legislation*. New York: Harper & Row, 1952.

Berlin, Isaiah. *Four Essays on Liberty*. New York: Oxford University Press, 1969.

Black, Eugene (ed.). *Posture of Europe, 1815–1940*. Homewood, Ill.: Dorsey Press, 1964.

———— . *Victorians: Culture and Society*. New York: Harper & Row, 1973.

Briggs, Asa. *The Age of Improvement*. London: Longmans, 1959.

Clark, G. Kitson. *An Expanding Society: Britain 1830–1900*. New York: Cambridge University Press, 1967.

Dahl, Robert A. *A Preface to Democratic Theory*. Chicago: University of Chicago Press, 1956.

Dahl, Robert A. *Democracy, Liberty, and Equality* New York: Oxford University Press, 1988.

"Declaration of the Rights of Man and of the Citizen." In Paul H. Beik, *The French Revolution*. New York: Harper & Row, 1970.

Dicey, A. V. *Lectures on the Relationship Between Law and Public Opinion in England During the 19th Century*. New York: Macmillan, 1952.

Dinwiddy, John. *Bentham*. New York: Oxford University Press, 1989.

Gray, John. *Liberalism*. Minneapolis: University of Minnesota Press, 1986.

Halevy, E. *The Growth of Philosophic Radicalism*. London: Faber, 1952.

Hallowell, John H. *The Moral Foundations of Democracy*. Chicago: University of Chicago Press, 1954.

Hamilton, Alexander, James Madison, and John Jay. *The Federalist Papers*. New York: New American Library, 1961.

Hartz, Louis. *The Liberal Tradition in America*. New York: Harcourt, 1962.

Hobhouse, L. T. *Liberalism*. New York: Oxford University Press, 1964.

Jefferson, Thomas. *Drafts of the Declaration of Independence*. Washington, D.C.: Acropolis, 1963.

Laski, Harold J. *The Rise of European Liberalism*. Atlantic Highlands, N.J.: Humanities Press, 1962.

Levine, Andrew. *Liberal Democracy: A Critique of Its Theory*. New York: Columbia University Press, 1981.

Lively, Jack. *Democracy*. Oxford, England: Basil Blackwell, 1975.

Locke, John. *Two Treatises on Government*. Edited by Peter Laslett. New York: New American Library, 1965.

MacPherson, C. B. *The Political Theory of Possessive Individualism*. Oxford, England: Hobbes and Locke, 1962.

———— . *The Real World of Democracy*. Oxford, England: Clarendon Press, 1966.

———— . *Democratic Theory: Essays in Retrieval*. Oxford, England: Clarendon Press, 1973.

———— . *The Life and Times of Liberal Democracy*. New York: Oxford University Press, 1977.

Mill, John Stuart. *Utilitarianism, Liberty*, and *Representative Government*, Everyman's Library, J. M. Dent and Sons, London, 1940. (With an introduction by A. D. Lindsay.) There have been many publications of these three essays by John Stuart Mill with critical introductory comments.

Palmer, R. R. *The Age of the Democratic Revolution*, 2 vols. Princeton, N.J.: Princeton University Press, 1959.

Palmer, R. R., and Joel Colton. *A History of the Modern World Since 1815*. New York: Knopf, 1971.

Read, Donald. *Cobden and Bright*. London: St. Martin's Press, 1968.

Rees, John C. *John Stuart Mill's On Liberty*. New York: Oxford University Press, 1985.

Revel, Jean-Francois. *Without Marx and Jesus: The New American Revolution Has Begun*. New York: Doubleday, 1971.

Rousseau, Jean-Jacques. *The Social Contract and Discourse on Inequality*. New York: Washington Square Press, 1967.

Rugiero, E. *The History of European Liberalism*. Boston: Beacon Press, 1959.

Sartori, Giovanni. *Democratic Theory*. New York: Praeger, 1965.

Sidorsky, David. *The Liberal Tradition in European Thought*. New York: Putnam, 1970.

Smith, Adam. *The Wealth of Nations: Representative Selections*. New York: Bobbs-Merrill, 1961.

Tawney, R. H. *Religion and the Rise of Capitalism*. New York: New American Library, 1954.

Thomson, David. *Europe Since 1815*, 2nd rev. ed. New York: Knopf, 1957.

―――. *Democracy in France Since 1870*, 4th ed. New York: Oxford University Press, 1964.

Thurman, Arnold. *The Folklore of Capitalism*. New Haven, Conn.: Yale University Press, 1937.

Weber, Max. *The Protestant Ethic and the Spirit of Capitalism*. New York: Scribner's, 1958.

Chapter
3

Democracy and the Economy

Socialism, the Welfare State, . . . Capitalism Again?

But man in society not only lives his individual life: he also modifies the form of social institutions in the direction indicated by reason—in such a manner . . . that will render them more efficient for securing freedom.

Sydney Oliver

Fabian Essays in Socialism

Our freedom of choice in a competitive society rests on the fact that, if one person refuses to satisfy our wishes, we can turn to another. But if we face a monopolist we are at his mercy. And an authority directing the whole economic system would be the most powerful monopolist conceivable.

F. A. Hayek

The Road to Serfdom

The year 1848 represents a watershed for European liberalism. From it, powerful and divergent currents began to flow. From Paris to Palermo, from Frankfurt and London to Budapest, Vienna, and Madrid, the poor, the workers, and the peasants who had left the countryside for the urban centers, led by students and intellectuals at their side, rose to take power away from the propertied classes in the name of *radical democracy* and *socialism*. Writing in the same year, John Stuart Mill commented on the industrial and technological achievements of the period and pointed out that they had improved the living standard of the middle classes only. "They have not as yet," he added, "begun to effect those great changes in human destiny, which it is their nature . . . to accomplish."[1]

The middle classes found themselves wavering. Some sided with radical democrats and the socialists and joined forces with them in an alliance that could not last. Others backed conservative groups—the nobility, the church, the landowners—that had resisted liberalism.

Using the three basic cores of the liberal democratic ideology as a guide, it is relatively easy to map out its evolution throughout the nineteenth century and to reassess its present position.

RADICAL DEMOCRATS

Radical democrats accepted the moral core of liberalism—civil rights, individual freedoms, freedom of press, religion, and association (though they insisted on the secularization of many of the functions that the church provided, such as education, and favored outright expropriation of its landed domains). They also supported the political core but interpreted it in Rousseauian terms: all political power should come directly from the people and a majority could make all decisions directly or through sovereign representative assemblies. They were against all voting qualifications and against any restraints on the exercise of popular will. They also began to express fundamental reservations about the economic core about capitalism.

Radical Democrats in England and France

A strong radical democratic movement developed in England roughly between 1830 and 1850. This was *Chartism,* a movement of middle-class reformers with working-class support. Their program (the Charter) seemed to be primarily political, calling for universal manhood franchise, equal electorate districts, "one man, one vote," annual parliaments, elimination of all property qualifications, and the secret ballot. The leaders, Feargus O'Connor, Francis Place, and William Lovett, attempted time after time to pressure Parliament into passing legislation in accordance with Charter, but without success.

But in addition to political reform, a strong group among the Chartists urged for social and economic reform. Sometimes they came close to the socialist ideas that were circulating in England and the Continent at the time. They demanded the regulation of work hours and wages as well as social benefits for the workers.

> Eight hours to work; eight hours to play
> Eight hours to sleep; eight bob [shillings] a day

---

[1]Cited by Asa Briggs, *The Age of Improvement,* p. 303.

was one among many Chartist slogans. Some of the Chartist leaders openly advocated socialist measures:

> It is the duty of the Government to appropriate its present surplus revenue, and the proceeds of national and public property, to the purchasing of lands, and the location thereon of the unemployed poor. . . .
>
> The gradual resumption by the State . . . of its ancient, undoubted, inalienable domain, and sole proprietorship over all the lands, mines, tributaries, fisheries, etc., of the United Kingdom and our Colonies; for the same to be held by the State, as trustee in perpetuity, for the entire people. . . .
>
> It is the recognized duty of the State to support all those of its subjects, who, from incapacity or misfortune, are unable to procure their own subsistence.[2]

In France during the same period, radical democracy took a more extreme form. Louis Blanqui, one of the early social reformers, moved very close to revolutionary socialism and led a number of armed uprisings against the governmental authorities. Louis Blanc, another social reformer, came closer to the Chartist position. He believed political reforms were essential, but it was the duty of the state to safeguard the "right to work." He urged the government to set up national workshops to employ workers, and he believed that such workshops would compete successfully with privately owned firms. As time went on, radical democracy in France increasingly moved in the direction of economic and social reforms—especially after 1848 when universal manhood suffrage, one of the major demands, was adopted. It raised the electorate overnight from a quarter million to nine million voters.

Thus, many radical democrats parted company with liberals on the definition of the economic core. They questioned the laissez-faire model of capitalism as it had been portrayed by Adam Smith. They were in favor of using the state in order to correct some of the evils and the uncertainties of the market, but they went beyond the mere search for corrective measures. They emphasized the importance of social and collective goals that could best be implemented by collective (i.e., state) action. They favored extensive state intervention not simply through legislation but through direct action and performance. Not just laws regulating child labor, but inspection and enforcement were demanded; not only poor laws providing for relief, but the actual operation of state workshops to provide employment to the poor. They demanded that the provision of social services be implemented directly by the public authorities.

Most radical democrats, however, stopped short of socialism. Their position was that the state should act and intervene where major social services and needs were involved, but without reaching out to expropriate property or to directly take over economic activities such as production and trade. They favored wide regulations and occasional direct controls but not the socialization of the means of production.

---

[2]Cited in G. D. H. Cole and A. W. Filson, *Working Class Movements: Selected Documents*, p. 79.

If we situate the radical democrats in terms of our basic cores of liberalism, we find them strong on the political core (leaning all the way to majoritarianism and popular sovereignty), strong on the moral core, but faithful to only a few of the basic principles defined as the economic core of early liberalism. In 1869, the French politician Jules Gambetta summed up the *political* program of radical democrats everywhere in his Belleville Manifesto and intimated at the same time the need for economic reform:

> I think that there is no other sovereign but the people and that universal suffrage, the instrument of this sovereignty, has no value and basis unless it be radically free.

He asked for

> the most radical application of universal suffrage; . . . individual liberty to be . . . protected by law; . . . trial by jury for every kind of political offense; complete freedom of the Press; . . . freedom of meeting . . . with liberty to discuss all religious, philosophical, political, and social affairs; . . . complete freedom of association . . . separation of church and state; free, compulsory, secular primary education; . . . suppression of standing armies; . . . abolition of privileges and monopolies.[3]

LIBERAL AND RADICAL DEMOCRATS: RECONCILIATION

With the exception of those who remained attached to the economic philosophy of Adam Smith, most liberals, and what we have called radical democrats, gradually came to terms. Liberals have accepted the full logic of democracy. Today the franchise has been extended in almost all democracies to cover all citizens, male and female, above eighteen. All of the many qualifications for voting based on literacy, age, residence, income, and so on, have been eliminated. Restraints on representative assemblies have been virtually lifted, except in cases where the chief executive is also elected directly by the people. In all existing constitutional monarchies, the monarch has become a mere figurehead.

The people were mobilized into large mass parties and these parties, in many countries, exercise a controlling influence over their representatives. In some instances provisions for referenda give the people an additional measure of direct democracy. Popular democracy and majority rule expressed through direct elections for or against the members and candidates of large national political parties have been accepted by all liberals and democrats to be the major source of policymaking. At the same time, the moral core of liberalism in the form of individual and minority rights has been reaffirmed.

There has also been a similar reconciliation between radical democrats and liberals with regard to economic matters. The liberals, as well as many other parties, even when they call themselves conservatives, have found themselves increasingly in agreement. State intervention to support economic activities in

---

[3]Cited in David Thomson, *Democracy in France Since 1870*, pp. 315–316.

the form of price and other controls is deemed acceptable; state intervention through direct or indirect means to stimulate economic activity is again deemed desirable; state regulation of a growing number of economic activities is viewed as indispensable; direct state involvement in providing for unemployment assistance and indirect and direct state action to provide for employment are now taken for granted in most democracies. Thus, the functions of the state are viewed not only as supportive or regulatory; they have actually become complementary to the private sector. This is the welfare state to which we return.

THE SOCIALIST IMPULSE

Socialism as a philosophy of life and as a scheme for the organization of society is as old as (perhaps older than) democracy or any other form of social, economic, or political organization. Some consider it, in fact, to have been prevalent among primitive societies where it has been suggested that land was collectively owned.

Socialism also represents an ethic diametrically opposed to that of private ownership and private profit and the inequalities that the free market may lead to. It is an ethic of an egalitarian and free society, from which the words "mine" and "yours" are eliminated.

Utopian Socialism

Utopian Socialists, beginning with Thomas More (1478–1535), through Francis Bacon (1561–1621) and Tommaso Campanella (1568–1639), down to some of the most important French and British Utopian Socialists of the nineteenth century, shared a set of common ideas.

1. They had an aversion to private property and the exploitation of the poor by those who owned the wealth, whether landed, commercial, or industrial. "Property is theft" was the curt aphorism of the French Socialist Proudhon. The Romantic poet Shelley voiced these early nineteenth-century socialist beliefs:

> The seed ye sow, another reaps,
> The wealth ye find, another keeps,
> The robes ye weave, another wears,
> The arms ye forge, another bears.

2. A passionate commitment to collectivism—the common ownership of wealth—was partly based on notions about primitive communism, and partly on ideas of mutual cooperation and social solidarity. Thus, socialism was seen as the way to extirpate strife, antagonisms, and selfishness. Utopian Socialists shared the nostalgic vision of the Roman poet Virgil about bygone ages:

> No fences parted fields, nor marks nor bounds
> Divided acres of litigious grounds,
> But all was common.

In a famous passage, Rousseau expressed similar thoughts:

The first man, who after enclosing a piece of ground, took it into his head to say, *this is mine*, and found people simple enough to believe him, was the real founder of civil society. How many crimes, how many wars, how many murders, how many misfortunes and horrors, would that man have saved the human species, who pulling up the stakes or filling up the ditches should have cried to his fellows: Beware of listening to this impostor; you are lost, if you forget that the fruits of the earth belong equally to us all, and the earth itself to nobody![4]

3. A passionate belief in what might be called "social collectivism" emphasized the interdependence and solidarity of social life—the "social nature" of men and women, as opposed to the individualistic or utilitarian ethic. Communitarianism was the supreme value; individualism, competition, and self-interest were detested.

4. There were divergent opinions among the early Utopian Socialists on *how* to bring about socialism. Some believed in violence and revolution, but did not spell out any details; others believed in persuasion and example. For instance, the British Socialist Robert Owen (1771–1856) set up a model textile factory in East Lanark, Scotland, where good working conditions and wages, and the participation of the workers in some of the profits, were to become a model to convince other businessmen that it was in their own interests to follow the same pattern. Most Utopian Socialists, however, believed in education. If men and women were properly educated, they would opt for socialism, and it was the task of the intellectuals to provide this kind of education.

5. Many, especially among the French Utopian Socialists, were what we would call today social engineers. In their opinion, society should be controlled and manipulated so that, under proper conditions and with the proper social organization, human beings could attain perfection—both moral and material.

Most of the Utopian Socialists were not democrats. They paid lip service to the moral core of liberalism but argued that liberal political and economic principles and practices could not bring about a just social order. A "new ideology" had to be imposed first or inculcated through education by an elite—by philosophers and intellectuals. The Utopian Socialists never managed to form a party or even a political movement, but their writings had a profound influence on the development of socialist thought.

Democratic Socialism

We have already noted that by the end of the nineteenth century there developed a gradual reconciliation between the proponents of liberalism and the radical democrats in the form of political democracy. A similar reconciliation was also beginning to take shape between democracy and socialism—one that developed throughout the twentieth century and accounts for what today is generally called *democratic socialism.*

Nineteenth-century democrats endorsed popular sovereignty and majoritarianism, while accepting the individual and civil rights that we have discussed

---

[4]Jean-Jacques Rousseau, *The Social Contract and Discourses,* book 1.

as the moral core of liberalism. This set the tone for state intervention to regulate the market, to correct malfunctioning, and to provide social service. But socialism, as first propounded by Marx and some Utopian Socialists, rejected the political core of liberalism. It favored revolution. However, revolutionary Marxism gave way by the end of the nineteenth century to "revisionism." In France, in Germany, especially in England, but also in Belgium, Holland, and the Scandinavian countries, socialist parties began increasingly to accept the logic and the techniques of democracy. Their goal was modified to bringing about social change through peaceful political means and established democratic procedures, and they became attached to the moral core of liberalism and its stress on individual and civil rights. Socialists began to consider these ideals as ends in themselves rather than as means to be used for the conquest of power. They became increasingly attracted to electoral politics, especially when Socialist candidates won appreciable numbers of votes at the polls. They began to see the proper instrument for change in democracy and realized that they could substitute democratic process for revolution and force.

The Fabians.   By the end of the nineteenth century in England, a number of intellectuals were expounding on socialism. Most important were the Fabians (who took their name from the Roman general Fabius, whose defensive "wait and see" tactics gradually weakened Hannibal's invading forces until they were defeated). The Fabians and the Fabian Society, which they established in 1884, relied on three forces: *time,* which meant that socialism would come about gradually; *education,* to persuade the elites and the people that socialism was a superior system, morally and economically, to capitalism; and *political action* in the context of democratic and parliamentary institutions. This meant the formation of a Socialist party that would present its socialist doctrine to the people for their approval. There was not even a mention of the use of force, and nothing about revolution: in fact, many of their socialist principles were inspired by the Bible. British socialism was steeped in moral, egalitarian, and humanistic values and sought human dignity and freedom in a society from which profit and selfishness had been removed.

The philosophic foundations of Fabian socialism were set forth in the *Fabian Essays,* published in 1889. George Bernard Shaw, one of the movement's leaders, wrote:

> It was in 1885, that the Fabian Society . . . set . . . two definite tasks; first, to provide a parliamentary program for a Prime Minister converted to Socialism . . . and second, to make it as easy and matter-of-course for the ordinary respectable English- man to be a Socialist.[5]

The Fabians favored socialization of the means of production, state controls, and broad welfare measures to bring about as much social equality as possible. They had no regard whatsoever for the economic core of liberalism and advocated drastic overhaul of the economy; in doing so, they went well beyond the simple

---

[5]George Bernard Shaw (ed.), *Fabian Essays in Socialism,* p. 33.

Sidney (1859–1947) and Beatrice Webb (1858–1943)

Sidney Webb, an Englishman of petit bourgeois background, spent over ten years in the service of the Colonial Office. In 1885, the year he joined the bar, he also joined the Fabian Society, a group of British socialists dedicated to the education of the British people in socialist principles. In 1889, Webb, along with other notable Fabians such as George Bernard Shaw and Graham Wallas, issued the *Fabian Essays in Socialism,* a book which was to become a classic of non-Marxist socialist thought. In 1887, Sidney Webb was married to Beatrice Potter, a woman of similar views. Both were heavily involved with social issues and active in the formation of the British Labour party. Sidney drafted its manifesto—*Labour and the New Social Order*—which served as the party's platform in the elections of 1918, 1922, and 1924.

regulation of social legislation advocated by radical democrats (and increasingly accepted by liberals). They favored the abolition of property and of the free enterprise system. Socialism was declared, however, to be an advanced form of individualism: "Socialism is merely individualism rationalised, organised, clothed, and in its right mind."[6]

---

[6]Shaw, p. 99.

Table 3.1   THE RISE OF THE LABOUR PARTY VOTE

General election	Seats contested	Members returned	Labour vote
1900	15	2	62,698
1906	50	29	323,195
1910 (Jan.)	78	40	505,690
1910 (Dec.)	56	42	370,802
1918	361	57	2,244,945
1922	414	142	4,236,733
1923	427	191	4,348,379
1924	514	151	5,487,620
1945	**640**	**393**	**11,632,891**

At the beginning of this century, in 1901, the Fabians and the leaders of the major British trade unions formed the Labour party and, by 1906, were running their own independent candidates for election. In the same year, they won 323,195 votes and secured twenty-nine seats in the House of Commons. Socialism had begun to gain the respectability that the Fabians wanted to give it (Table 3.1).

In 1918, Fabian intellectuals provided a definitive platform for the Labour party. The party declared the need for

> the gradual building up of a new social order based, not on internecine conflict, inequality of riches, and dominion over subject classes, subject races, or a subject sex, but on the deliberately planned cooperation in production and distribution, the sympathetic approach to a healthy equality, the widest possible participation in power, both economic and political, and the general consciousness of consent which characterise a true democracy.[7]

Socialism was explicitly and proudly endorsed by the Labour party, in order

> to secure for the producers by hand or by brain the full fruits of their industry, and the most equitable distribution thereof that may be possible, *upon the basis of the common ownership of the means of production* and the best obtainable system of popular administration and control of each industry and service [emphasis added].[8]

European Revisionism   In Western Europe it was revolutionary Marxism that remained the dominant intellectual force and inspiration of working-class Socialist movements, but in the latter part of the nineteenth century, democratic socialism (in the name of "revisionism") began to gain the upper hand.

Revisionism became a distinct ideological movement, based on the works of Eduard Bernstein, a German Socialist who produced the most comprehensive criticism of Marx and Marxism. He point out that:

---

[7]Quoted in G. D. H. Cole, *A History of the Labour Party Since 1914*, p. 65.
[8]Cole, p. 72.

1. The liberal capitalist system was not about to collapse, as Marx had anticipated.

2. The number of capitalists and property owners was increasing absolutely, rather than decreasing as Marxist theory stipulated it would. Thanks to the corporations and the stock exchange, a greater number of people began to "own" property in the form of stocks.

3. The capitalistic economy was generating an ever-increasing number of jobs as production became more specialized. The middle classes were, in fact, growing in number and changing in character. They no longer consisted of people who owned property, as in the past, but of new salaried personnel: technicians, engineers, white-collar workers, service personnel, civil servants, those in the liberal professions, teachers, and so on. Thus, instead of a pyramid with a huge base and sharp apex, the changing class structure under liberal capitalism was beginning to resemble a stepped pyramid in which blocks of decreasing width were superimposed upon each other.

According to Bernstein, class structure could be schematized, as shown on the left in Figure 3.1, as a stepped pyramid made up of many intermediate layers. This was contrary to Marx's view (to the right), which represents society as a smooth-sided pyramid, with the capitalist class at the apex.

4. As societies democratized, allowing for equal and universal franchise, associational freedoms, and the formation of political parties, strong working-class parties would be able to assume political power against the capitalist class, to use the state as an instrument for their own protection, and to secure a better allocation of goods and services. This would be accomplished through legislation and nationalizations. Bernstein felt that Marx had seriously underestimated the capabilities of the democratic state to intervene in favor of the workers and the underprivileged.

In light of these observations, Bernstein concluded that *Evolutionary Socialism* (the title of his book, published in 1899—ten years after the *Fabian Essays* were published) and not revolutionary socialism was to gain ascendancy. It was step-by-step and stage-by-stage development of socialism that would gradually replace capitalism.

Bernstein's analysis was persuasive. Revisionism was gradually adopted by the Socialist parties, and revolutionary socialism and its tactics were abandoned. Socialism became synonymous with *democratic socialism.* It accepted parliamentary government and elections and emphasized, almost exclusively,

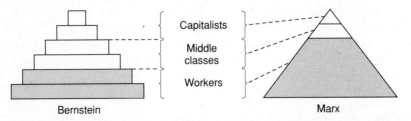

Figure 3.1 Bernstein's schematization of capitalist society (left) compared to Marx's (right).

political activity within the framework of bourgeois legality and democracy. It signified the abandonment of revolutionary class struggle. The workers were to devote themselves to improving their working conditions, their pension benefits, and their wages within the capitalistic economy, and to see to it that a larger share of the national wealth went to them and their families. The trade unions and democratic political action were to become the instruments for the realization of such tasks.

The Socialist movements and parties in Europe began to move, therefore, close to the position of the British Labour party. They, too, accepted the logic of democracy and began to rely more and more on elections, votes, and the conquest of political power through elections. In so doing, they endorsed fully both the moral and the political cores of liberalism but remained hostile to private property and the market economy, promising to socialize the means of production when they achieved full power. But, as with the British Labour party, their approach became gradualistic, even eclectic and pragmatic. Socialists on the Continent, especially the German Social Democrats (Table 3.2), began to propose only specific and selective measures, dealing primarily with the major industries. Small shopkeepers, manufacturers, farmers, and also many large industrial firms and groups would be allowed to operate on their own.

Revisionism thus mobilized a large percentage of the workers to favor democratic change and convinced them (not always completely) that they could promote and defend their interests within the democratic political institutions. Socialism, as such, remained the ultimate end, and strong Socialist parties, supported by the vote of the workers, were expected to press for, or undertake comprehensive measures for, the welfare and well-being of the workers. Even if Socialist parties would not gain a majority, they could still carry great weight

Table 3.2   THE STRENGTH OF THE GERMAN SOCIAL DEMOCRATS[a]

	Votes	Seats in Parliament (Reichstag)
1890	1,427,298	35
1893	1,786,738	44
1898	2,107,076	56
1903	3,010,771	81
1907	3,259,029	43
1912	4,250,401	110
1919	13,000,000	177
1920	11,100,000	184
1924	6,008,900	100
1928	9,153,000	153
1933[b]	**7,181,000**	**120**

[a]Since 1949, when the Federal Republic of Germany was established, the party has averaged about 37 percent of the vote.

[b]Last relatively free election before Hitler assumed full control.

within representative assemblies and could directly influence governments to adopt measures favoring the working class. Broad educational reforms, health, accident, and unemployment insurance, retirement benefits, paid holidays, the reduction of work hours, paid vacations, collective bargaining, welfare measures for the poor and the incapacitated, public works, reform in tax policies favoring low-income groups, and progressively higher taxes on middle and high incomes—these were essential and beneficial measures to ameliorate the conditions of the workers within the broad framework of both capitalism and democracy. Nationalizations could wait or be selectively undertaken under propitious political and economic circumstances. Gradually, a consensus evolved in the acceptance of the welfare state and of a mixed economy—combining state economic controls and social services with the market economy.

REFORMING CAPITALISM

Efforts to reform capitalism come from a variety of nonsocialist sources. The premise of a free market and a price mechanism reflecting the law of supply and demand gave way gradually to regulation. Overriding questions of health, education, unemployment, and poverty required regulatory legislation. Wild fluctuations in prices in the market called for controls, especially when they affected the prices of essential commodities like food and housing. Monopolies, which gave private owners control over needed commodities and hence freedom to adjust prices to satisfy the insatiable profit motive, had to be dealt with. Gradually, and especially in the twentieth century, economic liberalism underwent major reforms.

Keynesian Economics. Reliance on the automatic performance of the market—for the adjustment of prices, savings, and employment—came under serious reconsideration, thanks to the theoretical insights of the English economist John Maynard Keynes (1883–1946). According to Keynes, the market by itself could not provide a full utilization of resources, and the state should move into the picture with indirect controls.

By increasing the flow of money and decreasing the interest rates, there could be renewed investments, which would snowball into the creation of new jobs and hence more revenue to stimulate further demand. Thus unemployment would be absorbed and resources fully utilized. In the process, inflationary pressures would be avoided with appropriate tax measures. In this manner, capitalism would be both reformed and salvaged. The public authorities would become its guardian angel, and no structural modifications involving property rights, entrepreneurial freedoms and incentives, or state planning in the allocation of resources or in price-fixing would be required. "Keynesianism" resulted in policies adopted in a number of countries ever since the 1930s, including Nazi Germany and the United States, especially through the development of public works projects, public spending, and more generally through fiscal policy—including deficit financing. Today when we talk about "capitalism," we virtually always have in mind reformed capitalism, in which the public

John Maynard Keynes (1883–1946)

Considered by many as the greatest economist of the twentieth century, Keynes questioned the fundamental assumption of classic economists about the autonomy of the "economic laws" and opened the door for indirect state intervention. In both his *Treatise on Money* (2 volumes, 1930) and his *General Theory of Employment, Interest and Money* (1936), Keynes stressed the importance of monetary policy in providing for the full utilization of all resources, including labor. By manipulating the volume of money and the rate of interest through a central bank, the government could stimulate investment and employment (or, if needed, avert inflation). By lowering interest rates, for instance, it could stimulate investment, production, and employment. If this failed, and Keynes was particularly concerned in the years of the Great Depression with unemployment, the government could stimulate demand through "public works" that would simply put money in the pockets of many and thus stimulate demand, which in turn would stimulate investment and production. Keynes was not a socialist; he simply provided the best cure for the ailing free-market economy.

authorities, through fiscal policy and spending, play a determining role in the market.

The Welfare State   The major instrument for ensuring social and economic rights became the welfare state—the complex of public services and payments that correspond to "entitlements." The very magnitude of these entitlements is staggering. In the late 1970s, total government payments to individuals in various forms and through various services amounted to from 19 percent of the gross national product in the United States to as much as 40 to 60 percent in countries such as France or Sweden.

In all contemporary democracies the growth of social and economic rights calls for a series of choices, and this is what public policy is all about. Which services should be provided for everybody? What groups merit special attention? What are the limits below which poverty exists and should be prevented? The list is long, but by and large most democratic regimes have followed a similar route in establishing priority choices. Children and education have been at the top of the list, with minimal educational services provided. However, with ever-expanding requirements for schooling, a free college education was added in some countries, the United States being the first to do so.

The aged came next, with emphasis on pensions. In many countries today the age limit for retirement is set at sixty for women and sixty-two for men.

The third step came with legislation requiring the state to provide for employment or to cover the unemployed through special benefits (unemployment insurance). It is presently financed through compulsory contributions and public funds, and public subsidies have steadily grown. In Europe after World War II, a comprehensive scheme was developed, which provided for uniform payments and minimum income levels. In the United States, since the Social Security Act of 1935, an ever-expanding number of employees have been included, contributions have been raised steadily, and benefits have increased.

Health care was the fourth step. Originally undertaken by private and religious organizations, it has been increasingly assumed by government agencies either through insurance programs or through direct payments and services. Germany was the first country to develop a nationwide health program even before the turn of the century. England followed after the turn of the century, and in 1948 it introduced a most comprehensive medical care program: it nationalized all health services and hospitals and incorporated almost all the doctors into the National Health Service. Health care became free, a right of all citizens. In Sweden, a health insurance plan is mandatory, and every citizen receives health care free of charge. In France, medical expenses are covered through a system that combines insurance paid for by individuals with direct payments by the employer and the state. In the United States, it is only after age sixty-five that citizens become directly covered through the Medicare programs.

Although education, health, retirement, and unemployment coverage do provide some safeguards against unaffordable costs, the so-called safety net in the United States, is full of holes. Despite this supplementary income, there are millions who find themselves without adequate income—they are the poor. It is to plug these holes and support the poor that the income maintenance and public assistance programs have been developed everywhere. They are aimed at raising minimal income levels to tolerable ones. Minimum wages become a matter of public policy, and most democratic regimes have set a minimum floor below which wages cannot fall. But with a family to support, a minimum wage is often inadequate.

Various income maintenance programs are used to raise the family income. Tax exemptions, special benefits in the form of cash payments, rent allowances, food subsidies, special allowances for children, day care centers for working mothers, school luncheons, maternity benefits, and all sorts of other free services are calculated to do so.

Public assistance programs and related special treatment and payments are afforded to special segments of society. Although these programs also vary from one country to another, they are almost always available, at least for a given time. However, their purpose is to provide a family with a minimum income, not to equalize income, even if they lessen the distance between the rich and the poor. Security and often a small cushion of adequacy are all that can be expected.

Mixed Economy   *Capitalism*, as we have seen, is a system of social organization in which the means of production is controlled by private persons and firms who make all decisions on how and what to produce and on how benefits are to be distributed. In direct contrast, *socialism* calls for all decisions about production, distribution, and benefits to be made by publicly owned and publicly managed firms. These, of course, are only definitions—"ideal types." When some ownership, management, and decision making is in the hands of the state and some is in the hands of private persons and firms, we have what is referred to as a *mixed economy*.

Virtually all the so-called free-market capitalist economies, including the United States and Japan, are mixed economies. The state plays a critically important role, even when it does not own any of the means of production, which it often does, in deciding what and how much will be produced, how the distribution benefits will be made, and what they will be.

The state widely promotes business ventures and provides a great number of services (i.e., highway and airport construction, air traffic controllers, medical inspection and vaccines, and so forth). In all capitalist democracies, the state is a big employer—providing employment for 15 to 30 percent of those gainfully employed; it is the biggest contractor—for goods and services; it is the biggest spender. In all of these governments, the state plays a critical role in the determination of services and benefits. This has not changed appreciably either in England or the United States in the last decade. Similarly, and particularly in France, despite privatizations of many socialized firms, the state participates directly or indirectly in their operation. In Italy, Japan, and Germany many major industrial firms operate under the control of state-owned banks or under

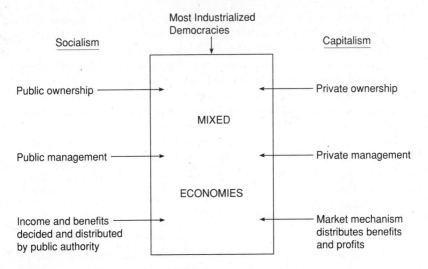

Figure 3.2 The socialist/capitalist mix.

semipublic financial and industrial "umbrella" organizations through which investment and production policies are made. Capitalism, in other words, as it
developed in Western Europe and elsewhere, has included powerful ingredients of statism and socialism. Not so incidentally, a kind of "people's capitalism"
has been developing in which workers own stocks through their pension funds
or profit-sharing arrangements with their employers.

How mixed is a mixed economy? The greater the portion of the economy
owned by individual firms who make decisions about production and the distribution of benefits, the closer we move in the direction of capitalism, and vice
versa (Figures 3.2 and 3.3). In most capitalist economies the "mix" is there. Just
to give you an idea, in the seven largest OECD countries,[9] public spending is
now about 39 percent of the gross national product (GNP); it was only 29 per-
cent in 1960. The state takes the following percentage of the GNP in taxes: Sweden, 57 percent; France, 43 percent; Britain, 39 percent; Italy, 38 percent;
Japan and the United States, about 30 percent. In many of these countries, significant areas of economic activity—public transportation, including the air-
lines, electricity and gas, nuclear energy, steel—are either owned and operated
by public agencies or are subsidized by the state.

For many, the welfare state and the growth of mixed economies represented a synthesis that has put an end to the bitter conflicts between capital and
labor and has transcended the ideological conflicts between Socialists on the
one side and liberals or conservatives on the other. This trend was one of the
reasons that prompted the noted sociologist Daniel Bell to announce the end of
ideology in the early fifties.

---

[9]OECD stands for the Organization of Economic Cooperation and Development, and provides,
among many other services, the best surveys of current economic trends.

Extent of State Ownership

	Posts	Telecommunications	Electricity	Gas	Oil production	Coal	Railways	Airlines	Motor industry	Steel	Ship building
Australia	●	●	●	●	○	○	●	◕	○	○	NA
Austria	●	●	●	●	●	●	●	●	●	●	NA
Belgium	●	●	◕	◔	NA	○	●	●	○	◑	○
Brazil	●	●	●	●	●	●	●	◕	○	●	○
Britain	●	◑	○	○	◔	●	●	○	○	○	●
Canada	●	◕	●	○	○	○	◕	◕	○	○	○
France	●	●	●	●	NA	●	●	●	◕	◕	○
West Germany	●	●	◕	◑	◕	◑	●	●	◑	○	◕
Holland	●	●	◕	◕	NA	NA	●	◕	◑	◕	○
India	●	●	●	●	●	●	●	●	○	◕	●
Italy	●	●	◕	●	NA	NA	●	●	◕	◑	◕
Japan	●	●	○	○	NA	○	◕	◕	○	○	○
Mexico	●	●	●	●	●	●	●	◑	◕	◕	●
South Korea	●	●	◕	○	NA	◕	●	○	◕	◕	○
Spain	●	◑	○	◕	NA	◑	●	●	○	◑	◑
Sweden	●	●	◑	●	NA	NA	●	◑	○	◕	◕
Switzerland	●	●	●	●	NA	NA	●	◕	○	○	NA
United States	●	○	◕	○	○	○	◕*	○	○	○	○

○ Privately owned all or nearly all   ● Publicly owned all or nearly all   ◕ 75%   ◑ 50%   ◔ 25%

*Including Conrail,
NA- Not applicable or negligible production.

Figure 3.3 This appeared in *The Economist* (December 30, 1978). I have adjusted the original table to include major privatizations that have taken place in England in the 1980s: aerospace, oil, Jaguar, telecommunications, Rolls Royce, British Airways, British Steel, electricity were privatized. In France, after a wave of nationalizations in 1981–1982, major sectors of the economy were denationalized in 1988. In all, 30 major banking and industrial units were returned to private hands. Thus, France's economy was becoming clearly "mixed" and moving in the direction of a free market. Extensive privatizations have been taking place throughout the whole of Eastern Europe. In Italy, Sweden, Mexico, Spain, Austria, and Brazil, privatizations are in process, while in China free market zones have been established and farmers have been freed from state controls. Reprinted by permission.

BACK TO CAPITALISM?

Some Recent Trends

Democracy, liberalism, radical democracy, democratic socialism, the welfare state—in successive waves, through the nineteenth century and into the twentieth, these movements have shaped a new consensus. Its major feature has been the reconciliation of individual and political rights and freedoms with direct state intervention in the economy and the provision of social services.

The concept of the triple core of liberalism helps us identify the consensus. Early liberalism stressed personal rights and civil rights—the moral core. This was retained by democracy, which also expanded the political core of liberalism by institutionalizing majoritarianism, organizing political parties, eliminating voter qualifications, and minimizing restraints on the power of the representative assemblies. Socialism maintained respect for individual and civil rights (the moral core), accepted the political core, and squarely introduced the question of comprehensive economic controls and social services. This is the essence of the welfare state. It is this consensus that is being shaken by the resurgence of capitalism.

Inspired by some of the works of F. A. Hayek, Ludwig von Mises, and more recently Milton Friedman, the "neo-liberals" or "neo-liberal conservatives," as they are often referred to, restate forcefully the tenets of the early economic liberals that we surveyed in Chapter 2. They argue that political, moral, and economic freedoms—the three cores of liberalism—are inextricably and organically linked. These freedoms stand or fall together. State economic controls inevitably invite political controls that lead to an authoritarian system of government.

William Buckley, reemphasizing capitalism as an ideology, makes the linkage between economic freedom and political freedoms:

> Economic freedom is the most precious temporal freedom, for the reason that it alone gives to each one of us, in our comings and goings in our complex society, sovereignty—and over that part of existence in which by far the most choices have in fact to be made, and in which it is possible to make choices, involving oneself, without damage to other people. And for the further reason that without economic freedom, political and other freedoms are likely to be taken from us.[10]

The arguments presented by neo-liberals are clear and pointed: bureaucracy leads to inefficiency; state controls and regulations stifle competition and are wasteful because they increase the cost of production. Furthermore, we become dependent upon bureaucratic and impersonal services for which nobody is responsible. In 1946, F. A. Hayek, a professor of economics at the University of Chicago, wrote *The Road to Serfdom*, in which he sounded the alarm. State

---

[10]William F. Buckley, Jr., *Up From Liberalism*, p. 166.

intervention and economic planning, he argued, and the end of individual economic freedoms would result in moral degradation for all of us and the ultimate loss of our political freedoms as well. The bureaucratic state would make choices for us—what to produce and what to consume, where to work and where to live, what income to make, and so on. The same theme is repeated by Buckley:

> What all conservatives in this country fear, and have plenty of reason to fear, is the loss of freedom by attrition. It is therefore for the most realistic reasons, as well as those of principle, that we must resist every single accretion of power by the State. [11]

Buckley provides the following list of particulars:

> to maintain and wherever possible enhance the freedom of the individual to acquire property and dispose of that property in ways that he decides on. To deal with unemployment by eliminating monopoly unionism, featherbedding, and inflexibilities in the labor market, and be prepared, where residual unemployment persists, to cope with it locally, placing the political and humanitarian responsibility on the lowest feasible political unit. [12]

In the last decade, no one has better expressed the position of the neo-liberals than Nobel Prize winner and economist Milton I. Friedman. One of his books, *Free to Choose* (written with his wife Rose), popularized the basic arguments against state intervention in the economy and the belief that such intervention will inevitably lead to controls that will undermine the moral autonomy of individuals and erode political freedoms.

Alongside the neo-liberal position, a second major argument has gained ground and relates to the efficiency of a free-market economy—where competition and free enterprise reign and where economic decisions are made in the market. It is an argument that has gained strength for two reasons. First, the economic crisis in many free-market democracies in the 1970s—with growing unemployment, inflation, and low rates of growth—was attributed to state regulation, the exorbitant growth of the welfare state, and government spending that did not stimulate the economy, as Keynes would have it. On the contrary, government produced, without taking into account the "defense establishment," a large bureaucracy to which resources were diverted; dependent upon this bureaucracy was now a growing number of recipients of welfare services. Second, the 1980s witnessed chaos and in the socialist "command economies" of Eastern Europe, the Soviet Union, and China, where the means of production had been socialized and where the state had become virtually the sole manager. This growing disarray in socialist economies reinforced the arguments of those who favored a return to capitalism. Without individual property linked to responsibility and risk, and without the market to reflect accurately consumer demands and to regulate prices, their economies, it was argued, had entered a period of chronic stagnation—far worse than that of capitalism during the Great

---

[11]Buckley, p. 179.

[12]Buckley, p. 202.

Depression of the thirties. This economic crisis also undermined private incentives and motivations, causing what some called an "egalitarian lethargy"! Unlike the Great Depression, however, it was a systemic collapse, and the socialist economies were unable to provide the seeds of their recovery.

Capitalism, therefore, simultaneously became the battle cry against mixed economy and the welfare state in many industrialized democracies and the driving ideology for many in Eastern Europe and even the Soviet Union who sought economic and political reform. For the industrialized democracies, the state had to be cut down to size; for Eastern Europe and the Soviets, it had to be thoroughly overhauled and democratized by disgorging the economy it had swallowed without being able to digest it.

The resurgence of capitalism is associated with the years of the Reagan presidency (1980–1988), the government of Margaret Thatcher in England (1979–1990), and the remarkable turnaround of the French Socialist party between 1982 and 1983. In the first case, the Reagan ideology was antistate and antiwelfare, emphasizing deregulation and so-called "supply-side" economics, whereby the state provides benefits and exemptions to those who own the means of production rather than helping the consumer and promoting consumer demand. The second case in England took the form of sweeping privatizations and efforts (not always successful) to reduce spending and welfare benefits. The third case in France was even more spectacular. Socialism and the socialization of major sectors of the economy were abandoned by the French Socialist government in favor of a return, first, to indirect forms of privatization in socialized sectors of the economy and, later, to an outright acceptance of the free market.

In Eastern Europe and the Soviet Union, the same phenomenon has been very much in evidence. The state is beginning to privatize by selling off nationalized sectors and firms, legalizing private property, and attempting to liberate the market from state subsidies and price controls. It is a process that links the return to the free market and the profit motive with the restoration of political democracy.

POLITICAL PARTIES AND THE SHIFT TO CAPITALISM

Everywhere the move is in the direction of capitalism, and this is reflected in the shift of the platform and the ideologies of all political parties. From the Communist party, excepting some diehards, to the British and other Conservative parties—all have moved, some more assertively than others, from socialism, a mixed economy, and welfare spending to privatizations, a free market, and economic liberalism.

Communist Parties   First and foremost, Communist parties throughout all industrialized democracies, but also in Eastern Europe and the Soviet Union, have undergone a significant transformation. They have abandoned their rigid commitment to the socialization of the means of production and in some cases, as in Italy and Spain, favor privatizations of nationalized sectors. They have also abandoned their commitment to class struggle and revolution. Instead, they have accepted democracy and majority rule and periodic elections. For all practical purposes, they have become reformist parties, with the Italian Communist party showing the way by renaming itself the Democratic Party of the Left.

Second, the Communist parties have lost strength everywhere and face collapse. In France, the strength of the Communist party has declined to about 8 percent of the vote; in Italy—the strongest Communist party in the Western world—the vote has declined to less than 25 percent. In Spain, the Communist party is down to about 5 percent; 9 percent in Greece; and about 10 percent in Portugal. There is a hard core of leaders and followers in all Communist parties that keep the old faith alive—revolution, nationalizations, and dictatorship of the proletariat—but they are getting old and disillusioned.

Throughout the whole of Eastern Europe, Communist parties have radically changed their stance. While they still favor a mixed economy with state controls, subsidies, and welfare measures, they have become increasingly reformist, arguing for privatizations and the free market. They have begun to praise individual initiative and free enterprise. In fact, in Eastern Europe, and some say even in the Soviet Union, as we will see in Chapter 7, communist ideology and the Communist parties face extinction.

Socialist Parties   Since the end of World War II, and more rapidly in the last decade, virtually all socialist parties abandoned their original tenets and have begun to endorse the free market. They continue to advocate state controls but only when the market can not provide needed services. The British Labour party, the German Social Democrats, and the French Socialists have abandoned the major tenet of socialism—the nationalization of the economy. After the first nationalization was instituted by the Labour party (1945–1951), during which coal mines, railroads, electricity, gas, iron, and steel were nationalized, the emphasis was put on welfare legislation, an equitable incomes policy, and efforts to meet the demands of the trade unions and to arrest inflation. Reconstruction of the economy, in order to maintain Great Britain's competitive position in the world economy, became a primary goal. Today the Labour party is divided, but the moderate wing is gaining ground. It is beginning to appeal again to the middle classes as a reformist party that accepts the free market even though it continues to favor welfare policies.

In Germany, the Social Democrats abandoned their commitment to socialization as early as 1959 in the Bad Godesberg Congress with the slogan "the state whenever necessary, freedom whenever possible." In office, the German Social Democrats undertook no major structural reforms of the economy. However, they introduced welfare legislation and maintained a wage policy that favored the workers, something that was made possible by the remarkable strength and competitiveness of German industry. But they lost the election in both 1983 and 1987 and again in 1990.

Perhaps nothing better illustrates the predicament of socialism than the rise and fall of French socialism. The French Socialist party came to power in May 1981—with the election of a Socialist president and a Socialist majority in

the National Assembly. It proceeded with speed and great ideological commitment to put into practice the Socialist blueprint: the nationalization of all banks
and of most of the major industrial sectors and the strengthening of the welfare
programs. Health, retirement, and unemployment benefits were increased;
paid vacations for the workers were extended to five weeks; wages were raised
and early retirement provisions were made. The intent of these reforms was to
achieve what virtually all other European Socialist parties, including the British
Labour party, had forsaken. However, by 1983, the French Socialists abandoned
their plan in the face of growing unemployment, high budget deficits, a growing
trade deficit, a high rate of inflation, and negative public opinion. They began
to turn to the private sector and to gradually privatize the firms they had nationalized, many of which showed deficits. From public management they
moved to private entrepreneurship. In the election of March 1986 it was the
conservative and centrist parties that won a majority in the National Assembly
and proceeded to privatize a number of firms—with assets of about 20 billion
dollars. When the Socialist President, François Mitterrand was re-elected in
1988, he promised not to return to nationalizations, but also not to allow any
further privatizations. Early in 1991, however, all major nationalized firms were
allowed to raise capital in the private market by issuing stocks and bonds. The
state would continue to own 51% of the assets, thus maintaining technically control. But in effect the French economy was becoming "mixed" and moving in
the direction of the free market.

   The Future of Socialism   It appears that socialism may have run its course
as virtually all Socialist parties have come to terms with, even if with reservations, a free-market economy. Socialism bequeathed a legacy—a social ethic of
equality, collective effort, and cooperation. It served well the working classes,
the underprivileged, and society as a whole. But what about its future? Without
a commitment to broad structural economic reforms and the socialization of the
means of production, without a strong advocacy of economic planning, unable
to suggest policies that can put an end to unemployment and rescue the underclass from its miseries, how can we distinguish socialism, even if it were to
remain faithful to the welfare state, from other parties? The answer at this stage
is that we cannot. What is next, then?
   The prospects for socialism lie in the efforts of socialist leaders to build vi-
able coalitions around certain issues that attract groups of voters, not in the pro-
jection of a new socialist philosophy, a new ideology about the state and the
economy. A new coalition is possible, which could begin with many Communists who have lost their faith. It is in this spirit that the Italian Socialists revealed their pleasure at the proposal by the Italian Communist leadership to
change its party name and to form a "broad reformist coalition." A second group
that could embrace such a coalition might be the environmentalists, and thus
the coalition could assume leadership for one of the potentially most powerful
movements in the upcoming decade, which we discuss in Chapter 12. A third
group to reach out to would be the feminists and women voters and to project
a vision of equality that would satisfy women's demands for the provi-

sion of social services that deal with women's issues. Fourth, there is the prospect of attracting the faceless underclass that will need to be mobilized and made conscious of its potential political strength by promising the services they need and hope for. There is also, finally, now that the Socialists have virtually forsaken the socialization of the means of production, the possibility of an alliance between them and progressive Catholic forces, many of them in Catholic and Christian democratic parties.

Christian Democratic Parties   Christian democratic parties founded in the nineteenth century reemerged with renewed strength after the liberation of Europe in 1945: in Germany, France, Belgium, Austria, Holland, and Italy. In the 1970s, these parties have surfaced in Portugal, Spain, and Latin America with new vigor. Their renewed strength was due to the synthesis they provided between *social Catholicism*, which was committed to social reform, and *liberal* or *democratic Catholicism*, which was committed to democracy.

Christian democratic movements had opposed fascism and participated in great number in the various resistance movements against the Nazi and Fascist regimes and the puppet regimes they established. The MRP in France ("Popular Republicans") became the largest single party in the year immediately following liberation. In the election of June 2, 1946, the MRP won 28.1 percent of the vote, and its leaders held key positions in the cabinets formed thereafter. In Italy, Christian democracy emerged as the largest single party after the liberation and, despite losses, has held this position ever since. Christian Democrats in the Federal Republic of Germany—replacing the old Catholic "Center" party—have continued strong ever since the end of World War II, heading the governing coalition for twenty-eight out of the last fourty-five years. In Switzerland, Norway, Austria, Holland, and Belgium, Christian democratic parties have continued to command the vote of 20 to 30 percent of the electorate. In the 1970s and 1980s, Catholic parties in Spain and Portugal reappeared and gained momentum. Beyond Europe, Christian democracy also developed, especially in Latin America. In Chile, Christian Democrats won the presidency in 1964 and commanded 31 percent of the vote in the election of 1973. They have opposed both military dictatorship and communism.

While they defend the interests and moral tenets of the church with regard to legislation concerning the subsidies, immunities, and freedoms for the church and the clergy, as well as legislation regarding primary education, divorce, and abortion, Christian democratic parties are no longer "confessional parties." They appeal to all citizens, irrespective of their religion, and they get the vote of many non-Catholics.

With the collapse of Communist regimes throughout Eastern Europe, after 1989 Christian Democratic parties resurfaced and showed strength in this part of the world; the Christian Democrats won as much as 46 percent of the vote in East Germany. Their vote ranged from 8 to 12 percent in Eastern Europe. And as it has been the case with Socialist and Social Democratic parties, Christian Democrats have veered increasingly in the direction of a market economy. This is clearly so with the Italian Christian Democrats and also with the German

Christian Democratic party, which won a majority in the first elections in a united Germany on December 2, 1990. It is even more so with the resurging Christian Democratic parties throughout Eastern Europe where, as we noted, the anti-Communist movements were linked with demands for economic freedoms. Christian democracy today is generally allied with liberal parties and groups that favor a free-market economy, even when the conscience of many Catholics is with social services for the poor and the underprivileged.

Environmentalist Parties   The small environmentalist parties that have sprung up throughout Europe (see Chapter 12) remain committed to state controls of the economy. Ironically enough, they are perhaps closer to genuine socialism than most of the Socialist parties. Their adherents advocate a plan to deal with industrial growth and environmental issues. Most of them consider capitalism to be the single major cause for the degradation of the quality of our lives and of the environment. But most of the environmentalist parties are in their infancy, and their political weight is small in England, Austria, Germany, Belgium, the Scandinavian countries, France, Eastern Europe, and the Soviet Union. What is even more relevant, however, is that a number of their leaders are beginning to come to terms with the notion that capitalism can be tamed and reformed to become compatible with environmental protection and regulation.

Liberal and Conservative Parties   Liberal parties throughout Europe, as is the case with the Democratic and Republican parties (including conservatives) in the United States (see Chapter 4), are the most outspoken advocates of economic liberalism—of capitalism. Conservatives in Europe have traditionally favored a paternalistic economy and state controls and regulations, including even nationalizations; now they have become advocates of deregulation and a free market. Both the British Conservatives under Margaret Thatcher (1979–1990) and the Gaullists in France, ever since the early seventies, have moved ever closer to the tenets of a free-market economy. They urged and brought about privatizations in the socialist sector of the economy, and they are committed to the reduction of taxes and government spending.

The political spectrum in Europe, North America and throughout the world is changing; a great number of political parties everywhere have shifted to the "right," as they come to terms with the free market economy and as they move from socialism to the mixed economy. The welfare consensus is eroding and a new consensus appears to be evolving away from statism and in the direction of individual economic freedoms, competition and profit incentives in the direction of a free market. The trend has been reinforced in the last decade by the growth of an international economy and free trade, which obeys the logic of a global free market and calls for the reduction of tariffs and state subsidies and controls. Related to this growth is the remarkable performance of the economies of the so-called newly industrialized countries (NICs)—Taiwan, Singapore, South Korea, Hong Kong, and perhaps Thailand and Malaysia. Events in these countries have reinforced the arguments of economic liberals. The state—any state—is at bay, and the welfare ideology that combined the socialist ethic of equality and state service is on the defensive. The association of political freedoms with a free market, particularly so in Eastern Europe and the Soviet Union, has strengthened capitalism as an ideology everywhere—at least for the time being.

CAPITALISM: PROBLEMS AND PROSPECTS

There are many critical problems with capitalism that should not be overlooked, especially now that it is being associated with the spread of democracy.

The Crisis of Rising Expectations

Everybody is familiar with the phrase "the revolution of rising expectations." It is common not only among poor nations, which have recently gained their independence and are underdeveloped, but also among peoples of the rich countries in Western Europe and the United States. The most characteristic manifestation of the "revolution" is that all people want *more of everything*—more wealth, a higher standard of living, better education, greater security, better health care, more participation in decision making, more leisure, and greater equality. The speed with which these expectations have escalated and have converged has created serious problems.

A crisis in modern democratic regimes is primarily caused by the disparity between ideology and institutional capabilities. Ideology conjures up a world of plenty and immediate fulfillment. It shapes the new moral imperatives of equality and of equal sharing in opportunities and benefits. However, institutions are slow to respond to the pressure, and as a result, democratic regimes are faced with the prospect of instability.

It is simply difficult to meet all the rising demands, not only because resources are limited, but because structural and institutional changes are needed in order to meet them. New services are required and new institutional mechanisms must be put in place. Even the most open and responsive systems experience a time lag between when demands are made and registered and when new mechanisms are developed to respond to them—let alone satisfy them.

The intensity and number of demands from minorities, professional organizations, trade unions, student groups, cultural associations, and so on (many couched in sharp ideological terms) threaten to overwhelm the existing democratic institutions. This is likely to cause upheavals in the institutional framework of democratic societies.

Social Costs

Private firms and industries whose major incentive is profitability often neglect basic social considerations and do not take proper steps to protect societal interests. For instance, virtually all industrial companies directly utilize goods that affect us all—the air we breathe, for instance, or the water we drink. Many of the activities of these corporations may adversely affect resources on which we depend for our very lives. Yet these industries do not assume a liability for the social predicaments they cause—leaving it to the state to do so. The public ultimately incurs the expenditure, while the companies pocket the gain. Similarly, industrial firms show little consideration for the community within which they operate; for example, they may sell themselves to another firm—domestic or foreign—for a profit. In all such cases the costs to the workers and the community are great. Capitalism appears, therefore, as an impersonal force, without social, human, or communal concerns.

Inequalities

Capitalist economies show a growing disparity between the wealthy and the poor.[13] We are beginning to refer to an "underclass"—the homeless, the unemployed, the unemployable, the mentally ill or handicapped, the drug addicted. Depending on the exact definition of the term—and there is none—the number is large and growing. In many Western European democracies, unemployment has become virtually chronic for as many as 10 percent of the workers. It has been rising in the United States between 1988 and 1990 and by 1991 it had reached almost 7 percent.

Moreover, on a worldwide basis, the disparity between a few wealthy nations (not more than twenty-five or thirty, as measured in terms of resources, gross national income, and per capita income) and all others, especially those of the Third World, has been growing. Since the capitalist economy is becoming increasingly an international economy, we may speak, therefore, of a growing *worldwide underclass*, excluded from the benefits that capitalism promises.[14] The poor throughout the world are migrating in despair to the industrialized, rich countries, where they hope to find shelter and food. Misery and poverty breed resentment and may incite violence. If so, not only the global economy will be held responsible, but its capitalist foundations, favoring free trade in goods and services and the free movement of capital as well as individuals, will be seriously questioned. So will political democracy with which the resurgence of capitalism is linked.

Any economic upheaval, even if not as severe as the Great Depression of 1929, will shatter the democratic political order that is rising. It will snap the links between economic liberalism (capitalism) and democracy, and weaken both. The coming decade or two will decide their future and our fate!

---

[13]See Kevin Phillips, *The Politics of Rich and Poor.*

[14]See Robert B. Reich: *The Work of Nations: Preparing Ourselves for 21st Century Capitalism.*

BIBLIOGRAPHY

Socialism

Bernstein, Eduard. *Evolutionary Socialism.* New York: Scribner's 1961.

Brucan, Silviu. *World Socialism at the Crossroads: An Insider's View.* Westport, Conn.: Greenwood Press, 1990.

Buber, Martin. *Paths in Utopia.* Boston: Beacon Press, 1958.

Cerny, Philip G., and Martin A. Schain (eds.). *Socialism, the State and Public Policy in France.* New York: Methuen, 1985.

Cole, G. D. H. *A History of the Labour Party Since 1914.* London: Routledge and Kegan Paul, 1948.

———— . *A History of Socialist Thought,* 6 vols. London: Macmillan, 1953–1960.

———— and A. W. Filson. *Working Class Movements: Selected Documents.* New York: St. Martin's Press, 1965.

Crossman, R. H. S. (ed.). *The New Fabian Essays.* New York: Praeger, 1952.

———— . *The Politics of Socialism.* New York: Atheneum, 1965.

Engels, Friedrich, "Socialism: Utopian and Scientific." In Robert C. Tucker, *The Marx–Engels Reader,* 2nd ed. New York: Norton, 1978, pp. 683–717.

Gay, Peter. *The Dilemma of Democratic Socialism.* New York: Columbia University Press, 1952.

Hancock, Donald M., and Gideon Sjoberg (eds.). *Politics in the Post-Welfare State.* New York: Columbia University Press, 1972.

Harrington, Michael. *Socialism: Past and Future.* New York: Little, Brown, 1989.

Joll, James. *The Second International, 1889–1914.* New York: Praeger, 1956.

Manuel, Frank. *Utopian Thought in the Western World.* Cambridge, Mass.: Harvard University Press, 1979.

Markovic, M. *Democratic Socialism: Theory and Practice.* New York: St. Martin's Press, 1982.

Shaw, George Bernard (ed.). *Fabian Essays in Socialism.* London: Allen and Unwin, 1958. (Reprint of 1889 edition.)

Wallace, Lillian Parket. *Leo XIII and the Rise of Socialism.* Durham, N.C.: Duke University Press, 1966.

Reforming Capitalism

Cyr, Arthur I. *Liberal Party Politics in Britain.* New Brunswick, N.J.: Transaction Books, 1977.

Galbraith, John Kenneth. *American Capitalism: The Concept of Countervailing Power,* rev. ed. Boston: Houghton Mifflin, 1956.

———— . *The New Industrial State.* Boston: Houghton Mifflin, 1967.

Goldthorpe, John. *Order and Conflict in Contemporary Capitalism.* Oxford: Clarendon Press, 1984.

Halévy, Elie. *The Growth of Philosophic Radicalism.* Boston: Beacon Press, 1955.

Heilbroner, Robert L. *The Limits of American Capitalism.* New York: Harper & Row, 1967.

Huntington, Samuel, et al. *Crisis of Democracy.* New York: New York University Press, 1975.

Berkowitz, Edward, and Kim McQuaid. *Creating the Welfare State: The Political Economy of Twentieth-Century Reform*, rev. ed., New York: Praeger, 1988.

Flora, Peter, ed. *Growth to Limits: The Western European Welfare States since World War II: Sweden, Norway, Finland, Denmark*, vol. 1, Berlin and New York: Walter de Gruyter, 1986.

———. *Growth to Limits: The Western European Welfare States since World War II: Germany, United Kingdom, Ireland*, Italy, vol. 2. Berlin and New York: Walter de Gruyter, 1986.

Jallade, Jean-Pierre, ed. *The Crisis of Redistribution in European Welfare States*. Stoke-on-Trent: Trentham Books, 1988.

Jordan, Bill. *Freedom and the Welfare State*. London: Routledge and Kegan Paul, 1978.

Keynes, John Maynard, Collected Writings of John Maynard Keynes, New York: St. Martin's Press, 1971.

Maier, Charles S. *Changing Boundaries of the Political: Essays on the Evolving Balance Between the State and Society, Public and Private in Europe*. New York: Cambridge University Press, 1987.

Paterson, William E., and Alastair Thomas. *The Future of Social Democracy in Western Europe*. New York: Oxford University Press, 1986.

Phillips, Kevin. *The Politics of Rich and Poor*. New York: Random House, 1990.

Schlesinger, Arthur, Jr. *The Age of Roosevelt*. vols. 1 and 2. Boston: Houghton Mifflin, 1957.

Schumpeter, Joseph A. *Capitalism, Socialism and Democracy*. New York: Harper & Row, 1950.

Thomson, David. *Democracy in France Since 1870*, 5th ed. New York: Oxford University Press, 1969.

Capitalism Again?

Bell, Daniel, and Irving Kristol (eds.). *Capitalism Today*. New York: New American Library, 1971.

Friedman, Milton. *Capitalism and Freedom*. Chicago: Chicago University Press, 1962.

——— and Rose Friedman. *Free to Choose*. New York: Harcourt Brace Jovanovich, 1980.

Hayek, F. A. *Road to Serfdom*. Chicago: University of Chicago Press, 1944.

———. *The Constitution of Liberty*. London: Routledge and Kegan Paul, 1960.

Kymlicka, Will. *Liberalism, Community, and Culture*. New York: Oxford University Press, 1989.

Lloyd-Thomas, David. *In Defense of Liberalism*. Cambridge, Mass.: Basil Blackwell, 1988.

MacFarlane, Alan. *The Culture of Capitalism*. Cambridge, Mass.: Basil Blackwell, 1989.

Novak, Michael. *The American Vision: An Essay on the Future of Democratic Capitalism*. Washington, D.C.: American Enterprise Institute for Public Policy Research, 1978.

———. *Spirit of Democratic Capitalism*. New York, Basic Books, 1983.

Reich, Robert B. *The Work of Nations: Preparing for 21st Century Capitalism*. New York, Knopf, 1990.

Seldon, Arthur. *Capitalism*. Oxford: Basil Blackwell, 1990.

Zysman, John. *Governments, Markets and Growth*. Ithaca, N.Y.: Cornell University Press, 1983.

Chapter
4

The Conservative Tradition

The good citizen is a law-abiding traditionalist.

Russell Kirk
What Is Conservatism?

*I*t could be said that conservatism is more a state of mind than a political ideology. In order to be conservative, one must have something to conserve—property, status, power, a way of life. Conservatives are therefore likely to be those who have power or wealth or status and who simply want to keep things the way they are. Also, a significant number of people—mostly among rural groups, those who live in small towns, the old, and the uneducated—cannot imagine something different, or are afraid of change. They too want to keep their way of life the way it is.

However, even if we were to define conservatism simply as the defense of the status quo and the rationalization and the legitimization of a given order of things—in other words as a "situational ideology"—we would find that conservative ideology has its own logic.[1] Conservative movements always and everywhere borrow from some of the same principles, irrespective of the particular situation they face at a particular time. They are the following:

1. Individual liberties are more important to conservatives than "equality."
2. Conservatives have a pronounced allergy for political power—and are against its concentration in the hands of anybody, especially the people.

---

[1] In a penetrating article, Samuel Huntington indicates that conservatism can be viewed as (1) an ideology that emanated from the aristocracy as it rationalized its position and interests against the French Revolution of 1789—*aristocratic conservatism;* (2) an ideology that contains substantive prescriptions about the organization of social and political life—*autonomous conservatism;* (3) an ideology arising from a given situation in which the status quo is threatened by the prophets and the activists of change—*a situational ideology.* Conservatism is "the articulate, systematic, theoretical resistance to change. It is primarily an ideology that defends the status quo." (In American Political Science Review, v. LI, June 1957, no. 2, pp. 454–473.)

3. They insist on an organic theory of society, involving a hierarchy of groups and classes and a cooperation among them—the community and its interests are always above the individual.
4. They have a respect for tradition and "inheritance"—that which is bequeathed to us from our ancestors.
5. Religion, with its reverence for authority, is dear to conservatives.
6. They distrust "reason" and the propriety of using it as a solution for social problems.
7. Almost all conservative ideologies are elitist. Some people are better equipped than others; some are superior, while some (generally the many) are inferior.

These principles were invoked throughout the nineteenth century as certain groups fought to maintain their position against the egalitarian and reformist principles of democracy, liberalism, and, later on, socialism and Marxism.

A final note: the terms "conservative" and "reactionary" should not be confused as they so often are. A conservative doesn't want change—but will acquiesce to it—at least to gradual change. A "reactionary," on the other hand, is often one who wants to change things radically in order to reestablish the past. A conservative is against rapid change; a reactionary is one who doesn't accept the change that has already taken place! Nor should conservatism be confused with authoritarianism. The latter favors a concentration of political power in the hands of a leader or a group, is against individual and political freedoms, rejects popular participation in almost any form, and accepts repression and the use of force.

CLASSIC CONSERVATISM: THE BRITISH MODEL

The best formulation of conservative ideology was given by Edmund Burke, in the latter part of the eighteenth century. The best implementation of it has been, through the nineteenth century and until today, that of the British Conservative party.[2] Variants of the British model could be found in Germany under Bismarck, in France during the so-called Orleanist period (1830–1848) and in some of its offshoots during the period of the Third French Republic (1871–1940), and in Gaullism. But almost nowhere on the Continent did an alliance of the aristocracy and the upper classes, the church, the monarchy, and the army lead to the "classic" form of conservatism tied to constitutional democracy that prevailed in England.

European conservatives often chose to reject constitutional democracy and representative government. In the United States there have been many variants of a conservative ideology, but the absence of a nobility and the success of the

---

[2]An excellent discussion of the evolution of conservative ideology can be found in Samuel H. Beer, *British Politics in the Collectivist Age*.

egalitarian ethic and liberalism account for the virtual absence of any genuine conservative movement or ideology that has had any impact.

Classic conservatism is characterized by certain basic propositions that relate to political authority, to a conception of society and the nature of the individual, and to the relationship between the national economy and the state.

The Political Society

Society, according to early British conservative thought, is organic and hierarchical. Classes and social groups fit together in the same way as do the various organs of the human body. One is indispensable to the others; it cannot function without them. Relations between them must be harmonious and balanced, and each group and each class performs the functions that are necessary to the others for the good health of the whole. Society is not like a machine, say a clock, in which the motions are eternally identical and where each part has no idea of what the other parts are doing. Rather, it is a combination of many parts, each one of which understands its role and perceives society as a whole. Unlike the machine, society knows it has a purpose; unlike a clock it grows and changes. "The whole," wrote Edmund Burke, "is never old, middle-aged, or young." It "moves on through . . . perpetual decay, fall, renovation, and progression."[3]

Society thus consists of interdependent parts—and all the parts are equally conscious of the interdependence. Each one does its own work, but what it does makes sense only when the whole is understood and valued. Farmers grow crops; soldiers keep order and give protection; priests improve our minds and souls; the leaders govern and balance the various parts. The parts working together almost lose the sense of their separateness. Society is not a "mixture" of various roles, groups, qualities, and activities. It is, as Aristotle said, much more of a "compound" in which the parts blend with each other to become something different from what they are individually. They become a society.

Different functions and roles inevitably suggest a hierarchical organization and social inequality. Some of society's roles are more important than others, and some people do more important things than others. This means that there must be a subordination of some individuals to others. Persons endowed by nature with certain qualities that others do not have should play the most important roles. Equality and freedom, as abstract propositions, are not acceptable to the conservative ideology. Instead, it emphasizes *rights* and *liberties*. These derive not from rational principles or from natural law but from specific institutional and legal arrangements, and from history and tradition. They give to individuals and to groups specific benefits, protections, and claims that are commensurate with their functions and roles. Nor is the idea of material equality for all seriously entertained. Material benefits should correspond to the talent shown and the work done.

---

[3]Edmund Burke, *Reflections on the Revolution in France*, p. 162.

Edmund Burke (1729–1797)

Edmund Burke was the most eloquent expounder of British conservative ideology. Originally, Burke appeared to be a liberal, arguing not only against the prerogatives of the crown and in favor of Parliament, but also for the autonomy of the colonies in North America. These views were expressed in *Thoughts on the Causes of the Present Discontents* (1770). It was the French Revolution and its excesses that accounted for his masterpiece, *Reflections on the Revolution in France* (1790), in which he presented arguments favoring tradition and prescription, and the sanctity of law and authority, while cautioning against anything but the most gradual expansion of popular participation in affairs of state.

The "whole"—this society that consists of the harmonious interdependence of many parts—is formalized in the Constitution. This is not a written document, and in fact there is no way, according to conservative thinkers, a constitution can be set down. The Constitution is a set of customs, understandings, rules, and especially traditions, that define political power and set limits upon its exercise. Power thus enshrined by habit, custom, and tradition becomes authority; that is, it is accepted and respected. In this way, it is the Constitution that binds the whole of the citizenry to its rulers, and the rulers to the citizenry within the nation. Conservatives, however, are not necessarily nationalists. To them the nation–state is a social and historical reality, the product of many centuries of common life and togetherness. But it is not a supreme moral value unless it has managed to embody justice and order. "To make us love our country, our country must be lovely" was the pithy comment of Burke.

Political Authority

In contrast to those who establish the foundations of political authority on contract and consent, conservatives find it in tradition, custom, and in what they call inheritance and prescription. Society as a living whole is the result of natural evolution. The Constitution of England and its various parts—the monarchy, the House of Lords and the nobility, the House of Commons, individual rights, the judiciary—are an "entailed inheritance." One accepts it, and lives on it, but cannot waste it. In a famous passage, Burke sees in the state something like a mystery: its parts and its majesty cannot be dissected, analyzed, and put back together in the same or in a different way. *The state cannot be made.* He wrote:

> The state ought . . . to be looked upon with . . . reverence. . . . It is a partnership in all science; a partnership in all art; a partnership in all perfection . . . between those who are living, those who are dead and those who are to be born. . . . Each contract is but a clause in the great primeval contract of eternal society, linking the lower with the higher natures, connecting the visible with the invisible world, according to a fixed compact sanctioned by the inviolable oath which holds all physical and all moral natures, each in their appointed place.[4]

Conservatives, therefore, have no use for the "contract" theory of the state propounded by the early liberals. The idea runs counter to the organic theory of society and to the role history and tradition play in the formation of a state. Burke insisted that even if there were a contract it was shaped by history and tradition, and once made "it attaches upon every individual of that society, without any formal action of his own." We are born into political society like our father and forefathers; we do not make it.

---

[4]Burke, pp. 139–140.

Change

Given the emphasis on tradition, conservative thought is generally opposed to change unless it is gradual. Our "partnership with the dead" should not be broken, for fear that this would undermine the living and those still to be born. Modifications become necessary, but on balance the past carries more weight than the present. As for the future, there are many would-be reformers and social engineers, and conservatives distrust them. Innovation is suspect, and Burke claimed it was prompted by "selfish temper and confined views." As a result, the conservatives fall back upon the existing and widely shared values that have kept the society together. Religion is one of the most important; so is common law and even prejudices. As Edmund Burke put it, "wise prejudice," consecrated by long usage, is "better than thoughts untried and untested."

Religion, tradition, the common law, and prejudice—all give the individual shelter and solace; they provide stability that in the last analysis is a higher value than change. All these things, together with the state and its organs, must be strengthened with the proper pomp and ritual that appeal to the common people. The crown itself is a symbol that, through ritual, secures support and obedience. More than fifty years after Burke, another British Conservative, Walter Bagehot (1826–1877), spoke of the "symbolic" or "ceremonial" part of the Constitution—the monarch—providing for the attachment of the common people and unifying political society. The cabinet, the prime minister, and Parliament were the "efficient part"—the government—though this was understood only by the elite and hardly appreciated by the common people.[5]

If change is to come, however, it must be natural and slow—one and the same thing for conservatives. Conservatives may even favor change in order to preserve. Change must reflect new needs and be the result of cautious adjustment with past practices. The British Conservatives *allowed* for changes in the Constitution, which they venerated; thus came about the gradual extension of the franchise, the ascendancy of the popularly elected House of Commons over the hereditary House of Lords, and the development of a civil service based on merit, as well as economic and social reforms. But they did so often under pressure, and with the aim of preserving what they valued most. In their efforts to slow down reform, however, British Conservatives remained firmly attached to the basic democratic principles of representative government, elections, and the rule of law.

Leadership

The purpose of the state and its leaders is to balance the whole and to create unity and commonality of purpose out of diversity. Government leadership and decision making should be entrusted to "natural leaders"—men or women of

---

[5]Walter Bagehot, *The English Constitution.*

talent, high birth, and property, who have a stake in the interests of the country and in its fortunes. As late as the middle of the nineteenth century, many argued in England that noblemen could own, outfit, and command whole regiments in the army, and the explanation given was simple—they cared more about England's welfare than did the common people. They had a greater stake in the defense of the country.

As a conservative put it recently, "Government is instituted to secure justice and order . . . and . . . the first principle of good government allows the more energetic natures among a people to fulfill their promise while ensuring that these persons shall not tyrannize over the mass of men."[6] Quality and not election should therefore be the source of leadership. Conservatives fought against the rapid extension of the franchise, acquiescing to it reluctantly, and did not accept the full logic of majority rule until very recently. The principle of one man–one vote was unacceptable, and the notion that decisions could be made by simple arithmetic majority could be entertained only when that majority, by long habits of obedience, had become self-disciplined. That would be when the majority had accepted the restraints that law and tradition had inculcated so as to act in accordance with the fundamental rules of the past.

The natural leaders hold the interests of the country in trust. They act on behalf of the people and the society. The trust, however, is almost a complete and blanket grant of power—it is not a delegation. Another way of explaining the same conservative notion of trusteeship is to refer to it as the theory of *virtual representation*. Today we agree that representatives represent their constituency, those who elect them, and the country in general, but their capacity to make decisions for us stems directly from elections and from the *mandate* they receive from their constituency or the electorate at large. Virtual representation, on the other hand, is the capacity to represent and make decisions by virtue of qualities other than mere election. Conservative thinking returns to the idea of birth and wealth. Persons who have one or both can represent the people and the nation by virtue of their position better than elected representatives. They are what in medieval times were called the *valentior pars* (the better part) of the community. This again shows the reluctance by conservatives to extend the franchise and accept majoritarianism.

Thus, the natural leaders should govern and the many should follow. This reflects the typical British conservative attitude, which still is evident today. Many of the members and leaders of the Conservative party still think that they are endowed with capabilities with which they can govern better than any other party and leadership. They still believe that they can hold the interest of the country in trust better than all others. They also think that the government has autonomous and independent powers to govern and that, once elected, it is free to exercise them. It is a government that once elected cannot be given instruc-

---

[6]Russell Kirk, "Prescription, Authority and Ordered Freedom," in F. S. Meyer (ed.), *What Is Conservatism?* p. 33.

tions or be delegated to do some things and not others. So, there is an element of authoritarianism and elitism still lurking in the hearts of all good conservatives, together with a certain distrust for the "common people" or the "masses."

Paternalism

While conservatives believe that the propertied classes and the landed aristocracy have special privileges, they also agree that such privileges and their exercise have corresponding social obligations. Here there is a strong element of paternalism, whereby the natural leaders have to cater to the well-being of the common people by providing them with relief when out of work and at other times improving their living conditions. Because of their organic theory of society, conservatives tended to subordinate economic interests to the overall interest of the collectivity. Social solidarity and social cooperation are given precedence over particular interests. Finally, the purpose of "the whole" goes beyond simple material considerations. The state is an all-encompassing agency for providing justice and order. It has a moral purpose to which particularisms and economic interests must yield.

For all these reasons, conservatives reject the utilitarian philosophy of economic liberalism. Self-interest, unrestrained competition, individualism, and the very notion that the society is held together by competing claims and antagonisms—such ideas are repugnant to them. They reject laissez-faire economics, or at best tolerate it on condition that individual effort and competition not be allowed to tear apart the fabric of the society. They accept economic individualism if it allows everybody to show his or her worth and capabilities; they reject it if it leads to sharp inequalities and social strife that would upset the balance of the whole. British conservatives have favored state intervention and welfare measures, unlike other conservative parties on the Continent and elsewhere.

Constitutional Government and Democracy

The British Conservatives and their Conservative party became strong advocates of constitutional and representative government. In contrast to the European conservatives, they did not waver in their support of democracy and parliamentary institutions. Authoritarian and totalitarian solutions appealed to only a negligible number of their leaders and followers. In this way conservatism, while representing the status quo groups, recognized the realities of social change and the necessity of guiding it and reducing its speed rather than arresting it altogether. Classic conservatives appear something like a well-controlled dam and not a bulwark against the forces of change.

After the nineteenth century, Conservatives not only accepted major economic changes, such as the establishment of Britain's welfare state and the nationalization of its industries, but they themselves also *introduced* social and economic reforms. In 1951, when the Conservatives replaced the Labour government, they assumed the direction and the management of the nationalized industries and the welfare system Labour had built. The Conservative party did not reject Labour's social economic and welfare legislation; it tried to slow their pace of reform until it judged society as a whole had time to adjust to it. Thus, British Conservatives reconciled themselves to a new social and economic order.

The Conservative party remains staunchly committed to democratic principles. While the authority of the leader of the party is given greater scope than in the case of other parties, notably Labour, the Conservative party developed into a mass party with 3 to 4 million members. It holds annual conferences, allows its various organs considerable autonomy, holds free debates in which policy resolutions come from the floor, and can be endorsed despite the opposition of the leadership. It now recruits its candidates for the House of Commons without consideration of their personal wealth and ability to contribute to their own campaign or to the party. In general, despite its affinities with the upper status groups and wealthier segments of the population, it has managed to appeal to and get support from many of the voters who belong to the working or lower middle classes. The marriage between the cottage and the throne that the great Tory leader of the Victorian period, Disraeli, had suggested, developed into strong ties between the people and the Conservative party leadership. As a result the party has survived as one of the two major political groups in England. Since 1945, it has held the reins of government for about twenty-five years.

To sum up some of the basic characteristics of classic conservative thought: there is a belief that society is like an organism; that its parts are hierarchically arranged; that authority should be entrusted to natural leaders. There is a rejection of individualism and egalitarianism; a strong belief in custom and tradition and an aversion to change; emphasis on religious and ritualistic symbolisms to solidify the union of the whole. Yet at the same time there is a strong commitment to a government under law guaranteeing individual rights, an acceptance of representative government, and with it an acknowledgment of the increased participation of all the people, an implementation of the welfare state, and above all, a rejection of authoritarian solutions. Conservatism has thus legitimized itself as an ideology consistent with democracy.

People who like change and innovation, and find themselves at odds with the conservative ideology, should not be particularly hasty in rejecting it. Classic conservatism, as portrayed here, was and remains a brake to rapid change. But it channeled the well-to-do and, more important, millions of voters, into accepting gradual and peaceful change. Conservatives have been distrustful of human reason and majoritarianism. But they never attempted to control the first or to outlaw the second. They (like the British Socialists) presented their position and policies in the context of democracy. The conservative ideology—in a sense the creature of the British ruling groups—tamed the class that formulated it, disciplined its followers to act within the logic of individual and associational freedoms, and accepted free political competition without which democracy cannot exist. By creating an ideology that taught the British ruling classes how to bend in order not to break, they legitimized not only gradual change but all change, if and when the electorate demanded it, and they prepared their followers to accept change, if not always with grace, at least without countering it with force.

AMERICAN CONSERVATIVES AND THE BRITISH MODEL

As we saw in our discussion of British conservative ideology, conservatives admire and try to preserve the past; they are elitist in that they believe in natural leaders; they accept only gradual and incremental change; they admire a well-balanced and hierarchically structured society, and they emphasize the need for authority. "Civilized man lives by authority," according to a (British-born) American conservative.[7] Conservatives believe that societies develop norms—that is, enduring standards of behavior—and that we obey them because of habit and tradition. "The sanction to norms," writes the same author, "must come from a source other than private advantage or rationality"—the two basic propositions used by liberals to explain our obedience to the state. The real source of authority and obedience "is tradition." For conservatives, "the good citizen is a law-abiding traditionalist."[8]

To most Americans these propositions are alien. "Man is created equal"; all of us are "endowed" with liberty. The American dream has been that change, through the manipulation of the environment in order to get more out of it, is equated with progress toward a better future, and a person's worth lies in achievement, not birth, inheritance, or status. As for society, it has no meaning and reality outside of the individuals who make it and can remake it. There is no hierarchy and no organic quality about it; there is no fixed subordination of some to others, and no structure of deference. The self-made person is still the symbol of Americanism, and of the constant restlessness, mobility, and change of Americans and American society. Law is but a convenient external standard that we set up and change to accommodate our domestic conflicts—hardly a norm maturing and gaining strength and respect with time until obedience to it becomes a tradition.

As noted earlier, economic liberalism became the dominant American political creed, and virtually all social thinkers called themselves liberals. Few dared called themselves conservatives until very recently. There was little to conserve and a lot to change and to conquer: more wealth to amass and greater material benefits to realize for all. Outside of individual effort and achievement neither norms nor "tradition" nor "wise prejudice," as Burke had put it, restrained the myth of material success and self-improvement that was the heart

---

[7]Kirk, p. 23.

[8]Kirk, p. 31.

of the beliefs of Americans. When the labor leader Samuel Gompers was asked in the latter part of the nineteenth century what it was that American labor wanted, he gave the answer that all Americans understood: "More!" In a society holding such an ideal, genuine conservatives were likely to find themselves out of place or, what amounts to the same thing, with no place for them.

The American political tradition therefore has few conservative authors or leaders in any way comparable to the British ones: Henry Adams, John Calhoun, Herman Melville, Brooks Adams, Irving Babbitt, and Walter Lippmann are among the best known. Calhoun, without any doubt, had a profound influence in the years until the Civil War. But his impact has not been a more lasting one than that of the others. The real classic conservatives—the "humanistic value preservers"—who venerate tradition, order, and natural law, have been very few indeed. The reason is that the American system and American society were made in the name of human reason and individual rights, not tradition. Real conservatives in the United States must either go directly to the British sources for inspiration, which they often do, or try to find the particular institutions and ideas that best correspond to the conservative ideology in the American experience, which they have tried to do. The only conservative ideology they claim to find is in the Constitution and in the thinking of the framers that produced it and, of course, in the political philosophy of some of them as it was expounded in the Federalist Papers.

American conservatives have tried to draw their inspiration from the Constitution because of its limitations on direct democracy and because of its emphasis on law. The American republic is "a government of law and not men." It is a republic and not a democracy—a state in which separation and the balance of powers make it impossible for any single branch of government to gain enough power to endanger the rights of the people. It is a system carefully engineered to make it impossible for a numerical majority to control all branches of government, at one and the same time, and to establish a tyranny—one that is considered just as bad as the tyranny of a minority or a group of men or of one man. Restraints are built into the system not only against the governmental organs, federal and state, but against the peoples as well. It is in this that American conservatives find the "wisdom of the framers."

Similarly, in the Federalist Papers which provide for a defense of the Constitution and embody the philosophy of the framers, notably James Madison and Alexander Hamilton, references are made and institutions are defended in terms that are close to British conservative ideas and vocabulary. Thus, the "electoral college," that was supposed to be free, once chosen, to elect the president, is viewed and defended as a body of wise men who are considered more reliable to make the proper choice than the people directly. The early mode of election for the Senate, by the state legislatures, again provided for an indirect mode of election whose purpose was to filter the popular choice. It is significant, however, that the electoral college has ceased to play the independent role it was supposed to play, and that the Senate is now elected directly by the people of the various states. Emphasis on law—a government of law and not men—remains an important ingredient of a conservative ideology, yet only a careful examination of the jurisprudence of the Supreme Court, the ultimate custodian of the Constitution, can answer to what extent. Furthermore, it should be remembered that nowhere did the Constitution grant power to the Supreme Court to declare acts of Congress unconstitutional and to set them aside.

This interpretation of the Constitution and the intentions of its framers as being essentially conservative and a reflection of a conservative ideology must be considered seriously. The framers were afraid of "the people," the majority, and they looked for "natural leaders." Many had a profound respect for tradition, but this hardly makes them and the Constitution, as it developed, conservative. Conservatives in England believed in the wise exercise of power and extolled established authority; they put politics and political wisdom above everything else except religion and divine or natural law; they thought, as we have seen, that a political society was a living organism to which material and functional interests were subordinated. Wise leadership kept this organism together.

The framers of the U.S. Constitution, on the other hand, feared political power. It could be abused and might be abused by anybody and everybody— even by "wise rulers." They were skeptical about the possibility of legitimizing power and creating a strong political authority. Their solution was to weaken authority as much as possible by fragmenting it and dividing it. The solution was a mechanical one—it reflected no belief in tradition, custom, or in natural leaders. Like the Newtonian physics which influenced the framers, the intent was to establish an equilibrium of forces and governmental organs.

This philosophy was fully consistent with the climate of opinion of the times. By downgrading the powers of the government and by providing for checks and balances for each and all its organs, the framers hoped to liberate society (i.e., the individual, the economy, voluntary associations, the churches, and so on) from the state and from political domination. The best government was the one that governed the least and left individuals free to pursue their material interest in the best utilitarian manner, and to maximize their pleasure and avoid pain as they saw fit. The "do-it-yourself man" of Benjamin Franklin was to emerge not only unfettered by political power, free of tradition and prescription, but also free from the wisdom of political elites and their natural leaders. This was, and remains, the very opposite of classic conservatism.

THE AMERICAN CONSERVATIVE IDEOLOGY

The doctrine of economic liberalism—emphasizing the market economy and competition, exalting the profit motive and private entrepreneurship, and building on the premises of self-interest in its pursuit of a world of social harmony and progress—was constantly contested in England, where it originated, and on the continent of Europe, where it never managed to gain a firm foothold. It provoked a strong reaction from intellectuals, Socialists, Christian reformers, liberal and traditional Catholic intellectuals as well as the Catholic hierarchy and was looked upon with strong repugnance by monarchists and the aristocracy. Liberals, buffeted from their right and their left, had to qualify economic liberalism by allowing for restraints and regulation of the market economy.

Economic Issues

In contrast, economic liberalism, or rather capitalism, flourished in the United States. It began to reflect the remarkable industrial growth which the country enjoyed after the Civil War and which continued until the Great Depression of 1929.

Andrew Carnegie (1835–1919) considered the search for and accumulation of wealth to be the central goal of our civilization, and found in the market and competition the best arena to test the caliber of men—their abilities and industry. As with the earlier Protestant ethic, Carnegie believed that wealth was an indication of divine grace and that it was bestowed only on industrious and frugal individuals. But he also believed that, commensurate with their station in society, the wealthy had a special duty to help the less fortunate through charity and other humanitarian endeavors.

In contrast to Carnegie's paternalistic capitalism, William Graham Sumner (1840–1910) suggested a pure individualistic ethic. Competition was to be the rule and success or failure would be determined in the marketplace. It would provide a selective mechanism to sort out the industrious from the lazy, the virtuous from the wicked. He contended that the search for equality, espoused by the Socialists, would bring only disaster. For Sumner, equality meant that the "worst would become the standard" and that it would pull down the rest to the lowest common denominator of competence, work, production, and wealth. Only through conflict, competition, and struggle could the best impose themselves and thus attain wealth for themselves and the society as a whole. As with Carnegie, the market became the best instrumentality for the "survival of the most able," just as nature had been for the "survival of the fittest" in Charles Darwin's theory of evolution. So that capitalism was the precondition of human progress. Conservatives therefore ask that the federal government move out of the economy; that if and when welfare measures are needed they should be undertaken at the state and local levels and not the federal one; that the federal budget and federal expenditures be sharply reduced; that income taxes and many other federal and state taxes be sharply curtailed. In effect, conservatives ask for the dismantling of much of the New Deal legislation and the welfare state.

The Moral Issues

Conservatives in the United States, however, and increasingly so elsewhere, move beyond the "economic man" and "rugged individualism," reaching out for "moral" issues that affect our society: violence and crime, pornography, premarital sex, abortion, drugs, and secular education. They join hands with the "religious right," which we discuss in Chapter 11. They favor, when it comes to

CAPITALISM—THE AMERICAN VERSION

1. The major actor in society—indeed the primary actor—is the individual who, using reason, is best suited to satisfy his or her needs and interests. The maximization of individual well-being (material wealth and profit) is the driving force of the economy. Consumer demand determines the supply of goods and the inventive entrepreneur provides them.

2. The free market is the most reliable and flexible mechanism for regulating supply and demand through the price mechanism.

3. Change (often used synonymously with progress) can be brought about through the dynamics of individual effort, competition, and entrepreneurship.

4. The individual, however, is not only an "economic man" to be left free to act according to his interests; he is also a moral man with a conscience, volition, and reason. To curb the economic efforts of individuals would be to seriously undermine their other freedoms and, most important of all, to deprive them of their right to pursue their own lives according to their individual best judgment.

5. The state must remain out of the market.

"moral" issues, restrictive legislative measures; they demand the death penalty; they ask for religious education in schools, for community controls against obscenity and pornography, and for strict antiabortion legislation. Moral issues are becoming just as important as economic ones. Alongside the emphasis on a free-market economy, these moral issues account for the strength of the conservative movement, and not only in the United States.

Reaganism and the Conservatives   Conservatives, by and large, supported Ronald Reagan. Both as a candidate and as a president, Reagan endorsed most of the conservative propositions. He was a fundamentalist on most moral-social questions (abortion, pornography, school prayer, etc.); he disavowed a "permissive" society by advocating greater police powers against suspected criminals; he opposed the ERA; he appointed conservative justices on the federal courts; and he strengthened national defense against the Soviets—he was the president who called the Soviet Union an "Evil Empire." Reagan emerged as the champion of economic liberalism, favoring deregulation, reduction in taxes and welfare spending, and a return to the market and free-enterprise economy. It is difficult to imagine a president who could be closer to the conservative positions while at the same time appealing to the center.

The conservative support began to wane, however, as Reagan had to compromise with the center of his party and with many of the Democrats who held a majority in the House of Representatives and in both houses of Congress in the last two years of his term in office. He was unable to sustain an interventionist policy in Nicaragua, and he began to shift his position on the Soviet

Union by considering and ultimately signing agreements on nuclear arms in December 1987. The Gorbachev visit to Washington that December, the signing of the treaty on missiles in Europe, and Reagan's visit to the Soviet Union in May 1988 were blows to the conservatives. Conservatives also became impatient with the lack of decisive measures for dismantling the welfare state and reducing government spending, and they fought for a constitutional amendment to set a limit on the federal deficit.

Subsequent events under the George Bush presidency—the meetings with Mikhail Gorbachev in 1990, the weakening of the Soviet Empire, the dissolution of the Warsaw Pact, which had brought Eastern Europe under the military control of the Soviet Union, the democratic revolutions in Eastern Europe, and the reunification of Germany—all spelled one and the same thing. Soviet communism appeared no longer to be a threat. These developments took the wind out of the sail of the anti-Communist and the anti-Soviet rhetoric of American conservatives. They continued to raise warning signals, but their followers began to lose interest.

Conservative intellectuals, however, are gaining prominence by addressing themselves to moral and economic issues. Speaking through the influential *National Review* and other journals, they are beginning to shape the country's political agenda. The outline for political action they present is familiar and finds many Americans in agreement: decentralization of the federal government in the direction of state and "community" control, lower taxes, dismantling of the welfare state, reduction of the federal bureaucracy, and, above all, emphasis on moral issues, including the restoration of religious education in schools to combat secularism.

Influential conservative research institutions and organizations expound the philosophy of conservatism, among them the American Heritage Foundation, the American Enterprise Institute, and the Bradley Foundation. Many organize political action and provide funding. There is the Conservative Caucus and the recently established Conservative Political Action Committee, under the direction of Republican Congressman Newt Gingrich, among many others. They sponsor candidates for election, seek and provide funds, and attempt to maintain in many states an identity separate from the Republican party on which, however, they continue to put pressure. With the old idols gone—Barry Goldwater and Ronald Reagan—and with President Bush failing to satisfy many of their aspirations, lower taxes for instance, they are determined to bring their weight to bear in nominations of candidates for the presidency and Senate.

But there are two issues on which conservatives may divide. With the Soviet threat gone, conservatives may split into two camps: "globalists" and "isolationists." The first wish to assert American hegemony and to maintain it through a strong military establishment and military intervention if needed. They supported the U.S. policy vis-à-vis Iraq. The second are beginning to revert to the old Republican faith in isolationism: to maintain America strong at home, U.S. leadership must emphasize economic development and moral values and let our allies—Western Europe and Japan, for instance, and of course, a reunited Germany—assume the burden and responsibility for their own defense. For the same reason, there may be a split between free traders and protectionists—the latter returning to the theme of unfair competition from abroad and the imperative of buttressing our national economy. Having entered what many consider a "mild recession" at the end of 1990, it is a theme that may gain momentum if the American economy were to continue to stagnate.

Deep, even if muddy, remains the soil from which American conservatives continue to draw—economic liberalism and free enterprise, hostility to big government, government spending and high taxes, a growing demand for state and community control, in line with deToqueville's interpretation of American democracy, and the full and firm reassertion of "moral" and even religious values and "law and order." Barring an economic depression or prolonged international conflict, these are the bread-and-butter issues for the American public as they are presented to them with renewed urgency by a growing number of conservative intellectuals.

BIBLIOGRAPHY

Bagehot, Walter. *The English Constitution*. New York: Oxford University Press, 1936.

Banfield, Edward C. *The Unheavenly City*. Boston: Little, Brown, 1970.

Beer, Samuel H. *British Politics in the Collectivist Age*. New York: Vintage, 1949.

Bellah, Robert N., Richard Madsen, et al. *Habits of the Heart: Individualism and Commitment in American Life*. Berkeley, Calif.: University of California Press, 1985.

Buckley, William F., and Charles R. Kesler (eds.). *Keeping The Tablets: Modern American Conservative Thought*. New York: Harper & Row, 1988.

Burke, Edmund. *Reflections on the Revolution in France*. New York: Bobbs-Merrill, Library of Liberal Arts, 1955.

Calhoun, John C. *A Disquisition on Government*. Indianapolis: Bobbs-Merrill, 1958.

Cecil, Lord Hugh Richard. *Conservatism*. London: Williams and Nurgate, 1912.

Diggins, John P. *Up From Communism: A Conservative's Odyssey in American Intellectual History*. New York: Harper & Row, 1976.

Filler's, Louis. *Dictionary of American Conservatism*. New York: Philosophical Library, 1986.

Hayek, F. A. *The Constitution of Liberty*. London: Routledge and Kegan Paul, 1960.

———. *The Road to Serfdom*. Chicago: University of Chicago Press, 1946.

Hearnshaw, F. J. C. *Conservatism in England*. London: Macmillan, 1933.

Holden, Mathew, Jr. *Varieties of Political Conservatism*. Beverly Hills, Calif.: Sage, 1974.

Huntington, Samuel. "The Conservative Ideology" *American Political Science Review*, Vol. LI, No. 2, June 1957, pp. 454–473.

Kirk, Russell. *The Conservative Mind*, rev. ed. Chicago: Henry Regnery, 1960.

———. (ed.). *The Portable Conservative Reader*. New York: Penguin, 1982.

Kristol, Irving. *Reflections of a Neo-Conservative*. New York: Basic Books, 1983.

———. *Two Cheers for Capitalism*. New York: Basic Books, 1978.

Meyer, Frank S. (ed.). *What Is Conservatism?* New York: Holt, 1964.

Nash, George H. *The Conservative Intellectual Movement in America*. New York: Basic Books, 1976.

Nisbet, Robert A. *The Quest for Community*. New York: Oxford University Press, 1953.

———— . *Conservatism*. Minneapolis: University of Minnesota Press, 1986.

Podhoretz, Norman. *Breaking Ranks: A Political Memoir*. New York: Harper & Row, 1979.

Rogger, Hans, and Eugen Weber (eds.). *The European Right: A Historical Profile*. Berkeley, Calif.: University of California Press, 1981.

Rossiter, Clinton. *Conservatism in America*, 2nd rev. ed. New York: Knopf, 1966.

Schuettinger, R. L. (ed.). *The Conservative Tradition in European Thought*. New York: Capricorn Books, 1969.

Sigler, Jay A. *The Conservative Tradition in American Thought*. New York: Capricorn Books, 1969.

Steinfels, Peter. *The Neoconservatives: The Men Who Are Changing American Politics*. New York: Simon and Schuster, 1979.

Viereck, Peter. *Conservatism: From John Adams to Churchill*. Princeton, N.J.: Van Nostrand, 1956.

Wills, Garry. In *Confessions of a Conservative*. New York: Doubleday, 1979.

COMMUNISM: THE VISION AND THE REALITY

In place of the old bourgeois society . . . we shall have an association in which the free development of each is the condition for the free development of all.

Karl Marx and Friedrich Engels
Communist Manifesto

*T*he Communist parties throughout the world that emerged after the Bolshevik Revolution of 1917 and the single-party totalitarian regimes they established were a harness to a vision—a vision of a free and egalitarian society and a peaceful world. This vision encompassed a world in which need and poverty, which dwarfed human values and impeded the full development of our individual freedoms, would come to an end; it encompassed a world in which material abundance would at last follow the remarkable growth brought about by the capitalistic world, but only after capitalism and the capitalist class had been destroyed and the means of production—the economy as a whole—had been socialized. Not only the workers, but all of us, would then gain our freedoms and shape our destiny instead of having it decided by the impersonal forces of a capitalistic market and the not so impersonal rule of those who control the means of production.

In this part, we first examine the vision—Marxism. Then, we turn to the reality—to the Communist regime as it was fashioned in the Soviet Union under Lenin and Stalin and copied elsewhere. We then take an overview of the collapse of communism as an ideology and of Communist regimes, except in some "last bastions"—in Cuba, North Korea, Albania, Vietnam and, for the time being, China.

Chapter
5

The Theory and the Vision

Marxism

Marx was a genius; we others were at best talented. Without him the theory would not be by far what it is today. It, therefore, rightly bears his name.

Friedrich Engels

*C*ommunism is literally an economic and social system whereby all the means of production are concentrated in the hands of the community or the state, and in which the production and allocation of goods and services are decided upon by the community and the state. Generally, however, communism has meant much more. It has been "an ideal, a political movement, a method of analysis and a way of life."[1] As an ideal, it promises an egalitarian society with production geared to need—a society in which the dream of abundance will be realized. As a political movement it represents the organization of men and women striving to attain freedom; as a method of analysis it sets forth propositions that explain the past and point to the future development of our societies; finally, as a way of life it portrays a new type of citizen for whom the communitarian and social attributes of human nature will gain ascendancy over egotism and private interest.

Whether taken singly, or all together as they usually are, the trends represent what communism has been—one of the most powerful myths and ideologies in history. It takes the form of a moral imperative—how to create a collective and social ethic that will override self-interest and do away with the demons of profit and private property, which are seen as the cause of subjugation of the many to the few.

---

[1]Alfred G. Meyer, Marxism: *The Unity of Theory and Practice*, p. 1.

Ever since antiquity, the theme of the *moral* superiority of communal ownership, in contrast to private property, interest, and individualistic aspirations, has been kept alive. It is defended in Plato's *Republic*, where no private property is allowed the rulers, the Guardians, in order that they can give their full attention to communitarian values and govern in the interest of the whole. The myth of communism appears and reappears in many religious writings in which property is viewed as the result of "man's fall." It is part of secular law and does not exist by "divine" or "natural" law. The theme reemerges with particular force in the writings of many Utopian Socialists in the decades after the French Revolution and well into the nineteenth century. After the Industrial Revolution, the dream of collective ownership, which would eliminate income inequalities and poverty, has been particularly potent.

Not until the middle of the nineteenth century, however, was the vision spelled out in the form of a political movement, and not until the end of the century did the ideology take on shape with the formation of Communist political parties. In 1917, communism gained ascendancy in one country, Russia. It spread after World War II with renewed vigor over Eastern Europe and beyond.

Almost a century and a half ago, in 1848, Karl Marx and Friedrich Engels wrote their now-famous *Communist Manifesto;* with it, they transformed communism from only a theory into a strong political movement. In the opening sentence they spoke of "a specter" that haunted Europe—"the specter of communism." It did indeed become a reality for many throughout most of the twentieth century. Communism, either in the form of established political regimes or as a powerful political revolutionary movement, inspired, mobilized, and organized for political action a greater number of people than any other political ideology had to date.

As with other ideologies, communism can be viewed in two different ways. First, we can look at it as a body of theory and philosophy. This requires us to examine and analyze it with one question in mind: How valid is its theory and underlying philosophic assumptions? Second, we can look at communism as a political ideology and movement. This requires us to examine the way in which its basic philosophic and theoretical propositions have been translated into an action-oriented movement (i.e., a political ideology). While the first level of analysis is important, we emphasize communism here as a political ideology and a movement for political action.

THE LEGACY OF MARX

It was Karl Marx and his associate Friedrich Engels who provided us, through their writings and their political activities, with the foundations of contemporary communism. Of the two, Marx was the dominant intellectual figure. He published major theoretical works on economics and philosophy and produced a series of pamphlets on various aspects of political tactics. After his death in

1883, Engels synthesized, some might say simplified, some of his ideas. When we speak of Marxism, however, we are referring to the combined work of Marx and Engels.

The Sources That Inspired Marx

Four sources combined to produce the overall synthesis that constitutes Marxism. They are:

1. Hegel's philosophy, especially his philosophy of history.
2. The works of the British economists, notably Adam Smith, David Ricardo, Thomas Malthus, and others.
3. The French Utopian Socialists, even though they were sharply criticized by Marx and Engels.
4. The social and economic reality of the mid-nineteenth century, particularly in England.

First, Hegel gave to Marx a dynamic and evolutionary theory of history based on conflict; second, the British economists provided him with a new objective analysis of economic phenomena in which all economic factors were viewed in abstract terms as commodities, or variables, relating to each other on the basis of demonstrable and quantifiable laws; third, the Utopian Socialists provided hints on the construction of a future society. As for the reality of British industrial society in the middle of the nineteenth century, it had a profound impact on both Marx and Engels. Working conditions were dismal, hours of work long, children and women were employed at starvation wages for twelve, fourteen, and sometimes sixteen hours a day, living conditions were abominable, and life expectancy low. The miseries of the workers contrasted sharply with the well-being of those who had land, property, and money (i.e., capital), and could employ others. Conditions like these provoked not only moral indignation but also widespread protest. Workers rebelled and destroyed the new machines for fear they would deprive them of work; regimentation in the factory under the new industrial order was deeply resented; and workers attempted to use their numbers against the employers who, in turn, made use of the instruments of coercion available to them.

The Rejection of Capitalism

For Marx, the rejection of capitalism is *not* based on moral or humanitarian considerations. It derives from what he considered to be the empirical reality of the capitalist economy. It obeys certain laws. Understanding them and studying them leads to the unavoidable conclusion that capitalism is doomed. Marx's anatomy of capitalism is also its autopsy!

The key to understanding capitalism and its inevitable demise is the notion of value, surplus value, and profit. The student can easily follow the Marxist critique of the capitalist economy by following Marx's own steps.

Karl Marx (1818-1883)

Born in Germany, where he studied law, philosophy, and history, Karl Marx and his family settled in London when he was thirty years old. There he began a lifelong collaboration with Friedrich Engels to develop a communist ideology and to translate it into political action. In 1848 they produced the *Communist Manifesto*, urging the workers to rise and take over the means of production for the exploiting capitalist class. In 1864 he founded the First International, whose purpose was to unite workers everywhere in a revolutionary struggle. A prodigious worker, a committed man, and also one of the most learned and creative minds of the nineteenth century, Marx, like Freud half a century later, suggested a new way of looking at social life and history. Accordingly, he saw material and economic conditions as responsible for the shaping of our values, morality, attitudes, and political institutions. Marx singled out property relations to be the key element and the exploitation of "have-nots" by the "haves" to be at the heart of liberal capitalism. It was, at the same time, the reason for a working-class revolution, and the vindication of communism. He wrote voluminously, but his major work is an analysis of capitalist economy in *Capital,* the first volume of which was published in 1867 and the second and third posthumously, by Engels, in 1885 and 1894, respectively.

1. Only labor creates value.
2. Machines, land, and all other factors of production create no new value. They pass on to the product a value equivalent to the portion of their value used as they depreciate during the process of production.
3. The capitalist (the entrepreneur) pays the worker only a subsistence wage.
4. The worker produces a value that is twice as much (generally speaking) as what he or she gets in wages.
5. The difference between what the capitalist pays the worker and what the worker produces is the *surplus value* pocketed by the capitalist.
6. All profits derive from the surplus value, though the actual profit does not correspond to the amount of surplus value extracted by a given capitalist.
7. In the market there is a fierce competition among capitalists. Each tries to sell more; a large volume of goods sold, even at lower prices, will bring added income.
8. This incites the capitalist to modernize and mass-produce, to introduce better machines, and to increase the productivity of labor.
9. A modern firm manages with fewer workers to produce and hence sell more. As a result, more and more workers are laid off.
10. Thus the modern firm can reduce prices by lowering its profit *per unit*.
11. Many firms that fail to modernize are gradually driven out of business. They employ more workers, pay out more in wages, and thus cannot compete with the lower prices the modernized firms set.
12. As a result, many firms have to close down. Capital becomes increasingly concentrated into fewer and fewer hands and in larger and more modern firms, in which more machinery and modern technology are introduced.
13. Capitalism reaches a point at which a small number of highly modernized large firms can produce goods efficiently and cheaply. However, with a great number of people out of work, there are not enough buyers for the products, so firms can no longer make a profit. Production becomes restricted.
14. Profit and private property, the great incentives of the Industrial Revolution, now become obstacles to the plentiful production of goods.
15. The legal forms of capitalism (private profit and private property) come into conflict with the means of production (efficiency, high productivity, and potential abundance).

This is the Marxist critique in a nutshell. The heart of capitalism and capitalist production is to be found in private property and profit. The purpose of production is *profit*—how the capitalist can get from the market a value for the product that is higher than the cost of production. The difference between what the entrepreneurs spend to produce and what they receive for the product is the *profit*—one of the most dynamic incentives for capitalist production and growth.

Marx develops an ingenious theory to explain profit. It is *the theory of surplus value*. The worker is paid wages that are determined by the market through the law of supply and demand. The daily wage corresponds to the price of goods the worker and his family need and consume in one day. During the same day, however, the worker has produced goods that have a much higher value. The difference between value produced (owned and sold by the entrepreneur) and what is paid out in wages is the *surplus value*. Marx contends that generally wages tend to correspond to not more than half of the value the worker produces. So the other half goes to the entrepreneur—to the capitalist. This is Marx's argument.

The Laws of Capitalist Accumulation and Pauperization

The quest for profit accounts for modernization; the technologically advanced firms with the newest machines benefit at the expense of the backward ones. Many firms go bankrupt, but the survivors accumulate in their hands an ever greater part of the capital. Fewer and fewer capitalists own the means of production, while more and more small firms disappear. The whole social structure becomes lopsided, with a tiny minority controlling production for the purpose of making profit; at the same time, the vast majority of the people have nothing but their labor to sell, precisely when it becomes all the more difficult to sell!

As more and more people are dispossessed of the means to produce, more and more fall into the class of the proletariat. Thus, as the firms develop more sophisticated machinery, a greater number of people find themselves living in a state of misery. Many cannot find work. Many become "marginals," moving from one place to another without a role, without skills, and in a state of constant deprivation and humiliation. They are the *lumpenproletariat*—the army of the unemployed and also the unemployable, the people from the countryside or those recently demoted from the middle or lower middle classes. They become a permanent fixture of capitalist societies.

The profit motive—a driving and dynamic motive in the early stages of capitalism—becomes a drag and an impediment in its most advanced stage. It pushes the capitalists to modernize and to accumulate capital and industrial equipment; it indeed makes production easier and much more efficient; *objectively speaking*, it makes it possible for human beings in a society to supply all their wants and more. Capitalism thus achieves a most remarkable breakthrough by creating all the material conditions for the good life. Marx is full of praise for the bourgeoisie and for capitalism when he views their historical role.

> The bourgeoisie has through its exploitation of the world market given a cosmopolitan character to production and consumption in every country. In place of the old wants, satisfied by the production of the country, we find new wants, requiring for their satisfaction the products of distant lands and climes. In place of the old local and national seclusion and self-sufficiency, we have intercourse in every direction, universal interdependence of nations.
>
> The bourgeoisie, by the rapid improvement of all instruments of production, by the immensely facilitated means of communication, draws all, even the most barbarian, nations into civilization. . . .

The bourgeoisie has created enormous cities, has greatly increased the urban population as compared with rural, and has thus rescued a considerable part of the population from the idiocy of rural life.[2]

Yet it is precisely at this advanced stage that the capitalistic economy can no longer provide for profits. By pressing heavily upon the middle class, and by creating a chronic state of unemployment among the independent artisans and small farmers, which reduces them gradually to the ranks of the poor and the dispossessed, many are being deprived of the means to buy things and meet their needs. Demand goes down and with it comes lower profit. To keep the rate of profit, the capitalist is now forced to produce less, to control prices, to develop monopolies in order to avoid competition, and to form cartels to keep prices up. Whereas profit was a positive incentive to industrial growth and production, now it becomes a shackle. It is at this point that capitalism has outlived its purpose—it can produce plenty, but there is no incentive to do so. It is at this point that Marx pronounces its death sentence!

The student will note that thus far there has not been a single note of moral approbation or disapprobation. Marx gives us a "scientific" account—that is, a description of what he sees happening, a description which fits his basic laws of the capitalist economy. They account for its inevitable demise.

The analysis of the laws accounting for the demise of capitalism, however, does not amount to a "rejection" of capitalism. People must become aware of something, become dissatisfied with something, and move actively against something in order for there to be a rejection. Rejection is a subjective phenomenon associated with a collective desire and consciousness and with concerted action. *This is the revolutionary side of Marxism.*

THE DYNAMICS OF THE COMMUNIST REVOLUTION

In contrast to his economic analysis, in which Marx set up theories and hypotheses and sought their confirmation in the empirical world of the capitalist economy, his whole notion of a revolution is the culminating point of philosophic speculation and is not amenable to the same rules of scientific inquiry. It includes: (1) a philosophy of history, (2) a theory of class struggles, (3) a theory of the state, (4) the historical act of "revolution," and (5) the utopian world to follow. We discuss each of these briefly.

A Philosophy of History

History has been defined as a set of tricks that the living play upon the dead. For Marx, there are no such tricks! For him, the living constantly interact with the dead. Men and women are both the product of history, bound by the

---

[2]Karl Marx, *The Communist Manifesto*, in Robert C. Tucker (ed.), *The Marx-Engels Reader*, pp. 469–500.

conditions it creates, and also the makers of history, in reacting to those conditions and changing them. But this is only within the limits that history itself
allows. How does this unfold? Marx answers by using the works of the German
philosopher Georg W. F. Hegel (1770—1831) to develop a theory of history
and change.

According to Hegel, history moves through conflict—a conflict of ideas.[3]
He believes that there is something like a divine will, an Absolute, destined to
finally unfold itself fully in the universe, but the process of unfolding is not evolutionary. It takes place through struggle between opposing ideas. The idea of
beauty has opposing it the idea of ugliness, the idea of truth that of falsehood,
the idea of liberty that of slavery, and so on. Throughout history and its various
stages, there is a constant and Homeric battle between opposing ideas, called
by Hegel *dialectic idealism*. It goes something like this: each phase in history
corresponds to the manifestation of certain ideas or an idea. It is called the *thesis*. However, it includes its opposite, its *antithesis*. Thesis and antithesis struggle with each other until the antithesis manages to absorb the thesis or to
combine with it in one form or another. This combination is called a *synthesis*,
representing a new stage in history. Every synthesis, in turn, becomes a thesis
that suggests automatically its antithesis, which comes into conflict with it to
lead to a new synthesis, and so forth. . . . A point comes *when history will have
exhausted itself—the best possible synthesis will have occurred*. God or the
Spirit will have fully unfolded itself in the universe!

Marx maintains the dialectic (the notion of conflicting opposites); he maintains the whole scheme of historical movement in terms of thesis–antithesis–
synthesis. However, he is clearly not an idealist. Writing in his preface to
Capital, Marx tells us himself how he changed the very foundations of Hegel's
philosophy of history while maintaining the basic structure.

> My dialectic method is not only different from the Hegelian, but its direct opposite.
> To Hegel, the life-process of the brain, i.e., the process of thinking, which under
> the name of "the Idea," he even transforms into an independent subject, is the de-
> miurgos (creator) of the real world, and the real world is only the external, phe-
> nomenal form of "the idea." With me on the contrary the idea is nothing else than
> the material world reflected by the human mind, and translated into forms of
> thought. . . . With Hegel (the dialectic) . . . is standing on its head. It must be
> turned rightside up again.[4]

Dialectic Materialism   Marx found in the material world, our senses, and
our working conditions—not in our ideas—the source of conflict and change.
This is what, in contrast to "dialectic idealism," has become known as *dialectic
materialism*. The stages of historical development—the specific contents of a
thesis, an antithesis, and a synthesis—are not to be found in the not-so-easily

---

[3]Georg W. F. Hegel, *The Philosophy of History*.

[4]Karl Marx, Preface to the second edition, *Capital*, Modern Library, p. 25.

observable world of ideas but in the empirical world, in our society. It is a momentous shift. The Hegelian abstraction now becomes a theory leading to hypotheses about human and social life that can be observed and tested.

Class Conflict

The major source and type of conflict are that amoung individuals and groups. It is not an indiscriminate conflict, haphazardly pitting individual against individual; it is highly structured. The conflict is between classes; it is a *class struggle. A class is defined in terms of the relationship individuals have to the means of production.* Very simply put, there are two classes: those who own property and those who do not. This has been the reality of social life and the basic source of conflict and change. Class struggle is the engine of dialectic materialism.

Each historical phase corresponds to new and different forms of private property. Landed property was the characteristic of the feudal period and the landed aristocracy; but within it money, gold, and commerce made their appearance. Artisans, small manufacturers, and merchants later emerged, with them commercial capital and finally manufacturing and industry. They were destined to become a new class, an antithesis, the *bourgeoisie.* The French Revolution of 1789 epitomized, in a way, the end of the landed aristocracy and the coming of the middle class to power, emphasizing new types of property and new productive forces. But the moment the capitalists and the various groups allied to them emerged, the antithesis was already present. It was *the working class*—a small cloud on the blue horizon of bourgeois capitalism. With no property of its own, with nothing to sell but its labor, and subject to the laws of capitalistic economy, the cloud of the working class grew bigger and bigger. The class struggle was on, presaging the storm and the inevitable revolutionary conflict between the workers and the bourgeoisie.

Infrastructure and Superstructure   In the constant interaction between society and environment, and in the constant class struggle that corresponds to various historical stages, human beings not only develop particular forms of property, they also change them. For each stage there is a particular set of ideas and norms, and these correspond to and are fashioned by the interests of the property-owning class. They rationalize and legitimize (i.e., make acceptable to all) the dominance of the ruling and property-owning class. This theory, which traces and attributes moral ideas and norms directly or indirectly to economic factors, is called *economic determinism*: it states that how and where we live and work fashion our ideas about the world. Capitalists have a set of ideas about society and the world that correspond to their interests and to their dominance. The workers begin to develop theirs to express their needs and interests.

In the Marxist vocabulary, the totality of factors that determine a person's relations to private property and work constitute the *infrastructure*: they are the material and objective social conditions. On the other hand, the way we look upon society—the ideas we have about it, in a word our ideology—is the *superstructure*. This superstructure includes religion, law, education, literature, even the state. It is an ideology fashioned by the dominant class, the one that owns property, and its view of society is forced upon all (including the workers) until a moment comes when they begin to question it.

Objective and Subjective Conditions   Each phase of the class struggle and each form of property relations differ in content from the preceding one. Bourgeois capitalism revolutionized the *objective economic conditions* of production. Division of labor, capital accumulation, technological progress—all these profit-inspired activities changed the world in the late eighteenth century and ever since. But by also creating a vast proletarian army, by divesting the lower classes of property, and by concentrating capital in a small number of firms, individuals, and banks, capitalism has ironically made it easier for society to replace the capitalist class. With this turn of events, a mass of people begin to demand the end of capitalist rule. These are the *subjective economic conditions*. A point thus comes when objective conditions (i.e., technology, concentration of capital, the capability of the economy to provide abundance) coincide with the subjective conditions (i.e., the will and the consciousness of the workers to take over the industrial apparatus created by the capitalist and to use it for the whole community). When subjective and objective conditions converge, it is the moment of revolution.

Note this carefully: the revolution was not, according to Marx, a matter of will, indignation, or even leadership. Conditions, both objective and subjective, must be ripe. The workers must gain full consciousness that they are a class and that they must demand a change in the existing property relations. Only then can revolution under the appropriate leadership be envisaged.

The Theory of the State

The state is viewed by Marx as part of the superstructure. It is used to keep the majority of the people, who do not own the means of production, under the control of the small minority who do. While many (including Hegel) see the state as the embodiment of noble purposes—rationality, an agency for social justice and protection, the equitable distribution of goods, an impartial umpire keeping and administering the rules and laws equitably—Marx sees it as the instrument of the capitalist class. It is a repressive agency—a policeman!

But the state is not the only agency of domination. The whole superstructure, as we have noted, is fashioned by the ruling class. Religion inculcates observance of bourgeois values and respect for property; the family and the laws of inheritance perpetuate the rule of property; the educational system socializes everybody to respect the capitalist ethic and, most important, private property; art and literature extol the same virtues. No matter where they turn, the workers and their children will confront the same values and principles, and many of them will be brainwashed into accepting them. The peculiar characteristic of the state, however, is that it is the only part of the superstructure that can use force. Hence it is necessary to use force against it.

The Revolution

Revolution, therefore, is necessary and unavoidable. "But what about democracy?" the student asks. "What about free and equal voting, freedom of association and of trade unions, of political parties and even of Socialist parties? What about the freedom of the majority to change the economy?"

The answer is complex. First, when Marx wrote, trade unions were only beginning to emerge; second, there were no Socialist parties, although some were just making their appearance; third, political parties almost everywhere were just about to become national parties with national organizations and members; fourth, outside the United States, universal suffrage did not exist or could not be freely exercised. Most important of all, however, Marx did not really believe that a capitalist system and the capitalist state would ever allow Socialist parties to gain ascendancy, nor did he believe that a majority would ever be allowed to challenge private property directly or to control production and the allocation of goods and services. If a majority did, the state would use force against it on behalf of the capitalists. Revolution, therefore, was necessary.

The Utopian Goal: The Communist Society

Marx gives us only a sketchy account of the Communist society to come after the working-class revolution. In fact, he provides us with what amounts to a two-stage program. The first corresponds to the transitional stage toward socialism, and the second is the ultimate one, the utopian level of communism.

In the first, the revolution is followed by the "dictatorship of the proletariat." The workers take over the state and all its instruments of coercion and use these instruments against the capitalist class. "The development towards communism," he writes, "proceeds through the dictatorship of the proletariat; it cannot do otherwise, for the resistance of the capitalist exploiters cannot be broken by anyone else or in any other way."[5] In contrast to all other dictatorships, however, this is one by the majority against the minority. Therefore, this is a dictatorship that corresponds to, and gradually becomes, a democracy of the people and the workers. The few—the capitalists—are excluded or suppressed by force.

As the state is now being used by the workers against the capitalists, its substance changes. It becomes the instrument of the many against the few. As the means of production become socialized, classes disappear, since there can be no classes without property. Without classes, there is no need for coercion. *The dictatorship paves the way toward its own disappearance and to the establishment of a classless and stateless society.* The state simply "withers away."

---

[5]Karl Marx, *The Communist Manifesto*, in D. McLellan, *Karl Marx: Selected Writings*, University Press, 1977 p. 237.

The second phase corresponds to communism. The economy, both production and distribution, is now in the hands of the community. Nobody can exploit anybody; "bourgeois rights" (individual rights) give their place to "common rights." The final and ultimate phase is reached with the collectivization of all the means of production, with the harnessing of production to common purposes, with the transformation of the state from a coercive power to a purely administrative one. The objective conditions of production bequeathed to the new society from capitalism can now be used to make the slogan *"From each according to his ability to each according to his needs"* possible.

This is the apocalyptic or utopian element. And although Marx did not go to the lengths some earlier Utopian Socialists did, he shared their general optimism and was influenced by it. Crime would disappear, the span of life would increase, brotherhood and cooperation would inculcate a new morality, scientific progress would grow by leaps and bounds. Above all, with socialism spreading around the world, war, the greatest blight of humankind, and its twin, nationalism, would have no place. International brotherhood would follow. Engels waxes enthusiastic over the prospects and goes so far as to declare that, with the socialist revolution, humanity will complete its "prehistoric" stage and enter for the first time into what might be called its own history. Until the revolution, he claims, society submits to outside forces while the majority of humans within a society submit to a ruling class. After the revolution a united classless society will be able, for the first time, to decide which way to go and what to do with its resources and capabilities. For the first time we can make our own history! It was to be, in Engels words, "the ascent of man from the kingdom of necessity to the kingdom of freedom."[6]

The skeptics were now confronted with the anatomy of capitalism, a theory of history, a theory of revolution, a theory of state—all of them pointing in the same direction, toward a Communist society. With it, of course, the laws developed by Marx to explain the economy, the society, and history would come to an end, and individuals and the society would be free to make their own laws and shape their own future. It was this Marxist vision that provided the intellectual basis for the Bolshevik Revolution and that inspired Lenin to whom we now turn.

BIBLIOGRAPHY

Avineri, Shlomo. *The Social and Political Thought of Karl Marx*. New York: Cambridge University Press, 1968.

Berlin, Isaiah. *Karl Marx: His Life and Environment*, 3rd ed. New York: Oxford University Press, 1963.

---

[6]Friedrich Engels, "Socialism: Utopian and Scientific" in Robert C. Tucker, *The Marx–Engels Reader*, p. 716.

Berstein, Eduard. *Evolutionary Socialism.* Translated by E. C. Harvey. New York: Schocken, 1961.

Bober, M. M. *Karl Marx's Interpretation of History.* New York: Norton, 1965.

Bottomore, Tom (ed.). *Modern Interpretations of Marx.* Oxford: Basil Blackwell, 1981.

Burns, Emile. *An Introduction to Marxism.* New York: International Publishers, 1966.

Cohen, G. A. *Karl Marx's Theory of History.* New York: Oxford University Press, 1978.

Cornforth, Maurice. *Communism and Philosophy: Contemporary Dogmas and Revisions of Marxism.* London: Lawrence and Wishart, 1980.

Fromm, Erich. *Marx's Concept of Man.* New York: Frederick Ungar, 1965.

Gottlieb, Roger S. (ed.). *An Anthology of Western Marxism: From Lukacs and Gramsci to Socialist-Feminism,* New York: Oxford University Press, 1989.

Gregor, James. *A Survey of Marxism.* New York: Random House, 1965.

Hegel, Georg W. F. *The Philosophy of History,* translated by J. Sibree. New York: The Colonial Press, 1900.

Heilbroner, Robert L. *Marxism: For and Against.* New York: Norton, 1980.

Kolakowski, Leszek. *Marxism and Beyond: On Historical Understanding and Individual Responsibility.* Translated by Jane Zielonko Peel. London: Pall Mall Press, 1969.

———. *Main Currents of Marxism,* 3 vols. Translanted by P. S. Falla. Oxford, England: Clarendon Press, 1978.

Kolakowski, Leszek, and Stuart Hampshire (eds.). *The Socialist Idea: A Reappraisal.* London: Weidenfeld and Nicolson, 1974.

Lichtheim, George. *Marxism: An Historical and Critical Study,* 2nd ed. New York: Praeger, 1965.

Luxemburg, Rosa. *Selected Political Writings.* Edited by Dick Howard. New York: Monthly Review Press, 1971.

Marx, Karl. *Capital, A Critique of Political Economy.* Modern Library, 1925.

Marx, Karl, and Friedrich Engels. *Selected Works.* New York: International Publishers, 1968.

McLellan, David. *Karl Marx: His Life and Thought.* New York: Harper & Row, 1973.

———. *Karl Marx.* Baltimore: Penguin, 1976.

——— (ed.). *The Karl Marx Reader.* New York: Oxford University Press, 1977.

———. *Marxism after Marx.* Boston: Houghton Mifflin, 1981.

Meyer, Alfred G. *Marxism: The Unity of Theory and Practice.* Ann Arbor: University of Michigan Press, 1963.

Seliger, Martin. *The Marxist Conception of Ideology: A Critical Essay.* Cambridge, England: Cambridge University Press, 1977.

Tucker, Robert C. (ed.). *Philosophy and Myth in Karl Marx,* 2nd ed. New York: Cambridge University Press, 1972.

———. *The Marx–Engels Reader,* 2nd ed. New York: Norton, 1978.

Wolfe, Bertram, D. *Marxism: One Hundred Years in the Life of a Doctrine.* New York: Dial Press, 1965.

Chapter
6

The Reality
Leninism and Stalinism

The organization of the Party takes the place of the Party itself; the Central Committee takes the place of the organization; and, finally, the dictator takes the place of the Central Committee.

Leon Trotsky
Our Political Tasks

With Lenin, Marxist ideology and revolutionary tactics were given a new sharpness and urgency. Lenin was able to take the theoretical Marxist blueprint and adapt it not only to a revolutionary movement in Russia in the early part of the twentieth century but also to the independence movements of the colonial world. The first successful revolution in the name of Marxism, the Bolshevik Revolution, was made under his leadership in Russia on November 7, 1917.

Joseph Stalin succeeded Lenin in 1924 and became in a true sense the builder of Soviet communism. He remained in power for almost thirty years until his death in 1953. Collectivization, economic planning, rapid industrialization, the expansion of Soviet power, and also a one-man authoritarian government are associated with his rule. During the same period of time, Communist regimes were established in many parts of the world. They were built upon the Leninist-Stalinist model.

LENINISM

Lenin faithfully accepted the body of Marxist thought and devoted a good part of his life to defending it against its many critics. His two most important contributions to communist thought can be found in two pamphlets—*What Is to Be Done?* (1903) and *Imperialism, the Highest Stage of Capitalism* (1917). In the first, Lenin developed a new theory for the organization of the proletariat through the Communist party; in the second, he attempted to show that the highest stage (and last stage) of capitalism was inextricably associated with colonial wars among capitalist nations. In a third long essay, *The State and Revolution* (1918), he elaborated on such key concepts as the revolutionary takeover of power, the period of the dictatorship of the proletariat, and the final stage of communism where the state was to disappear and material abundance become a reality. But his most important contribution, as the head of the Russian Bolshevik party, was to make a revolution and to preside over its consolidation.

Lenin's Revolutionary Doctrine

The greater part of Lenin's life was devoted to the development of a revolutionary doctrine. In *The State and Revolution* he summarized the Marxist theses: the state is the product of the irreconcilability of class antagonisms and the agency of the capitalist class; liberal democracy is another name for capitalism, ensuring domination of the workers; law and the state are instruments for the domination of the ruling class against the working classes; and, of course, revolution and the triumph of the working class are both desirable and inevitable.

The revolutionary stages Lenin envisages are the following:

1. The armed uprising of the proletariat, under proper leadership.
2. The seizure of political control by the workers, in the form of a temporary "dictatorship of the proletariat," against the remnants of the capitalist classes.

Lenin's concept of dictatorship was as succinct as it was brutal. "The scientific concept of dictatorship [of the proletariat] means neither more nor less than unlimited power, resting directly on force, not limited by anything, not restricted by any law or any absolute rules. Nothing else but that."[1]

3. The socialization of the means of production and the abolition of private property.
4. Finally, the slow "withering away of the state" as an instrument of coercion and class oppression, and the emergence of a classless, stateless society.

The Communist Party

What does Lenin mean by a revolution of the working class *under proper leadership?* Marx's position was that objective economic factors and the class consciousness of the workers world move in parallel. The maturing of capitalism would mean the maturing of the social (i.e., revolutionary) consciousness of the workers.

Lenin posits from the very beginning, however, the need for leadership and organization. The working class—and particularly the Russian working

---

[1]Lenin, quoted in Bertram Wolfe, "Leninism," in Milorad M. Drachkovitch (ed.), *Marxism in the Modern World*, p. 69.

Lenin (1870–1924)

Vladimir Ilyich Ulyanov ("Lenin" was originally a pseudonym, but became the better-known name) spent his childhood—a happy one according to all accounts—in the province of Kazan. After receiving his law degree, he was arrested for revolutionary activity and exiled to Siberia. In 1900 he was allowed to go abroad where, as a professed Marxist, he pursued his revolutionary activity with remarkable energy. He formulated, and imposed on his followers, a program for a highly centralized party consisting of trained revolutionaries.

The collapse of the tsarist armies and the democratic revolution of February 1917 found Lenin in Switzerland. He managed to negotiate with the German government for a passage across the front line between the German and Russian armies; on the night of November 6–7, 1917, the Bolsheviks seized power and Lenin was made chairman of the new government. By 1918, Lenin had established what amounted to a dictatorship. He dissolved the Constituent Assembly after the Bolsheviks failed to get a majority in the elections, but his main attention was given to the war against the tsarist loyalists. Not until 1920 did the Russian Civil War come to an end with the victory of the communist forces.

class—could never develop revolutionary consciousness by itself. An elite, organized into a Communist party, would have to educate the masses, infuse them with revolutionary spirit, and inculcate in them class consciousness. This would lead them toward the revolution and, ultimately, communism. *Dialectic materialism is brushed aside here to be replaced by a theory of voluntarism.* The Communist party is based on the will and dedication of Marxists. They are the revolutionaries. They can make the revolution irrespective of the prevailing social conditions.

A number of consequences, both at the theoretical and tactical levels, follow these assumptions.

Elitism   The party is to be composed of gifted individuals who understand Marxism and therefore understand the direction of history better than the rest of the people. The leaders of the party are particularly endowed with scientific knowledge and foresight that the common people lack. Leadership is likely to come not from the ranks of the working class but from "outside"—from middle-class intellectuals who are able to comprehend the totality of the society's interests and hence promote socialism. They are trained in Marxist dialectics and can discern the historical pattern leading to socialism. This party is the *vanguard* of the proletariat. It speaks and acts on behalf of the proletariat.

Organization of the Party   The rank and file of the party is united with its leaders by bonds of allegiance and common action, but also obedience and discipline. They must be prepared for any kind of action, legal or illegal, at any time. "The one serious organizational principle for workers in our movement," Lenin wrote, "must be the strictest secrecy, strictest choice of members, training of professional revolutionaries."[2] The party has to be organized on the basis of *democratic centralism*, according to which:

1. All decisions are to be made in an open and free debate by the representative organ of the party, the congress.
2. Once a decision is thus made, it is binding upon all. No factions are to be allowed within the party and no minority within the party is permitted either to secede or to air its grievances in public.
3. All officers of the party—secretaries, the Central Committee, and other executive organs—are elected indirectly from the lowest membership upward.
4. All decisions and instructions of the party executive officials are binding upon all inferior organs and officers.

The organization of the Soviet Communist party thus became increasingly hierarchical. Orders for action flowed from top to bottom. Throughout his whole life Lenin was able, despite opposition, to hold the supreme decision-

---

[2]Wolfe, p. 78.

making power in his hands and to control the nomination of local party leaders. The party did not tolerate dissent and, under Lenin's leadership, indulged in purges in the years after the revolution. He invented the notion "enemies of the people." It was during this same period that thousands of so-called wreckers, saboteurs, petit bourgeois, and many others were jailed, and sentenced to death.

From Lenin's model of the party, it is obvious that he had no respect for democracy. "Lenin and his friends [insisted] upon the need of absolute authority by the revolutionary nucleus of the party." The revolution was to be "the supreme law." "If the revolution demanded it . . . everything—democracy, liberty, the rights of the individual—must be sacrificed to it."[3] Accordingly, Lenin had no scruples at all in dissolving democratically elected bodies when the Bolsheviks were in a minority. The party was to be the single guiding spirit and the governing body of the nation.

Colonies and World Revolution

In *Imperialism: the Highest Stage of Capitalism*, published in 1917, Lenin attempted to show that the highest and last stage of capitalism ("monopoly capitalism") corresponds to a period of control by the big banks and trusts that have investments in overseas colonies, the division of the world into colonial areas of domination and exploitation, and wars. The most important thesis of the book, however, was that capitalism had become a world phenomenon despite the uneven economic development of the various countries and the backwardness of the colonies.

If capitalism had indeed become a worldwide phenomenon, if the imperialist nations had divided the world among themselves, and if they had managed to blunt the revolutionary class consciousness of their workers by providing them with benefits and advantages that were being extracted from the colonial peoples, where would the revolution come from? For Lenin, as we have seen, it would have to come from trained revolutionaries, well organized and sharing a common will. But where would the revolution take place?

The answer given by Lenin, with the support of Leon Trotsky, was that one should not wait for the stages of capitalistic development to unfold themselves. It was tactically necessary to push for revolutionary seizures of power anywhere in the world rather than wait until each and every country had reached the level of maturity required by Marx and Engels. The capitalistic chain which bound the world had some weak links, particularly its colonies, where it was vulnerable because colonial peoples began to demand what many liberal bourgeois leaders had advocated for themselves—national independence, political rights, equality, and so on. One step in the fight against capitalism, therefore, was to try to snap the chain at any of its various weak links. Communists were asked,

---

[3]Isaiah Berlin, "Political Ideas in the Twentieth Century," in *Foreign Affairs*, vol. 98, April 1950.

in the name of Marx, to promote revolutions in countries where the peasantry and not the workers represented the most numerous social group; they were to do this in the name of nationalism rather than internationalism. From a tactical point of view, every colonial independence movement that succeeded was a break in the capitalistic chain and hence a victory for Communist Russia.

It was a masterly tactical twist designed both to defend communism in a backward country like Russia against potential enemies (and in so doing defend Russia as well) and to expand and export the Communist revolution made in Russia to virtually anywhere in the world.

Conclusion

Emphasis on political and revolutionary tactics, no matter what the objective conditions, are the hallmarks of Leninism: reliance on the human factors of will, leadership, and organization irrespective of their social contents; and the subordination of everything else to political organization, political will, and leadership to make the revolution. Very often this is referred to as the theory of *substitutism*. With Marx, the working class develops the consciousness to make the revolution and establish communism, thus substituting itself for the whole of society. With Lenin, the Communist party substitutes itself for the working class and speaks for the interests of the working class. It is then the executive and higher organs of the party, the Central Committee, that speak for the interests of the working class, which speaks for the interests of the whole. But since the same Central Committee controlled the world Communist movements, it also spoke for the interests of all the Communist parties, which spoke for their respective working classes, that spoke for the world community! It takes only one more step for the single leader to substitute for all the others in order to arrive at the logical outcome of such an organization—the subordination of *everything* to the leadership of *one* man. Such was the essence of Stalinism.

STALINISM

The name of Stalin is becoming as remote to many students as that of Napoleon. But still for many contemporary Communists, inside and outside the Soviet Union, Stalin and Stalinism remain important and highly controversial. A member of the Russian Communist party and an associate of Lenin, Stalin succeeded him after his death in 1924. After five years, during which he managed to eliminate all opposition within the Communist party, he became its absolute ruler. While Lenin was backed by his enormous prestige and was respected for his intelligence and writings, Stalin relied on the organization he had built with the party as well as outright force. Stalin institutionalized in his own person the dictatorship of the proletariat: not bound by any law, indeed being above any law.

Stalin succeeded Lenin at a moment when the revolutionary spirit in Russia, and everywhere else, was at an ebb. Long years of strife, civil war, and

Joseph Stalin (1879–1953)

Born in Georgia, Stalin became the head of the Communist party of the Soviet Union after Lenin's death in 1924. Though originally a lesser figure among the Communist leaders who made the revolution, and lacking the literary, oratory, or intellectual talents of many of them, Stalin nevertheless assumed a controlling position within the organization of the party, becoming its Secretary General, and his rule prevailed. He launched what is generally called the Second Revolution, collectivizing agriculture and socializing all the means of production. His rule, which lasted until his death, saw the rapid increase of Soviet power, economically, internationally, and militarily. But it was in substance a personal dictatorship based on the most ruthless application of force and terror, and it is characterized by many as a great betrayal of the original principles upon which the revolution was predicated.

economic hardships had disillusioned a number of revolutionary leaders and undermined the morale of the party's rank and file. A party organizer above all, Stalin wove within the Central Committee of the party and within the regional and district committees a web of personal and organizational contacts. He controlled the appointments of Communist party members to local and district administrative jobs; he was in charge of party admissions; he was asked to reorganize and purge the administrative apparatus of the state and assume control of the police. He used these powers in order to consolidate and promote his own personal position within the party.

No Internal Democracy

Another indication of the demotion of the status of the party was the lack of any genuine free deliberation and criticism among its assembled delegates. Congresses, whenever they were convened, spent their time in giving their approbation without any debate to the resolutions of the leadership. After 1930, not a single protest was raised; not a single dissenting voice or vote expressed. The slate of candidates for the various exective organs was prepared in advance by Stalin and his immediate associates and was always approved unanimously.

The Police

The new organ, which in effect replaced the party, was the police, which operated directly under Stalin. It was the duty of the police to maintain communist legality. Lenin had used it to first operate against "deviationists" and "dissenters," but it was always understood that it was to be an adjunct of the party acting on its behalf. But by 1935, the secret police became the instrument of control and intimidation not only of the society as a whole but also vis-à-vis the party. Party members were totally at its mercy as were high-placed party officials. The secret police gradually became the most feared coercive and punitive force. It had its own private army (including tanks), a huge network of spies and informers, and was in command of the forced labor camps where the inmates—variously estimated to range from 3 to 4 million to as many as 10 million over the whole Stalinist period—were interned. Terror thus became an instrument of government.

The Organization of the Communist Party

The organization and functions of the Communist party under Stalin represent the ultimate development of what Lenin had started. The party remained an *elite* composed of loyal and energetic members. Its mission was to maintain and further the cause of Soviet socialism and to educate the masses into socialism.

Its membership continued to be relatively small. Sometimes it was described as the "chief of staff of the proletariat," sometimes as "the teacher" of the Russian masses, and at other times the "vanguard of the working class and the masses." It grew into an exclusive organization which controlled every aspect of governmental and social life of Soviet society.

The Leninist conception of the hierarchical relationship between leadership and rank and file hardened into an institution. The role of the leader began to be expounded upon in a semireligious, semi-Byzantine manner: he was omniscient and omnipresent, he was the father of the people, his word was law. There was in Stalinism a marked similarity to the despotic paternalism of the czarist regime.

The development of this concept of leadership is also related to the internal development of the party organization. Decision-making powers became concentrated exclusively in the hands of the executive organs of the party, and any semblance of democractic centralism was abandoned in favor of rigid centralization and control from the top. Nominations to party posts were made from above and not by the rank and file. Criticism was allowed only when leaders would permit it, and only on subjects selected in advance by them; periodic purges accounted for a constant turnover of the rank and file and middle-echelon officers and organizers.

The Economy

In 1929, Stalin introduced what is often referred to as the "Second Revolution" or the "Revolution from Above." All means of production and all private property were socialized, and agriculture was collectivized. The Communist party became the political instrument for controlling society and bending it to the task of rapid industrialization. This entailed a rigorous centralization and bureaucratic control of the national economy—what is often referred to as a *command economy,* which is now being challenged in the Soviet Union. Economic targets were formulated over five-year periods (the Five-Year Plans) with priorities and specific quotas. Capital investment—the building of factories and industrial equipment—and the training of the labor force took precedence over consumption. Education became an indispensable part of industrialization, because technicians, scientists, skilled workers, engineers, and service personnel such as doctors, administrators, accountants, and so on, were vital to economic growth.

Force and Incentives

The overall effort amounted to a radical overhaul of Russian society. In the name of socialism, the task was to create what socialism should have inherited, an industrialized society. Three basic incentives could be used. The first was propaganda and persuasion: to extol the myth of socialism and incite people to communal efforts and sacrifices. But ideological exhortation has limits, and Stalin had to fall back on the two classic means of encouraging compliance: the carrot and the stick. The carrot was monetary incentive; the stick, force.

He who did not work would not eat. Income was to be proportionate to the quality and quantity of work done; inequality of income was declared to be unavoidable. Trade unions that favored equality of pay were put in their place—their leaders arrested and eliminated; the right to bargain was abolished, and the right to participate in the decisions of the plant manager were withdrawn.

The differences in pay created a salary structure that began to resemble that of the capitalistic societies, with the right of certain individuals to save and get interest, to pass on some of their gains to their heirs, to provide their children with better education, and to enjoy special advantages for vacation, leisure, and travel. There was even status—the recognition that they belonged to an elite class consisting of the top group of the *intelligentsia* (the Russian word denotes a very large class of people, comprising all groups other than workers and farmers). In recognition of their services and as an added incentive, they were allowed membership within the party—thus bestowing upon them political status as well. The percentage of workers and farmers within the party decreased correspondingly.

Force took a number of forms and served many purposes. It was used against those who did not work, or did not work regularly, and failed to live up to the quotas assigned to them. These people found their way to labor camps, and their disappearance was only a reminder to others of what they might have to face. Force was also used directly to create regiments of workers in labor camps who were responsible for tasks that nobody else would take (except for very high pay), such as mining of gold, lumber cutting, and road construction. In a more comprehensive sense, force was also a constant reminder, even to those who received a good pay for their work, that any relaxation or negligence would be followed by swift punishment.

SOVIET DOMINATION: THE COMINTERN

How would the Communist parties and the movements that sprang up almost everywhere after the Bolshevik Revolution be organized? The answer was the Third International—the Comintern—founded in 1919. The Communist parties that formed in many countries agreed to coordinate revolutionary strategy and tactics. There were thirty-five national parties in the Comintern when it was founded. By 1939—on the eve of World War II—the number had grown to about sixty.

The Twenty-One Conditions

What bound all these new Communist parties and movements together in the Third International were the famous twenty-one conditions set forth by Lenin. The same (or almost the same) characteristics of discipline, organization, and loyalty that Lenin imposed upon his Bolshevik party were required of all other national Communist parties. Some of the conditions for Communist parties everywhere were as follows:

- They must accept absolute ideological commitment to communism.
- They were to assume direct control over their communist press and publications.
- They accepted the principle and practice of democratic centralism (i.e., the compliance of the rank and file to the instructions of the higher authorities and the obligation not to allow any factions to exist within their party). Reformists, revisionists, trade unionists, were to be ruthlessly eliminated from their ranks.
- Underground and illegal organizations and activities were to be established, and party members should be ready for illegal work.
- A pledge was taken to make special efforts to undermine and disorganize the national armies.
- Pacifists and pacifism were not to be tolerated.
- All Communists undertook the obligation to give aid and support to revolutionary movements of colonial peoples.
- They were ordered to break with all trade unions affiliated with the Second International.
- Communist members in national parliaments were mere delegates of the party.
- All Communist parties in the world undertook to support the Soviet Union and "every Soviet republic."
- The Communist party program for every country had to be accepted by the executive committee of the Third International.

In this manner Lenin transformed the Communist movement into a worldwide organization to counter the worldwide grip that he claimed the capitalists had established. Any threats on the part of the capitalists against socialist Russia would meet with the resistance of this well-organized force everywhere outside of Russia.

With the offices of the Comintern in Moscow, the Soviet leadership under Stalin established its control over all other parties. Aside from ideology, many organizational and financial ties linked the individual Communist parties of various countries with the Soviet Union. Seven Congresses of the Third International were held and, in the beginning, there was freedom on the part of delegates from abroad to express their points of view and engage in dialogue. Soon the choice of these delegates became controlled by the Soviets, and the Congresses simply confirmed the "line" suggested by the Soviet leaders.

In 1943, the Third International was formally dissolved. The reasons given were that the various Communist parties in the world were "mature" enough to take care of their own programs and tactics and move about in their own way. The dissolution, however, was meant to placate the Western Allies (especially the United States) by showing that the Soviet Union was no longer bent on world revolution. But the Third International had played its role—it had coordinated tightly the Communist movements throughout the world according to Soviet designs and had solidly infused the belief that the defense and protection of the Soviet Union were the ultimate duties of all workers.

STALINISM: CONTRADICTIONS AND STAGNATION

For a long period of time, the Marxist vision sustained the communist reality, fashioned first by Lenin, and then worked out in its political and economic structures by Stalin, despite the disparity between the two. Such is the force of a grand ideology. Communist visionaries, ideologues, and intellectuals simply refused to examine the Stalinist reality because of the vision. Soviet leaders, on the other hand, exploited the vision to impose their rule and gain support both at home and abroad. Nonetheless, the disparities could not be accepted for too long. Some were noticeable even before Lenin's death—notably the imposition of a single-party rule by a party that allowed no free debate; the growing role of the police; the silencing of opposition by force; and the efforts to impose total communism upon a backward economy—in which 75 percent of the people were peasants. The disparities became more glaring, however, after the consolidation of the Stalinist regime. The party came under the complete domination of a single person—Stalin—who ruled by ruse and force like an Oriental despot.

With Stalin, revolutionary ideology and revolutionary movement became state and party orthodoxy. Speculation, argument, and debate gave place to imposition and dogma. Arguments, or even mere disagreements, were magnified to mean treason. Persuasion gave place to force, and the state and the police became the agencies to administer it, frequently against the party itself. Marxism was now presented in simple didactic terms to settle every dispute, especially when the presentation of the ideas was made by Stalin himself. Marxist ideology became a catechism repeated through all the socializing mechanisms available to the party—the party agitators, the press, the schools, the radio, the universities, the trade unions, and so on. The state and its bureaucracy, instead of withering away, grew and so did the totalitarian reach of the party; the use of force became, through the police, institutionalized into a permanent instrument of terror to exact compliance; all forms of public debate and argument were silenced—with all the media coming under the control of the appropriate party organs, just as it was the case under the authoritarian regimes that had sprung up in Germany and Italy. All societal groups and associations—professional, cultural, religious—were subordinated and came under the control of the party, including the family and the church. The state became the sole owner of property and the sole manager of the economy.

A despotism that was so reminiscent of the czars was but one of the developments that could not be reconciled with Marxism. But it was also the economy that failed to live up to the vision as well. The first decades of socialist buildup called for rapid mobilization of resources and was relatively successful. Under Stalin, Russia did indeed industrialize but only in the building of an industrial infrastructure that other countries had attained much earlier. Coal, cement, iron and steel, oil, rapid urbanization, and housing construction—the quantitative targets of the Five-Year Plans were impressive. Until well into the sixties, the authoritarian nature of the regimes, including even the police and the *gulags*, was ignored or even excused because of the vision of modernization and economic abundance promised by communism and by all those who believed that a planned and socialist economy was superior to capitalism; this was the conclusion of many Western European and American intellectuals as well. But the command economy, even in the days of Stalin, began to show inevitable weaknesses. First and foremost, it was unable to produce consumer goods—to meet the rising expectations of the Soviet citizens; second, and glaringly so, the collectivized agriculture could not produce enough food; third, inflexible mechanisms for the transport of goods were unable to move them from the producer to the consumer; and, even worse, planners were unable to manage so that materials needed in industrial firms could arrive in time and their products leave the factory on schedule. The socialist economy was unable to make the critical shift in the direction of diversification and experimentation and to introduce up-to-date technology.

With the economy stagnating, another of the Marxist visions began to fade away—that of equality. For a long time, a kind of ideological trade-off had been made between democracy (political freedoms) and equality (economic freedoms and satisfaction of economic needs, for all). The first was to be sacrificed to the second, *for a time*. The democracies of the West, it was claimed, gave the citizens equality of opportunities only; socialism provided them with real material equality. In the first there were formal rights; in the second substantive rights. Increasingly, however, it became apparent that this was not so. In a stagnating economy, the political oligarchy—notably the party members, the bureaucrats, the army officers, the police, and selected members of the intelligentsia—began to assume economic and social privileges that gave them a higher standard of living and access to special services. Political power became increasingly synonymous with privilege. Special food stores for shopping, vacation spots, and advantages for the education of their children were added to their higher benefits and salaries. Abuses and corruption inevitably followed. The vision appeared flawed as the communist ideology seemed to have become but a shield that protected a new political elite. It began to be looked upon with disdain by the rest of the population—including the populations of many nationalities whose standard of living was well below the level of the Russians. Joining the Communist party, and professing to be a Communist, was but a way for many to ensure their future and careers. The party gradually became a vast bureaucratic machine for maintaining the privileges accruing to its members. The ideology that sustained and nurtured it began to decline rapidly.

Waiting for . . . Gorbachev!

In 1956, after a short power struggle, Nikita Khrushchev, who replaced Stalin as General Secretary of the party and Chairman of the Council of Ministers of the Soviet Union, gave a "secret report" to the delegates of the Soviet Communist party at its Twentieth Congress. He criticized Stalin sharply for the many crimes committed during his long stay in office.

> Comrades! . . .
>
> After Stalin's death the Central Committee of the party began to implement a policy of explaining concisely and consistently that it is impermissible and foreign to the spirit of Marxism-Leninism to elevate one person, to transform him into a superman possessing supernatural characteristics akin to those of a god. Such a man supposedly knows everything, sees everything, thinks for everyone, can do anything, is infalliable in his behavior.

Only minor reforms were undertaken, however, in the economy, the society, and hardly any in the organization and rule of the party. Among them the most important were:

1. The control that the Soviet leadership once exercised over the other Communist parties in the world declined. References were now made to polycentrism, with multiple and independent centers of Communist rule, and to "national communism" in which Communist parties would follow a path dictated by specific national conditions and not by the Soviet leadership according to the Soviet model.
2. The "inevitability" of conflict between communism and liberal democracies gave place to "peaceful coexistence." In great part this was due of course to the development of nuclear weapons—and the "mutual assured destruction" they would bring upon all.
3. Stalin came under increasing criticism both with regard to the political practices he used and with reference to the kind of socialism that developed. His name was gradually removed from every corner of Soviet life. He was no longer regarded as one of "the founders" of communist ideology. Efforts to rehabilitate some of the Communist leaders who were put to death or "disappeared" during his reign have been successful. Many of the Communist leaders executed by Stalin were proclaimed innocent in 1988. Finally, but only in 1989, Gorbachev admitted that Stalin's "guilt is unforgiveable."
4. Stalin, as the leader—omniscient and omnipotent—was replaced by "collective leadership." The General Secretary of the Party, however, continued to maintain his ascendency. Yet the servile adulation and deference were gone. Through the party, Stalin's successors continued to exercise control, but it was no longer the direct and personal iron grip that Stalin held through the police and through outright intimidation and force.
5. The police and its arbitrary practices came under control, thanks to the development of some general rules and procedures to curb and subordinate it.

Little else was changed, however, until the mid-eighties. The official ideological orthodoxy of the party remained immune from criticism. The "dictatorship of the proletariat" continued to be proclaimed. The state in the hands of the Communist party maintained its coercive traits and Soviet military power dominated Eastern Europe, stifling by force national uprisings. Little was also changed in the economy. It continued to operate under the same bureaucratic and centralized controls, and the disparity between its progress (or rather lack of progress) and that of the Western world became manifest. The command economy was unable to provide for the consumer, and the standard of living of the Soviet citizen declined. The Soviets began to experience their own kind of "stagflation"—increased centralized controls by a burgeoning privileged Communist elite, with fewer and fewer goods for the population.

BIBLIOGRAPHY

Berlin, Isaiah. "Political Ideas in the Twentieth Century." *Foreign Affairs*, April 1950.
Bialer, Seweryn. *Stalin's Successors*. New York: Cambridge University Press, 1980.
Borkenau, F. *The Communist International*. London: Faber, 1938.
Braunthal, Julius. *History of the International 1914–1943*, 2 vols. New York: Praeger, 1967.
Conquest, Robert. *The Soviet Political System*. New York: Praeger, 1968.
Conquest, Robert. *The Great Terror: A Reassessment*. New York: Oxford University Press, 1990.
Deutscher, Isaac. *Stalin*. New York: Oxford University Press, 1949.
Djilas, Milovan. *The New Class: An Analysis of the Communist System*. New York: Praeger, 1957.
——— . *The Unperfect Society: Beyond the New Class*. New York: Harcourt Brace Jovanovich, 1969.
Drachkovitch, Milorad M. (ed.). *Marxism in the Modern World*. Stanford, Calif.: Stanford University Press, 1965.
Gorbachev, Mikhail. *Perestroika*. New York: Harper & Row, 1987.
Lacqueur, Walter. *Stalin: The Glasnost Revelations*. New York: Scribner's, 1990.
Lenin, V.I. *What Is To Be Done?* New York: International Publishers, 1969.
——— . "Imperialism: The Highest Stage of Capitalism" and "The State and Revolution." In *Lenin: Selected Works in One Volume*. New York: International Publishers, 1971.
NcNeal, Robert H. *The Bolshevik Tradition*. Englewood Cliffs, N.J.: Prentice-Hall, 1975.
Medvedev, Roy. *Let History Judge—The Origins and Consequences of Stalinism*. New York: Columbia University Press, 1990.
Meyer, Alfred G. *Leninism*. New York: Praeger, 1957.
——— . *The Soviet Political System: An Interpretation*. New York: Random House, 1965.
Miliband, Ralph. *Marxism and Politics*. New York: Oxford University Press, 1977.
Plamenatz, John. *German Marxism and Russian Communism*. New York: Longmans, 1954.
Schapiro, Leonard. *The Communist Party of the Soviet Union*, rev. ed. New York: Vintage, 1978.
——— . *The Government and Politics of the Soviet Union*. New York: Vintage Books, 1978.
Shub, David. *Lenin: A Biography*. New York: Penguin, 1976.
Simon, Gerhard. *Church, State, and Opposition in the USSR*. London: C. Hurst, 1974.

Solzhenitsyn, Aleksander. *The Gulag Archipelago,* 3 vols. New York: Harper & Row, 1974–1979.

Stalin, Joseph. *The Essential Stalin.* Edited by Bruce Franklin. New York: Anchor-Doubleday, 1972.

Trotsky, Leon. *History of the Russian Revolution.* Ann Arbor: University of Michigan Press, 1952.

Tucker, Robert C. (ed.). *Stalinism: Essays in Historical Interpretation.* New York: Norton, 1977.

———— . *Stalin in Power—The Revolution from Above.* New York: Norton, 1990.

Ulam, Adam B. *The Bolsheviks.* New York: Macmillan, 1968.

———— . *Stalin: The Man and His Era.* New York: Viking, 1973.

Wolfe, Bertram D. *Three Who Made A Revolution.* New York: Delta/Dell, 1964.

Chapter
7

The Collapse of Communism

The Myth was transformed into Lie . . . ; for Soviet Socialism as actually realized was a fraud in terms of the Myth's own standards. This Lie could be made to appear to be the truth, and the fraud concealed for a time . . . by the combination of terror and drumbeat indoctrination. . . . The collapse of the Lie under glasnost *is destroying acceptance of the system itself.*

"Z" (for Martin Melia)
"To the Stalin Mausoleum"

Despite minor reforms undertaken after Stalin's death and as late as the seventies, the contours of the Soviet regime changed little—a single party controlling the society in the name of communism and imposing an ideology that was becoming increasingly irrelevant, with a centralized and bureaucratized command economy increasingly unable to provide for economic growth and satisfy the consumers' needs.

It was only in the eighties, and more specifically after Mikhail Gorbachev became Secretary–General of the Communist party in March 1985, succeeding at fifty-four a line of old party stalwarts, that reforms began to affect the party, the regime, and the communist ideology. But it was not before the end of 1989 and in 1990 that radical reforms were undertaken, or made necessary, that affected the very citadel of communist orthodoxy—the rule of the single party and the command economy. By 1990, the very fabric of the Soviet polity had been torn apart and its future became uncertain. Dramatic change also took place in the Eastern European satellites—in Poland, East Germany, Czechoslovakia, Hungary, Bulgaria, and Romania, spreading even into isolated and small Albania. In each and every case, there was a profound crisis in communist ideology and communist institutions, which we survey in this chapter. It is a crisis in which many see the worldwide collapse of communism.

To appreciate the magnitude of change, let us recall the essential features of the communist totalitarianism:

1. The ideology is official, that is, espoused by the leadership to the exclusion of all other ideologies. It is total and comprehensive and everything becomes subordinate to it. Society is to be restructured in terms of the posited ideological goals.
2. The purpose of the single party is to control, intimidate, and govern. It is the major vehicle of political mobilization and recruitment. No political competition is tolerated.
3. All associations, all groups, and all individuals are subordinate to the party, the state, and the leader. There is no cultural pluralism. Education, literature, art, music, architecture—all must yield and conform to the overriding objectives and goals of the political ideology. Groups and individuals, family life, social and recreational activities, the schools, and the economy must all be synchronized with the political regime. All must "march in step" with it.
4. The use of violence is institutionalized through the police and other specialized instruments of coercion and intimidation.
5. The party directly, or through the state, has a monopolistic control of mass communications and overall economic activities.

DECLINE OF THE COMMUNIST IDEOLOGY

Even before the period of stagnation (1964–1985), the official communist ideology, and with it the Communist party, had begun to weaken. It lost its mobilizing force as the disparity between its promise and reality became apparent; it became especially irrelevant to the young for whom Marxism and Stalinism appeared dogmatic and incapable of resolving new societal, domestic, and international problems, or for that matter, of explaining the successes of Western and American free-market economies whose doom had been clearly spelled out by all Marxists. Socialists, technicians, academics, and in general the growing professional class within the Soviet society became restive at first, disillusioned during the years of stagnation, and downright critical throughout the 1980s.

Yet until today, no counterideology to confront communism had emerged. This was the result of two reinforcing factors, prevalent both in Russian and Soviet history. Until 1917, ideologies that had emerged in Russia had never taken hold by gaining popular support. Anarchism, conservatism, liberalism, democratic constitutionalism, or socialism never crystallized into political movements that gained widespread support. To be sure, the peasantry reclaimed the land. "We are yours but the land is ours," its leaders proclaimed to the Czar, but this was the substance of their demands, except for some utopian schemes involving collective village ownership proposed by some intellectuals. The church followed a servile attachment to the autocracy. The aristocracy did, by and large, the same, and the emerging bourgeoisie in the latter half of the nineteenth century was too weak to gain any representation. Group life, associational life, and intermediary institutions linking authority with participation and consent did not exist and, as a result, no ideology was formulated to confront the czarist despotism.

With the coming of the Soviet revolution, whatever group and political life existed—in the church, the trade unions, and nascent political parties and groups—was destroyed, as we have seen, in the name of a single all-encompassing ideology professed by an elite and enshrined in the Communist party. So when the Communist regime began to falter, there were no potential centers from which a new reformist anticommunist ideology could spring. As one intellectual close to Gorbachev put it in assessing the impact of communism on the Soviet society: "When you have destroyed all natural structures of life— in the family, the state, in religion—then how can you recreate them?"[1] Or more to the point: How can they reassert themselves?

The decline of communism that we are witnessing today is associated, therefore, only with the reemergence of ideological fragments rooted in past history: anarchism, ethnic manifestations, workers' strikes, a return to religious attachment, nationalist anti-Soviet protests in virtually all fifteen republics of the Soviet Union. Grass-roots citizens' groups have emerged representing a host of claims, ranging from demands for religious freedom to environmental movements and anti-Semitic protestations. Curiously enough, the peasantry has not seized the opportunity to reclaim the land that had been collectivized. The ruthless liquidation of private farmers by Stalin may well have stifled their secular aspirations to own their land. Communism—or the term increasingly used, "socialism"—remained the only ideology and it still is. If there was a "revolution," as Gorbachev dubbed *perestroika*, it had none of the characteristics of a genuine revolutionary movement involving a coherent set of principles.

It is the lack of a new ideology, while the old one is withering away, that has amounted to a genuine crisis of authority and institutions. The communist institutions in place have been weakened, but the new ones in the process of being set up lack legitimacy because of the lack of a coherent set of values to sustain them. The crisis in ideology became a crisis of institutions, and the continuing ineffectiveness of institutions intensifies the crisis in ideology.

Many claim that Gorbachev and some of his associates were, from the very beginning, committed to the liquidation of Marxism as an ideology. They had to move slowly, however, first within the top leadership of the party, then in the Central Committee, and then among the party members before they reached out to seek popular support. It is highly doubtful Gorbachev had this in mind. Reforms undertaken at first in the name of *perestroika* and democratization were not the result of ideologic reflection but the children of necessity. The economy had come to a virtual standstill and the food supplies were dwindling; at the same time, burdens upon the Soviet system, because of military and international commitments, were growing heavier. All Gorbachev offered at first was a reformed Communist party. Reforming the party, weeding out inefficient

---

[1]*New York Times*, April 1, 1990.

and incompetent bureaucrats, and decentralizing the state and the command economy became necessary, but in all cases they were made in the name of communism.

A New Ideology?

It was only in November 1989 that Gorbachev provided, in a major address on "Revolutionary Perestroika," what pretended to be a new ideology. There was a forceful declaration favoring privatizations and the liberalization of the market and a gradual democratization of the political process. Yet Gorbachev continued to cling to the Communist party and to its monopoly on political power. He insisted that he was a Leninist. "We are using the Leninist method," he proclaimed. "We must analyze how the future arises from reality." He explicitly rejected the Stalinist method that imposes "ready-made recipes on society and adjusts reality to these recipes."

It was the "Leninist method" that led Gorbachev to the conclusion that the political regime and the command economy should be drastically reformed in the direction of the free market and cultural and political pluralism. He propounded, however, new humanitarian goals. The centerpiece of socialism is "Man," according to Marx, and despite Marx's shortcomings in predicting the course of capitalism and the dynamics of the capitalist economy, socialism remained for Gorbachev "the ideal." He promised a new revolution not from above but "from below." He suggested the growth of a grass-roots and participatory socialism to replace statism. "Perestroika," he claimed, "has shown that only the drawing of people into social and public affairs as a responsible field of activity will make it possible to overcome their alienation, close the gap between personal and common interest and change the activity of the individual in all spheres of life." After giving an outline of a variety of economic and social reforms that, in many cases, sounded like an endorsement of democratic socialism as practiced in the Scandinavian countries, Gorbachev returned time after time to the cure-all—the Communist party. "Developing the independent activities of the masses and promoting democratization of all spheres of life under a one-party system is a noble but very difficult mission for the Party. . . . And a great deal depends on how we cope with it." Even after February 1990, when the monopoly of the Communist party was officially abandoned by revising the Constitution, Gorbachev was asking it "to elaborate and generate political and ideological platforms that are recommended to the society and the state."[2]

Speaking before the Central Committee on February 6, 1990 on the draft platform that was to be submitted to the Twenty-Eighth Party Congress, Gorbachev declared again his ideal of a "humane, democratic socialism" and called

---

[2]Mikhail Gorbachev, "The Socialist Idea of Revolutionary Perestroika," *Pravda*, November 26, 1989, translated by the Soviet Embassy Information Services.

for the "restructuring of the party as a democratic force." "We remain committed to the choice made in October 1917," he said, "to the socialist idea."

No new doctrine has emerged, no new vision has dawned, no new comprehensive programs developed. Even the position of the Communist party continues to remain uncertain. An end to its political monopoly was decided in February 1990, but Gorbachev remained its leader, exhorting it to new efforts, even if in the name of pluralism and democracy! The collapse of communism, therefore, amounts to an internal collapse—some call it an "implosion." There has not been as yet a "democratic" revolution in the Soviet Union—there has not even been a broad, coherent, reformist movement to challenge communism. The fabric that Stalin had woven—the personality cult, the rule of the nomenklatura, the command economy and the huge bureaucracy that managed it, the party that derived privileges and benefits, the secret police that pervaded the lives of all, the conformity imposed by the party upon nationalities—was taken apart stitch by stitch. The garment hangs in shreds, but no other has been sewn. Public response to an ideology of liberal democracy and economic liberalism has remained lukewarm, in contrast to the appeal of nationalist, ethnonationalist, religious, and sectarian movements.

THE "OPENING": *GLASNOST* AND *PERESTROIKA*

After becoming Secretary–General of the Communist party in March 1985, Mikhail Gorbachev consolidated his power in the Politbureau, the Central Committee, and within the party as a whole. By the middle of 1986, he was vigorously advocating a policy of "openness"—a liberalization of the political system (*glasnost*) and an economic restructuring (*perestroika*).

The aim of *perestroika* was and remains to decentralize and ultimately dismantle the huge bureaucracy that plans, directs, and implements industrial and agricultural production and trade. The central bureaucracy was to be replaced by smaller functional units at the regional and local levels, right down to the business firms and their managers. They would be free to plan production, secure labor and raw materials at the best possible prices, establish their own budget, and seek benefits from their products. "Profits" would be realized through both an increase in productivity and efficiency, which would reduce costs, and through creative marketing practices that would increase sales and income. Such moves would inject some flexibility into the system so that production could be increasingly geared to consumer demand, needs, and tastes. There could even be competition among firms; for example, differential profits and wages could be established and a special bonus for productivity could be granted. In other words, the Soviet economy would move in the direction of the "capitalistic" world in order to spur growth.

Glasnost is the term used to denote reforms undertaken to liberalize the political regime by allowing for greater public debate within and outside the political party, in the press, on radio, and on television. Moreover, *glasnost* sought to develop procedures through which public officials—mostly party

Gorbachev's expression—open and argumentative—seemed to portray a new era of openness.

members—could be scrutinized and held accountable. It was not originally interpreted as a move toward democracy; there was no pretense, as we have seen, of abandoning the monopoly of the single party, nor was there a desire to publicize the deliberations of the higher decision-making units of the party. Only some democratization at the grass-roots level and in local elections was envisaged and implemented. More important at this stage was Gorbachev's new policy of "openness," reflected in the photograph of the Soviet leader on this page. Dialogue, debate, reexamination of the roots and the destiny of the Soviet society and the Soviet Union, and the liberalization of societal forces, including the economy, were gradually introduced.

"We are for a diversity of public opinion," Gorbachev proclaimed, "for a richness of spiritual life. We need not fear openly raising and solving difficult problems of social development, criticizing and arguing. It is in such circumstances that the truth is born and that correct decisions take shape." Gorbachev further asserted that critical inquiry should also be directed to Soviet history and the reconsideration of the role of revolutionary leaders—including, above all, Stalin and many of his victims. In short, Gorbachev was urging the Russians, for so long treated as subjects, to become citizens—free to participate, equal before the law, and protected from personalistic and dictatorial regimes, such as the one shaped by Stalin. He also opened a wide window to the world. "Peaceful co-existence," he seemed to indicate, was no longer enough. The present and the future require "interrelatedness" and "interdependence," cooperation and solidarity. This outlook was necessary, he said, because of technological changes, the role of mass communications, world environmental and resource problems, the social and economic problems in the developing countries, and, above all, human survival from the dangers of nuclear weapons.[3]

Without doubt, the move toward economic freedoms (and efficiency) and political freedoms (and political responsibility) became one of the most exciting prospects for the Soviet society. The inertia of the past, the heavy hand of a bureaucracy that has institutionalized itself over so many years, the preferential treatment and privileges that go with the top decision-making jobs—among the politicians, the managers, the military, the bureaucrats, and the Soviet intelligentsia in general—seemed all to be in jeopardy if public officials were to be freely scrutinized and criticized (see Table 7.1).

The End of the Communist Party Monopoly and Political Pluralism

It was not until 1988, and particularly between 1989 and 1990, that change reached a critical point. It became radical; it questioned, at least indirectly, the communist ideology and its regime. In effect, it put an end to both, as genuine democratic and some liberal economic reforms were initiated by Gorbachev and his associates and began to be implemented. The "Soviet Bloc" split into its parts—with Eastern Europe, Latvia, Lithuania, and Estonia claiming independence. Within the Soviet Union itself, the federated political units (the republics) moved also to assert their will as independent entities.

The Single-Party Monopoly   Until the end of 1989, Gorbachev favored, as we noted, reforms within the party and by the party. Communism and the party, he asserted, had a vital role to play in the democratization of the society and in economic reforms. He urged the Communist party to lead the way. Yet in February 1990, by a virtual unanimous vote, the Central Committee put an end to the party monopoly. Article 6 of the Constitution, the very cornerstone of Leninism, which we discussed earlier, stated:

> The leading and guiding force of Soviet society and the nucleus of its political system and all state organizations and public organizations is the Communist Party of the Soviet Union . . . armed with Marxism–Leninism (it) determines the general perspectives and the development of society.

---

[3]Quotes from excerpts of a speech printed in the *New York Times*, November 3, 1987.

Table 7.1 SIX YEARS OF CHANGE UNDER GORBACHEV, 1985–1991

March 1985	Gorbachev assumes power and promises to reform the economy.
April 1985	Before the Central Committee of the party, Gorbachev introduces *perestroika*—a policy aimed at reforming the Soviet bureaucracy and the rigidities of the command economy.
March 1986	Communist Party Congress approves Gorbachev's resolution favoring "true revolutionary changes in the economy" in the direction of liberalization.
November 1987	On the occasion of the seventieth anniversary of the Bolshevik Revolution, Gorbachev acknowledges Stalin's crimes, favoring reconsideration of the history of communism in Russia. Censorship is loosened; freedom to publish and criticize encouraged. But democratization provides the ethnic republics—Armenia and Lithuania, for example—the justification to reassert claims of independence.
March 1989	In freely held elections for the newly established Congress of People's Deputies, many Communist leaders are defeated, but the majority remains in the hands of the party.
November 1989	Gorbachev produces a long manifesto in which he endorses Marxism as the only force capable of reviving the system and reemphasizes the guiding role of the Communist party. He urges development of a communism "with a human face."
February 1990	The monopoly of the Communist party is formally abandoned by the Central Committee, and the Constitution is revised accordingly.
March 1990	Elections are held in the Soviet Socialist Republics and in many cities. In Russia, the Ukraine, and Byelorussia, the independent pro-democracy candidates make significant gains. In some major cities—Moscow, Leningrad, Kiev—they gain outright control.
March–June 1990	Constitutional changes—confirmed by the Central Committee—create a new all-powerful presidency, and Gorbachev is elected by the Congress of People's Deputies as the first president.
July 1990	The Twenty-Eighth Congress of the Communist party meets. Gorbachev maintains his leadership but is sharply criticized by both the conservatives and the democratic reformers. The latter blame him for not moving ahead rapidly with reforms in the economy.
December 1990	Congress of People's Deputies convenes to consider constitutional changes that give to President Gorbachev additional powers and to debate a new Union Treaty. A proposal to change the Union of Soviet Socialist Republics to the Union of Soviet Sovereign Republics is defeated. A new post of Vice President is created and Gennadi I. Yanayev, a loyal and long-time official of the Communist party, is nominated for the post by Gorbachev and endorsed by the Congress. He declares himself to be a Communist to "the core of my soul." Many of the liberal democratic reformers withdraw. Major legislation regarding the economy, property rights, and the new Union Treaty has yet to be enacted.
March 17th, 1991	A referendum on the "Union Treaty" is overwhelmingly endorsed, but both the wording of the referendum and the answers to specific questions included in the referendum in various Republics clouds the popular verdict.
March 31st, 1991	Georgians participate massively in a referendum and favor overwhelmingly the independence of Georgia.
June 12th, 1991	The wavering pro-democracy forces get a powerful boost when Boris Yeltsin is elected President of the Russian Republic, which accounts for over half of the Soviet Union's population, in a free and open election. He wins 60 percent of the vote, defeating all other cadidates, including the Communist Party candidate, on the first ballot.

The abolition of Article 6 signaled an "opening" to other parties and groups—already tentatively organized—to compete in national and state (republic) elections. But it meant much more: it signified that the Communist party relinquished its role as the educator and the guide of society. The ideology embodied in communism, therefore, was no longer deemed to embody the truth. Other emerging ideologies, speaking through newly founded associations, parties, and groups—including the church, nationalist and patriotic organizations, and, above all, ethnonational minorities—asserted their own claims. They could compete freely with the Communist party on a footing of equality. Political pluralism was in the air, and by the end of 1990 a great number of political organizations had mushroomed.

Elections and Growing Pluralism   Elections have underscored not only the emerging political pluralism but also a growing political disarray. By the end of 1990, the number of independent political groups in the USSR continued to mushroom:

1. National "popular fronts" of the non-Russian peoples of the Soviet Socialist Republics and other territories have begun to focus on securing national independence.
2. "Popular fronts" in the Russian republic, encompassing large cities or regions of the republic, began to assert themselves.
3. Russian nationalist groups have formed.
4. Independent groups, usually called "clubs," have been established in over a hundred cities across the USSR.
5. Parliamentary groups, or factions, of delegates have been elected to national and regional parliaments; these include groups of various political orientations, from the most radical to the most conservative.
6. An antinuclear movement has gotten under way in Kazakhstan, part of a burgeoning environmentalist movement in the USSR.
7. National and cultural groups have formed to defend the identity of ethnic and cultural heritages.
8. Religious groups have become active again.

With each new session, the Congress of People's Deputies provides a more open forum for the expression of popular sentiments and for the exercise of pressure on the central leadership from below. Delegates in the Congress have coalesced into several "blocs" that amount to loosely organized parties.

But the prospects for pluralism go beyond the present multiplicity of groups and movements. It affects the Soviet *Union* as one political entity—the Soviet federation—which consists of many ethnic groups and distinct nationalities living in the fifteen union republics (or states) and in numerous other local and territorial units. In the republics of Russia, the Ukraine, and Georgia (but also in the Baltic republics of Latvia, Lithuania, and Estonia), non-Communists have assumed political control. Virtually all the Soviet republics—thirteen out of the fifteen to be exact—have asserted their intention to become "independent" or have asserted that their own legislative enactments have precedence over Soviet law. If Soviet law conflicts with the law passed by the legislature of a republic, it is the latter that a republic will enforce.[4] This was precisely the argument made by the South before the Civil War became inevitable in the United States.

New Governmental Institutions

In the midst of a profound ideological crisis, with the communist ideology dying without giving place to another, with relatively free elections in which oppositional groups asserted their strength, with rampant ethnic violence and movements in favor of the independence of a number of Republics against the central Soviet authority, we can begin to understand the frequent institutional changes introduced by Gorbachev to cope with the crisis and, even more, the constant tinkering with the institutional reforms he introduced.

New governmental institutions were established, superseding the Communist party. The Congress of People's Deputies now elects a smaller body, the 542-member Supreme Soviet, to conduct the actual legislative business of the state. While the earlier Supreme Soviet had functioned merely as a rubber stamp for the party leadership, lending the facade of democratic legitimacy to its decisions, the newly reconstituted Supreme Soviet has become an increasingly important institution for the representation of societal interests and the exercise of social control over the institutions of government. It is far less subject to control by the party leadership than the Congress, and its members subject the prime minister and other members of the government—whom it elects—to careful scrutiny and, often, powerful criticism.

In March 1990, Gorbachev mobilized the delegates to the Congress of People's Deputies to push through legislation favoring the creation of a powerful Soviet presidency. And he secured his own appointment as president for a five-year term, not through the party but through the Congress, without having to stand for popular election. The new president is commander-in-chief of the armed forces and can declare war. He also appoints the leading members of the government, subject to confirmation by the Congress of People's Deputies and the Supreme Soviet. The most distinctive, and inherently controversial, powers granted to the president by the constitutional reforms of March 1990 are the ability to issue decrees that have the force of law for the entire territory of the USSR; the power to dissolve the Supreme Soviet in certain circumstances; and the power to impose martial law on areas of the Soviet Union.

A new "presidential council" was established, and a reorganization and redistribution of executive authority and functions have allowed it to operate as a kind of cabinetlike advisory body to the president. Together with the plan to submit the presidency to direct popular election in the future, these changes have brought the Soviet Union closer to the establishment of a strong "semi-

---

[4]This is currently referred to as "the war of laws"!

presidential" system of government.[5] In this manner, Gorbachev began to develop a basis of power outside the Communist party; he is now beholden to elected representative bodies that include non-Communist delegates.

The Twenty-Eighth Congress of the Communist party, held in June–July 1990, further undermined the party. Policy now is to be made by a president (Gorbachev) and his "presidential council" subject to the scrutiny of the legislative bodies. Many within the presidential council—even if not Gorbachev—are *not* members of the Communist party. Many of them are heads of the Soviet Socialist Republics. In fact, a number among the most prominent leaders withdrew from the party, while powerful conservative leaders of the Communist party disappeared from the Central Committee. Those who resigned from the party assumed important posts in the presidencies of the Russian and Ukranian republics and as chief administrative officers in major cities, Kiev, Moscow, and Leningrad among them.

Reform of the Economy

Side by side with the political reforms we outlined, comprehensive reforms of the economy have been contemplated. They all point in the same direction— toward economic liberalism. In the last omnibus proposal introduced by President Gorbachev in November 1990, the following measures were outlined, to be implemented over a period of time:

1. Freedom of producers to produce for profit.
2. Competition among producers.
3. Gradual deregulation of prices.
4. Privatization of the land and farming.
5. Gradual incorporation of the Soviet economy into the international economy.
6. Finally, the dismantling of the huge bureaucracy—in the economic plan and in the economic ministries.

These reforms are staunchly resisted in the name of ideology by the millions of bureaucrats (most of them party members). They strike also at the "entitlements" of major segments of the society—workers, retirees, salaried personnel, and farmers. To many they are as revolutionary as the Bolshevik Revolution of 1917!

To add to the overall disarray the Soviet Socialist Republics are in the process of developing their own economic reforms independently of the Soviet Union. They are beginning to enter into trade agreements with each other and even with foreign countries independently of the Soviet authorities; they have even threatened to print their own money and declare it as the only legal cur-

---

[5]For a full discussion, see Roy Macridis and Steven Burg, *Introduction to Comparative Politics*, chap. 8.

rency; they have stated—and this is far more noticeable in the three Latvian republics, but also in Armenia—that their citizens will not be recruited into the Soviet army; and some have set up their own police, defying, at times, the all-powerful Secret Police.

THE STATE OF THE UNION

Without a new ideology to replace the old, faced by powerful, even if disorganized, opposition and the continuing erosion of the economy, Gorbachev began to lean upon the forces from which he had never dissociated himself—the Communist Party apparat, the Secret Police, the bureaucracy and the Army. Uprisings in the various Republics and the professed desire of many among them to separate their economies, their laws, and even defense and foreign policy from that of the Soviet Union accounted for a backlash in the name of law and order and unity. On March 17th, 1991, a referendum was held throughout the whole of the Soviet Union. The question that called for a yes or no vote was:

> Do you consider it necessary to preserve the Union of the Soviet Socialist Republics as a renewed federation of equal sovereign republics, in which human rights and the freedom of all nationalities will be fully guaranteed?

More than 80 percent of eligible voters voted and 76 percent voted "Yes." Such an overwhelming positive response would have seemed to put an end to the matter and strengthen the position of the Soviet leader, giving him time to address himself to the pressing economic issues facing the country. Yet both the question asked and even the answers given continued to cast a spell of ambiguity for which Gorbachev began to be blamed. Did the "yes" mean yes to the proposed federation—to the overall authority of the central government? Or was the stress put on the equality and sovereignty of the republics? The first would entail the continuation of the supremacy of the central government; the second would lead to autonomy and even the outright independence of the republics. Even greater ambiguity was caused by the fact that in individual republics, the wording of the referendum was changed or new questions were added. In Kazakstan the wording was changed, striking out "federation" and replacing it with "union of sovereign states"; in other cases, the vote for a union was to be on the basis of a declaration of sovereignty by the Republic involved. In Ukraine, for instance, 90 percent of the voters expressed the wish that Ukraine become an independent state. Furthermore, in six of the fifteen republics—the referendum was boycotted (in the Baltic Republics, in Moldavia, Georgia and Armenia).

In the midst of uncertainty and the continuing erosion of the economy, and demands for independence by the Union Republics, it seemed that perestroika and glasnost had run their course and Gorbachev began to lean increasingly on the conservative forces. The army, the K.G.B. (Secret Police), the top and middle echelons of the Communist party, the bureaucracy, came out in support of "law and order" and the use of force to preserve the Union, while resisting economic liberalization. They all seemed to share the same distrust for the West and for liberal democracy that characterized the Russian Empire before and after the Bolshevik Revolution of 1917. Facing them, the pro-democracy forces appeared to weaken. Without a new ideology to mobilize the masses, however, a return to communist authoritarianism appeared unlikely; but without broad supports for democracy, it, too, may fail. What is needed above all in the Soviet Union today is a comprehensive new political ideology that is not yet in sight.

THE COLLAPSE OF COMMUNISM IN EASTERN EUROPE

Communism—as an ideology and a political and economic regime—collapsed in Eastern Europe, within a matter of less than two years. During 1989 and 1990, Communist regimes disappeared in Poland, East Germany, Czechoslovakia, Hungary, and have been tottering in Romania and Bulgaria. In Yugoslavia, the Communist party has virtually collapsed, and ethnic conflicts have brought the country to the brink of dissolution. Throughout all of Europe, only in Albania did the Communist leadership maintain a shaky rule!

There are many reasons for so precipitous a collapse of communism in the Eastern European countries. All these countries had one thing in common: the revolt against Communist regimes was profoundly nationalist and it sought independence from Soviet domination and from the indigenous Communist parties that had been imposed by the Soviet leadership. The weakening of the Soviet capabilities to maintain its control and the liberalization within the Soviet Communist party and the regime triggered the pent-up demands for national independence. Related to the Soviet Union's failure with its command economy, the Eastern European societies suffered the same economic stagnation as the Soviet Union. Experimentation with market economics and individual entrepreneurship had been carried out, but it ran against the common grain of communist orthodoxy and was looked upon with suspicion until the Soviets began to entertain thoughts about instituting the same reforms. When this happened, the revolt against both communism and Soviet domination became irresistible. The revolt affected all the mainstays of communist ideology and of their regimes.

The End of Communist Party Monopoly and Governance

The stranglehold of the party ended, for all practical purposes, first in Poland, where widespread dissatisfaction had produced repeated confrontations between the state and society in the past and led in 1979 to a grass-roots trade-union movement—Solidarity. After failing to silence resistance through repression, the near-collapse of the economy finally forced the Polish regime to permit, at least partially, democratic elections through which Solidarity finally broke the Communists' political monopoly. In June of 1989, Solidarity won an overwhelming victory in the first free parliamentary elections, in effect putting an end to Communist rule. In August 1989, a new government was formed, headed by Solidarity, but with Communist participation. After introducing radical economic reforms, this new government proceeded in July 1990 to oust all Communists from the Council of Ministers. Finally, in December 1990, the leader of Solidarity—Lech Walesa—was elected president.

In Hungary, declining economic performance led to conflict within the Communist political elite over the future course of reform, and this conflict soon spilled over into society. Under the pressure of increasingly frequent and growing demonstrations demanding democratization, the Communist leadership rapidly fragmented, and the party disintegrated. By spring 1989, it was clear that a new, more democratic, and more pluralistic order was emerging in Hungary, as opposition groups coalesced into parties. In an attempt to break with its own past, the Hungarian Communist party changed its name, abandoned any claim of political monopoly, and negotiated an agreement with opposition forces on the calling of free elections.

Growing impatience with authoritarianism in East Germany provoked popular demonstrations and uprisings that the police could not contain. Thousands of East Germans fled to West Germany in 1989, and mass demonstrations calling for democratization took place in Leipzig and other cities. A "new" Communist leadership attempted to win popular support by making concessions to the people's desire to travel, including the momentous opening of the Berlin Wall. But continuing demonstrations forced the ousting of the Communist party, clearing the way for the emergence of a non-Communist regime in East Germany as well.

In Czechoslovakia, mass demonstrations beginning in mid-November 1989 toppled the Communist leadership by the end of December. And in Romania mass demonstrations overthrew the Ceausescu regime—in effect a personnel tyranny—in the last days of 1989 (see Table 7.2).

Democratization and Liberalization: The Regime and the Economy

By and large, 1989 was a year of demolition! But in its wake, the year 1990 began a reconstruction—during which democratic practices and institutions were reaffirmed and confirmed. In the first free elections held in 1990 throughout virtually all Eastern European states that had been dominated by Communist parties, the verdict was overwhelmingly against them. In Czechoslovakia (June 8 and 9) the Communist party received only 14 percent of the vote; in East Germany (March 18), only 18 percent; in Hungary (March 25–April 8) two communist parties—one "reformed" and the other unreformed—managed 11 percent; in Poland in the elections for the Senate held earlier (in June 1989), Solidarity won 92 of the 100 seats; while in the Presidential election of December 1990 there was no Communist candidate. The leader of the Solidarity, Lech Walesa,

Table 7.2   TRANSITION IN EASTERN EUROPE: THE COLLAPSE OF COMMUNISM,
1989–1990

January 1989	*Poland* Communist party agrees to negotiations with Solidarity opposition. *Hungary* Communist party leaders promise multiparty system.
April 1989	*Poland* Communist leader Wojciech Jaruzelski and Solidarity leader Lech Walesa reach agreement on partly democratic elections to parliament.
May 1989	*Hungary* Demolition of "iron curtain" begins with removal of barbed wire from Hungarian–Austrian border.
June 1989	*Poland* Solidarity wins overwhelming victory in first partly free parliamentary elections; gains control of strengthened parliament.
August 1989	*Poland* Solidarity-led government is elected by parliament, with Tadeusz Mazowiecki as prime minister. Non-Communists lead social and economic ministries, Communists head military and security ministries with non-Communist deputies, and Jaruzelski remains as president.
October 1989	*East Germany* Flow of refugees to West Germany, through Hungary and Czechoslovakia continues as internal demonstrations for change increase in size and frequency. *Hungary* Communist party reorients itself toward more liberal political program and renames itself Socialist party; parliament revises constitution to end Communist political monopoly, allowing multiparty system. *Bulgaria* Protest rally leads to promise of reform by Communist leadership.
November 1989	*East Germany* Shakeup of Communist party leadership fails to stem either flow of refugees to West or rise of internal unrest; politburo resigns; Berlin Wall is opened and free travel to West permitted; Communist leadership promises free elections. *Czechoslovakia* Opposition groups form "Civic Forum" alliance; despite efforts by Communists to retain power through concessions, opposition forces prevail; Communist party renounces monopoly of power and concedes need for free elections. *Bulgaria* Longtime Communist party leader, 78-year-old Todor Zhivkov, is ousted; replaced by 53-year-old Petar Mladenov, who begins to carry out a program of modest political liberalization.
December 1989	*Czechoslovakia* New government, with non-communist majority is formed; Vaclav Havel elected president of Czechoslovakia by parliament. *Romania* Local protest against harassment of ethnic Hungarians escalates, with support from ethnic Romanians, into mass demonstrations against Ceausescu tyranny; Ceausescu and wife are arrested and executed.
January 1990	*Yugoslavia* The League of Communists (Communist party) of Yugoslavia convenes an extraordinary Congress at which it renounces its constitutional monopoly of political power and endorses a multiparty political system. *Poland* Communist party (Polish United Workers Party) formally disbanded and reconstitutes itself as a non-Communist but Socialist-oriented party known as Social Democracy of the Republic of Poland.
March 1990	*Hungary* First free multiparty elections produce electoral victory for democratic opposition; the moderate-to-conservative "Democratic Forum" wins 24.7 percent of vote, the more radical Alliance of Free Democrats wins 21.4 percent, and the Independent Smallholders' party wins 11.8 percent. *East Germany* First free multiparty elections produce electoral victory for alliance of conservative democratic opposition.

Table 7.2 (*Continued*)

April 1990	*East Germany* Conservative democratic coalition led by Christian Democrats forms government.
December 1990	Lech Walesa, the former leader of Solidarity, is elected president in Poland, replacing General Jaruzelski, the only remaining representative of Communist rule; beginnings of "de-Stalinization" and liberalization in Albania, where an opposition Democratic party is formed.

won. In Bulgaria (June 10 and 17), the ex-Communists, running under the label of a Bulgarian Socialist Party, received 47 percent of the vote and sought to form a coalition cabinet. Only in Romania (May 20) did the Communists running under the label of National Salvation Front that included a number of political groups, won a majority of 66 percent of the vote—a vote whose validity has been contested.

With the ousting of the Communist party from power, new political institutions were introduced. They all copied Western European democratic constitutions. Legislative assemblies were freely elected and were given the power to freely legislate and to control the government; the executive was vested either in a presidency or in a cabinet, elected by the legislatures or by the people and responsible to them; judicial review was restored and the independence of the judges guaranteed. The Secret Police, the pillar of Communist regimes, was dismantled or purged and its powers now carefully circumscribed. Pluralism—political and cultural—has been reaffirmed. Political democracy, in other words, as we understand it, and as some of the Eastern European countries had experienced it in the past on different occasions, has returned.

Economic liberalism has been espoused and private property reinstated; socialized industries are being dismantled and privatized; the market is gradually replacing the command economies everywhere; and it is expected that the freeing of prices and the end of subsidies will follow. Even stock markets to buy and sell shares and channel investment are emerging. Collectivization of agriculture—where it had been established—is gradually giving place to private farms. Capitalism, as we discussed it in Chapter 3, is making a comeback. The Eastern European governments are looking west to Europe—to the European Common Market that will be fully integrated by 1992, hoping to become associated with it in one form or another.

Far more clearly than in the Soviet Union, democracy and economic liberalism seem to be in the process of replacing communism throughout Eastern Europe. But the question remains whether democracy and a free-market economy will provide the needed mobilization and commitment to sustain the difficult period of transition from Communist rule and a command economy to democracy and individual entrepreneurship. Much will depend on the durability and the effectiveness of a newly found democratic consensus as an instrument to reconcile societal and economic conflicts that cripple many

Eastern European societies. In other words, the new democratic ideology that has replaced communism has yet to gain legitimacy.[6]

THE LAST BASTIONS

Communist regimes, together with the ideology that nurtured them, seem to be in the process of being swept away almost everywhere. There are some, however (we can call them the "Last Bastions"), that are resisting change and remain defiant in proclaiming their commitment to communism and in maintaining the rigid one-party authoritarian rule. They include North Korea, Albania, Cuba, Vietnam, and notably China. Among some African regimes that have paid lip service to communism as an ideology to rationalize military rule, Marxism is also rapidly waning—but not military rule!

In the remaining Communist regimes, the reaction to Gorbachev's "opening" was a defiant rejection of the changes made or contemplated and a reassertion of the true faith. In North Korea, where the military and political dictatorship of Kim Il Sung has ruled the country for over thirty years and where the "cult of personality" of the leader emulates the one Stalin enjoyed, the leadership reaffirmed its intention to "safeguard the principles of socialism—no matter what." Intimidation, repression, and indoctrination have been reinforced, and the vigilant control of the police strengthened. In Albania, where a communist-style dictatorship has been in force ever since the end of World War II, the reforms in the Soviet Union and Eastern Europe were first attributed to "revisionism"—a departure from Stalinist orthodoxy and rigid controls. Some protests were nipped in the bud and again the Segurami—the Secret Police—reinforced its vigilance. But for how long it will prove successful remains to be seen. By the end of 1990, there were clear indications of a reform movement. In Cuba, where communism was proclaimed as the official ideology in 1961, the reaction to the changes in the Soviet Union and Eastern Europe was swift. There would be no "Castroika"! Conceding that "difficult days are ahead," Fidel Castro proclaimed Cuba to be the "last bulwark of socialism" and had sharp words for revisionism and revisionists. There has been no relaxation of the single-party rule, of the role of the police, or a move in the direction of liberalizing the economy. Cuban socialism, with a strong dose of nationalism directed against "Yankee imperialism," remains firm. Similarly, in Vietnam, the Communist party and the command economy are organized along Stalinist lines. Here the Communist regime maintains its intransigent posture. In its most recent "Platform for Building Socialism in the Transition Period," released on December 1, 1990, the Vietnamese Communist party asserted: "In certain

---

[6]By the end of 1990, and early into 1991, there was already evidence to indicate that Eastern European countries including Eastern Germany faced a crisis associated with the introduction of a free market and privatizations; ethnic conflicts have also intensified.

countries the Communist parties have even lost their leadership role. Hostile forces are taking advantage of these errors and difficulties to launch a counter offensive with a view to abolishing socialism. . . . Socialism will regain its vitality and . . . will prevail."[7]

China: Mao and Beyond

China is of course the most important of the countries that remains Communist. It presents a special case. "Maoism" was the label for the Communist movement and its ideology that developed in China under the leadership of Mao Tse-tung and continues now after his death. "Chairman Mao" was, for more than forty years, the undisputed leader of the Chinese Communist party and the head of the Communist government in China after the civil war (1946–1949) and until his death in 1977. But there has been a high degree of fluidity, and at times downright instability if not chaos, in the development of the Chinese Communist system, both during Mao's leadership and after his death. The following ideological and institutional stages of the Chinese Communist regime since its inception can be outlined:

1. A period of consolidation but also of education and mobilization in the principles of socialism (1949–1953).
2. The move in the direction of economic planning and socialism (1953–1956), followed by a period of liberalization, known as the "Hundred Flowers" campaign.
3. A massive effort to industrialize, known as the "Great Leap Forward" (1957–1960).
4. A subsequent period of retreat from the goals of rapid industrialization that lasted until 1965.
5. The "Cultural Revolution" (1966–1969), again followed by a period of consolidation until 1972.
6. The period since Mao's death when, after a brief conflict between "moderate" leaders and "revolutionaries" (who hailed from the period of the Cultural Revolution and claimed to be Mao's intellectual heirs), the moderates have gained the upper hand. Their emphasis has been on stability, industrialization, and modernization, with the help of capitalist countries in Western Europe, and even the United States itself.
7. In the 1980s we again witness a period of flux in which "capitalistic" incentives in the economy and especially in agriculture are being tried side by side with socialist modes of production—a period indeed in which China may alternate between the two.
8. The early 1990s present a struggle between the forces of democratization and economic liberalization and the forces of a wavering party oligarchy.

---

[7]Quoted in *The Economist*, December 8–14, 1990, p. 35.

The constant flux—the constant dialectic between a democratic and participatory urge and Communist control and domination—continues, and events both in the Soviet Union and Eastern Europe have only sharpened it. In China, the democratic and participatory urge is directed against an aging party leadership, and yet the party maintains its political monopoly, has refused any genuine democratic reforms in allowing for political competition, and has denied freedoms to the press, the intellectuals, and the universities. The confrontation with students and intellectuals (and some workers) in Tiananmen Square in June 1989 only highlighted the tension between liberal and democratic forces and the party leadership. After wavering at first, the party leaders decided to take repressive measures against the advocates of democratization and asked the army to intervene. Hundreds apparently died, and many more were arrested or went into exile. The Communist party reasserted its role and political monopoly and accused the Soviet leadership of deviations from the socialist model.

Three developments, however, all related to the Tiananmen Square repression, should be noted. All indicate the growing weakness of the party and its aging leadership. First, the top leadership divided until the faction opposed to democratic reforms won out. But the dissenters remain and some of them have resurfaced. Second, the leadership of the Communist party, which favored repression, was unable to mobilize public support—the army was solicited. But any alliance between the party and the army is likely to undermine the party's legitimacy and its claim of political supremacy. Third, the army itself appeared divided, with some officers favoring democratization and others supporting the hard line that was eventually taken. Finally, economic liberalization—in agriculture, manufacturing, and trade—initiated more than ten years ago is strengthening the prospects of deregulation and of a market economy. All in all, there are signs that suggest that the ruling elite in China is divided and that the claim of the Communist party to remain the sole custodian of the country's political life may be in jeopardy.

Will the Last Bastions Fall?

With what was the citadel of worldwide communism—the Soviet Union—in disarray, the remaining Communist regimes, including China, find themselves in a serious predicament. The Soviet Union has been for most of them, at one time or another, the source of ideological truth, the banker that provided them with needed resources, and the supplier of weapons and military technology. The Soviet ideology is now murky, its funds limited, and its willingness to come to the aid of friendly regimes in serious doubt. The protector is gone! All of the remaining Communist regimes therefore face the same ideological uncertainty—all will experience the same economic and political crisis. Several observations can be made about these last bastions, and some predictions as well.

1. The socialist command economies everywhere face the same crisis. Central controls and bureaucratization have led to blatant inefficiencies, corruption, low productivity, and a decline in the national and per capita product, in con-

trast with the free-market economies. The leadership in almost all of these regimes has been forced to tinker, in one way or another, with the economy by adopting some measures that allow for private incentives and by freeing the market, but within a strictly controlled command economy.

2. All the last bastions face the need to make reforms and to meet the demands of the people. To ensure political participation, they only promise to democratize the single party, to cleanse it, and to renew its links with "the masses." This has been the case with Vietnam and Albania, but the same is true in China and Cuba. All refuse to abandon the party monopoly.

3. As the Soviet subsidies decline, alternate sources of support must be sought in international trade. The more these regimes do so, the more vulnerable they become to the logic of the international economy and, hence, the less they can maintain their control over their economies. Tourism in Cuba; German loans for Albania; the opening of the Chinese market to the United States and Japan, and the need to export to both; demands by the Vietnamese for economic aid—all point in the same direction.

4. Given the rapid expansion of worldwide communication networks, the people in all these regimes are beginning to become conscious of the disparities between their standard of living and that of the so-called capitalist world. This is clear for many Chinese, as they get signals and messages from Taiwan, Hong Kong, and Japan, to say nothing of the tens of thousands of Chinese students studying in the United States and Western Europe. Signals reached the Albanians even in their isolated corner of the Balkans.[8] The Cubans themselves listen to radio programs from the United States and elsewhere in South America and can watch TV programs, including news, sports, and commercials beamed from Key West in Florida. A sort of a black market in public opinion is growing that no regime can control.

5. In virtually all of these remaining Communist regimes—even in Cuba—the leadership is getting old. The heroic years of the revolution are over and the vision is beginning to wear off, especially among the young who know little of the past and assess their regime in terms of present performance. There is a genuine intergenerational conflict today that pits the majority of the population against its Communist leadership. The Marxist ideology, so precious to those who fought for it, is becoming irrelevant to most. Nowhere is this phenomenon clearer than in China where very old men remain at the top in the Communist party.

---

[8]By the end of 1990 the Albanians began to demonstrate and some managed to flee the country; in the early months of 1991 there was a massive exodus into Greece and Italy, despite promises by the Communist leaders to allow for open and free elections. On March 31st, 1991, the promised elections were held. The Communist Party won 68 percent of the vote and the Democratic Party, received about 30 percent. The Democratic Party won overwhelmingly in all cities, but in the countryside, where more than 70 percent of the Albanians live, the Communists maintained their hold. Violent demonstrations followed and an offer by the Communists to the opposition to form a coalition cabinet indicated that change was in the air. The last communist bastion in Europe seemed ready to fall.

The Communist leadership in all of the "last bastions" is desperately trying to cling to power, and the ways to do it are uncertain, to say the least.
One is to reinforce repression with the help of the military; the second, and the
one most often used, is to promise to undertake incremental reforms through
the democratization of the party and the liberalization of the economy. Such
reforms, however, inevitably whet the appetite for more. They may undermine
and perhaps displace the political elite in power. Caught between two choices—
repression or reform—the future of the Communist regimes still in power remains uncertain.

There is, finally, the critical question of "ideology." As is the case with the
Soviet Union, there is no new ideology to replace communism. Despite statements favoring democracy and liberalization, none of these countries has had
any attachment to a democratic ideology and democratic practices. The "democratic alternative" is in doubt.

EPILOGUE: A WORLD WITHOUT COMMUNISM?

The vision of a communist world, as formulated by Marx in terms of a new
body of social and economic theory and sharpened by Lenin into a political
weapon for the conquest and consolidation of political power by a single party,
became a reality first in Russia. The vision and the Leninist party became
vehicles for the establishment of an autocratic regime, fathered and nurtured
by Stalin and his heirs, until a sharp disparity became evident between the
Soviet "reality" and the Marxist vision. Yet, as we noted, until the late seventies
Soviet communism was considered by many loyalists and intellectuals in Russia
and the West, but also where it had gained ascendancy in China, Eastern
Europe, Cuba, Vietnam, and some other countries, as a progressive and liberating force.

Historians and theorists will argue for a long time about the cause of the
Communist collapse. Some will claim that the reasons for the Stalinist autocracy
lay deep in the Russian political culture and that the failure of the socialist command economy was due to the very backwardness of Russian society; other will
argue the exact opposite—that Stalinism was but a necessary authoritarian device to bring about rapid industrialization. The ideological vision of abundance
spurred many to work and accounted for their allegiance both during the heroic
years of industrialization (1929–1940) and in the years of the war against Nazi
Germany (1941–1945). With industrialization, the growth of new technological
and managerial elites, and the spread of education, the ideology and the party
could no longer harness the society into one single plan. Technology itself
spawned new means of communication, new professional groups, and new demands. The monolithic and hierarchical structure began to crack and to fragment. Communism became the victim of its success! There are others who will
hail the stamina and successes of democratic societies in the West and in the
United States. "Containment," suggested by George Kennan in 1947, worked
well and put pressure on the Soviet economy and society until the leadership

itself and many of its supporters began to realize the weakness of their system. There will be, finally, sociologists and philosophers who will argue that in the name of Marxism a huge intellectual fraud was perpetrated upon us all. Marxists claimed that capitalism led to a growing alienation of the individual. It was a "false" ideology into which we were socialized. It distorted human nature and made us all slaves to things alien to our free nature. Many will now point out that perhaps the reverse was true—that it was communism that imposed a false ideology, contrary to human nature, and in the process caused alienation and misery. Therefore, the demise of communism and the collapse of the Communist regimes will be viewed by them as a reassertion of the true human nature—prone to selfish interests, needy of individual fulfillment, attached to property, as Aristotle and many others have argued, and in search of self-gratification. The alienated individuals have reclaimed their true selves, just as Marx had asked the workers to do, but in doing so have caused the collapse of communism.

Whatever the reasons and causes, the collapse of communism as an ideology and system of governance has created a set of unanticipated problems. It leaves the societies in which it was implemented in complete disarray. In contrast to all other authoritarian regimes—military, despotic, tyrannical, nationalist, including even German national socialism—communism destroyed the societal forces in the name of its revolutionary vision. Human motivation was altered; self-interest grounded out; participatory mechanisms shaped in a way that secured the domination of a political elite. Conformity replaced consent and command replaced free initiative. Individuals even lost the ability to plan their own lives, since the all-powerful state determined the course for each individual by promising to care for it. With communism gone, the societies over which it ruled may well be compared to the land where a huge flood is receding. It is in shambles but the landmarks we take for granted; self-articulation, self-interest, entrepreneurship and initiative, the joys and poisons of private property, the ability to assume responsibility and to take risks, and, finally, the ability for sustained grass-roots action and associational life have to be learned all over again.

Communism, therefore, left all the societies over which it reigned with no opportunities to reshape a new ideology. Under these circumstances, political, regional, local, ethnic, and religious forces will surface and inevitably come into conflict with each other. In fact, the many conflicts that have already emerged in various countries of the Communist world may lead, as we noted, to authoritarian solutions in which a combination of military imposition with the Leninist practices of a single-party organization may gain the upper hand.

The challenge for democracy as an ideology and as a system of governance is to fill the vacuum created by the collapse of communism. It is a challenge that will unfold in the years and decades to come—first in Eastern Europe, then in the Soviet Union, and ultimately in many of the "last bastions" of communism. Will democratic political institutions and liberal economic structures be able to meet the challenge? This, in a true sense, is what "a world without communism" is all about.

BIBLIOGRAPHY

Brzezinski, Zbigniew. *The Grand Failure: The Birth and Death of Communism in the Twentieth Century.* New York: Scribner's, 1989.

Brown, F. J. *Eastern Europe and the Communist Rule*, Duke University Press, Durham and London, 1988.

_____. *Surge to Freedom, The End of Communist Rule in Eastern Europe*, Duke University Press, Durham and London, 1991.

Gorbachev, Mikhail. *Perestroika.* New York: Harper & Row, 1987.

Hosking, Geoffrey. *The Awakening of the Soviet Union.* Cambridge, Mass.: Harvard University Press, 1990.

Kagarlitsky, Boris. *The Thinking Reed: Intellectuals and the Soviet Union from 1917 to the Present.* Translated by Brian Pearce. New York: Routledge, 1989.

Laqueur, Walter. *The Long Road to Freedom: Russia and Glasnost.* New York: Scribner's, 1989.

Macridis, Roy, and Steven Burg. *Introduction to Comparative Politics: Regime and Change.* New York: HarperCollins, 1990.

Melia, Martin ("Z"). "To the Stalin Mausoleum." *Daedalus*, Winter 1990.

Medvedev, Roy. *On Socialist Democracy.* New York: Knopf, 1975.

Schammell, Michael. *Russia's Other Writers: Selections from Samizdat Literature.* New York: Praeger, 1971.

Shlapentokh, Vladimir. *Soviet Ideologies in the Period of Glasnost: Responses to Brezhnev's Stagnation.* Westport, Conn. Greenwood Press, 1990.

Other Reading

"Eastern Europe . . . Central Europe . . . Europe." *Daedalus*, Winter 1990.

Two excellent surveys of the Soviet economy have appeared in *The Economist*. "A Survey of Perestroika: Ready to Fly?" April 20, 1990 and A Survey of the Soviet Union—"Now What?" October 20, 1990.

Three

THE AUTHORITARIAN RIGHT

Preventing the sick from making the healthy sick . . . this ought to be our supreme object in this world. . . . But for this it is above all essential that the healthy should remain separate from the sick, that they should not even associate with the sick.

Nietzsche

The Genealogy of Morals

*E*xtremist authoritarian movements, like those of the Nazis and Fascists, developed everywhere in Europe after World War I. They spread to Central Europe, Portugal, Spain, and the Balkans in the 1930s. They affected countries with strong democratic traditions like France, and even England. Liberal democracy was threatened everywhere. The Fascist and Nazi regimes did away with some of the most basic freedoms that the civilized world had built up over many centuries. They proclaimed force at home and war in the international community as the highest of values. Their discrimination against certain races, nations, and creeds was taken to the point of not only advocating, but actually implementing, their methodical destruction.

Despite the upsurge of democracy in Eastern Europe and its first uncertain steps in the Soviet Union, as well as the decline in military dictatorships in many parts of the world, the authoritarian temptation is ever-present. Authoritarian ideologies and movements lurk in all democracies—especially in those that are not fully legitimized and where there are serious social, ethnic, religious, or racial strains. Authoritarianism is always in our midst.

In this part, we first examine the intellectual roots of right-wing authoritarianism and the ideology of the political movements they spawned. Second, in Chapter 8, we look at the most virulent manifestation of authoritarianism—the Nazi ideology in Germany and the Nazi regime (1933–1945).[1] We then turn to some manifestations of right-wing extremism in the United States and elsewhere.

THE INTELLECTUAL ROOTS

Many authors, philosophers, sociologists, anthropologists, and political scientists contributed to the formulation of an antiliberal and antidemocratic body of doctrine. Some would have taken pride in the movements and regimes that borrowed from their thinking; others would have rejected them outright as a gross distortion of what they had thought, written, and taught. The major ideas used by the right-wing parties were elitism, racialism, Social Darwinism, irrationalism, the exaltation of violence, the notion that the group has a reality superseding that of the individual, and nationalism. Lenin's conception of a revolutionary party based on will also played an important role, as did the reaction against industrialization by many social groups who felt threatened by it.

Elitism

Liberal assumptions of equality and participation had not been accepted by many conservatives. The latter spoke in terms of natural leaders—that is, persons with special endowments and with a special stake in the country that entitled them to have special leadership roles. Throughout the nineteenth century a number of authors advanced new arguments to justify the rule of the few, whether by government or by an elite, and they believed that the majority was simply incapable of self-government.

Elites derive superiority from intelligence, knowledge, manipulative skills, or sheer physical courage. One sociologist distinguishes between gifted individuals and the mass of mediocrities who follow them.[2] He asserts that competition takes place only among elites—the people follow like sheep. Democracy, he claims, is nonsense, a better name for it would be "mobocracy." Robert Michels, in a much-quoted book on political parties, had observed and documented the same phenomenon of elitism within Socialist parties that claimed to be open, egalitarian, and democratic.[3] They were run by an elite. In all such organizations there is an "iron law" of oligarchy.

---

[1] Italian fascism (1922–1944) had traits that were very similar to nazism. In fact, it preceded nazism by more than ten years. But the Fascists never managed to unite and permeate the society with their ideology as the Nazis did in Germany, and fascism did not develop a racist component. We frequently refer, however, to fascism even though we focus our attention on German nazism.

[2] Vilfredo Pareto, *The Mind and Society.* New York: Dowe, 1963.

[3] Robert Michels, *Political Parties.* New York: Free Press, 1962.

The German philosopher Nietzsche reached even more extreme conclusions. He identified leadership with the "heroic man" who has the will to power and the desire to dominate. The "superman," he predicted, would emerge and rise to power to impose his law and his will upon the "spineless multitude" with its Christian "slave morality." The future belonged to heroes unconstrained by law and conventional morality who would set their own morality and make their own law for all to follow. Lenin, too, without subscribing to the "superman" theory, emphasized that only a few, an elite, could organize the Communist party and speak on behalf of the workers and lead them to the promised land of communism.

Irrationalism

Early in the nineteenth century, another German philosopher wrote a book characteristically enough entitled *The World as Will and Idea*.[4] It began with the ominous phrase, "The world is my idea. . . . " What this means is that rational and scientific discourse is inadequate to provide us with the understanding of the world surrounding us and that "knowledge" is a matter of intuitive communication that alone can provide full "understanding." Knowledge thus becomes entirely subjective. Much later, the French philosopher Henri Bergson also stressed the intuitive aspects of learning—the mystical communication of the subject with the outside object.[5] It is thanks to intuition that we "know" an object by "entering into it." Science, reason, measurements, observation give us only a relative, partial, and fragmented knowledge; intuition supplies an "absolute" one. "The spirit has never had more violence done to it than when mere numbers made themselves its master," wrote Adolf Hitler.

Myths and Violence

But what is the relevance of intuition or instinct to politics? Simply that logic, persuasion, and argument cannot move people and cannot sustain a political system. In politics the counterpart of intuition is the "myth,"—that is, an idea, a symbol, a slogan that moves people into action because it appeals to their emotions. They become attached to it and they feel for it. The "crowd" or the "masses" act and can be much more easily moved when their emotions are aroused. They act in terms of stereotypes, prejudices, and instincts, not in terms of reason and proof. The myth unites them and gives purpose and meaning to their lives far better than logical exposition and reasoning. After

---

[4]Arthur Schopenhauer, *The World as Will and Idea*. Translated by E. P. Payne. New York: Dover, 1968.

[5]Henri Bergson, *The Two Sources of Morality and Religion*. Notre Dame, Ind.: University of Notre Dame Press, p. 177.

all, it was the great philosopher Plato who had defined a myth as a "golden lie" to be propagated by the philosopher–king in order to keep the people united and under control. All people were to be taught that they were brothers and sisters because they had the same parents, and were to accept inequalities as natural. Myths can take a variety of forms—racial supremacy, racial purity, national superiority and strength, the dictatorship of the proletariat, the resurrection of ancient empires, the reassertion of tribal bonds, the emergence of the superman, and so on.

Georges Sorel, the French revolutionary syndicalist (1857–1922), used the myth explicitly as a vehicle for moral, economic, and social revival.[6] The myth that he considered as potent as the Christian belief in the Second Coming was that of the general strike, by which he meant the development of a state of mind among the workers favoring the violent destruction of the existing social order. Violence would organize the workers, form the battle lines, and marshal them to war against the society. Their "sentiments," properly aroused by an elite, would lead to revolution. The myth of the general strike, therefore, called for a state of permanent violence. Violence, Sorel argued, is ennobling in itself, but it also helps people develop the moral courage to distinguish them from bourgeois cowardice and rationality. He wrote:

> Proletarian violence, carried on as pure and simple manifestation of the sentiments of class war, appears . . . a very fine and heroic thing; it is at the service of the immemorial interests of civilization. . . . It may . . . save the world from barbarism.[7]

Lenin never accepted Sorel's overall philosophy, but he nonetheless endorsed the need for violence.

Social Darwinism

Charles Darwin's theory of evolution and the notion of the survival of the fittest was quickly, and unwarrantedly, transferred to the social and the international order. In its new setting it became known as Social Darwinism. According to Darwin, "survival" means that some species survive while others perish in the course of adjusting, or failing to adjust, to the environment and to each other. Transposed to human society, the term was taken to mean that those who manage to survive or to succeed are superior to those who are unsuccessful or perish. Conflict between individuals and groups, and especially races and nations, was declared to be a natural and necessary process

---

[6]Georges Sorel, *Reflections on Violence*, New York: Macmillan, 1961.

[7]Cited in Lane W. Lancaster, *Masters of Political Thought*, vol. 3. Boston: Houghton Mifflin, p. 296.

for the selection of the best and the elimination of the weak and incompetent. The elites in power arrive at their position through struggle; but they are likely to be displaced through struggle if they begin to lose the qualities that brought them to the top. The struggle for survival is likely to affect them just as it affected the dinosaurs.

Social Darwinism has been used by liberals to justify economic competition and economic individualism. Right-wing totalitarianism has used it to justify competition and conflict, especially among elite races and nations, and to legitimize the supremacy of some individuals on the grounds of biological superiority. Some nations are considered superior to others and need more territory than others; some races are considered superior to others. Those that are superior are the "master race," while those that are inferior are the "slave races."

Throughout the nineteenth century, sympathy for racial theories was widespread, and Social Darwinism reinforced previously developed racist theories. French and British authors had discoursed on racial differences and were responsible for the establishment of cultural, biological, and moral criteria of superiority and inferiority. They concluded that the white race, and some of its various branches, was superior. The Nazi regime came to a most horrifying decision to exterminate the Jews—a fate that was also reserved for other "inferior races."

The Group Mind

As we pointed out, liberalism freed individuals from all attachments to groups and status that defined and structured their activities. The individual became the driving force within the social and political system. The formation of associations, and even the existence of the state, was traced ultimately to contractual and voluntary relations and individual consent. There was nothing "real" outside of the individual, to whose will, consent, and rationality all economic, political, and social institutions were traced. Throughout the nineteenth century, however, this position was strongly contested by those who argued that "individuals," as such, were a mere fiction, and that their ideas and values, and ultimately their reasoning, derived from group values. Marx argued, too, that individual attitudes and ideas were determined by the class to which an individual belonged.

Anthropologists and sociologists claimed to have discovered the "group mind" in tribal groups. People living in tribal societies could not clearly distinguish between "I" and "we"; individual morality, value judgments, and attitudes coincided fully with tribal or collective values and attitudes. In this way the group was larger than its parts, the individuals, and preceded them. Even more, group and collective ideas had a coercive character: the individuals were constrained by them, and their lives were to be understood only in terms of conformity and compliance to such groups. It was group solidarity, not individual morality, that counted most.

Thus, studying and understanding groups was a better way of understanding society than studying the individual who was nothing else but the sum total of the group images and pressures weighing upon him. Only the group was real. It took but one step to move to larger collectivities, notably the nation. The nation was real and not the individuals who made it; the morality of the nation was the morality of the individual; individual judgments had to yield to national judgments and imperatives. Therefore, the nation and nationalism became a superior moral force.

Escape from Freedom

Erich Fromm published a melancholic book in 1941 entitled *Escape from Freedom.* He claimed that there was one basic psychological need that liberalism had ignored. It was the individual's desire to belong, to be attached to groups or to hierarchies that make decisions, and to be part of the whole with fixed obligations to it and fixed rights deriving from it. Feudalism had provided such a setting, and its destruction had uprooted the individuals from their traditional groupings. Individuals found themselves desperately in need of similar ties to anchor their existence—ties that liberalism and industrialization had broken. Totalitarianism was in essence a return to group values and to authority; it was a response to the intense need for "belongingness," which, he claimed, was much stronger than reason and self-interest. Liberalism and the historical phase of liberalism were therefore nothing but an interlude between the structured life of the feudal society of the past and the subjection to the totalitarian regimes of the future. The latter amounted to a revolt of the individuals against the burdens of freedom and free choice that liberalism had imposed upon them.

Against the Bourgeois Mentality

Bourgeois values were a major target of criticism throughout the nineteenth century. The peaceful but unheroic existence of the citizen; the constant search for material gains and satisfactions; the compromising spirit that democratic liberalism fosters; the smugness of the wealthy and their ability to manipulate representative institutions to their advantage, while paying lip service to equality and freedom; the subordination of all values to material considerations—all this was repugnant to many intellectuals and philosophers, as well as workers. In a reaction, many writers extolled courage, violence, emotions, and instincts. They sought to find new binding ties in common adventures that liberalism downgraded and to help the "true" individual realize himself or herself; to find a way of life that was closer to nature but further away from reason; closer to instinct and intuition but further away from material interests; closer to feeling but away from science. It was in essence an exaltation of bygone romantic values of valor, adventure, and physical strength.

The "group mind" in action: The Führer arrives at a mass rally in Nuremburg in 1935.

The Historical Moment

As we pointed out, ideas may hibernate for a long time until circumstances bring them back to life to transform them into powerful political ideologies and movements. Defeat in World War I in 1918 and the ensuing Great Depression in 1929 were precisely the circumstances that accounted for the rise of German authoritarianism—the Nazis and their conquest of political power. The Great Depression—the most severe crisis capitalism had experienced— was of critical importance in the rise of the Nazis, and it carries a special message. Wherever and whenever economic conditions deteriorate sharply, political legitimacy of the democratic regime in power declines sharply and antidemocratic movements rise. It is a message that we should keep in mind as we assess the prospects of democracy today—especially in the new democratic regimes recently established.

Because of the economic depression, nazism appealed to a growing number of people and voters. Unemployed workers, farmers, the lower middle classes, and particularly the middle classes, war veterans, and university students found the combination of nationalist and unifying slogans, with the promise of economic reform, irresistible. Conservative groups, fearing loss of income and status, joined forces with the disaffected, the romantics, the nationalists, and the unemployed.

The remedy suggested was that of a strong state that would overcome internal divisions and cleavages—a new economic system that would set aside private interests and even private profit in favor of unity and cooperation with common social and national goals. It was the formula used in Italy by the Fascists and in Germany by the Nazis, and by all other antidemocratic nationalist movements throughout Europe. It is a standard formula—patented by many precedents but always ready for use!

Chapter
8

The Nazi Ideology and Political Order

For the Weltanshauung [the ideology] is intolerant ... and peremptorily demands its own, exclusive, and complete recognition as well as the complete adaptation of public life to its ideas.

Adolf Hitler

Mein Kampf

A historian of Germany entitles his chapter on German Nazism "Germany Goes Beserk."[1] It is only a mild comment on what occurred in one of the most advanced and civilized nations of the world. Nazism should be a constant reminder to all of us—no matter how special the conditions in Germany appear to have been—of how fragile the bonds of reason and law are and of how vulnerable we *all* may be to political fanaticism under certain circumstances.

German authoritarianism became a political reality when the leader of the Nazi party, Adolf Hitler, came to power in January 1933. Hitler immediately set about organizing the new system, the Third Reich,[2] implementing many of the promises he had made. Most notably, these included the abolition of the institutions of democracy, military preparations for worldwide domination, and the establishment of a single party. The Nazis managed to bring virtually all Germans and all elements of German society under their control. Germans were made to "march in step" to the tune of the Nazi party. This was the meaning of the famous term *gleichschaltung*—the "synchronization" of all aspects of social life with the political ideology and objectives of the Nazi party.

---

[1] K. S. Pinson, *Modern Germany*, p. 479.

[2] Third Reich was an expression intentionally used to indicate continuity with the German Empire (1871–1918) and the Holy Roman Empire.

THE ROAD TO POWER

The beginnings of the Hitler movement can be traced directly to the aftermath of World War I, and also to the rich background of German antidemocratic literature and right-wing political extremism.

Defeat in World War I caused a great disillusionment and eventually a desire for revenge. The discontent was focused on the Versailles Treaty, which had stripped Germany of its colonies and imposed a heavy burden of reparations, but there were also other factors. First, the galloping inflation of the early 1920s was unprecedented in the economic history of any nation. The inflation wiped out savings, pensions, and trust funds and made salaries and wages dwindle with the passage of every day, week, and month. It created a state of acute panic among the middle classes.

A second important factor was the reaction to Communist revolutionary movements. Revolutions actually took place right after World War I, and Communist regimes were installed temporarily in parts of Germany. Private groups and armies, led by officers and war veterans, took it upon themselves to stop the leftists. Often aided by the police and whatever remained of the German Army, they began to wage war against the Communists and their sympathizers. Many of these veterans and their organizations rallied to the Nazis and formed the hard core of the Nazi party.

The Nazi party was founded in 1921. Its original program included the usual nationalist and racist themes but also promised social and economic reforms that were downright socialist: land reform, nationalizations, and the "breaking of the shackles of capitalism." It also attacked the political and economic elites, and identified the "domestic" and "outside" enemies of Germany as the victorious powers—notably England and France, the Jews and "international Jewry." It was a small party at first. Few paid attention to its founding. After the economic Depression of 1929, however, the Nazis began to make rapid gains and soon emerged as the strongest party (see Table 8.1).

There were a number of reasons for the rapid growth of the Nazi party. Leadership was consolidated in the hands of Hitler—the Führer. Uniforms, a special salute, pomp and ritual, and, above all, discipline and activism appealed to many, especially the young. In 1931, some 35 percent of the party members were below the age of thirty. Party membership began to grow—especially after 1928–1929 when there were about 100,000 members, to 1.5 million by 1933, and up to about 4 million at the beginning of World War II.

Special shock formations were established. The SA (Brownshirts) and, after 1934, the SS (Black Guards) grew in numbers to almost equal the German army. At the slightest provocation they engaged in street fights or attacks against leftists and opposition leaders, whose headquarters they sacked and burned. Anti-Semitic demonstrations and acts of violence were common. All this was testing the will of the Nazis, preparing them for further action and intimidation.

A number of front organizations were created to strengthen the party's appeal and to recruit more members and sympathizers. In 1931, the Hitler Youth

Adolf Hitler (1889–1945)

The Führer, ironically enough, was a non-German. Hitler was born in Austria in 1889. A poor student given to prolonged moods of melancholia and day-dreaming, he found himself in the army, where he served with the rank of corporal with apparent diligence and courage. Defeat enraged him and he sought scapegoats in the "cowardice" of the civilians and the "conspiracy" of the Jews. Without any formal education—he wanted to be an architect and tried painting—he had read much of the nationalist literature.

After World War I he found himself in Munich, capital of Bavaria, where he founded the NDASP (the Nazi party) in 1921. After the abortive effort to seize power in 1923, he received a light sentence and spent the months of his imprisonment writing what became the political bible of Nazism, *Mein Kampf* (My Struggle). It was the Depression and the frustrations and political conflict associated with it that provided the climate for his ascent to power. On January 30, 1933, President Hindenburg asked him to become Chancellor of Germany, and he assumed full powers until his "Thousand Year Reich" ended with his suicide in the ruins of Berlin on April 30, 1945.

Table 8.1. ELECTIONS AND THE NAZI VOTE

Legislative elections

1924 (May 4)	1,918,300 (32 deputies)	6.0%
1924 (Dec. 7)	907,300 (14 deputies)	3.0%
1928 (May 20)	810,000 (12 deputies)	2.6%
1930 (Sept. 14)	6,409,600 (107 deputies)	18.3%
1932 (July 31)	13,745,800 (230 deputies)	37.4%
1932 (Nov. 1)	11,737,000 (196 deputies)	33.1%
1933 (March 5) Nazis in power	17,277,200 (288 deputies)	43.9%
1933 (Nov. 12) Nazis in control	39,638,800 (661 deputies)	92.2%

Presidential election

1932 (March) 1st ballot	11,339,288 (Hitler)	30.1%
2nd ballot	13,418,051 (Hitler)	36.8%

Source: Koppel S. Pinson, *Modern Germany,* 2nd ed. New York: Macmillan, 1966. Reprinted with permission of Macmillan Publishing Company. Copyright © 1966 by Macmillan Publishing Company.

numbered only about 100,000. In 1933–1934, it was close to about 4 million members, and at the outbreak of the war in 1939–1940 it approached almost 9 million. In addition, there was a Hitler Student League, an Officers' League, a Women's League, a workers' Nazi organization (the Labor Front), and many others representing every academic, social, and professional group in the country. The party gradually became a state within a state with its private army, tribunals, police, and military formations all spreading the Nazi doctrine far and wide and creating within Germany a strong Nazi subculture. It had its own cult, slogans, and morality; they were antirepublican, racist, and nationalist.

With the economic depression, the Nazis made the breakthrough that led them to power in 1933. They became a mass party as the election results show, but they also attracted the attention and support of the conservative forces and the army. The business community and the financial elites opened up their purse, and the party's treasury was again full. The Nazis and their leader broadened their appeal to catch, if possible, every group, every section, and every occupation and profession.

Nazi Pledges

To the farmers, the Nazis promised "green democracy" and "soil-rooted" pure communitarian values as well as protection and subsidies. They pledged to uphold the rural values and traditions that were menaced by urbanization.

To the workers, they promised jobs. Between 1929 and 1932, unemployment had shot up from 1 to 6 million. Many employed and unemployed workers began to join the party and to vote for it. The depression had weakened the trade unions, and left-wing workers were hopelessly divided between socialism and communism.

To the army, the Nazis promised rebuilding and an end to the Versailles Treaty.

To the middle classes, they promised special measures to arrest the decline of their income and give them security; above all, they promised to do away with the dangers from the left by eliminating communism. These promises appealed especially to the lower middle classes—merchants, artisans, shopkeepers, civil service personnel, clerical personnel, and so on.

The Nazi party promised a special place to the young. The future was theirs. "Make room for us, you old ones," was one of their battle cries.

Propaganda was developed into a fine political art along clear-cut lines suggested by Hitler: repetition of the same simple slogans and themes; appeal to the emotions; propositions that clearly distinguished the negative from the positive—"this *is* the truth, *they* lie," "*we* can, *they* cannot"; simple answers to complex problems—"*we* shall solve unemployment by giving jobs to all"; emphasis on nationalism and national togetherness—"*we*" (Germans) against "*they*" (Jews, plutocrats, capitalists, communists, and so on). These propaganda themes were to be strengthened by direct action taken against opponents. Truth lay not in demonstration but in belief *and* in action. A Nazi was someone who believed and strengthened his belief by acting. Force became the best vindication of belief.

In the 1932 presidential election the Nazi candidate, none other than Hitler himself, received 36.8 percent of the vote. More than one-third of German voters wanted him as their president!

THE NAZI IDEOLOGY

Nazism as an ideology and a political movement began as a gesture of negation, but there was also the formulation of a number of "positive" themes and propositions on the basis of which the new society would be constructed. Some of them were addressed to the immediate situation, others to long-range social, economic, and political problems created by liberalism and the threat of communism.

Negative Themes

The negative themes of Nazism were many:

1. *Against class struggle*   The notion of class, developed by Marx and endorsed by all Communist parties, was inconsistent with national unity. As such, it was only an extension of the idea of conflict and competition developed by liberals and Marxists. The Nazis claimed that the notion of class was incompatible with the communitarian values of the German people and the German nation. Germany was "one"!

2. *Against parliamentary government*   According to the Nazis, parliamentary government leads to the fragmentation of the body politic into parties and groups jockeying for position, compromising their particular interests, and forming unstable governmental coalitions. The "real" national interest was neglected. A common purpose could not develop from such a fragmentation of the national will. "There is no principle which . . . is as false as that of parliamentarianism," wrote Hitler in *Mein Kampf*.

3. *Antitrade union*   Unions express the sectarian and class interests of the working class. However, the workers were also Germans and citizens. They had to be integrated into the community like all others instead of pitting themselves against other Germans.

4. *Against political parties*   Like representative government, political parties expressed special ideological or interest particularisms, splitting the nation. The national purpose called not for parties but for one movement embodying it. Such a movement, even if it were called a party, should be given monopoly of representation. Hence all other political parties should be outlawed, and a one-party system instituted.

5. *Against the Treaty of Versailles*   The Versailles Treaty, imposing an inferior status upon Germany that deprived it of its army and required it to pay reparations, had to be eliminated. But more than that, the existing international system that perpetuated the supremacy of some nations—notably England and France—should be drastically altered to give freedom and space to Germany.

There were a number of other comprehensive negative themes that inevitably blend with some of the "positive" formulations of the Nazis.

6. *Anti-Semitism and racialism*   Anti-Semitism had been a common phenomenon in many countries of Europe stemming from religious prejudices, cultural differences, and economic rivalries. The Jews were blamed as responsible for both liberal capitalism *and* for communism. There were extravagant myths attempting to show that the Jews were plotting the domination of the world. This was the case with a document (fabricated by nineteenth-century anti-Semites) called *The Protocols of the Elders of Zion*, in which the Jews were said to set forth their plans to conquer the world. This was widely used by the Nazis. They added a new twist, however—that Jews were biologically inferior. They were therefore not only dangerous because of their ideas, their beliefs, and their plans to conquer the world (how inferior people could do it was never explained), but because their very presence within Germany endangered the purity of the German "race." There were only half a million Jews in Germany at

the time Hitler assumed power and over 65 million Germans—that is less than 0.7 percent. More than 200,000 Jews managed to escape the country by 1938. Those who remained were viewed as a germ just as virulent as botulism. It had to be isolated first and then exterminated.

As soon as the Nazis came to power, they began to reduce the German Jews to the status of nonpersons. They could not keep their businesses; they could not receive any social benefits. They were relegated to special neighborhoods; they were constantly harassed and intimidated by the members of the Nazi party, the SA, and its various front organizations; they were arbitrarily arrested, could not engage in any gainful occupation, had their belongings confiscated, and were forced to pay special levies to the state authorities that invariably went to the Nazi party members. Intermarriage was prohibited, and existing intermarriages annulled. The Nazis developed the long-range policy of exterminating all Jews that led actually to the destruction of European Jewry wherever the Nazi armies gained a foothold.

Given its basis, German anti-Semitism left no room for compromise. But the same biological discrimination also threatened other groups and nations that the Nazis found dangerous or "impure"—Slavs, blacks, and so on.

7. *Anticommunism*   If anti-Semitism derived from racist allegations, anticommunism stemmed primarily from political and international considerations. It was aimed not only against Communists at home, but against the "fatherland of communism," the Soviet Union. It called not only for the elimination of the German Communist party, but also for the elimination of international communism as spearheaded by the Soviet Union. The ideological crusade against communism would thus serve the secular strategic, economic, and geopolitical goals of Germany. It was part and parcel of the *Drag Nach Osten*—the German drive eastward.

"Positive" Themes

Every negation advanced by the Nazis (what they planned to do away with) naturally called for an affirmation (what they planned to do instead). It is therefore only in this sense that I am using the term "positive."

Anti-Semitism suggests racialism and the purity of the race; antiindividualism, a communitarian ethic transcending the individual; antiliberalism, a new political organization; and the anti-Versailles posture, the erection of some new kind of international order. It is the combination of the reasoning behind many of the negations that resulted in the new and dynamic synthesis of social and national life. No matter how morally repugnant, it must be analyzed and discussed if we are to grasp the full and ominous implications of the Nazi movement and regime.

1. *Nationalism and racialism*   To understand the character of Nazi German nationalism, we must distinguish it from other nationalist movements. There were liberal nationalist movements in the wake of the French Revolution of 1789 identifying with the principle of nationality and demanding that people sharing the same national background—a common history, culture, language,

religion—live within a given territory, the nation–state. This is basically the principle of self-determination, allowing peoples to form their own state. There have also been conservative nationalist movements which have extolled national virtues and asserted their superiority over others; they stress national integration and unity at the expense of particularisms, regionalisms, and even individual freedoms. But such nationalist movements are content to see the values they assert cultivated and strengthened within the nation–state. They are not expansionist.

Nazi nationalism was both racialist and expansionist. While insisting on the superiority of Germanic values, it also proclaimed the superiority of the German race and the desirability of imposing its superiority upon others. Aryans were superior not only to Jews buy also to Slavs, Turks, Greeks, French, and so on. And among the Aryans, the Germans were the superior race because they had managed and, thanks to the Nazis, forever intended to keep their race "pure." They would not allow for a "mongrelization" similar to what they claimed had occurred in the United States. They were the *master race* destined to dominate all others. This racialist doctrine, coupled with extreme nationalism, led to the inevitability of war.

2. *Expansionism* The valor of the race could not be proven by assertion only. It had to be demonstrated on the proving ground of war and conquest. The master race was to be a race of warriors subduing lesser races. Germany was to conquer, and Berlin would become the capital of the world. But in addition to racism there were ideological, economic, and strategic reasons to justify an expansionist and warlike policy. A totalitarian system is "total" at home because it tries to subordinate everything to its ideology and control. It cannot allow competing units to exist. But the same is true in international terms. The logic of totalitarianism calls for the elimination of competing centers of power everywhere.

Economic reasons were also advanced. One was the notion of "proletarian" nations; another that of "living space." According to the former, World War I had allowed some nations to control the world's wealth—for example, England, the United States, France—while other nations like Germany, Italy, and even Japan were poor, "proletarian," without colonies, raw materials, and resources. Similarly, some nations had ample space at their disposal: the French, British, and Dutch had their colonial empires. The Soviet Union and United States had immense land at their disposal. Others nations did not, however, and Germany, without colonies, was squeezed into the center of Europe, while it population was growing and its needs increasing. Land would therefore have to be reapportioned to meet the German needs. To this argument yet another one was added—the distinction between "young" and "old" nations, suggesting growth against decay. In historical terms, Germany was "young" compared to England or France and needed "living space" and land into which to grow.

Thus the conquest of territory and the destruction of neighboring nation–states became an essential element of the Nazi ideology, and a long-range policy goal. It could not be attained overnight. The elimination of Soviet Russia (an old bulwark against German expansion to the east and also an ideological foe) and France (the spearhead of the "plutocracies," especially England and the United States) would have to come first. The Japanese and the Italians were offered only tactical alliances in the expansionist German ambitions. Their position in the international order that the Nazis would build would have to be settled later.

3. *Communitarianism*   The elimination of all freedoms and their replacement by a single "freedom"—that of obeying the party that represented the German community and the leader of that party—was the essence of German totalitarianism. It was central to the building of a new political system that would replace liberalism and capitalism. All parties, all organizations, all associations, all religious groups, and churches would become subordinated to the communitarian will. After the Nazis came to power, freedom of press, of association, and of speech ceased to exist. All parties were abolished. The individual—alone, free, independent, thinking his or her own thoughts—would give place to the "new individual" imbued with communitarian and nationalist beliefs as dictated by the leader and the party. The individual and the community would become one. Dissenters were, of course, not to be tolerated; they were executed or sent to concentration camps. But individuals who tried to remain aloof and distant from the national community were declared to be "asocial." They had failed to respond to the demands of the party and the community; they were not fully mobilized; they were not one with the nation.

Communitarianism called for constant participation; it aimed to inculcate a spirit of individual attachment to the whole and a readiness not only to obey but also to sacrifice everything for the general interest as defined by the Nazis. Communitarianism also suggested the need to subordinate private interest in the economic sphere to general social goals and, thereby, the subordination of the market economy to the party and the leader. The early Nazi ideology was distinctly anticapitalist, and it advocated the supremacy of national goals over all economic interests.

4. *Leadership ("Führerprinzip") and the party*   In what ways do communitarian values manifest themselves? One way is the direct participation of all in decision making—claimed to be the practice of the early Germanic tribes. A second way is for the community to select its representatives. This notion of representation was given a particular twist by the Nazis. They accepted it but they rejected free elections. The Nazi party "represented" the German people because it was in tune with the people and expressed directly the desires of the nation. Within the party, its leader instinctively and intuitively acted for the whole. It is the leader, therefore, who best expresses the communitarian values.

Within six months after it came to power, the "monopoly" of the Nazi party was legalized. The National Socialist Workers' party constituted the *only* political party in German. Whoever undertook to maintain the organizational structure of another political party or to form another political party was to be punished with penal servitude up to three years.

Communitarian aspirations gave a populist trait to nazism. It claimed to embody values and principles that stemmed directly from the people—the *volk*. It was the "people's spirit"—the *volksgeist*—that was tapped by the party and was represented by it. Hence the party, in the name of this unique representative quality, claimed to be the only vehicle of representation and the very essence of direct democracy. But because of this, it also claimed to be an entity above the state and to control the state while acting on behalf of the community. In the last analysis, the state was nothing but an agency, an instrumentality of the party, and all its offices and officials were subordinate to the party.

The leadership principle is the cornerstone of nazism and the institution that best combines authority and control with "representation." It is a principle that cannot be easily defined since it can be only "understood" by those who experience it. The leader decides everything and everybody must obey. He can delegate his authority to others but can never give it up. He is the law and hence above the law. He can legislate and then change that legislation overnight. His will is arbitrary, absolute, and superior. He can set procedures and change them at will. He is free to appoint his successor, just as a Roman emperor could make his horse a consul, or send him to the slaughterhouse!

But why do people obey? The link is the mystical and intuitive link between leader and followers. He speaks for the people and the people agree with him because he speaks for them! And where his authority does not quite prevail, the leader has at his disposal formidable instruments of coercion, intimidation, and downright terror to elicit obedience.

The Subordination of the Society

The vast majority of Germans acquiesced in the Nazi takeover, often with enthusiasm. They showed remarkable loyalty throughout Hitler's stay in power. Many did so out of self-interest; how many submitted out of fear is difficult to tell. Let us see how the various "social groups" reacted to the coming to power of the Nazis and their regime.

The Army   Diminished in status, reduced in numbers, bearing the brunt of defeat, and hostile to communism and left-wing movements, army officers saw, in the coming of the Nazis, the prospects of their rehabilitation. Never at ease with republican institutions, the army's position was that it either should be a dominant force in the society or a separate and distinct entity for training soldiers, maintaining order, and making war. It would not play a subordinate role. After World War I, many of its officers joined right-wing vigilante organizations against Communists and leftists. Throughout Hitler's rise to power, prominent officers cooperated with him or gave him a helping hand. He promised the rehabilitation of the nation and saw war as an answer for past failures. As General Blomberg testified at the Nuremburg trials: "Before 1938–1939 the German generals were not opposed to Hitler. There was no ground for opposition since he brought them the success they desired."[3] It was only when the fortunes of

---

[3] Cited in Pinson, p. 508.

the war began to turn against Germany that a number of generals became impatient with Hitler and some even conspired to assassinate him.

Civil Service   German civil servants, federal and state, responded with satisfaction to Hitler's program and supported his regime. The Nazis seemed to represent the basic values of order, centralized authority, and national integrity to which they were accustomed. Once it became clear that party members would not replace them, the support of the bureaucracy was overwhelming. It was strengthened by generous promotions and increases in salaries.

Yet bureaucracies are accustomed to an orderly way of doing things. They accept hierarchical relationships and a careful structuring of inferior–superior lines of command. They are committed to a rational detached, and impartial way of reaching decisions and implementing them; they are concerned with efficiency. The Prussian, and later on German, bureaucracy was always considered to be both well-organized and efficient. As a result, the frequent intrusions into it of the Nazi leaders, and the ultimate power they had to intervene and make decisions themselves, alienated some civil servants, forced the resignation of others, and often created confusion. However, at no time during the Hitler regime was there an open defiance on the part of the civil service.

The Church   Religious groups tried to maintain a certain distance from the Nazis, but an effort was made to eliminate some and to bring the two major churches, Catholic and Lutheran, under control. Jews were quickly isolated and their synagogues burned; Jehovah's Witnesses were presecuted. A Concordat was signed with the Vatican giving the Catholic church some autonomy—the right to hold services, raise funds, and distribute pastoral letters to the faithful. But the Concordat also legitimized the Nazi state in the eyes of many Catholics. They were particularly receptive to Nazi anticommunist pledges and, during the war, considered it their patriotic duty to support the fatherland, especially when it was against the Soviet Union.

The Lutheran church maintained a distance from the state, distinguishing political from spiritual matters. Political obedience was one thing, and the worship of God another, but the Lutherans gave their support to the Nazis as citizens, whatever their innermost thoughts might have been. Even to those for whom Hitler was a tyrant, obedience to the state was an obligation and prayer the only answer.

Individual Catholic prelates and Lutheran pastors occasionally raised their voices against the Nazi regime and its atrocities, but they were the exceptions to the general passivity of the churches.

Business Groups   As for business groups, they gave their full support and cooperation once the "socialist" pledges that were in the original platform of the party were abandoned. Neither private property nor business profits were tampered with, and the antilabor and antitrade union measures satisfied them fully. Business elites cooperated closely with the Nazi leaders, trading favors and benefits with them.

The Middle Class, Farmers, and Workers   Germany had never experienced a genuine middle-class liberal movement as had England, France, and the United States. Rapid industrialization was grafted upon semifeudal and authoritarian social structures. Paternalistic and hierarchical relationships were the rule. The middle classes *fitted* themselves into these structures instead of creating their own kind of political and social relationships—egalitarian and participatory. They felt more at home with authoritarian solutions and hierarchical relationships, and hence they were inclined to accept nazism and the authoritarian and nationalist philosophy it represented. Furthermore, the Nazi anticommunist ideology and its intention of doing away with trade unions reflected the middle-class fear of the working class and their political parties. The overwhelming majority of middle-class voters elected the Nazis and supported them throughout their stay in power. The lower middle classes, the petit bourgeoisie—insecure, patriotic, and antisocialist—gave them their full support as they sought a niche in the Nazi order.

Similarly, the farmers gave the Nazis overwhelming support. The rustic virtues the Nazis extolled were also theirs: protection in the form of higher tariffs provided them with added revenue; anticommunism appealed to their traditional nationalism and conservatism. Small towns and rural communities voted overwhelmingly Nazi.

It was only the workers, then, who seemed to demur. But even among them it was only the politically and ideologically organized and committed, those who belonged to trade unions or were in the Communist and Socialist parties, who provided the opposition. The unemployed, as we pointed out, tended to join the party in return for promises of employment. With the coming of World War II in 1939, full employment was attained and the labor force was by and large materially better off than it had been at any time since before World War I. There was no organized opposition.

The Economy

The Nazis failed to implement their original economic program. They did not nationalize the monopolies—on the contrary, every effort was made to encourage concentration and cartelization; they did not confiscate war profits or unearned income; they did not undertake land reform and did not take over uncultivated lands and transform them into peasant cooperatives. Populist and socialist promises were forgotten when they came to power. Some of the Nazi party's leaders, many of whom had taken these promises seriously, were massacred in 1934.

Nazi economic policy consisted of a series of improvisations to meet the political objectives of rearmament and war. There is no doubt that the economy was subordinated not only to political and ideological exigencies, but also to the necessity of planning or waging war. From the very start, controls were put on foreign exchange. Special efforts were made to promote investment and direct it to key areas of economic activity; to secure raw materials and, when it became necessary, to produce them at home (as, for instance, with synthetic gas and rubber). In general, the emphasis was put on reducing imports and promoting self-sufficiency. Property, however, both individual and corporate, was respected.

Political and ideological imperatives prevailed. But the economy was not absorbed by the state; it was not nationalized. It became subordinate to the state and the party—a subordination that most other countries had experienced in time of war. Similarly, the churches, even if they remained submissive, maintained their autonomy under Nazi surveillance. And although various associations—business, legal, professional, and academic—were infiltrated by the Nazis and made to march to the tune of Nazi ideology, they, too, retained their identities.

All and all, the economy and the civil society even if subdued, subordinated, and infiltrated were never destroyed—they maintained their distinctiveness. This is one of the major differences between Nazi authoritarianism and communism. After the defeat of Germany and the collapse of the Nazis in 1945, the societal forces managed to reassert themselves. With the collapse of communism, on the other hand, as indicated, what followed was a societal vacuum.

AUTHORITARIANISM: INTERPRETATIONS AND PROSPECTS

What are the prospects for authoritarianism? Is right-wing authoritarianism dead? With the reunification of Germany in 1990, many ask the same question: "Will it happen in Germany again?" Before we answer, let us survey the major theories—the major explanations for right-wing authoritarianism.

The Marxist Theory   A classic interpretation widely used by many authors is the Marxist one, formally endorsed by the Communist Third International. According to it, nazism corresponds to the "last stage of monopolistic capitalism." It is spearheaded by the most extreme and expansionist elements of the capitalist class in an effort to maintain its rule at home and subjugate other peoples and their economies. Expansionism and war are two of the remaining means available to the capitalists faced with economic depression and the growing contradictions of their system that Marx had anticipated. The evidence was considered clear: both nazism and fascism geared the economy to war, distracting the people from their economic problems by appealing to their nationalism and by preparing them for war. They maintained private property and profits and destroyed the trade unions and working-class parties.

The Modernization Theory   Another theory views authoritarianism in terms of economic modernization. As the industrial and nonagricultural sectors gradually gain, there is a shift of power from the traditional landed and commercial elites to industrial and banking groups. Industrialization accounts for an influx of farmers into the cities and for urbanization and rapid growth in the numbers of industrial workers. These shifts bring about a new type of political mobilization and new political parties that attempt to recruit the workers, the urban masses, and also the disgruntled peasants. Invariably, such a mobilization frightens the middle classes and the industrial elite groups who begin to favor repressive and integrative solutions.

Psychological Interpretations   Authoritarianism has been viewed by many authors as a psychological phenomenon. People react to a "threat" or to "alienation," both of which occur during the development of industrialization and the concomitant creation of a "mass society." A mass society corresponds to the breakup of most intermediate social structures—village, family, neighborhoods—and many traditional institutions that structure and shape individual values, attitudes, and life. The ultimate result is the "atomization" of society. As the old groups disintegrate, the individuals find themselves alone and lonely. A reaction sets in in favor of communal and integrative ideologies.

The perception of threat strengthens authoritarian appeals when the threatened individuals belong to groups that are comfortable, relatively well-off, and satisfied with their lot. Such is the case with the middle classes, which enjoy a higher income and a better status than farmers or workers or lower middle-class individuals. They are, according to some authors, the key to the door to power for right-wing leaders. There is hardly any doubt that the middle classes, both in Germany and Italy, gave their full support to the Nazis and the Fascists in order to protect themselves against threats to their income and status. They sought protection against trade unions and workers, and found it.

As with the previous theories, this psychological interpretation fails to provide a satisfactory and general explanation. If Germany was a mass society in 1933, so were the United States and England. Why did right-wing extremism gain the upper hand in one country but not in the others? Similarly, if the middle classes were "threatened" in Germany, so were they threatened in other industrialized systems, including the United States, during the Great Depression. Why did they seek defense in a totalitarian system in Germany but not elsewhere? Why were antidemocratic solutions sought in some countries and not in others? A theory that does not provide us with the explanation of as many occurrences as possible is not satisfactory.

Managerial Revolution?   Totalitarianism and totalitarian regimes have been viewed by some as representing a "managerial revolution" to replace the inept political leadership of democratic regimes. The economic structure of capitalism, they argue, changes. Property is not in the hands of only a few; it is widely dispersed among stockholders. Property owners cannot and do not make decisions: their managers do. Decision making is therefore increasingly concentrated in the hands of a managerial elite that enters into close contact with other elites, not only in the economy but also in the army and the civil service; it even enters into close cooperation with labor leaders. In other words, it is a coalition of persons with technical skills in production, management, administration, and group organization.

It is this new managerial elite, then, that makes the major decisions in the economy (often through planning): production levels, the establishment of economic priorities, the utilization of resources, the supply of money, income distribution, wage policy, and so on. Gradually, the democratic institutions become an obstacle to this *de facto* government of experts and managers who control the heights of the economy and society.[4] Authoritarianism in the form of fascism or nazism has been viewed accordingly as the triumph of the technocrat and the expert—of a power elite which finally does away with democracy for the sake of efficiency and organization.

The difficulty with this interpretation is that is assigns a role to rationality, knowledge, and technical expertise that neither the Fascists nor the Nazis valued. On the contrary, in both systems there was a constant struggle between the political ideological propositions, utopian or downright irrational, and the imperatives of rational management. There were constant conflicts between the economic managers and the party or the state, between the army officers and the party, and between the economic planners and the party leaders. In fact, fascism and nazism amounted to the predominance of politics over technical roles and considerations such as competence, organization, management, and efficiency.

Personality Theory   Considerable ingenuity has gone into efforts to show that authoritarianism appeals to and receives widespread support from individuals with a particular type of personality—the "authoritarian" or "potentially authoritarian." A number of attitudinal traits combined constitutes a "syndrome" or a "pattern" of the authoritarian personality: anti-Semitism, nationalism, fear of outsiders or aliens, conservative political outlook, strict family upbringing. Persons showing this syndrome are likely to be found among the lower middle classes, the workers, and the uneducated. Similarly, persons suffering from various types of anxiety, even paranoia, who are unable to make decisions and choices and often are afraid of the outside world, divest themselves easily of their freedoms in favor of authoritarian leadership which provides some degree of fixity and stability in their lives.

But there is no adequate evidence to attribute fascism or nazism and membership in and support for authoritarian movements to particular personality types. To begin with, both Nazi and Fascist movements received strong support from the middle classes, to say nothing of university students—persons, that is, with relatively comfortable backgrounds and higher education. Support was lowest from the working classes, where many of the traits associated with an authoritarian personality would be found. Second, even if we concede that there is an authoritarian upbringing in German families, a random distribution

---

[4]James Burnham, *The Managerial Revolution.*

of political attitudes, ranging from authoritarian to democratic, would show only marginal differences for various countries of Europe and elsewhere.

Is There One Interpretation?   All the interpretations given of authoritarian movements provide us with only parts of an explanation. In some cases, it may well be that levels of modernization provided a setting; in other cases, the lonely uprooted individual may have sought shelter in unity and communitarian effort; in others, authoritarian solutions were sought by business and financial groups to defend the economic system that provided them with profits; in still others, the middle classes and the lower middle classes, confronted with loss of income and status, revolted against democracy and liberal institutions. No single interpretation will do; and even if all of them are put together, they do not point to the set of conditions that will inevitably lead to authoritarianism.

Prospects

As we have noted, ideologies often go through a process of ebb and flow. Right-wing extremism and authoritarianism have deep roots, and it is not at all unlikely that, given certain conditions, they may surface again. Many of the conditions for the rise of authoritarian movements and regimes continue to be present. The mass society has become even more impersonal and atomized because of rapid modernization and technological development. Individuals are very much "alone," and their discontents and frustrations may lead them to espouse unifying and communitarian themes. The liberal ethic that continues to emphasize individual effort and to promise material well-being has raised high expectations for abundance. But it has also undermined some of the basic intermediary "control mechanisms" of society—like the church, the school, trade unions—and in so doing, weakened the structures of deference, mutuality, and obligation. The political parties seem unable to hold people together around common programs and to pattern and regulate their expectations accordingly. The democratic society has been reduced to a myriad of competing and conflicting groups (some refer to them as molecular groups), each one of which tries to maximize its benefits and advantages. It is not unlikely, therefore, that new authoritarian parties may try to capture the frustrations and discontents of the many who are not satisfied with their position and material well-being. All that may be needed for virulent extremist movements to emerge is a severe international crisis or another serious economic crisis. Such a crisis could cause a resurgence of revolutionary leftist parties, of one denomination or another, that would put the elites and the middle classes on the defensive. It could bring forth a movement or a regime that would attempt to control group particularisms, to replace representative institutions, to set aside political competition, and to manipulate public opinion around nationalist and communitarian themes. Force would replace consent, even if only to a degree, and propaganda would replace persuasion. In other words, the prospects for extremist antidemocratic movements remain very much alive. So does the rich ideological background from which they can draw.

What About a United Germany?   Now we are ready for the questions we raised: "How likely is the return of nazism in Germany? After its reunification in 1990,[5] will Germany assume the same nationalist, antidemocratic, and racialist posture?" There are Germans and German territories still outside of Germany; there is the memory of defeat and humiliation in 1945; there are internal problems that may cause a resurgence of racism, namely, more than 4 million foreign workers in Germany today, among them Turks and North Africans; there is also the realization dawning upon the Germans that with unification Germany has once more attained the rank of a major power in the world, with a worldwide role to play. National strength requires unity that may lead to national exaltation and reassertiveness. There are some who believe, therefore, that rightwing authoritarianism is likely to return.

There are developments, however, that point in the opposite direction. First, German unification has been attained by democratic means with an emphasis on new economic arrangements in the direction of the free market for East Germany. Second, ever since 1945, West Germany (the German Federal Republic) prospered and a new middle class has grown—liberal in outlook, with democratic parties and a democratic constitution. Third, the old elites that cooperated with Hitler—the Junkers, the army, and big business—no longer hold the power and influence they did; in fact, the old elites were destroyed by the Nazis and the new ones grew under a democratic regime that lasted for more than 45 years and that has now been extended to East Germany. Fourth, Germany—a united Germany—remains part of the European Community and has fully accepted the jurisdiction of the European Parliament, the European Commission, and the European Court. It is difficult to see it launch on nationalist and expansionist ventures.

Finally, in the last forty years a more egalitarian and participatory political society has emerged to replace the previous structures of deference and obedience. It had been often said that German revolutionaries who attempted to commandeer trains to transport their militants sought to buy a ticket first! Obedience had been ingrained into the German culture. It is no longer so, and it is more difficult to envisage a return to the political conformism that the Nazis imposed and exploited. However, in light of the interpretations of authoritarian extremism that we discussed and also of the special circumstances that may recur, notably an economic depression, there is no reason to exclude the possibilities of authoritarianism. No society—even less the German society—is immune!

---

[5]After World War II, Germany was divided into two: West Germany (German Federal Republic, with a democratic constitution) and East Germany (German People's Republic, with Communist party domination).

THE RETURN OF THE EXTREME RIGHT IN EUROPE

Almost half a century after the defeat of the Nazis and Fascists in Europe, right-wing extremism is surfacing again. The ideology revolves around the same old staples: racism, xenophobia, and nationalism. Its springboard is also what it was in the early thirties: the insecurities and anxieties that arise from an economic crisis, unemployment, and international tensions. Its political manifestations, tame for the time being, may well become increasingly intransigent.

The spearhead of the extreme right today is in France—it is the National Front, a party organized and led by Jean-Marie Le Pen. It is dedicated to the preservation of the purity of the French nation and its culture, and is directed against the immigrant workers (and their families) in France. There are more than 4.5 million immigrants in France today and at least half of them are Muslims from North Africa or from the African colonies of France. Le Pen's movement seeks to deny them citizenship, education, and employment and to repatriate them. Muslims speak a different tongue; they have a different religion (mosques have sometimes been built close to the French medieval cathedrals), different laws and customs (some practice polygamy), and they produce children at a much higher rate than French citizens or Europeans. They refuse to assimilate; they want to maintain their cultural, religious, and linguistic identity as well as their attachment to the countries they came from. However, since they also want to and do work in France, they are accused of depriving French citizens of jobs at a time when unemployment remains high.

In the elections for the European Parliament in 1984 and again in the legislative election of 1986, the French National Front received almost 10 percent of the vote; and finally to the surprise of all Jean-Marie Le Pen received 14.4 percent of the vote in the presidential election held on April 24, 1988. In many opinion polls more than one-third of the French "agree" or "agree more or less" with the positions taken by Jean-Marie Le Pen. For a time, the National Front was considered as a transient reaction to special circumstances—the rapid increase of immigrant workers from North Africa and unemployment. It seems, however, to have stabilized. Its hard core may represent less than 10 percent of the French public, but it operates within a favorable climate of opinion that may increase its strength. The major political parties have been unable to settle the status of foreigners and immigrant workers—especially North Africans—and to establish clear criteria for them on how to become citizens or face repatriation. Islamic fundamentalist movements are spreading throughout North Africa—especially in Algeria and Tunisia—and may create domestic and international problems that will provoke a backlash to swell the ranks of Le Pen's movement.

Right-wing parties like the French National Front have mushroomed in England, Belgium, and Holland, while similar movements are developing in Denmark and the Federal Republic of Germany. They have all taken up the same slogans of nationalism, xenophobia, and racism, although they have not yet challenged democracy and the democratic institutions of the countries where they have surfaced. A severe economic or foreign policy crisis could propel them into action against the "aliens" and the "undesirables" in the name of national unity and national independence. Once in power, they could jettison the protections that constitutional government and democracy provide.

In the legislative election held in Denmark on May 9, 1988 the right-wing Progress party received 9 percent of the vote. In the last parliamentary elections held in Austria on October 7, 1990, the extreme right-wing party—the Freedom party—doubled its popular vote to 18 percent from a little over 9 percent in 1986. It stands for full Austrian sovereignty by putting an end to its status of neutrality, favors restrictions on immigration and the flow of immigrants from outside, notably Eastern Europe, and a return to "law and order." Its members are young—under forty—and many of its slogans are reminiscent of those used by pro-Nazi sympathizers in the 1930s.

Right-wing authoritarian movements, which may be joined by disgruntled Communists, are spreading in the Soviet Union and Eastern Europe. They are all nationalist, xenophobic, and anti-Semitic. One such movement—Pamyat—in the Russian republic favors the reestablishment of old traditional and religious Russian values and emphasizes the primacy of Russia. It is anti-Western and antidemocratic, and its following has been growing. In Yugoslavia, new parties have sprung up in the various republics, stressing their independence and the subordination or exclusion of nonnationals. This is notably the case with Croatia, where right-wing nationalists have gained a majority. In the name of nationalism, right-wing movements in Romania were formed by the Hungarian minority, only to provoke the organization of counterformations by Romanian nationalists. In some instances, such movements have assumed many of the characteristics associated with nazism or with pre-World War II Fascists—uniforms, emblems, martial outlook, and paramilitary organizations. They all threaten the new and fragile democracies as they did in the years between World War I and World War II. Extremists are active everywhere—even in the United States—to which we now turn.

THE EXTREME RIGHT IN THE UNITED STATES

"Extremism," writes Seymour Martin Lipset with particular reference to American political history, "describes the violation, through action or advocacy, of the democratic political process." Despite sporadic flareups from what has come to be called the American "extreme" or "radical" right, the democratic process in the United States has held remarkably well. Extremist movements hardly ever succeeded in synthesizing their various negations into a program or an ideology or in transforming them into some kind of positive political formula in order to seek, let alone gain, broad national support and political power.

The strains and stresses of American society, however, have spawned extremist movements. Most but not all of these have come from the right. They have been movements of disaffection appearing in "periods of incipient change"; they are addressed to groups that "feel deprived" or feel "that they have been deprived of something they consider important" and also to particular groups whose "rising aspirations lead them to realize that they have always been deprived of something they now want."[6] Under such circumstances, and unless there is a deep commitment to democracy, the growth of authoritarian movements becomes a distinct possibility. Underlying economic factors have always played a crucial role in the rise of extremist movements, but in the American experience ethnic, racial, and religious factors have been more important. Only since World War II have economic as well as international and genuinely ideological political factors begun to gain prominence.

The Know-Nothings

One of the earliest extremist movements was the Know-Nothing party that developed in New England, with particular strength in Massachusetts, in the 1820s. It was primarily composed of workers and artisans who feared that the influx of immigrants would depress their wages and drive them out of work. They advocated the exclusion of immigrants and wanted to prevent their participation in politics. Direct action was often taken against foreigners: members were supposed to "know nothing" about such action. Even if wages appeared to be the central issue, psychological factors played an important role. In an expanding economy, there could be work both for immigrant workers and also for the indigenous Anglo-Saxons. But the very fact that "foreigners" would attain the income of the native workers appeared to the latter an affront to their position and status within the community.

The Ku Klux Klan

The Ku Klux Klan (KKK) emerged in the South right after the Civil War, to intimidate blacks and thwart the federal measures taken to give them citizenship and extend constitutional rights after they had been freed. It was a regional movement based on community and vigilante organizations and gangs, designed to keep blacks out of politics and the economy, to deprive them of access to property, and to keep them at the level of farmhands and unskilled workers. It also kept a tight control on all whites suspected of showing tolerance and sympathy to blacks. In the years following World War I, the Klan had a particularly strong revival, emerging not only as the advocate of white supremacy but also as the champion of "Protestant" and native superiority over all immigrant and non-Protestant religious groups. It became the proponent of the purity of Americans—against Italians, Jews, Mexicans, Japanese, and so on. At one point in the 1920s, it numbered more than 4 million members and extended beyond the South into the Southwest and California. It exerted a strong influence over the Southern state legislatures.

The Klan did not directly challenge the Constitution. It gave it, however, a special interpretation favoring state rights and state autonomy. It was unwilling

---

[6]Seymour Martin Lipset and Earl Raab, *The Politics of Unreason*, p. 428.

to see individual protection and civil right extended to the groups and the minorities it had singled out. It favored restrictive and repressive legislation, and when it was not forthcoming, resorted to direct violence with burnings, intimidation, evictions, and not infrequently lynchings.

Like the Know-Nothings, the Ku Klux Klan's membership consisted of low-income and low-status groups: artisans, shopkeepers, unskilled workers, and farmers who had moved from the farm to small towns. Their leadership came from petty officials—police officers, small-town businessmen, realtors, and an assortment of veterans. Local ministers of various Protestant denominations played an important role and added biblical zest and justification to the movement, especially in the campaign against Catholics and Jews. In general, the movement preached religious orthodoxy and conformity, the simple values of rural life and the small town against the big city, and was against American entanglements abroad. It was fearful of industrialization and modernization because they were changing American society and shifting the weight of population and economic and political power into the cities and away from the countryside. The movement against the immigrants was a desperate effort to vindicate the position of white, small-town, low- and middle-class Protestant America, and to maintain its economic, social, and political status in a changing world.

Father Coughlin

The first genuine ideological and national extremist right-wing movement was spearheaded by Father Charles E. Coughlin, a Catholic priest, between 1928 and 1940—the years of the Great Depression. Unemployment peaked at a level of about 9 to 10 million until 1939, despite the New Deal measures. Not only did blue-collar and white-collar workers suffer, but also the farmers, the middle classes, and many of the manufacturing and trading groups. Fascism had triumphed in Italy, and the Hitler movement had begun its upward climb in Germany. Democracy, as we have seen, was on the defensive, and socioeconomic conditions in the United States were ripe for a strong movement against it. Father Coughlin tried to exploit all this.

His movement had many of the characteristics of an authoritarian right-wing movement similar to those in Italy and Germany. First, it purported to be a mass movement. According to surveys conducted at the time, almost one-third of the American people "approved" of what Father Coughlin said. What he said was not addressed to native Americans. It did not pit them against immigrants: it almost did the reverse. It struck at the major American institutions and the elites, pitting the "small man" against the "establishment."

A second important feature of the movement was its anti-Semitism. It endorsed the racist doctrines of the Nazis and described Jews in the same racist terms. But there were other special factors—one of them manifestly religious, exploiting the Catholic bias against the Jewish faith. It viewed the Jews as an "internationalist element," distinct from the American melting pot. The infamous and malicious *Protocols of the Elders of Zion*, which, as we have seen,

Hitler had publicized, were frequently broadcast and printed in the various pamphlets of the movement.

Its third feature was anticommunism. Communism was a threat both because of its antireligious appeal and also because of its emphasis on class. This was in opposition to the national and communitarian philosophy Father Coughlin wished to impart.

Although a staunch nationalist and an isolationist, Father Coughlin began to lean increasingly in the direction of the Nazi and the Italian models, favoring support of both countries. Just before the demise of his movement in 1940 (by this time its popularity had waned, and at the beginning of the war it was outlawed) he identified fully with the cause of the Nazis to the point of declaring himself to be a "Fascist."

His program had all the familiar "antis": it was anti-elite, anti-Semitic, anti-internationalist (except, as noted above, his support for Hitler and Mussolini), anti-democratic, anti-liberal, anti-capitalist, and against the Constitution. It was one of the first movements to directly advocate the overhaul of the Constitution of the United States. It also suggested a new social order against *both* big capital and big labor. The name of the movement, characteristically enough, was The Union Party for Social Justice, and it merged with other extremist groups to form the National Union. It preached unifying and communitarian themes.

The social configuration of its support was not dissimilar from the one found in the early stage of nazism and fascism. It came from lower middle-class groups and from rural areas and small towns; there was considerable support among the middle classes, and higher support among Catholics and the unemployed in the urban and industrial centers.

Joseph McCarthy

It was a convergence of many factors that both sharpened and deepened the content and the thrust of the American extreme right in the 1950s. The major ones were similar to those that accounted for the emergence of fascism in Italy after World War I: profound discontent with the settlement that followed World War II. Many in the United States felt that the Russians had strengthened their position and began to search for scapegoats. Senator Joseph McCarthy found one in "international communism" and its agents in the United States. Singlehandedly, he began to mount a campaign against not only Communists but also their sympathizers—left-wingers and liberals—the so-called "fellow travelers." The term included intellectuals, university professors, members of the "Northeastern establishment," bankers, and supporters of the United Nations. Not only Democrats but also Republican leaders—even President Eisenhower—were accused. McCarthy, in many highly publicized appearances and through investigations conducted by his Senate Committee, discovered "hundreds," of card-carrying Communists in the State Department. He claimed that agree-

Senator Joseph McCarthy, whipping up anti communist hysteria in New York in 1954.

ments at Yalta and Potsdam during and after World War II were engineered by the fellow travelers to give undue benefits and advantages to the Soviet Union and to deprive the United States of its victory.

While McCarthy never managed to organize a national movement, national response was widespread and positive. This was the period of "The Great Fear,"[7] when wholesale purges of "crypto-Communists" occurred in the federal government, universities, the army, and the trade unions. It was also a movement which began to show clearly the impact that the media of communication, especially TV, can have in creating a "national" state of mind. McCarthy and his activities were widely publicized.

Conspiracy theories are common in extremist movements. With Hitler, it was the conspiracy of the Jews and the failure of the civilians to support their soldiers in war that played an important role. The conspiracy of the Communists against the United States was a notion that satisfied many conservatives and appealed to others who felt that the international position of the United States was slipping. In a peculiar way the McCarthy crusade also appealed to the forces of nativism that we found in the Know-Nothings and the Klan. There were the "ins," the good Americans; and the "outs," the Communists, fellow travelers, crypto-Communists, immigrants, left-wing liberals, and so on.

---

[7]David Caute, *The Great Fear: The Anti-Communist Purge Under Truman and Eisenhower.*

The John Birch Society

Founded in 1958 by a candy manufacturer, Robert H. W. Welch, Jr. (who died in 1985), the John Birch Society has maintained that it exists to educate the public on the threat of communism. Its official ideology can be found in the John Birch Society Blue Book, and it should be noted that in contrast to other extremist organizations it does not espouse political violence.

The movement, named after a captain in World War II killed by the Chinese and seen as the first "hero" of the Cold War, opposes social and welfare legislation. Its followers consider social security as socialism and they call for the elimination of a graduated income tax. They claimed that Presidents Roosevelt, Truman, and Eisenhower were Communists and conspired with Russia to deplete U.S. power. The John Birch Society disapproved of all efforts leading to an arms treaty with the Soviet Union and would like the United States to withdraw its recognition of the USSR. In addition, they oppose the United Nations. Welch said that he wanted the country to move toward "a militant form of Americanism."

During its heyday in the 1960s, the Society had 100,000 members, an annual budget of $8 million, and 400 bookstores nationwide carrying its message. Recently, under the leadership of Thomas Hill, membership seems to have stabilized around 50,000. It publishes a monthly newsletter, the *Bulletin*, and *American Opinion*, a magazine issued eleven times a year.

Fringe Movements

Minuscule groups of extremists keep mushrooming throughout the land. They constantly question political compromise and political tolerance, sometimes through the pulpit and the ballot, often with overt acts of defiance and violence. By and large, they preach white supremacy and many trace their origins to the KKK; many are overtly anti-Semitic and some are against Catholics and the new immigrants from Asiatic and Latin American countries. They all share a common anticommunist and anti-Soviet posture, drawing from the literature of the John Birch Society and the legacy of McCarthyism. In line with the evangelicals, they actively preach a return to traditional and moral values, but they do not shy away from violence. They appeal to poor farmers and the marginal groups in small towns in Middle America—those most threatened by economic changes. It appears that each group acts independently of the others and that the seeds of intolerance and militancy they sow have not found fertile soil. What are some of these movements? And what is their overall impact, if any?

1. "Minutemen" was the label for an extremist vigilante organization founded in 1960 by Robert DePugh, a Missouri businessman, with the purpose of training Americans in guerrilla warfare They would be used to fight the Communists after they had taken over the United States (an event the Minutemen saw as highly probable) either through internal subversion or invasion. Membership estimates ranged from DePugh's claim of a high of 25,000 to a low of

500. Several groups of Minutemen were seized with illegal arms caches that included rifles, submachine guns, explosives, mortars, and antitank weapons. DePugh himself was arrested in July 1969 and sentenced to a ten-year prison term. Little has been heard of the Minutemen since then.

2. The Populist party, founded in 1984 as an arm of the Liberty Lobby, is intensely nationalistic and racist. Their motto is "America First." Claiming to be a revival of the nineteenth-century Populists, the party managed to receive 66,000 votes in the 1984 presidential race (they were on the ballot in not more than twelve states).

The agenda of the Populist party is quite clear. "[It] will not permit any racial minority, through control of the media, culture distortion or revolutionary political activity, to divide or fractionalize the majority of the society in which the minority lives." Its weekly newsletter, *The Spotlight*, claimed a subscription list of "over" 50,000 in October 1984.

3. Lyndon LaRouche has formed a group within the Democratic party with some notable success in party primaries. He claims that there is an international conspiracy against the United States that includes Pope John Paul and Queen Elizabeth of England and has accused many prominent American statesmen of conspiring with Soviet leaders to impair U.S. power.

In 1980, LaRouche received 177,784 votes in Democratic presidential primaries, representing 0.09 percent of the total votes cast. In 1982, a LaRouche candidate opposing Maryland Congresswoman Barbara Mikulski, Debra Freeman, won 19 percent of the Democratic primary votes.[8]

4. Some of the smaller groups include (a) The Liberty Lobby, founded in 1955 in Washington, D.C., which claims a membership of some 200,000 who subscribe to the *Liberty Ledger* and the monthly *Liberty Letters;* (b) the Nationalist Socialist White People's Party, under the leadership of Lincoln Rockwell, with a handful of members; (c) the National Socialist Party of America, based in Chicago; (d) the National Association for the Advancement of White People, with about 6000 members; (e) the National Socialist Movement, founded in 1975 with chapters in twenty-two states; (f) the White Aryan Resistance, based in California with about 5000 members; and (g) the Invisible Empire of the Knights of the Ku Klux Klan, committed to the protection and maintenance of distinctive institutions, rights, privileges, principles and ideals of pure Americanism and to the defense and preservation of the Constitution as originally written and intended.

In the last decade extremist groups have remained active. In times of discontent, depression, and violence in the big cities, the gospel of Christian white supremacy finds support and votes. In the Louisiana election for the U.S. Senate held on October 7, 1990, David Duke, identified with the KKK, received 44 percent of the vote. In great part it was of course a protest vote, an expression

---

[8]"The LaRouche Democrats," Steven Strasser and Ann McDaniel, *Newsweek*, April 16, 1984, p. 31.

of dissatisfaction with economic conditions, especially by the lower middle class rather than a vote for the philosophy of the KKK. But all extremist parties thrive on protest and dissatisfaction. Similarly, violence in the cities—especially in New York City—accounts for the growth of the Klan membership and the emergence of other extremist groups.

Among the white supremacist groups, the Aryan Nation and some of its off-shoots—such as the Anti-Tax Vigilante Group, the White Patriot Party, and the Christian Identity—continue to agitate. Some of their spokespersons claim that blacks are "God's mistake" and that Jews are "Satan's offspring." These extremist groups are scattered through the Midwest and the far West but seem to have lost some ground in the South.

There are also a number of minuscule "hate groups," which according to the U.S. Attorney General totaled about 200 in 1989. They are responsible for numerous incidents of racial violence in schools, churches, and synagogues. The most extremist group among them are the "skinheads," consisting mostly of 13- to 25-year-olds. They indulge in indiscriminate acts of violence, almost for the sake of violence. Without central organization, leadership, or ideology, they simply defy and reject the norms and substance of civilized life. But there are also some 3000 or so neo-Nazi skinheads, predominantly in the Pacific Northwest, responsible for many acts of violence.

A feeling of frustration, resentment, and impotence has always provided the best climate for the growth of extremist movements, which invariably come up with simple answers to complex problems and nationalist solutions to endemic social and economic difficulties. Currently, they are dispersed, but in a turbulent political landscape, the voices of violence and "unreason" could grow loud, and coalesce under one leader. Under certain circumstances—economic depression or military setbacks—they could unite to challenge the foundation of constitutional government and democracy.

BIBLIOGRAPHY

Abel. Theodore. *The Nazi Movement: Why Hitler Came to Power.* New York: Atheneum, 1965.

Allen, William Sheridan. *The Nazi Seizure of Power: The Experience of a Single German Town.* New York: New Viewpoint, 1973.

Aycoberry, Pierre. *The Nazi Question.* New York: Pantheon Books, 1981.

Bracher, K. Dietrich. *The German Dictatorship.* New York: Praeger, 1970.

Bruce, Steve. *The Rise and Fall of the New Christian Right: Conservative Protestant Politics in America, 1978–1988.* New York: Oxford University Press, 1990.

Bullock, Alan. *Hitler: A Study in Tyranny.* New York: Harper & Row, 1971.

Burnham, James. *The Managerial Revolution.* Bloomington: Indiana University Press, 1973.

Carsten, F. F. *The Rise of Fascism.* Berkeley: University of California Press, 1980.

Dalton, Russell, and Manfred Kuechler (eds.). *Challenging the Political Order: New Social and Political Movements in Western Democracies.* New York: Oxford University Press, 1990.

———— . *Interpretations of Facism.* Cambridge, Mass.: Harvard University Press, 1977.

DeFelice, Renzo. *Fascism: An Informal Introduction to Its Theory and Practice.* New Brunswick, N.J.: Transaction Books, 1976.

Fried, Richard M. *Nightmare in Red: The McCarthy Era in Perspective.* New York: Oxford University Press, 1990.

Gallo, Max. *Mussolini's Italy.* New York: Macmillan, 1973.

Germani, Gino, *Authoritarianism, Fascism, and National Populism.* Transaction Books, New Brunswick, N.J. 1978.

Gregor, A. James. *Interpretations of Fascism.* Morristown, N.J.: General Learning Press, 1975.

Heiden, Konrad, *Der Fuehrer.* Boston: Beacon Press, 1969.

Hitler, Adolf. *Mein Kampf.* Boston: Houghton Mifflin, 1962.

Joes, Anthony James. *Fascism in the Comtemporary World.* Boulder, Colo.: Westview Press, 1978.

Karsten, F. L. *Rise of Fascism.* Berkeley, University of California Press, 1980.

Kater, Michael. *The Nazi Party.* Cambridge, Mass.: Harvard University Press, 1983.

Langer, Walter C. *The Mind of Adolf Hitler.* New York: New American Library, 1978.

Laqueur, Walter. *Fascism: A Reader's Guide.* Berkeley: University of California Press, 1976.

———— , and George Mosse. *International Fascism.* New York: Harper, 1966.

Lee, Stephen J. *The European Dictatorships, 1918–1945.* New York: Routledge, 1987.

———— . *The Making of a Stormtrooper.* Princeton, N.J.: Princeton University Press, 1979.

Merkl, Peter H. *Political Violence Under the Swastika,* Princeton, N.J.: Princeton University Press, 1975.

Mussolini, Benito. *My Autobiography.* New York: Scribner's, 1928.

Neumann, Franz. *Behemoth: The Structure and Practice of National Socialism,* 2nd ed. New York: Oxford University Press, 1944.

Pinson, K. S. *Modern Germany,* 2nd ed. New York: Macmillan, 1966.

Reich, Wilhelm. *The Mass Psychology of Fascism.* New York: Farrar, Straus & Giroux, 1970.

Smith, Dennis Mack. *Mussolini's Roman Empire.* New York: Viking, 1976.

Tannenbaum, Edward R. *The Fascist Experience.* New York: Basic Books, 1972.

The American Right

Barnhart, Joe Edward. *The Southern Baptist Holy War.* Texas Monthly Press, 1988.

Bell, Daniel (ed.). *The Radical Right.* New York: Doubleday, 1964.

Bozell, L. Brent. *Dialogues in Americanism.* Chicago: H. Regnery Co., 1964.

Caute, David. *The Great Fear: The Anti-Communist Purge Under Truman and Eisenhower.* New York: Simon and Schuster, 1978.

Crawford, Alan. *Thunder on the Right: The "New Right" and the Politics of Resentment.* New York: Pantheon Books, 1980.

Epstein, Benjamin, and Arnold Forster. *The Radical Right.* New York: Vintage, 1967.

Fachre, Gabriel J. *Religious Right and Christian Faith.* Erdmans, 1982.

King, Desmond S. *The New Right: Politics, Markets and Citizenship.* Chicago: Dorsey Press, 1987.

Kymlicka, B. B., and Jean V. Mathews. *The Reagan Revolution?* Chicago: Dorsey Press, 1988.

Lipset, Seymour Martin, and Earl Raab. *The Politics of Unreason: Right Wing Extremism in America, 1790–1970*. Chicago: University of Chicago Press, 1978.

Macedo, Stephen. *The New Right v. the Constitution*. Cato Institute, 1986.

Roelfs, H. Mark. *Ideology and Myth in American Politics: A Critique of a National Political Mind*. Boston: Little, Brown, 1976.

Shapsmeir, Edward. *Political Parties and Civic Action Groups*. Westport, Conn.: Greenwood Press, 1981.

Viguerie, Richard A. *Establishment vs. the People: Is a New Populist Revolt on the Way?* Chicago: Regnery Gateway, Inc., 1984.

Four

OLD VOICES AND NEW

1. Nationalisms . . . and Internationalist Movements
2. The Religious Impulse: Liberation Theology and Religious Fundamentalism
3. Feminism
4. Environmentalism
5. Ideologies of Revolution

What is truth? asked jesting Pilate,
and would not stay for an answer.

Francis Bacon
"Of Truth"

*T*his part deals with several significant movements and ideologies now being voiced throughout the world. They include (1) nationalism and some of its contemporary manifestations, often referred to as "ethnonationalism"; (2) liberation theology and religious fundamentalism, which we discuss under the heading of "The Religious Impulse"; (3) feminism; and (4) environmentalism. We also survey (5) some extremist revolutionary ideologies.

All these ideologies and movements, so disparate at first glance, have a number of things in common: all of them borrow a great deal from past ideologies—nationalism, anarchism, early Christian thought, utopian socialism, Marxism and Leninism, and even early liberal and democratic thought. The wine seems to be the same old heady wine, but one will find it mixed with many recent vintages. All of these ideologies demand the realization of long-unfulfilled imperatives: they all seek redemption "now and here." "This is our world" and "we must set it right," they all seem to affirm. They all share a profound, almost religious, sense of righteousness, of what is morally right and must be done, and of what is morally unacceptable and has to be destroyed. Some put great emphasis on human will—on our freedom to change and improve radically the circumstances that surround us. Others, however, notably nationalism and religious fundamentalism, invoke traditional values. With the collapse of communism and the resurgence of democracy, some threaten democratic institutions, as we point out in our concluding chapter.

Chapter
9

Nationalisms

This happy breed of men, this little world,
This precious stone set in the silver sea . . .
This blessed plot, this earth, this realm, this England

Shakespeare

Richard II

Without a country . . . you are the bastards of humanity. Soldiers
without banner . . . you will find neither faith nor protection.

Mazinni to the Italians, c. 1850

*P*eople who once every four years watch the Olympics or who occasionally
turn their TV to U.N. debates cannot help but marvel at the number of
nation–states with their delegates, flags, athletes, diplomats, and national an-
thems stressing the same themes—pride and strength, unity and loyalty to the
fatherland or the motherland, military glory, a call to action and sacrifice, an
assertion of superiority, and a demand for utter devotion. "Our fight for our
land will never cease; it was ours and it will be ours forever and ever" (Uganda);
"Fatherland, fatherland . . . thy sons swear to breathe their last on thine alter"
(Mexico); "Onward *enfants de la patrie* . . . The day of glory is before you"
(France); "Germany, Germany above all others" (Germany); "Sweet land of liberty . . . " and so on. Ours continues to be a world of nation–states. Today there
are more than one hundred and seventy. Within nation–states there are also
ethnic groups and "nationalities"—Basques, Bretons, Tamils, Catalans, Corsicans, Armenians, Macedonians, Moldavians, Kurds, Ukrainians, Georgians,
Ibos, Azeris, Welsh and Scots, Native Americans, and so forth—each with their
own identity.

Nationalism has proved to be one of the most tenacious ideological bonds
binding human beings together into separate political communities. Its values
may vary, the particular content of the citizen's attachments may change, but
fundamentally the nationalism is identified in terms of a common feeling of togetherness that separates the "we" and the "they." Nations are invariably defined in terms of a *community* and in terms of the *loyalty* of the individual to

the community. It is a common mind, with common habits—moral, social, cultural, and political—common ancestors, common character, common race, common symbols, common language, a corporate will, and a common soul. Loyalty is invariably described in terms of dedication, sacrifice, subordination, love, and affection. Nations are either a "motherland" or a "fatherland," evoking the obedience and affection that children supposedly owe to their parents.

Even if we take it for granted, nationalism is something relatively recent. It is primarily a political ideology that developed in Europe in the latter part of the eighteenth century and throughout the nineteenth century. After the end of World War II, in 1945, it spread to the so-called Third World (the then colonies in Africa, Asia, and the Middle East), and also Latin America. Like all political ideologies, nationalism is an instrument for the acquisition of political power by certain groups and the organization of political power on the basis of new principles—notably popular participation. Hugh Seton–Watson defines nationalism as "a policy of creating national consciousness within a politically unconscious population,"[1] and he notes that its purpose was precisely the mobilization of a population behind new leaders and social forces. Nationalism was, and remains, a unifying ideology aimed at manufacturing consent on the basis of a strong appeal and symbols of identification. Its aim is to generate emotional supports, create a state of exaltation and sacrifice, and provide for loyalty.

NATIONALITY, NATION–STATES, STATES, AND NATIONALISM

Some clarifications are needed in order to better understand the dynamics of nationalism.

Nationality denotes an ethnic and cultural identity, based on common values. A *state*, on the other hand, is a political organization holding and exercising supreme power through its various agencies over a given people within a given territory. A state may include a number of "nationalities." The most illustrious example of such a state was the Austro-Hungarian Empire that until 1918 was a political administrative organization governing Slavs, Slovenes, Croatians, Italians, Montenegrins, Hungarians, Poles, Austrians, Czechs, and quite a few others. A state, in other words, may be "multinational." The best examples today are the Soviet Union and Yugoslavia and, as we will see, both the Soviet Union and Yugoslavia are going through a process of dissolution as the various nationalities assert their separate autonomous claims to the point of demanding political independence. Multinational "states" seem to be in the process of being devoured by their "ethnic" and "nationality" parts!

---

[1] Hugh Seton–Watson, *Nations and States*, p. 449.

A *nation–state,* in contrast to a nationality (which is not a state) and to a state (which is not necessarily based upon a common nationality), is supposed to be *both a state and a nationality.*[2]

Nationality and Nationalism: Objective and Subjective Factors

The terms *nation* and *nationality* began to appear only in the seventeenth century, to denote the emergence of a consciousness of a common identity of people in a given territory. People in a given location began to gain awareness of something they had in common as distinguished from others. There was a common sharing and a common predisposition for sharing. A people's feelings and a common predisposition accounts for the nation. The nation-state may be viewed, to put it very simply, as the creation of the individuals who comprise it; it exists and derives its existence from the support and the consent the individuals give to it. As a French publicist put, *it is the result of a contract or of a "daily referendum."*[3]

The nation may also be viewed as having a separate reality outside and beyond the consent of the individuals who make it up. It is an objective and historical reality that overwhelms the individuals. Historical and other reasons give it a transcendental quality and a moral superiority that impose themselves upon the individuals. According to this view, individual freedom and morality cannot be attained except within the nation and in terms of the national values and beliefs. The nation, in other words, is "real"; the individual is not.

Objective Factors   The most common traits with which nationality is associated remain: (1) language; (2) religion; (3) a consciousness of common traditions and history and a will to maintain them; and (4) a common territory. When no common territory exists, as was the case with the Jews and the Greeks and the Poles, it was the memory of the common territory they occupied in the past that kindles their desire to regain it or to reclaim it. The same is true today for Armenians, Azeris, Kurds and many many other nationalities.

The authors of nationalism have stressed at different times one or another of these objective factors.

Religion was particularly important in the period of the formation of national consciousness. Religious wars were fought to both emancipate the state

---

[2]Curiously enough, the most succinct definition of a nation was given by Joseph Stalin: "A nation is an historically evolved, stable community of language, territory, economic life and psychological makeup manifested in a community of culture." Add "common political authority," and you have a nation–state. Joseph Stalin, *Marxism and the National Question,* Foreign Languages Publishing House, Moscow 1954, p. 8.

[3]Ernest Renan, "What Is a Nation?" in Hans Kohn, *Nationalism: Its Meaning and History,* pp. 135–140.

from the Papacy and to create internal unity, which was endangered both by papal control and by the existence of religious minorities.

Language was an important criterion used by a number of authors, especially German. It was a common and distinct vehicle that bound people together, creating a special bond among its users. But, as the case of Switzerland shows conclusively, it is not a necessary condition.

Race was used primarily, as we have seen, in the twentieth century by the Nazis to show the unique traits of the German nation. It is supposed to refer to specific biological traits which are not always clearly perceived or agreed upon.

Ethnicity is a broader term that may or may not include race but usually refers to a number of the common cultural attributes. Both race and ethnicity are terms indiscriminately used in Europe as well as in Asia and Africa. Some groups perceive themselves or are perceived by others as a "race" or as an "ethnic group" and often as both.

The *common past* has been constantly invoked, and when it could not be easily found, every effort was made to manufacture it by rewriting history.

Geography—a common territorial basis—is invariably invoked. Nations like an individual had to have "a home," a space under the sun.

Subjective Factors   All the objective traits we outlined—religion, language, common history, and so on—may exist and may be commonly shared by a given "nationality." Nationalism, however, becomes an ideology and a movement only when it translates this self-consciousness into a demand to form a state. The subjective element is an element of will and purpose. Nationalism asserts the validity of the objective factors of nationality for *certain* political purposes; it affirms their uniqueness and often their exclusiveness. It is not only the will to live together but to have a government. It is the assertion that such a purpose has an inherent claim to be heard and to realize itself; it is a purpose that is presumed to be morally just. In this sense nationalism is, as Elie Kedourie writes in one of the most penetrating studies on the subject, "a doctrine *invented* in Europe at the beginning of the nineteenth century. . . . [It] holds that humanity is naturally divided into nations, that nations are known by their characteristics . . . and that the only legitimate type of government is *national* self-government."[4]

Nothing better exemplifies the differences between those who stress objective factors from those who rely on subjective ones in defining a nation—the first relying on history, language, religion, and tradition and the second on subjective factors—than the conflict between Germany and France over the provinces of Alsace and Lorraine occupied and annexed by the Germans in 1871. Ernest Renan, the French publicist, in his famous essay *What Is a Nation?* (1882), was willing to accept the verdict of the people given through a referendum. The Germans, on the other hand, asserted their claims in terms

---

[4]Elie Kedourie, *Nationalism*, p. 77.

of historical right. "These provinces are ours by the right of the sword," wrote a German nationalist, "and we shall rule them by the virtue of a higher right. . . . *We desire, even against their will, to restore them to themselves*" [emphasis added].[5]

Self-determination is the demand made by a nationality to become a state. It became a doctrine when it was expressly stipulated in the famous Fourteen Points that President Woodrow Wilson issued as the guidelines for building a new political order in Europe after World War I.

"Self-determination," Wilson declared, "is an imperative principle of action, which statesmen will . . . ignore at their peril." World War I, he claimed, "had its roots in the disregard of the rights of small nations and of nationalities which lacked the union and the force to make good their claim to determine their own allegiance and their own form of political life." He suggested among other things, in the form of guidelines for the Peace Conference that was to follow the hostilities that ended in 1918, "a readjustment of the frontiers of Italy . . . along clearly recognizable lines"; "the freest opportunity of autonomous development" for the peoples of Austria–Hungary; the redrawing of some of the frontiers in the Balkans "along historically established lines of *allegiance* and *nationality*"; "an absolutely unmolested opportunity of autonomous development" for the national minorities within Turkey; "an independent Polish state . . . inhabited by indisputably Polish populations."[6]

It is in the name of nationalism and self-determination that old multinational political organizations and empires gradually broke down until by the end of World War I most European nationalities became nation–states. The Austro-Hungarian and the Ottoman empires broke up under the force of nationalist movements. The Czarist Russian Empire showed signs of disintegration and the Bolsheviks stepped in to consolidate their control; but now that control, too, has begun to unravel.

ROUSSEAU AND NATIONALISM

Everybody seems to agree that the great French philosopher, Jean-Jacques Rousseau (1717–1778) is the "father" of modern nationalism. For some he was a romantic—stressing emotions instead of reason and believing that psychological attachments were far more potent than agreements derived from rational calculations and expectations. The nation was an emotional and a spiritual entity. For others his theory of popular sovereignty helped identify the state with the people; still others consider that Rousseau was the first to see in nations the best expression of community life. Others see in him the precursor of totalitarian-

---

[5]Kohn, *Nationalism*, p. 61.

[6]Presented on February 11, 1918. Cited in Alan P. Grimes and Robert H. Horowitz, *Modern Political Ideologies*, pp. 501–503.

ism—the development of irrational and conformist national themes couched in terms of national superiority that led to the subordination of the individual.

It was Rousseau's theory of the "general will," but more particularly the distortion of this theory by others, that leads us directly to the exaltation of communitarian and national feeling. For Rousseau the general will was in fact the will of all the people—but only on condition that they were right! The people were sovereign and would and could act rationally only if they abandoned their direct and immediate personal interests and acted as social beings by putting the interests of the whole above their own. His theory assumed that people in a community could reach a consensus. But under what conditions, and how?

Nationalism was to become the answer. By injecting the same values and feelings, by stressing unifying themes, by exalting what unites, by inculcating through education, ritual, and at times even force common national bonds or strengthening those that exist, nationalism would shape the people as a whole to develop a common frame of reference from which an agreement, a general will, would result. Nationalism becomes thus a unifying ideology—a powerful emotional force. "Everything for my fatherland; nothing for myself." The citizen becomes a patriot.

The political leader, the prophet, the legislator is called upon to distill the rules and the institutions that will establish and consolidate a common frame of reference—a feeling of togetherness, a national mind. Moses, according to Rousseau, "gave" to the Jews their nationality of which they were only dimly aware. He built "a nation out of a swarm of wretched fugitives who possessed no arts, no arms, no talents, no virtues, no courage and who—with not a single square foot of territory that they might call their own—were in truth a troop of outcasts upon the face of the earth. . . . He imposed rites upon them and ceremonies to be performed within the bosom of their families. . . . It was Moses who dared transform this gang of servile migrants into a political body— *a free people*."[7]

Mazinni (1805–1872), an Italian nationalist, expressed Rousseau's nationalism even more forcefully by telling the Italians, who were still divided into many states: "Without a country you have neither name, token, voice, nor rights, no admission as brothers into the fellowship of the Peoples. *You are the bastards of humanity.* Soldiers without banner, Israelites among the nations, you will find neither faith, nor protection; none will be sureties for you."[8] The Jewish people took notice and began their long struggle, after the middle of the 19th century in the name of Zionism, for the establishment of Israel.

The French Revolution

It was the French Revolution of 1789 that asserted the sovereignty of the people *and* the nation. But it was also the French Revolution that through its various

---

[7]Grimes and Horowitz, "Considerations on the Government of Poland," p. 469.

[8]Grimes and Horowitz, "The Duties of Man," p. 496. Italics added.

stages highlighted the distortions of Rousseau's ideas. The revolution began as an assertion of individual freedoms and popular sovereignty. It finished with an absolutist ruler—Napoleon—and an expansionist nationalism that changed the map of Europe.

With the overthrow of the monarchy in 1792, the French Revolution quickly established patriotism, the unqualified attachment to the nation–state, as the highest ideal and as the most intimate bond among the people. Rituals, national festivals, symbolisms, national songs were all used to create a solidarity among the French. A system of national education was instituted to propagate patriotic values. Every attempt was made to wipe out regional and linguistic particularisms in favor of cultural unity, territorial integration, and centralization. The republic was to be "one and indivisible." Compliance with the revolution and its policies was promoted everywhere, requiring coercive measures that gradually were transformed into an outright tyranny. A revolutionary leader spoke of "the *tyranny of liberty* against despotism."

The last phase of the revolution produced an expansionist nationalism and a desire to conquer and subdue other peoples in the name of liberty *and* France. French men and women were made to "march in step" with the nationalist ideology, not only in Napoleon's battlefields but also at home. "The citizen is born, lives and dies for the fatherland" was the inscription that all French could read in every municipality where they lived. "Oh sublime people! Accept the sacrifices of my whole being. Happy is the man who is born in your midst; happier is he who can die for your happiness," exclaimed Robespierre. The citizen–patriot gradually became transformed into the citizen–soldier, willing to die for his country. General Charles de Gaulle—the most eminent French political leader of the twentieth century—wrote in the same vein: "France is not really herself unless in the front rank. . . . France cannot be France without greatness."[9]

Thus we find in the manifestation of French nationalism the traits that appear again and again in many national independence movements throughout Europe: a revolutionary fervor associated with the destruction of the aristocracy and the economic and social order it represented; an effort to devise slogans to unify the country and to break down all internal barriers; the creation of new national symbols to mobilize the people and inculcate in them common values, and thus elicit their support; and, finally, the assertion of national virtue and right over individual citizens, and over other peoples as well.

Throughout Europe, nationalism played the same important role in forging tightly integrated communities. It was strongly related to the rise of the middle classes and the destruction of the feudal structures. Politically speaking, it was a vehicle for the acquisition of power by the middle classes by mobilizing the masses as they had never been mobilized before. Controlling "their minds and souls" was a source of far greater power than any ruler or class

---

[9]Charles de Gaulle, *The War Memoirs*, vol. 1, *The Call to Honor* 1940–42 (Transl. by Jonathan Griffin). New York: Simon and Schuster, 1955, p. 3.

appealing to status, tradition, authority, or divine right had ever claimed or possessed before.

Traditional Nationalism

The French nationalism that came with and after the French Revolution was an intensely ideological phenomenon that broke from tradition and the past. It attempted to restructure society and formulate a new way of life, a new nation. This was not the case with traditional nationalisms as they grew in response to the French nationalism, especially in Germany. French nationalism was a matter of will and future oriented. Traditional nationalism, on the other hand, sought its source in the past and was portrayed as a natural phenomenon, not an act of political will.

German nationalists, influenced by Rousseau, naturally selected from his writings what suited them best. Johann von Herder (1744–1803) sought the German national spirit in the "people"—the *Volk*—as it had developed from the time of the German tribes. Herder also "legitimized" nations and nation–states by claiming, as so many others have claimed since, that they were "willed" by God and that the diversity of nations represented His will. Men and women could best fulfill themselves within nations.

Traditional nationalism was reinforced not only by biological and racial arguments but also by cultural ones. The purity of the German language indicated, among other things, its cultural superiority. A German writer, Johann Fichte (1762–1814), called upon Germany to assert its "cultural" supremacy. Some asked that all those speaking the German language be united into one fatherland. Others, long before the Nazis, asserted the racial purity of the Germans. Unification and independence were in the air, and German philosophers extolled the state as the embodiment of the purest ideals of the Germans. It was the Prussian state that ultimately was to become the vehicle of German national unification in 1871.

What characterized German nationalism, therefore, was its conservative emphasis. It looked to the past; it appealed to the establishment groups; it was part of the political tradition and culture, not "made" as in the case of French nationalism during the revolution. The same was true with many Eastern European nationalisms, notably the Russian one, which stressed religion as one of its primary forces and only indirectly race and language.

GERMAN NATIONALISM: THE 1990 VERSION

When Germany became a nation–state in 1870 after defeating France and annexing Alsace and Lorraine (two French provinces), the architect of unification, Chancellor Otto van Bismarck, called it "a victory . . . a divine judgement such as has never been seen, inscribed in letters of fire upon the tablets of history." In these words, he was expressing the traditional and transcendental point of

The Romantic painter Delacroix (1798–1863) painted *Mother-France*. She is portrayed with her children, who flock behind the flag and mount the barricades in the name of Liberty.

view of German nationalism. On October 3, 1990, Germany (after being divided into two after World War II) was reunited. Nobody invoked divine intervention. Unification was accomplished in very much the same way two companies agree to merge. It was accomplished when the peoples of East Germany agreed by open vote to unite with West Germany and accepted its democratic constitution. It was a liberal and democratic unification accomplished by the consent of all parties involved.

In the very heart of Europe where it burned for so long, the fiery vision of German national unity was now inscribed upon the common tablets of economic and social cooperation—a common currency, common social security benefits, the need for investments, and the prospects of employment for all. Chancellor Helmut Kohl, the architect of the unification of 1990, emphasized democracy, pledged to respect the frontiers of the new Germany, and expressed on numerous occasions Germany's responsibility for the atrocities committed by Hitler's regime against other nations and peoples, especially the Jews. He firmly committed the new Germany to membership in the European Common Market. The fatherland was to become a part of Europe instead of striving to dominate Europe. Traditional nationalism appeared to be giving place to a democratic and liberal vision.

British and American Nationalism

The early awakenings of nationalism in England and in America—in England going back to the Elizabethan period and in the United States beginning in the decades before and after the Declaration of Independence—were closely associated with individual freedoms and toleration. Pride in the Constitution and in individual liberties characterized this early Anglo-Saxon form of nationalism. It derived from an individualistic ethic; it reflected the proclamation of the virtues and the initiative of the individual, not of the collectivity. Even a conservative like Edmund Burke, who admired the British national institutions, never subordinated religion, tradition, and rights to the nation. He loved his country only as long as his country served them well. One must love one's country, he pointed out, only if it is "lovely."

As for the United States, the main assertion of nationalism lay in the creation of a republic best exemplified in the Constitution. The country remained wide open to immigration, and as succeeding waves of immigrants came from England, Scandinavia, Germany, Ireland, Italy, Poland, and elsewhere, it lost whatever distinctive ethnic, cultural, or religious characteristics it might have claimed. As for its history—the Boston Tea Party, Lexington, Concord, Bunker Hill, and so on—it was repeated in the schools and in literature. It strengthened and maintained the political symbolism of individual freedoms and constitutional government. American "nationalism" remained political in character: it meant an attachment to the Constitution and to the individual rights spelled out. It was *civic* loyalty that counted.

Both in England and in the United States, of course, the assertions that the fatherland is above the individual were made, but not as often and not as convincingly as in Europe. No nationalist ethic developed that subordinated the individual to the collectivity; no religious, historical, or cultural bonds were imposed upon the individuals in the name of the nation; no uniformities of thought and action were shaped in the name of an overriding national reality and goals.

Of course, such views about American and British nationalism must be taken with a grain of salt. It is true that the two countries have remained relatively far more open and tolerant than others and that nationalism never managed to mobilize the people in one overriding conformist ethic as other nationalisms did in Europe. But there were frequent assertions of national supremacy in both countries. In England, Rudyard Kipling and many others spoke of the "white man's burden"—the self-appointed duty of the British to civilize and educate the masses of the colonial peoples, which were under their control. Both cultural and racist considerations entered into the formulation of English nationalism. By the end of the nineteenth century in the United States as well, there was a strong nationalist ideology with a revealing vocabulary. It claimed a "manifest destiny" for the Anglo-Saxon nations, like the United States, and an important role in world affairs for these nations as they assumed their share of domination and tutelage of "lesser" peoples. Considerations that were religious, political, economic, and not infrequently racist entered into this American form of nationalism. And the effort to exact civic conformity and loyalty around national symbols was and remains ever present. Deviations from the national and political ethos of American liberalism have been often branded as "un-American," and at times was viewed as synonymous with treason.

NATIONALISM IN ACTION: A HISTORICAL OVERVIEW

Three major waves of "nationalism" have swept over the globe ever since the French Revolution, and we are now witnessing a fourth wave. Each and all of them are associated in general (with the German nationalist movement of the nineteenth century being the exception) with the breakdown of multiethnic or colonial empires—the Austro-Hungarian Empire in Central Europe, the Ottoman Empire in the Balkans and the Near East, the colonial empires of Britain, France, and others, and more recently, the weakening of the Soviet Union. Most, beginning with the French Revolution, are also linked with the spread of democratic and liberal ideas, even though Marxism, at its height, provided some ideological tools for the uprisings of the colonial peoples after World War II. We are witnessing, at present, a fourth and last wave—we can call it *ethnonationalism*. It is, as an ideology, an extension and a continuation of past nationalist movements, borrowing from the same vocabulary and, by and large, articulating the demands of distinct ethnic groups living within a state to emancipate themselves by asserting their identity and attempting to translate it into political autonomy or political sovereignty. They all attempt to translate *nationality* into some form of *statehood*.

The first wave solidified France as a nation–state and planted powerful seeds throughout Europe. The seeds grew throughout the nineteenth century into movements for national independence and statehood among many of the European nationalities—Czechs, Slovenes, Hungarians, Serbs, Greeks, Italians, Catalonians, Bulgars, Romanians, and Poles. In the name of nationalism, they stormed the citadels of centralized power and began to nibble at the periphery. Hungary carved its autonomy in what became the Austro-Hungarian Empire in 1867; in the name of antiquity and after centuries of struggle, Greece gained its independence from the Ottoman Empire in 1827; agitation in Italy confronted the last papal states and led, when the Papacy withdrew, to its national unification in 1870. Powerful messages for independence reached out to the Serbians, Czechs, Slovaks, and Croatians. As empires were tottering, new ones were born—in the name of nationalism. Germany became one in 1870, when Prussia was able to unify the various independent principalities, confederations, and kingdoms into one German nation–state. At about the same time, the United States, too, asserted its national unity after a bitter Civil War.

The second wave comes after the end of World War I in 1918. The Austro-Hungarian Empire was definitively dismantled, disgorging a number of national states—Hungary, Czechoslovakia, Austria, Yugoslavia—and bringing Serbs, Croates, Slovenes, and others together; Romania and Bulgaria emerged as independent states; Greece liberated most of its nationals from Turkey. Poland, at long last, became an independent state, accommodating within its borders most

of the Poles. Finland, Latvia, Estonia, and Lithuania rid themselves of the csar-
ist yoke without falling into the centralizing vortex that the Bolsheviks fashioned. By and large, the Wilsonian idea linking national self-determination,
democracy, and statehood was realized—even though democracy did not survive for long! It was impossible, however, to accommodate all ethnic minorities
and to create political borders that corresponded fully to ethnicity and nationality. Some newly founded and some old states continued to include ethnic
groups that longed to join their brothers and sisters across their political borders
or to change the borders of their states and bring them in.

The third wave swells after the end of World War II and follows the logic
of previous nationalist movements. In virtually the whole of the colonial world,
the "lower breeds"—the arrogant term of the British nationalist poet Kipling—
began to demand independence. The colonial empires—England, France,
Belgium, and Holland—began to crumble as the Austro-Hungarian and
Ottoman empires did. The British and the French moved out of the Middle
East to be replaced by new states reflecting nationalist political movements—
Iran, Egypt, Syria, Israel, Tunisia, Morocco—and, in some cases, by artificial ones as in Iraq, Algeria, Libya, Kuwait, the Arab Emirates, Oman, and
Jordan.[10] In the whole of Sub-Saharan Africa, movements of national liberation
led to the formation of new states. Between 1945—the end of World War II—
and today, at least sixty new states emerged in Africa, the Middle East, the
Caribbean, and Asia, most of them basing their right to be so on the principles
of nationality. The logic linking statehood and nationhood—real or alleged—
seemed irresistible.

The New Wave in Communist States

The fourth—but not necessarily the last—wave of nationalism is associated with
the liberalization policies in the Soviet Union and Yugoslavia. Nationalist independence movements have been rising against the Communist regimes that
kept them under control for some seventy years in the Soviet Union and for
almost half a century in Yugoslavia. They clearly show that communism was
unable to tame nationalisms.

Marx, Lenin, Stalin, and Nationalities   Marxist ideology and theory underestimated the force and tenacity of nationalism. It was summed up in the pithy
statement we find in *The Communist Manifesto:* "The working men have no
country." Nationalism, Marxists claimed, was but one of the many ideological
devices used by the capitalist class to distract the workers and to detract them
from their revolutionary mission. Nationalism belonged to the superstructure.

---

[10]For instance, in the 1930 Faisal, the king of Iraq wrote: "I say in my heart full of sadness that there
is not yet an Iraq in the Iraqi people." In the 1950s, before the Algerian rebellion began, Ferhat
Abbas, who became one of its leaders, proclaimed that he had looked in vain everywhere, including
in the cemeteries, to find traces of Algerian nationality.

If religion was the opium of the people, nationalism (and the inevitable wars to which it led) was an equally powerful opiate to give the workers a false ideology and a false sense of identity, contrary to their interests: to eliminate capitalism and to establish a proletarian international socialist world.

Lenin shared the same conviction. But as a great tactician, he had realized, as we noted, that nationalist movements could be used against the imperialist powers—in India, Iran, Egypt, and elsewhere in the colonial world—in order to weaken the capitalist countries and pave the way to their downfall and the collapse of capitalism as a worldwide system. It was a deviation from Marxist theory, but a necessary one to bring about the downfall of capitalism.

Stalin also discussed the concept of nationality and nationalism. "Self-determination" had been used by the Bolsheviks to promote nationalist uprisings against the czar. The right of nationalities to secede was formally granted by the Soviet constitution. However, Stalin never departed from the Marxist notion that nationalism was a bourgeois ideology and that the moment communism had been established—through the expropriation of the means of production and the development of a classless society—the workers, not only in the Soviet Union but throughout the world, would abandon their nationalist attachments. With the development of socialism in the USSR, it was expected that national particularisms would gradually wither away.

Stalin's remarks on nationalities in the Soviet Union are of special interest, especially since they embodied the official Soviet ideology until 1985 and have only been qualified but not quite abandoned yet. (For today's nationalities, see Table 9.1.) Speaking in 1921 to the Tenth Congress of the Communist party of the Soviet Union, he said:

> Whereas private property and capital inevitably disunite people, inflame national enmity and intensify national oppression, collective property and labour just as inevitably bring people closer and undermine national oppression. . . . The establishment of a Soviet system in Russia and the declaration of the right of nations to political secession have brought about a complete change in the relations between the toiling masses of the nationalities of Russia; they have undermined the old national enmity, deprived national oppression of its foundation, won for the Russian workers the confidence of their brothers of other nationalities, not only in Russia, but also in Europe and Asia, and have raised this confidence to a pitch of enthusiasm and readiness to fight for the common cause. The creation of Soviet republics in Azerbaidjan and Armenia has been productive of similar results and has put an end to national collisions and the "age-old" enmity between the Turkish and Armenian toiling masses and between the Armenian and Azerbaidjanian toiling masses. The same must be said of the temporary success of the Soviets in Hungary, Bavaria, Finland and Latvia. The consolidation of the Soviet republics and the abolition of national oppression are two aspects of one and the same process of emancipation of the toilers from imperialist bondage.[11]

---

[11]Joseph Stalin, "Theses on the immediate Task of the Party in Connection with the National Problem," address delivered at the 10th Congress of the Communist Party of the Soviet Union in 1921.

Table 9.1   MAJOR NATIONALITIES IN THE SOVIET UNION: READY TO ASSERT
THEMSELVES

	In thousands	percentage
Russians	143,500	51.73
Ukrainians	43,500	15.68
Uzbeks	14,800	5.34
Byelorussians	9,760	3.52
Kazakhs	7,470	2.69
Tatars	6,600	2.38
Azerbaijanis	6,270	2.26
Armenians	4,580	1.65
Georgians	3,800	1.37
Tajiks	3,450	1.24
Moldavians	3,165	1.14
Lithuanians	2,985	1.08
Turkmenians	2,400	0.87
Kirghiz	2,240	0.81
Germans	2,000	0.72
Chuvash	1,790	0.65
Jews	1,750	0.63
Bashkirs	1,470	0.53
Latvians	1,445	0.52
Mordvinians	1,140	0.41
Poles	1,140	0.41
Estonians	1,030	0.37
Other peoples	11,115	4.00

Source: Peoples of the World: A Historical and Ethnographic Reference Book. Moscow: Nauka, 1988, p. 543.

In the same vein, Krushchev declared in 1959:

"With the victory of Communism on a world-wide scale, state borders will disappear, as Marxism-Leninism teaches. In all likelihood only ethnic borders will survive for a time and even these will probably exist only as a convention. Naturally these frontiers, if they can be called frontiers at all, will have no border guards, customs officials or incidents. . . . "[12]

A Soviet policy on nationalities was based accordingly on the assumption that

1. Soviet socialism would gradually supersede nationalism and nationalities.
2. Soviet socialism would create a new fraternal union.

---

[12]Quoted in Zbigniew K. Brzezinski, The Soviet Bloc. Unity and Discord. Rev. Ed., Harvard University Press, 1967, pp. 451–452.

3. The various forms of national expression—language, culture, historic traditions, literature, religion, and so forth—would give way to the unifying trends of the new socialist culture.
4. The Communist party, the vanguard of the proletariat, would lead the way to the creation of the new fraternal union—and beyond, to internationalism.
5. Finally, the Communist party would gradually grind out nationalist predispositions and particularisms by weeding them out—by force, if necessary, just as we weed the beautiful garden we are growing.

Nationalist Movements and the Soviet Union

Today, both in Yugoslavia (see Figure 9.1), to which we make only passing reference, and in the Soviet Union, demands for autonomy and independence from various national and ethnic groups are escalating.

Figure 9.1 Yugoslavia: Republics and autonomous provinces.

In the Soviet Union, four categories of "nationalities" and correspondingly of nationalist movements should be considered. First, there are the nations of Eastern Europe dominated by the Soviets since 1945 by direct economic and military controls and through the Communist parties the Soviets had managed to impose—Poland, Czechoslovakia, Hungary, East Germany, Romania, and Bulgaria. All of these countries were established nation–states before World War II and have now managed to reclaim their national independence.

Second, there are the Baltic republics annexed by the Soviets during World War II—Estonia, Lithuania, and Latvia—but also a part of Romania (Moldavia). The first three had been independent states and have already proclaimed their intent to become sovereign again. Moldavians are struggling to do likewise.

Third, and most important, there are the "republics" *within* the Soviet Union. They had been a part of the Czarist Empire and of the Soviet Federal Union ever since 1920—the Ukraine, Georgia, Armenia, Byelorussia, Azerbaijan, and others—fifteen of them. Some of them are manifesting their wish to secede—to declare their independence from the Soviet Union.

Finally, there are smaller ethnic and nationalist movements within the individual republics; they are what we call *ethnonationalisms*. They demand autonomy, border changes, and, at times, even outright independence. For instance, the Crimean Tatars wish to move from Uzbekistan back to the fertile lands of the Crimea; the Armenians in Nagorno–Karabakh wish autonomy from Azerbaijan and hope to join their brothers in the Armenian republic, which in turn wishes its independence; the Ossets in Georgia wish to move into the Russian Union Republic, which also aspires to independence; the Volga Tatars wish to form a new republic with the Bashkir Muslims.

Ethnic groups within the various Republics of the Soviet Union have been asserting themselves (Figure 9.2). Some demand autonomy from the Republics within which they are located; others seek to separate from the Republic in which they are situated and join their ethnic brothers and sisters that live in a different Republic—with ethnic identities being defined mostly in terms of religion, language, common traditions, and historical experiences. The move towards ethnic autonomy stretches across the vast Soviet land from Kaliningrad (the former German Konisberg) in the west, where the citizens want to create an autonomous political unit to be known as "people of Konisberg," all the way to Vadlivostok, where Ukrainian settlers want to establish an autonomous Ukrainian Republic in the southeastern corner of the country. In between there are the Poles in Byelorussia who want their autonomy, Moldavians, near the Black Sea, pressing for union with Romania, and Crimean Tatars forced into Uzbekistan near Tashkent by Stalin who wish to return to the Crimean peninsula by the Black Sea. In Kazakhstan, there are more than 100 ethnic groups in conflict with each other. But this gives only a sketchy account of the complexity, intensity and extent of ethnic conflicts. The Volga Tatars, the Mongols, the Uzbek Muslims, and ethnic Germans are demanding autonomies while in Turkmenia the Persian speaking majority is at odds with the Turks each claiming the land of the other.

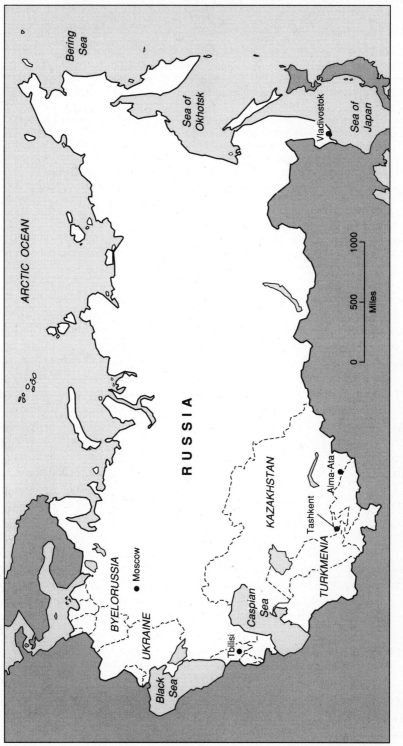

Figure 9.2 Ethnic subdivisions within the Union of Soviet Socialist Republic.

Figure 9.3 Ethnic enclaves in Central Europe

Poland: Germans expelled from Poland after World War II and their descendants have organized themselves. There are ethnic Germans in Poland, but the number is unknown.

Czechoslovakia: The Slovaks seek a loose federation; the Czechs prefer a more centralized republic.

Yugoslavia: Serbians, Croatians, Montenegrins, Macedonians, Bosnians, Slovenans, Albanians, and some minor ethnic groups. In Kosovo, ethnic Albanians are rising against Serbian control; the Croatians are moving toward independence; and the Slovenes have declared formally their intention to become independent.

Hungary: Ethnic Hungarians in Romania have revived their ethnic claims.

Romania: Hungarian claims (the Hungarian minority in Romania is estimated at about 8 percent of the population) have provoked a Romanian nationalist backlash. In the meantime, Moldavia (formerly a part of Romania and now in the USSR) is asserting its independence against the Soviet Union.

Bulgaria: The ethnic Turks whose number is estimated at about 1 million—about 10 percent of the population of the country—have been feuding with the Bulgarians. Repressive measures have forced some of them to flee to Turkey.

Despite Stalinist repression during which, in the name of Marxism, nationalities saw their national heroes vilified, their national traditions shelved, their written scripts and printed books gone in the vaults of public libraries, their languages gradually cede ground to the Russian official language, and their deep-rooted religious feelings and practices scorned and outlawed, nationalities have remained defiant and alive. After 1985, with the coming of Gorbachev and *perestroika,* they began to reassert themselves—sometimes with an explosive force that revealed a vitality that showed all of us that an ideology repressed for long may return with renewed force. They have taken a number of forms that are reminiscent of the previous waves of nationalism we have discussed: the search for and identification with past national symbols; the resurgence of religious identity—among Greek Orthodox, Muslims, and others; the renewed efforts to use their native language or dialect, teach it in schools, and make its use official; a return to national folklore and the restoration of national heroes, long forsaken by the official propaganda. All such nationalist assertions are directed against the center—against the Soviet federation and its organs.[13]

It was only in 1990, speaking before the central committee, that Gorbachev conceded that "ethnic problems are no fantasy; they are real and waiting to be solved by *perestroika.*"[14] How remains to be seen, as the Soviet Union is facing the prospects of fragmentation into its many and multiple ethnic components. There has been nothing in Gorbachev's statements to indicate that he has abandoned the notion that socialism is the best framework within which nationality problems can be resolved.

---

[13]The same is the case among Croatians, Slovenes, Montenegrins, Albanians, and others, as they make their claims against Yugoslavia.

[14]Quoted in *Pravda,* February 6, 1990. Translated in *News and Views from the USSR,* Soviet Embassy Information Department.

With the collapse of Soviet power and the Communist regimes, ethnona-tionalisms are on the rise throughout Central and Southeastern Europe as well (and of course in Yugoslavia). Czechs against Slovaks, Ethnic Hungarians in Ro-mania against Romania, ethnic Turks in Bulgaria, and so on. Ethnic strife ev-erywhere may undermine many of the newly founded democratic regimes (see Figure 9.3).

Figure 9.4 The Nemesis of the Kurds
Not only are the Kurds a nation of over 20 million without a state,
but they have had the misfortune to live in an area—Kur-
distan—that straddles five states. About 9 million live within the
borders of Turkey, another 5.5 million or so are in Iran, at least
3.5 million have survived in Iraq, and about half a million live
within the borders of the Soviet Union. They have survived per-
secution and repression almost everywhere and, at least in Iraq,
have been the victims of attempted genocide. Their nemesis
(the name of the ancient Greek goddess of blind and undeserved
retribution) is the tacit collusion of the states within which they
live. If and when the Kurds claim autonomy within one of the
states where they live, fear springs in all other states that "their"
Kurds will do likewise; furthermore, any separatist movement
among the Kurds anywhere sends nationalist and separatist signals to other nationalities to do likewise through the whole region of the Middle East and beyond. Kurdish claims for
autonomy are held at bay by the tacit alliance against them by all
states in the region. Yet the United Nations whose Charter proclaims "respect for the principle of equal rights and self-
determination of peoples" and the international community
seem incapable to save the Kurds from their nemesis!

But ethnonationalist movements are not confined to Eastern Europe and the Soviet Union; we are witnessing their presence throughout the world. The Basques in Spain are on the move; in Quebec, which claims to be a "distinct society" within the Canadian federation, the Mohawk Indians assert their independence; and in Sri Lanka, the Tamils are waging war to preserve their autonomy while the Kurds face extinction (Fig. 9.4).

In all parts of the world, enthnonationalist movements—some seeking autonomy, others agreeing to live within a loose federation, and still others seeking separation and sovereignty—are tearing apart some newly founded states. In Ethiopia, Sudan, Kashmir, Morocco, and India, ethnonational (often religious) minorities daily confront each other and the state within which they live. One should also be extremely alert to potential ethnonationalist movements by Muslim fundamentalists (Chapter 10) everywhere in North Africa, the Middle East, Indonesia, but also in some countries of the European community, where immigrant workers, many of them Muslims, amount to as much as 5 to 8 percent of the population. In the whole of the African Sub-Saharan continent, tribalisms that have many of the characteristics of ethnonationalisms are also on the rise.

Ethnonationalist movements are in the process of becoming the most virulent ideology today. But they do, by and large, derive from the same old ideology of nineteenth-century nationalism. The bottles are the same old bottles, but the wine appears at times headier. It is nurtured and ripened by the many discontents that our industrial society has spawned—impersonality, uncertainty about employment as technology requires a higher level of education among workers, a feeling of deprivation that rising expectations for economic growth and prosperity have heightened, ignorance and poverty. Like religious fundamentalism, with which many ethnonationalist movements are linked, they aim to provide a safe and secure home, a common center of loyalty and attachment, a feeling of togetherness in the reassertion of old values and traditions shared and cherished for so long. The call of ethnonationalism resembles the call for the revival of old neighborhoods that we heard about or dreamed. It is part and parcel of a movement for small and manageable social units that we believe we can control, instead of the distant and impersonal forces that seem to rule our lives. Ethnonationalist emotions and attachments are so powerful that at the least sign of actual and perceived discrimination, the ethnonationalist wine. . . . boils over.

BLACK SEPARATISM IN THE UNITED STATES

Nothing displays more clearly the importance of ideology than the lack of Afro-American ethnonationalist separatism in the United States. A little more than 10 percent of the people in the United States are black. Brought to American until 1808 as slaves or born and raised in slave plantations until 1863, they were people without rights under the law, without property, deprived of their skills and education. In some states, slaves were not allowed to learn to read or

Martin Luther King (1929–1968)

Martin Luther King was without a doubt one of the most prominent American political figures of the twentieth century—though he never held public office. Deeply influenced by Gandhi and his philosophy of "passive resistance," King was well versed in religion and philosophy before turning to social and racial relations and becoming the leader of the "nonviolent revolution" which swept the country in the fifties and sixties. Through preaching, demonstrations, and marches and the organization of the Southern Christian Leadership Conference, he mobilized blacks and whites and became the most inspired moral voice on civil rights. Rejecting the demands for "black power" and "black separatism," which other black leaders advanced, King argued for the full entitlement of blacks in American society. And progress was made: First, in 1964, with the Civil Rights Act, which abolished segregation in all public places, and then in 1965, with the Voting Rights Act, which abolished all discriminatory voting practices that had been widely followed in the south and elsewhere. King's "dream" was that of a society of equals in which the distinctions of color would be done away with. He was assassinated on April 4, 1968.

write. They were at the mercy of their white owners. The Civil War led to their emancipation and their political enfranchisement. But soon thereafter, discriminating practices developed. The blacks were for all practical purposes disenfranchised in the majority of states and remained without protection of the law, the right to vote, or the opportunity to learn the skills that would provide for a better life and income. They were excluded from the American liberal mainstream. Yet in contrast to most all other ethnic minorities in so many other parts of the world, the prevalent ideology among blacks in the United States has been to join, rather than to reject, the mainstream of American liberal values, to become part of it and to be integrated within it. Louis Hartz's *The Liberal Tradition in America* provides perhaps the best answer for the lack of black separatism. The overwhelming liberal ethos in America—stressing equality of opportunity and individual effort—could not be arbitrarily interpreted to exclude men and women because of their color. At the same time, it exercised an overwhelming attraction for blacks—it promised them the equality that they wanted and of which they were deprived.

There were many other reasons, however, for the lack of a black separatist movement. One reason was *the lack of education among blacks*. They were deprived of education for a long time, which made it difficult for them to gain a consciousness of their position and to translate it into a distinct and organized political movement. Second, they lacked a clearly identified territorial base—a territory in which they lived, as is the case with the Basques in France, or the French in Quebec, or the Croatians in Yugoslavia, or even the Scots and the Welsh in the United Kingdom, and the Corsicans in France. To be sure, a preponderant percentage of blacks lived in the South, but after World War I, and even more so since World War II, the blacks who moved in search of employment to the urban centers of the North and the West began to outnumber those who remained in the South. The black population dispersed throughout the United States. Their predicament, economic or social, remains a national phenomenon; it is not associated with a given region, area, or state to which national resources have not been properly allocated, as it is with Soviet Georgia. The arguments of "internal colonialism" and "regional deprivation" could not be advanced in order to reinforce territorial separatist claims. Third, in contrast to most separatist movements, no common and different language existed for the blacks. They all spoke and wrote—when they were allowed to learn how— English. Finally, as the economy developed and the most overt forms of discrimination ended, blacks appeared less and less a homogeneous social force. They became increasingly differentiated on the basis of income, status, skills, and lifestyles. Some had fully entered the "mainstream" and became its supporters; to many, the mainstream continued to beckon. Even if most blacks remained out of the mainstream, the hope had been kindled that they too would "overcome," and become a part of it.

Without a clearly identified territorial base, without a commonly shared consciousness of their traditions and past, without a common and separate language, without a common social and economic identity or even a commonly shared sense of exploitation—which goes with "class"—the blacks, excluded and invisible to all others for so long, became increasingly visible to each other and to all as Americans.

Separatist Movements

The most spectacular phenomenon of American society remains the lack of black separatism and the lack of ideologies to promote it. There are only a few ideologies that can be mentioned. Black "nationalism" is associated with Marcus Garvey (1887–1940) and his movement, the Universal Negro Improvement Association, founded in 1914 in Jamaica and transferred to Harlem in 1920. Its platform advocated Negro nationhood, Negro race consciousness, inculcation of "ideals of manhood and womanhood" in every Negro, self-determination, and racial self-help and self-respect.

As stated in the platform, Africa was to be "territory" for the blacks in the same way that Israel was to be a home for the Jews, according to the Zionists. This meant that the liberation of Africa, virtually all of which was under colonial rule at the time, had to be undertaken. In the meantime, race consciousness would enhance the unity and cultural identity of all blacks—and Garvey was a segregationist. Racial self-help required the development of black capitalism and a black economy, and again Garvey was particularly instrumental in the building of black businesses and cooperatives. The founding of the African Orthodox Church just about completed all the elements of "nationality" to be imparted, namely economic autonomy, cultural autonomy, religious autonomy, and racial separateness. Self-determination would follow with a plea for the political independence of all blacks in Africa and of those who went to Africa and for the political independence of Africa from the colonial yoke.

It is interesting to note that at no time did Garvey assert or claim any territory of the United States as a "home" for the blacks. It was only in the years after World War I that a small group, under communist inspiration, asked for a "Negro republic" in the "Black Belt" of the South, a proposal that was not seriously considered by any of the black leaders. Instead, Garvey's dreams died with him, and until almost 1965 black activism focused instead on ending all discriminatory practices and attaining integration in education, jobs, law and political representation, and social life. This theme was strengthened by the massive move of blacks from the South to the booming industrial centers in the North, the Midwest, and the West, and also by some critical decisions of the Supreme Court in favor of integration. It was also strengthened by the assertion of the blacks themselves in favor of integration under the leadership of Martin Luther King, Jr., and others and in cooperation with liberal groups among the whites and a number of white political leaders—notably John F. Kennedy and Lyndon B. Johnson. Boycotts, marches, and demonstrations gradually brought down segregation.

Malcolm X

Yet it was at this juncture that a strong black nationalist movement emerged in the late 1960s first under Malcolm X (1925–1965), and the black Muslims and

Malcolm X

Malcolm X was the preeminent figure among African Americans who rejected the goal of integration. Born Malcolm Little, he replaced his "slave name" with an X, a symbol of his unknown African ancestry. Malcolm argued that blacks had no need to prove themselves to whites who had kept them subservient throughout American history, and should not seek participation within a society fundamentally based on racism.

Malcolm X believed that Islam is the historical and appropriate religion for African Americans, and that Christianity is a religion borrowed from whites. He became a charismatic spokesman for Elijah Muhammed and his Black Muslim movement, but split away after a pilgrimage to Mecca convinced him that the movement shared many racist and materialistic traits with Christianity. After this split, Malcolm X founded the Muslim Mosque and the Organization of Afro-American Unity.

John Henrik Clark, (*Malcolm X: The Man and His Times.* Toronto: MacMillan Co., 1969) writes that Malcolm X expressed "black pride, black redemption, black reaffirmation." He was assassinated in 1965.

---

the Organization of Afro-American Unity, and later under the Black Panthers, among other groups, including white radical organizations like the Students for Democratic Society. Malcolm X gradually began to view the situation of the American blacks in the broader contexts of American capitalism. It was American exploitive capitalism, he argued, that accounted for their inferior status, and it was the destruction of capitalism that would liberate the blacks. It was not, therefore, a matter of appealing to black nationalism. Nationalism in itself could become, Malcolm X argued, a reactionary force and, even after emancipation, could keep black people under subjection. Black nationalism should become simply a component in the struggle against class oppression and exploitation everywhere in the world. Only a *revolutionary* nationalist movement could attain this. Only a movement such as socialism, which promised profound and radical change in the structure of the economy and the society, could liberate the blacks and the downtrodden.

The Black Panthers

The Black Panthers moved a step closer to this revolutionary position. Inspired in part by the revolution in Algeria against the French, the victory of Castro in Cuba, and the independence of almost all colonies in Africa during the 1960s, they saw the situation of the blacks as a phenomenon of "internal colonialism" and hence saw the redemption of the blacks only in terms of a revolutionary struggle against colonial masters in the United States and everywhere. The Black Panthers asked for "independence" at home; they set up their own cabinet with various ministers and organized paramilitary groups for self-defense. But they viewed the success of their movement in the context of a worldwide revolutionary struggle in which nation–states would give place to ethnic and cultural groupings cooperating with each other in a socialist world. This is what was meant by *intercommunalism*. No other specifics were given and no demands were made for any form of black autonomy or "territorial" autonomy within the United States. If the class structure in America was altered and if capitalism were superseded by a socialist commonwealth, only then would the position of blacks become safe and their lot equal with those of whites. Black nationalism was viewed as almost identical with the colonial emancipation movements. Its vision, however, remained far more difficult to realize for lack of a territorial base or "home." For Garvey it was Africa; for the Panthers, the world—a socialist world.

Garvey, Malcolm X, the Black Panthers, and other small black organizations that advocated positions ranging from separateness and autonomy to revolutionary struggle and socialism, never captured the following of even a minority of the blacks in the United States. In the last thirty years only a handful attempted to reject completely their "Americanism," stressing their roots and their past with Africa or Islam. Some have reached out to their black-Hispanic origins, stressing their ties with Cuba and the Caribbean; some converted to Islam; some even tried to familiarize themselves with African dialects. Only tiny minorities began to seek identities outside of the American world to which their ancestors had been forcefully transplanted and which was the only world they had known.

In 1984 and again in 1988, the political symbol and leader of the blacks became Jesse Jackson, who ran for the presidential nomination of the Democratic party within the "system." Throughout his candidacy, Jackson asked for the support of all people (even if particular emphasis was put on the so-called Rainbow Coalition of blacks, women, Hispanics, and other minority groups) and sought equal representation in the electoral process and within the Democratic party for all minorities and blacks. He also reached out to solicit the support of whites. Jackson identified the blacks in political terms—as a political force that could be organized within the context of democracy and had to be counted upon, just as other ethnic groups and movements were, including labor, in the past. In this sense, he remained solidly in the tradition of Martin Luther King—the tradition favoring the full integration of the blacks as citizens within the United States on the basis of equality of opportunities for all and equal treatment to all. Today the only true separatist movement is represented by a religious leader, Reverend Farrakahn, but he has a very small number of followers.

But the American myth—the American ideology of equality and individual freedom—cannot be sustained unless they are both realized. Freedom—political and individual freedoms—may have been attained and with them go immense opportunities for all. But if adequate material means and services are lacking, those deprived over a long period of time will reject the validity of the myth. The message of Malcolm X continues to blur the vision of Martin Luther King.

There is every indication that poverty afflicts the blacks far more severely than any other group of the population. Over thirty percent of blacks live below the line of poverty (with an income of about $13,000 a year for a family of four) as compared to ten percent of the whites. At least forty percent of all black children live in families (usually headed by women) that are below the poverty line. Unemployment among the blacks runs twice as high as for whites. Despite affirmative action and massive welfare spending, education and training and the opportunities for employment have not improved among blacks ever since the vision of the Great Society was outlined by Lyndon Johnson in the early sixties, despite the notable successes of blacks in securing elective office. Even more ominous is the return of what amounts to a *de facto* segregation: the whites live in the suburbs and their children are educated in virtually all-white schools; the blacks live in the inner city where schools are inadequate, poverty rampant, and crime and drugs a daily fare. The two communities—black and white—are drifting apart—culturally, educationally, economically, in terms of lifestyles and expectations. Neither the army, nor the political leadership, nor sports or the churches provide adequate linkages between blacks and whites. The ghetto, many claim, is becoming a national phenomenon, dividing the American society in two.

Advocacy of black separatism, many point out, would be a prescription that is worse than the disease: it will divide the society even more and affect all of us adversely. But ideological fervor and protest, we have pointed out in this book, do not always stem from a rational calculation of benefits and losses. They often spring from powerful emotional impulses that human degradation produces. Black rejection and separatism may yet challenge the complacency of the American liberal myth.

BEYOND NATIONALISM—INTERNATIONALISM?

Are the nationalist and ethnonationalist impulses we surveyed unavoidable and inevitable? Is the ideology of nationalism to remain so powerful and pervasive as to splinter our political world to a myriad of exclusive and conflicting units? For unless we find a way to reconcile the needs of nationalisms and the imperative of political unity and order, nationalist and ethnonationalist ideologies may lead to what Thomas Hobbes called "a war of all against all." Is there a new ideology emerging to counter and accommodate nationalisms—big and small? This is the question we address in this second part of the chapter.

Cosmopolitanism

Cosmopolitanism as an ideology is the exact opposite of nationalism. According to it we are all citizens of the world. Literally, "cosmopolis" means a world–city or a world–state—from *cosmos* (the world) and *polis* (a city). Cosmopolitanism is based on an ideology of universal values deriving from our human nature, but does not exclude separate nationalities or even nations. They can exist side by side under fixed and common standards and rules that apply to all individuals and nations to guide their relations on the basis of equality. A common law, for example, an international law that is binding upon all, or a common political authority, or an international organization something like a United Nations, provides for order and the swift settlement of disputes and the protection of the rights of all, irrespective of individual, racial, cultural, or national differences. Cosmopolitanism allows for many cultures and many nationalities to live side by side, but in the last and ultimate sense there is but one law, one polis, one state.

The Stoics   The first genuine movement toward cosmopolitanism was a reaction against the Greek city–states (the small sovereign states into which ancient Greece was divided, just as our own world today is divided into nations). It came during the second and third centuries before Christ and was expressed by the Stoic philosophers. They preached simple human virtues, argued in favor of equality for all, and insisted that there were common and universal principles for all people that derived from human nature. They were against the artificial distinctions and exclusive loyalties the city–states had created. Their belief was that, since all people are part of a divine will or God (*Logos*), they are all alike and should be treated as brothers and sisters. They called for the city–state to give way to the imperative of equality and brotherhood. It was a universalistic ethic.

The Stoic philosophy was followed by Christianity. It, too, was based on the broadest universalistic assumptions; it preached equality and brotherhood and focused on the spiritual quality of life that would bind people together and give only minimal powers to the state. The world would be one for all—Greeks and barbarians, Phoenicians and Romans, Corinthians and Carthegenians. All the faithful constituted one community—universal and peaceful. The Vicar of Christ (later the Pope) would be the spiritual leader.

The Roman Empire

Yet it was not Christianity nor the Papacy but the Roman Empire (31 B.C.–476 A.D.) that became the first and truly cosmopolitan arrangement that we know. The Roman Empire included virtually all the peoples and "nationalities" of Europe and parts of Africa and the Middle East; it established common measures, standards, and currency; it abolished all boundaries; and it developed an efficient communication system and a centralized administration that gave protection to all. Above all, it established a system of law for all and the proper judicial organization to administer it.

While the Roman armies and administration maintained the integrity of the empire, it was the Roman law that united the various peoples within it. During the early days of the empire, Roman civil law applied exclusively to Roman citizens and to any conflicts arising among them. Gradually, however, a new kind of law emerged that applied to disputes among all individuals—Roman and non-Roman alike. Similar to the common law that developed much later in England, Roman law was developed by special judges, case by case, first throughout all the provinces in Italy and later throughout the entire Roman Empire. It became known as the *ius gentium*—something like international law. It was simple, avoided formal procedures, allowed for rules of equity, treated all equally, and constantly adjusted itself to the changing nature of economic and social relations. All citizens of the empire—Scythians and Egyptians and Greeks and Romans—had access to it. Gradually, as the *ius gentium* evolved and developed general rules and principles, many began to confuse it with "natural law," a law consonant with human nature and therefore valid for all. It was a universal law—truly cosmopolitan.

What made the Roman Empire the first truly universal political organization, however, was citizenship. Citizenship in Rome was originally granted only to those born of Romans. But gradually many people began to be assimilated even though they were not "Romans." In 212 A.D., a famous edict was issued by Emperor Caracalla proclaiming all those living within the empire and, of course, the children to be born, to be Roman citizens. Thus every person became a citizen of the then known world, recognizing (or submitting to) one authority, with access to a common law and a common judge, free to move from one place to another, and assured of equal protection.

This was the farthest ever that the institutionalization of cosmopolitanism ever went! The Roman Empire was not a "nation"; it had no "spiritual" entity and no "soul"; it had no common language and no common culture or "race." It was an administrative, judicial, and military organization that included many ethnic and religious groups. It did not impose uniform values, except when some emperors tried to outlaw or to impose Christianity. It was, as we would say today, a multiethnic, multiracial, multireligious, multilingual system in which all peoples could work, trade, and live. It provided for order and peace.

There were some other manifestations of cosmopolitanism after the fall of the Roman Empire. One was the Papacy—the spiritual head of the universal community of believers representing Christendom. The "Holy Roman Empire" represented the legacy of the Roman Empire and remained more of an assertion than a reality. After the fifteenth century, the Papacy was unable to impose its spiritual rule over the faithful. Schisms developed and national churches appeared with king rather than pope as their head. The king became "Pope and Emperor in his own kingdom" defying all the universalistic claims of the church. All aspirations to keep the Holy Roman Empire began to fade and they eventually died with the end of the seventeenth century.

Liberalism, Marxism, and Cosmopolitanism

Both liberalism and Marxism are internationalist and cosmopolitan ideologies. This is implicit in liberalism and quite explicit, as we saw, in Marxism. In fact, liberalism represents the essence of individualism—of men and women preoccupied and devoted to the satisfaction of their wants and pleasures, of a government that governs the least, of freedom of trade and movement. Nation–states, both large and small, should not interfere in economic life; should not engage upon destructive wars; should not try to impose heavy tariffs that would disrupt the free flow of goods and undermine a division of labor that would spread gradually throughout the world. Order, security, and peace were the conditions for economic prosperity, and governments in nation–states were to be responsible for maintaining them but for little more. Thus the middle classes would gain ascendancy and create a vast commercial brotherhood among nations in which individual and economic freedoms would keep governments limited and under control.

When applied to the international community, liberalism remained individualistic. It rejected mass appeals, mass movements, and unifying communitarian themes. It portrayed nations and the international community in terms of myriads of individuals interacting with each other; a society of "economic" men and women attached to professions, jobs, wealth, and profit recognizing no superior moral or political authority other than their own conscience and their own interests. Wherever they could set up a business and make profit was their fatherland, Rousseau hinted scornfully. In addition to economic individualism and commitment to profit, early liberals also shared what we described earlier as a "common moral core," which had cosmopolitan and universalistic aspirations. All men and women were free; all of them were endowed with rights; all of them should be secure in their person and property; all of them should be free to speak, think, and worship as they pleased; and ultimately all of them should be free to participate in forming a government and controlling its conduct. Human nature in this sense was not determined by national characteristics—it transcended them. Irrespective of their nationality and despite differences in language and habit, human beings had more in common with each other than their apparent national differences would indicate. It was not *human* for a German to be only a German or for a Frenchman to be only French. Their humanity was stronger than their nationalities. A stranger was a fellow human being. It followed that the spread of liberalism would reinforce the spirit of cosmopolitanism and internationalism and bring the civilized peoples of the nations of the world closer together.

Marxism, like liberalism and curiously enough for almost identical reasons, aspired to a cosmopolitan order. The working class was to be the genuine and liberating force that would overcome the prejudices and emotions of bourgeoisie nationalisms. The workers from Budapest, Paris, Berlin, and London would join hands in asserting common interests and universal human values. It did not come to pass!

With the demise of Marxism as an ideology almost everywhere, is it possible that the renewed emphasis on democracy and liberalism will provide a new cosmopolitan ideology? Economic interdependence and free trade, for instance, require an international order to safeguard them from nationalist movements. There is no ideology as yet to sustain interdependence, globalism, and an international order. There are no widely accepted international institutions and organizations to implement such an ideology. Heartfelt worldwide needs to protect the environment, regulate world resources, avert wars, and protect human rights may gradually bring them about. But if a liberal international order is in sight, we are only dimly aware of it.

INTERNATIONALISM AND INTERNATIONALIST ARRANGEMENTS

Ever since the ancient Greeks tried to group their small city–states into a confederation, innumerable efforts have been made by states and nations to establish regional arrangements. The most spectacular effort to date has been the European Common Market, established in 1956 by the Treaty of Rome to include initially the Benelux countries (Belgium, the Netherlands, and Luxembourg), France, the German Federal Republic, and Italy. In 1972, England, Denmark, and Ireland became members and were joined by Greece, Spain, and Portugal in the 1980s. Committed first to economic unity and economic integration, its ultimate goal was to bring about "political union." Similar efforts have been made (and often unmade) by Arab states, sometimes in the name of Islam or pan-Arabism, and among the Latin American and African states with the Organization of American States and the Organization of African Unity, respectively.

Regionalism

We think of a region as a given geographic area comprising a number of states where common beliefs and practices exist and within which various forms of communication—both economic and personal—are strong. We assume and expect that within a given region, defined in this manner, regional values and attachments will promote cooperation and inhibit conflicts among individual nation–states. In fact, we tend to assume that regional values and regional institutional arrangements may supersede national entities to lead ultimately to regional institutions and regional loyalties. This has not come about. If we limit ourselves to the period since World War II, individual nation–states have mushroomed while all efforts to build regional organizations, institutions, and genuine regional loyalties and ideologies have failed. No regional ideology has developed to supplant nationalisms. Neither liberalism nor Marxism has produced one. We talk about "French" liberalism or "British" liberalism and, until recently, about "Chinese Marxism" as opposed to the "Soviet" or the "Yugoslav" one. In the European Common Market that brought together nations with strong affinities, few of the citizens of the member states put the regional organization they have established above their nation–states. First and foremost are their loyalties to their own countries. There have been some efforts spearheaded by intellectuals—"Europeanists" and "Federalists"—to promote a supranational idea and doctrine, but they are only a handful and have been unsuccessful thus far. Even Islamic religious leaders have failed as yet to bring any semblance of unity to the "Arab nation."

CONCLUSION

No matter where we turn, we continue to be faced by the same stubborn reality—nationalisms, nations, and nation–states. A noted English author writing forty-two years ago (when World War II had come to an end and with it, many had thought, the dawn of a new era of internationalism) pinpointed all the defects of nationalism. "What has to be challenged and rejected," he wrote, "is the claim of nationalism to make the nation the sole rightful repository of political power and the ultimate constituent unit of world organization."[15] The claim has not been rejected yet!

Large or small, nationalism continues to shape the minds and the attachments of all of us—whether it is about Panama for the United States; New Caledonia for the French; the Palestinians in the search for a homeland; the Irish in their efforts to dislodge the British from Northern Ireland; the Czechs, the Slovaks, the Slovenes, the Croatians, the Armenians, and all the other nationalities in their efforts to establish a sovereignty. It provided a moment of exaltation to the Argentines when in 1982 they sent their navy and army into the Falkland Islands, miscalculating the immediate and profound nationalist response on the part of the British. A bitter war went on for three months over these remote and inhospitable islands in which both British and Argentines became emotionally involved. Nothing could show more aptly how seductive the old-time religion of nationalism remains. Like Rupert Brooke, a young British poet buried on a small Greek Island after dying in combat in World War I, many of the British soldiers buried in the Falklands will continue to whisper to the generations to come the same gospel that Shakespeare put in Richard II's famous lines:

> Think only this of me:
> That there is a corner of a foreign field
> That is forever England . . .
> A dust whom England bore, shaped, made aware.

If nationalism is, as it has been alleged, "the last refuge of scoundrels," most of us continue to remain scoundrels in our hearts and minds!

BIBLIOGRAPHY

Alter, Peter. *Nationalism*. New York: Routledge, 1989.
Bracey, John H., et al., eds. *Black Nationalism in America*, Indianapolis, 1970.

---

[15]Edward Hallet Carr, *Nationalisms and After*, p. 63.

Bruilly, John. *Nationalism and the State*. Chicago: University of Chicago Press, 1985.

Carr, Edward Hallet. *Nationalism and After*. London: Macmillan, 1945.

Deutsch, Karl W. *Nationalism and Its Alternatives*. New York: Knopf, 1969.

———. *Nationalism and Social Communication*, 3rd ed. Cambridge, Mass.: The MIT Press, 1981.

——— et al. *Political Community in the North Atlantic Area*. Princeton, N.J.: Princeton University Press, 1957.

Forsyth, Murray (ed.). *Federalism and Nationalism*. New York: St. Martin's Press, 1989.

Franklin, John H., and Alfred Moss, Jr. *From Slavery to Freedom*, 6th ed. New York: Alfred Knopf, 1988.

Gellner, Ernest. *Nations and Nationalism*. Cambridge, Mass.: Basil Blackwell, 1987.

Gerassi, John. *The Coming the New International*. New York: World Publishing, 1971.

Grimes, Alan P., and Robert H. Horowitz. *Modern Political Ideologies*. New York: Oxford University Press, 1959.

Hayes, Carlton T. H. *Essays on Nationalism*. London: Macmillan, 1937.

Hinsley, F. H. *Nationalism and the International System*. London: Hodder and Stoughton, 1973.

Hobson, John A. *Imperialism*. Ann Arbor: University of Michigan Press, 1965.

Horowitz, Donald L. *Ethnic Groups in Conflict*. Berkeley: University of California Press, 1985.

Kedourie, Elie. *Nationalism*, rev. ed. London: Hutchinson, 1961.

Keohane, R. O., and Joseph Nye. *Transnational Politics*. Cambridge, Mass.: Harvard University Press, 1972.

King, Martin Luther, Jr. *Stride Toward Freedom: The Montgomery Story*. New York, 1962.

———. *Why We Can't Wait*. New York, 1964.

Kohn, Hans. *Nationalism: Its Meaning and History*, rev. ed. New York: Van Nostrand, 1965.

———. *The Idea of Nationalism*. New York. Collier, 1967.

Malcolm X. *Autobiography of Malcolm X*. New York: Ballantine, 1965.

Mayall, James. *Nationalism and International Society*. New York: Cambridge University Press, 1990.

McNeil, W. H. *The Rise of the West*. Chicago: University of Chicago Press, 1963.

Meinecke, Friedrich. *Cosmopolitanism and the National State*. Princeton, N.J.: Princeton University Press, 1970.

Ronen, D. *The Quest for Self-Determination*. New Haven, Conn.: Yale University Press, 1979.

Rothschild, Joseph. *Ethnopolitics—A Conceptual Framework*. New York: Columbia University Press, 1981.

Seton–Watson, Hugh. *Nations and States*. Boulder, Colo.: Westview Press, 1977.

Smith, Anthony. *Theories of Nationalism*. London: Duckworth, 1971.

———. *Nationalism in the Twentieth Century*. New York: New York University Press, 1979.

———. *The Ethnic Origins of Nations*. Cambridge, Mass.: Basil Blackwell, 1988.

Snyder, Louis L. *Global Mini Nationalism: Autonomy and Independence*. Westport, Conn.: Greenwood Press, 1982.

Stalin, Joseph. *Marxism and the National Question*. Moscow: International Publishers, 1934.

Tilly, Charles (ed.). *The Formation of the National States in Western Europe*. Princeton, N.J.: Princeton University Press, 1975.

Walker, Connor. *The National Question in Marxist Leninist Theory and Strategies.* Princeton, N.J.: Princeton University Press, 1984.

Waltz, Kenneth. *Man, the State and War: A Theoretical Analysis.* New York: Columbia University Press, 1954.

Watson, Michael. *Contemporary Minority Nationalism.* New York: Routledge, 1990.

Chapter
10

The Religious Impulse
Liberation Theology and Religious Fundamentalism

Render to Caesar the things that are Caesar's and to God the things that are God's.

St. Mark 12:17

Most all great religions ordain our temporal lives in terms of transcendental values. When we think of religion, we think of contemplation, inwardness, and a preparation for the life hereafter. "My kingdom is not of this world," Jesus Christ proclaimed. The kingdom of God is separate and very different from earthly kingdoms. The "church" does not pretend to assume or exercise temporal powers. The "secular sword"—politics—is in the hands of kings, monarchs, peoples, and governments. The "spiritual sword" is less visible. It is addressed to matters of sin and salvation and binds the faithful in an intricate web of faith, ritual, and sacraments. Within the civil society, it is the mission of the church to "evangelize"—to spread the "good tidings" and to convert pagans, agnostics, and "heretics." The mission of all religious orders has been to save us *from* the world in which we find ourselves temporarily.

Again, all great religions have developed a set of principles derived from revered sources in terms of which the faithful must behave. Whether it is the Bible or the Koran or the Torah—it is always the "Book" that spells out divine guidance. Churches, synagogues, mosques, and shrines where the faithful congregate to worship become the centers of religious activity; they set the standards of religious behavior and often can impose sanctions that, even when not supported directly by the law, are just as painful as legal sanctions: to be deprived of Holy Communion may be far more painful for a devout Catholic than a jail sentence.

Despite their transcendental emphasis, religions, all religions, therefore, directly influence behavior. They influence our perceptions about civil obligations, about our relationships with each other, about our family lives, and about the education of our children. Religion has spurred protest, revolution, even the assassination of a "bad king"—a tyrant—or, as the occasion called, counselled submission and obedience. No matter where, we find religious beliefs to make up a good part of the political fabric we wear—of our political attitudes. Whether a "superstructure" or not, to use the Marxist vocabulary, religion is a far more potent source of ideology and morality than class or state. And it is with religion as an ideology that we are concerned in this chapter, and only with reference to two most important and relevant political manifestations: liberation theology and religious fundamentalism, particularly Islamic fundamentalism and the fundamentalist movement in the United States—the Evangelicals.[1]

In our discussion we do not attempt any theological analysis or evaluation. We treat the religious origins only as ingredients that shape political ideology. Our question is always the same: How does the religious ingredient influence politics?

LIBERATION THEOLOGY

Liberation theology, as it has developed in the last thirty years, is a call for action, headed by bishops, many clergy, and laypersons, especially in the Catholic church, addressed to all but especially to the poor and the downtrodden of the Third World in order to redress, in the name of Christ, the social wrongs inflicted upon them—abject poverty, illiteracy, exploitation, and powerlessness. Liberation theology has spawned new forms of religious organizations that question the hierarchical organization of the church—especially the Catholic church. It has gained roots among populations where poverty has been endemic, where illiteracy is widespread, and where the law provides no security or protection. It claims to be a new religious movement addressed and applicable to the underdeveloped societies of the world, and it has been particularly in evidence in Latin America—in Colombia, Brazil, Peru, Nicaragua, Chile, El Salvador, and Guatemala. Though many of its leaders received training in European religious institutes, it is a truly indigenous intellectual and ideological movement addressed by native theologians and intellectuals to the social ills plaguing the Third World. Its major inspiration, however, came from the Second Vatican Council (1962–1965) and from a number of papal encyclicals that called upon the church and Catholics to spearhead social and political action.

Background

Ever since World War II, churchgoers, Catholic or not, began to experience a growing sense of dismay and indignation at the poverty, misery, and helplessness of the mass of people in many of the underdeveloped areas of the world. In most Latin American countries, daily income, social assistance, educational facilities, and health services are dismally low or nonexistent. Redress is im-

---

[1]It should be noted that not all Evangelicals are fundamentalists, as we point out later.

Gustavo Gutierrez

Gustavo Gutierrez was born in Lima, Peru, in 1928. He began his higher education at the National University in Lima, studying medicine. During the time that he attended the National University, Gutierrez was active in a number of political groups. After five years Gutierrez discontinued his medical studies and enrolled in a course in philosophical and theological studies and sought to enter the priesthood. These studies began in Chile but soon Gutierrez traveled to Europe, where between 1951 and 1955 he studied at the University of Louvain. He is a professor of theology at the Catholic University in Lima, Peru, and a national advisor for the National Union of Catholic students.

Gutierrez's *A Theology of Liberation* is considered by many scholars to be the definitive statement on the theology of liberation. Gutierrez's emphasis is on the theoretical rather than on the ideological movement associated with liberation theology itself. Gutierrez traces the origins of theological reflection since the early days of Christianity to a new and evolving orientation which stresses social *praxis*, a commitment to critical reflection, and a renewed commitment on the part of the church to the disenfranchised, the poor, and the destitute.

---

possible among the societies still ruled by dictators and military regimes—characteristics of underdevelopment, that often shield the ruling class. From a political standpoint, the poor are powerless. They are unable to organize and articulate their demands, unable to participate in any decision, constantly at the mercy of a minority that abuses its power instead of promoting a degree of sharing that would raise the level of consciousness and participation of the masses. How does a society raise the people from their poverty and ignorance and give them a place consistent with their humanity?

One answer has been economic modernization, and many regimes, including military ones, have espoused it. But modernization in Latin America has involved an imitation of Western methods: a growth of investment (by borrowing from abroad) and a reliance upon free enterprise and the market. It has been advocated by intellectuals and economists and by some theologians, too. It was to be a modernization decreed from above, consistent with the social, political, and economic structures that prevailed; it was to be gradual and incremental.

This type of modernization as an answer to problems of poverty was disavowed by others. The reasons given were briefly the following: the Latin American economic structures were so closely tied to the world economy, or rather the U.S. economy, that they were in a state of "dependency." They could not develop the autonomy and freedoms and the means to modernize in order to serve their own needs and purposes. They were but an adjunct of American capitalism. There was no way to break the cycle of dependency except

Leonardo Boff

Leonardo Boff was born in the town of Concordia, Brazil, in 1938. He pursued his studies in Brazil (Petropolis, Curitiba) and Europe (Ludwig-Maximilian Universitat in Munich, Wurzburg, Louvain, and Oxford). He is a Franciscan. Boff has been a professor for over a decade at the Petropolis Institute for Theology and Philosophy, where he teaches courses in systematic theology. He has written a number of books and numerous articles on theology and liberation. He is perhaps best known for his recent summons to Rome in September 1984 to explain his views on liberation theology before the pope and the Congregation for the Doctrine of the Faith, headed by Joseph Cardinal Ratzinger. One of his more recent books, *The Church: Charisma and Power,* was formally criticized in March 1985 by the Congregation.

by undertaking major structural reforms of the economy and the society, some in the direction of socialism.

The church doctrine especially in the Catholic Church began to change accordingly. The pope himself had pointedly referred to the uneven distribution of goods among nations, and in a number of his pronouncements had sharply criticized both the abuse of power and the abuse of wealth and property; he had expressed his particular concerns for the poor. On three occasions—at Medellin in 1969, in the *Letter Addressed to the People of the Third World* (1976), and in the Council of Latin American Bishops at Puebla in 1979—the contours of a liberation theology were outlined. They were fleshed out by many theologians—many from the Third World.

THE PHILOSOPHY OF LIBERATION THEOLOGY

A new body of thought developed before and ever since Vatican II that raises fundamental questions on the historical role both of Christ and the church and even more searching questions about the role and position of the church in society. Let us try to outline the philosophic assumptions of the theory of liberation theology and then discuss it as a political movement.

The Theory

Traditionally, the church viewed history as a temporary stage in our lives as compared to eternal life. The objective historical circumstances were not a matter of concern to the church when viewed with reference to the splendor of life hereafter. Orthodoxy, the maintenance of the true faith regardless of historical circumstances, was the church's central concern. In contrast, liberation theologians consider the church to be a vital agency of history, molding historical conditions and reflecting on these historical conditions. The gospel itself, and especially the role of Christ, is viewed as a historical basis for reform and change. Liberation theology therefore places its major emphasis on action—on the correct praxis or orthopraxis (*ortho* meaning correct and *praxis* meaning action) as opposed to orthodoxy (*ortho* meaning correct and *doxia* meaning belief). Indeed, the true faith can be found only in the proper action in line with Christ's life and teachings. Praxis—*action*—therefore becomes the essence of faith.

Critical Reflection   Not only does the concept of orthopraxis signal the significance of service and action, but it also requires that theology become a form of critical reflection, not just in a doctrinal sense but with regard to economic, political, and social issues. If praxis is to be advocated, guidance must be provided as to when and how to act. Critical reflection, derived from secular theories and the reading of the "signs of the times," serves to guide praxis. Present realities are confronted, and through the proper reflection, the seeds of future praxis are implanted. Praxis situates the church within historical realities and demands of it specific commitments and service. This means that the theologian should become engaged where domination and oppression run rampant, and where the poor clamor for their own salvation here on earth. But what is the truth behind the needed action—behind the correct ("ortho") action?

In analyzing society, liberation theologians use new tools to evaluate the present social, political, and economic realities. The analytical tools that help in critical reflection are derived from the social sciences: sociology, economics, politics, anthropology, and the behavioral sciences. Many also moved in the direction of Marxism.

The Marxist Option

The urgent task before Christians is to change society in order to improve the lot of the poor—indeed in order to eradicate poverty. But poverty arises because of faulty societal and economic structures, both national and international. Poverty can be alleviated by radical economic reforms in the direction of socialism. As liberation theologians put it, the preferential option for the poor is a socialist option.

The socialist option stems from an *analysis* of the society that—and here is the major source of controversy—borrows from Marxism. As we have seen, Marxism assumes the confrontation of two classes: those who own the means of production and those who do not—the workers for Marx, or the "poor" for the liberation theologians. In the same manner in which Marx assumed the workers would gain consciousness of their predicament and would rise to replace the property holders and socialize the means of production, the liberation theologians want to impart a reformist and even revolutionary consciousness to the poor to undertake the same task. The poor must improve their position by their own action and their own organization as the level of their awareness and consciousness improves. Self-reliance, community action, and spontaneous movements for reform and rectification of social evils are the means available to the poor, for the poor, and by the poor. In the process, local, community, regional, or national movements of the poor in their respective societies must keep their distance from international capitalism, which is blamed for the dependency of so many Third World countries and the concomitant subjugation of the poor to a local capitalist or bourgeois class. Liberation movements have to confront both their local oppressors and the international capitalist forces. When it comes to Latin America, this means "Yankee Imperialism."

In the eyes of liberation theologians, then, the church assumes the task of leading a revolutionary movement by one class, the poor, against the local and international forces of capitalism that account for their plight. It becomes, in the name of an inevitable class struggle, an agency of revolution and reform to bring about socialism and social justice. According to Gutierrez, class struggle is an "objective reality" and "the liberation" of the poor is "not an act of generosity or charity or Christian brotherhood"—though it may include them. It is, in his words, "a demand for the construction of a new social order."[2] Class struggle pitting the poor against the capitalist class appears to be inevitable and perhaps desirable if the poor are to regain their position as human beings by their own efforts. In this sense, commitment on the part of the clergy for the poor and their liberation appears to be, even in the name of class struggle, the epitome of religious commitment.

In choosing to associate its theology with secular theories, which explicitly or implicitly adopted Marxist analysis and terminology, Latin American liberation theology became associated, at least in the eyes of Western observers and some Vatican officials, with Marxism. In fact, the terms used (i.e., class struggle, alienation, dialectic, imperialism, proletariat, and so on) were directly borrowed from the Marxist vocabulary.

Collective Sin

Liberation theologians, particularly Leonardo Boff, went so far as to suggest the notion of institutionalized violence and sin. This notion derives from and is embedded in the social structure; it relates directly to groups and classes; it says that the owners of the means of production or wealth (the landowners, for instance) who oppose and exploit the poor are—by virtue of belonging to the same group or class—all sinners; they collectively represent a regime bent upon violence, which is sinful.

According to this notion, the redemption of the poor and the exploited lies in their collective struggle against the class that commits the sin. Violence must be met by counterviolence—by revolution. That is the only way to achieve lib-

---

[2]Gustavo Gutierrez, *The Power of the Poor in History*, especially ch. 6.

eration. This analysis comes close to the Marxist theory of class struggle and the ultimate liberation of the proletariat by revolution. The Marxist categories are used, even if couched in terms of theology. The individual is viewed with regard to his or her position in a given group rather than by his or her own volition, his or her own acts, and his or her own morality and reason. "When Christians take cognizance of the link between the personal and structural levels," writes Boff, "they can no longer rest content with conversions of the heart and personal holiness at the individual level. They realize that if they are to be graced personally, they must also fight to change the societal structure and open it up to God's grace."[3] Injustice is embedded in a given structure that must be changed or destroyed, if necessary. God's grace should extend beyond the individual to the structures—to groups, to classes, to political regimes. The church, therefore, has an obligation to act here in our world to change the socioeconomic structures that account for injustice.

The Voice of the Poor and Political Action (Praxis)

In Latin America, and in the Third World in general, the poor constitute the vast majority of the citizenry—peasants, a good percentage of Indians, the landless migrant farmhands, migrant workers, marginals, the urban poor. They remain separate from the centers of power and decision making, uneducated and unorganized. The church provided them with inadequate help and services in the past, and its emphasis on evangelization was not consistent with everyday needs and expectations. The last rites were still administered, but on a social scale it was far more urgent to see to it that infants did not die at birth and that life expectancy increased. Love your neighbor—yes; but what if your neighbor is the police officer who put your son in jail? There was also another problem, closely associated with the role of the church to help the poor. There were not enough priests even for religious services, let alone societal education and reorganization.

It soon became necessary to dispense with the formal education of priests and to establish seminars and workshops in which priests could be quickly trained (and some ordained). A Theological Education by Extension (TEE) program was developed, comprising study centers, lay training centers for missions, clinical pastoral education centers, community-based educational centers, pastoral education cells, groups for study and mutual care, centers of reflection on liberation movements, and a number of ad hoc centers to discuss immediate community problems.

Evangelization (the teaching and the bearing witness of the gospel) soon became superseded by the notion of social service. What would a priest—a lay or ordained "priest," a "missioner," or a "delegate"—be expected to teach the peasantry or the poor? The word of God, to be sure. But in various discussion groups, meetings, and seminars, social questions—about the lack of water, the

---

[3]Leonardo Boff, *The Church: Charisma and Power*, p. 85.

lack of schools and health clinics, the heavy taxes, the exactions of those in a position of political or military power, the lack of food and housing—questions of everyday life, and the need to satisfy urgent wants began to be raised. Religious and moral questions inevitably became related to everyday needs and predicaments. How can we all be brothers, according to the Bible and Christ's teaching, when we live under such unequal conditions? Where is mercy and kindness when only few have access to a clinic but the many do not? Where is the "humanity" of the many, without access to a school or even a church? A theological seminary that discusses these questions inevitably becomes transformed into a social sciences or social services seminar!

The Second Vatican Council's call for social reform and political participation could only strengthen the missionary zeal of the many clergy—and also the urgency shared by lay Catholics (as well as other Christians)—to reach out to the masses and help improve their lives. What developed was literally an explosion of new community ecclesiastic organizations, not only to educate and evangelize, but also to organize and make the poor conscious of their predicament but also of their potential power. To put it simply, new parallel "churches" were established under the name of "base Christian communities"—*communidades eclesiales de base*. There are over 4 million Brazilians who participate in the more than 50,000 Christian "base ecclesiastical communities." The church followers who comprise these base communities represent such societal segments as "labor unions," "Indian groups," "slum organizations," "activist feminist groups," and "peasant movements." They discuss the Bible and apply its religious teachings to everyday political life. In this sense the meaning of praxis appears clearer. It is action within historical circumstances, informed by history *and* the gospel, in order to transform them.

The base ecclesiastical communities today consist of a large network of communities comprising millions, headed by ordained or newly trained priests or lay surrogates, providing and giving awareness to many, not only of the Word but of the need of social and political action. They are the new ministers of God whose function, however, is to make the many and the poor conscious of their predicament and their power. Their function is no longer to proselytize and evangelize but to "conscientize": to make conscious, educate, and create a new dimension of personal and social awareness and, of course, political action.

Conclusion

To the ever-shifting winds of change so much in evidence throughout the Third World, a new ideology—liberation theology—has been added. Many of the Latin American bishops are uncertain about its scope and its Christian credentials; others espouse it. The Vatican itself seems deeply concerned about the adoption of Marxist analysis by its clergy. The erosion of Marxist ideology, however, may also take the wind from the sails of liberation theology as a potentially revolutionary movement. Movements spurred by liberation theology may begin to merge with Christian democracy and seek action through political means, notably the political parties and the ballot. The Vatican would favor such a

---

Reverend Jean-Bertrand Aristide

On December 16, 1990, Reverend Jean-Bertrand Aristide, a firm adherent of liberation theology, was elected President of Haiti with 70 percent of the ballots cast in what appeared to be the first open and free election in this country. In line with Vatican policy, he had to withdraw from the priesthood to devote himself to his office as advocate "for the poor." While other priests advocating liberation theology have been active and many have held important public offices throughout Latin America, this is the first time one has attained the highest office. But how long, remains to be seen.

---

course, and many progressive Catholics, especially in Latin America, would prefer it. But whatever develops, one thing is clear: by arousing and educating the heretofore excluded and by making them conscious of their power, liberation theology may have paved the way to what it sought to accomplish—to make the wretched of the earth here and now conscious of their miseries and incite them into political action to improve their lot.

RELIGIOUS FUNDAMENTALISM

The term *fundamentalism* is relatively new.[4] Even though it was used first in the United States for some Protestant sects, it applies to a variety of religious sects and movements among Muslims, Protestants, Hindus, Jews, Greek Orthodox Catholics, and Roman Catholics. They all share a hostility to the changing social mores of modern society—its emphasis on material values and gratification, the emancipation of women, divorce, the loosening of the family bonds, and the predominant emphasis on secular values to the detriment of religious and moral education in schools. Fundamentalist movements become overtly political in order to maintain the hard core of religious beliefs and traditional practices that are being threatened by the changing social environment. They reach out to preempt social change that undermines their values.

---

[4]For the discussion in this section, I am indebted to two papers: "Contemporary Fundamentalism" by Lazarus–Yafeh, Hava, *The Jerusalem Quarterly*, No. 47, Summer 1988, pp. 27–39, and the unpublished paper of Yaakov Ariel, "Fundamentalism in Christianity, Islam and Judaism." Dr. Ariel is with the Department of Religious Studies, The Hebrew University of Jerusalem.

Common Characteristics

All religious fundamentalist sects share common orientations and values.

Dogmatism   Most all religions, organized in churches, synagogues, mosques, and temples, are inherently dogmatic and authoritarian. Each and every one propound the truth and show the greatest intolerance for the beliefs of others. Foremost among them, for a long time, was the Catholic church, which refused, until the latter part of the nineteenth century, to accept democracy, freedom of conscience, majority rule, and the right to vote. Protestant sects displayed rigidity as well and imposed conformity. John Calvin (1509–1564) imposed, in the name of a reformed church, a rigid moral and religious code upon his congregation in Geneva. Various Protestant sects in New England imposed an iron spiritual rule of obedience on their members. Those who could not stand it left with their followers to adjacent areas, only to impose upon their members the same orthodoxy they had defied. Religious fundamentalism carries the same characteristics of rigidity, disciplinarianism, and conformity to the extreme, seeking to impose its views to the exclusion of all others.

Otherworldliness and Messianic Spirit   Fundamentalists do not care about the outside world. Their beliefs and their message are not addressed to secular matters. They are concerned with the sacred. The secular society and nation–states are, strictly speaking, irrelevant. This is true for the "Arab nation," for Israel, and for the United States. Ours is only a temporary life on earth, and we will all return to God. Hence the only activities to which we should devote our energy are those consonant with the word of God.

Subordination of Political Power   Political power should be subordinate to religious power. The Bishop, the Rabbi, or the Ayatollah should have the last word on societal issues. Whenever possible—as in Iran—they should govern. Compromises are inevitably made with the secular authorities, but the intrusion of "religious men" is becoming increasingly obvious as they try to influence political leaders and voters. Fundamentalist rabbis have tried to impose their religious preferences in a number of instances (sometimes with success) on Israel's political leaders—even from outside Israel; American fundamentalists are beginning to rewrite the agenda of American politics; the spread of Islamic fundamentalism is changing the political order everywhere in the Middle East and North Africa. Not unlike Calvin in Geneva many centuries ago, holy men wish to reestablish divine rule wherever they can and to the maximum degree possible when they cannot!

The Inerrancy of the "Written Word"   All fundamentalists believe in a literal reading of the holy script and in the "inerrancy" of the Bible or the Koran. It represents the word of God or Allah—it is the truth. And it is ultimately the Scriptures that should take the place of political constitutions.

Belief in the Supernatural   All fundamentalists believe in what we might call supernatural explanations and events. God is sending us messages that we should take into account. Similarly, "Satan" is ever-present and must be combatted. Explanation, therefore, moves from the logical canons of induction, deduction, inference, generalization, and proof into a world of divine intervention and revelation. Many, especially among the American fundamentalists, believe in individual mystic "experiences"—in specific events that show God's grace. To quote from the Bible, "Angels came and ministered into . . . [them]." Even some American presidents have experienced such visitations!

Against Science   Fundamentalists reject science when science differs from their beliefs—which is quite often. They reject any critical interpretation of the Bible and any historical or archaeological evidence that may be at odds with it. They reject Darwin's evolutionary theory, arguing for the fixity of the species, and believe that the universe was created in a few days—it was not a matter of gradual evolution and change.

Charismatic Leadership   Many of the fundamentalists believe in charismatic leadership. There is one version of the truth and one "leader" who embodies it and will implement it. In this sense, they are at odds with democratic thought. Throughout Islam, there is an ongoing effort on the part of a leader to gain ascendancy by invoking some relationship with the lost Prophet. In the Catholic faith, the pope remains the Vicar of Christ and he is "infallible."

Subordination of Women   A common trait in all fundamentalists is their perception of the role of women. While accorded "high respect" as mothers in the family, they are deemed clearly inferior in all other societal roles. A strict separation of the sexes is prescribed by fundamentalists—and this is notably so among Muslim (and some Jewish) fundamentalist sects, but not among the Evangelicals, at least not to the same degree.

Moralism   When it comes to "moral values," the fundamentalists everywhere are in agreement. The family is indissoluble; sexual promiscuity is condemned; the use of alcohol and, naturally, drugs must be severely punished. In Iran, as it was in Calvin's Geneva, special "police units" supervise the implementation of these prescriptions. Fundamentalists believe in censorship to eliminate pornography and to avoid violence on TV. In short, they want to have the media conform to a moral code. They also believe that religious education is necessary in schools where it is not provided—as in the United States.

A "New" Society   All these traits give us the common "profile" of fundamentalists. It is an ideological profile that amounts to a political vision of the world. It is a political ideology that promises to fashion a new society. But what kind?

1. It is a simple uncomplicated world with fundamental values imposed by a select group of "holy men."

2. It is one in which truth is there, ready-made like a water fountain. It is in the "Book."
3. It is a masculine society; women are subordinate to men.
4. It is a static society—the word of the Bible is "inerrant." No new ideas are to be allowed if they cast any shadow upon the literal interpretation of the Bible.
5. It is an authoritarian society—in which all must follow the religious doctrine and practice enunciated by the highest religious authority.
6. It is an ascetic society in which every effort is made to subordinate many pleasures and joys, in art, literature, entertainment, and other forms of individual expression, to the imperatives of a moral code and religious worship.
7. It projects a world in which all sects are intolerant of each other. They surround themselves with religious walls that invite constant conflict among them.

Muslim Fundamentalism: Iran and Beyond

In no other country has Muslim fundamentalist ideology been more fully realized than in Iran. The founder—Ayatollah Ruhollah Khomeini, a theologian, who was elevated to the stature of an Ayatollah (a "reflection of Allah") and subsequently became Grand Ayatollah—had one and only one overriding purpose: to establish an Islamic republic, supervised, if not controlled, by the Ayatollahs, to cleanse the Iranian society of Western and secular influence that became obvious during the years of the Shah's rule (1954–1979).

Khomeini promised to return the society to its Islamic traditions and to liberate the Muslim masses throughout the world. He waged a political war against the Shah for destroying the Iranian culture, persecuting the clergy, establishing a dictatorship, and allowing foreigners to control the state and the society. "God has formed the Islamic republic. Obey God and his Prophet and those among you who have authority [i.e., the clergy]. It is the only government accepted by God on Resurrection Day." "We do not say," he added, "that the government must be composed of the clergy but that the government must be directed and organized according to the divine law, and this is only possible with the supervision of the clergy."[5] This, in a nutshell, is pure Islamic fundamentalism.

But Khomeini appealed also to nationalism, national independence, and democracy. His plea against the Shah's dictatorship appealed both to the poor and downtrodden, who, in an industrializing society, continued to be deprived of the benefits of economic growth, and also to Iranian students and intellectuals who favored democracy. In fact, the Ayatollah found great support among the university students of Teheran and elsewhere. But his major appeal was to

---

[5]The citations come from the excellent article by Raymond H. Anderson: "Ayatollah Ruhollah Khomeini, 89, Relentless Founder of the Islamic Republic" (*New York Times*, p. B11, June 5, 1989).

the *mullahs* (the clergy) and the mosques. They acted as revolutionary transmission belts, linking him with the masses at a time when all media were censored and controlled by the official government. When the Ayatollah returned to Iran from exile in Paris in 1979, he was hailed by the mobs, and within a few short weeks, he took power. He was vested with lifelong supreme authority as the religious leader—a charismatic leader.

Secure in power, he proceeded to impose Islamic fundamentalist ideology upon the society: thousands were executed for dissent, including students, intellectuals, and leaders of Communist Party; foreign workers were dismissed in favor of Iranian workers; the university was purged; women were forced to retreat to their traditional positions and roles, and made to wear veils and full-length gowns; drug addicts and drug peddlers were summarily executed. Homosexuals and prostitutes met the same fate. ("If your finger has gangrene," the Ayatollah opined, "you cut it before gangrene spreads to your body."[6]) Alcohol was prohibited, and all religious Islamic practices were strictly enforced. The press and the media came under tight control; music was banned from radio and the state-controlled TV; and, of course, the masses came under the control of the Hezbullah (the Party of God) whose leadership was in the hands of the *mullahs*. Ayatollah's rule was a splendid demonstration of *jihad*—a "holy war" against the evils and vices of a society that had strayed away from the word of the Koran, but also against the forces outside that were inimical to it, including Muslim secular regimes like those of Iraq, Syria, and Egypt. This messianic spirit—a trait of all fundamentalist movements—may well have accounted for the eight-year war with Iraq, a secular, self-styled, socialist, modernizing society.

Thus Iran, in the name of religious fundamentalism, nationalism, and anti-Westernism, has become an authoritarian regime. It is a regime that constantly evokes traditional values and is addressed to the vindication of past values. It is a regime the eschews the concepts of enlightenment, rationality, science, and the institutions and practices of liberalism, where power is legitimized in religious terms. It is a regime that is dedicated to the elimination of all infidels, especially the state of Israel. It is also a regime that, after unifying the society around the basic myths it proposes, now wants to impose its ideology and political practices abroad—particularly among the Shiite Muslims who are spread throughout the region. It is dedicated to Islam. In terms of leadership, the organization of the single party, the conformity the regime has attempted to exact, the religious mythology that it has elevated into an official ideology, and the mobilization and use of force, the Iranian regime is truly totalitarian.

The clergy has recruited and organized a paramilitary force, the Revolutionary Guards, about 150,000 strong. They are the eyes and ears of the clergy, the dogs that sniff out treason and silence opposition. Whenever the spiritual arm of the clergy cannot assure conformity, the secular arm they forged is called

---

[6]NYT *Ibid.*

upon to enforce it through intimidation and assassination. The party and the Revolutionary Guards permeate the society. They control family life, impose religious conformity, appeal to the young to join the army for both material and heavenly rewards, and punish those who fail to volunteer. They also deal out swift justice to anyone who violates religious taboos.

Over and above the party, the mosques, the Revolutionary Guards, and the Parliament, there are three institutions that stand supreme. The first is the Supreme Religious Guide. The second is the Assembly of Experts (eighty-three clergymen), which was established in 1983 to decide Khomeini's succession. The third is the Council of Guardians, a very small group of clerics (with scholarly reputations) who go over legislation, government decrees, and orders to check their conformity with the religious faith. They are, in a sense, the highest court. Finally, there is the army. Purged of all pro-American or pro-Western elements, it is now manned with converts and new recruits and serves faithfully the religious–political leadership. Unable to win the war against Iraq, the army maintains nonetheless its position and prestige. It is and probably will remain an obedient instrument of the Islamic revolution that it hopes will extend beyond the borders of Iran. In the meantime, dissenters and critics have been eliminated at home, and those who live abroad have been the victims of terrorist attacks and threats. Salmon Rushdie is in hiding somewhere in England, sentenced to death for blasphemy contained in his book *The Satanic Verses*, which parodied some religious observances.

Beyond Iran Muslim fundamentalism is spreading. In Sudan, the National Islamic Front (an outgrowth of Egypt's Muslim Brotherhood) has gained control in alliance with a military junta. The secular constitution was set aside to be replaced by Islamic religious law—the *charia*. In the local elections held in Algeria on June 12, 1990, the Islamic Salvation Front, advocating the establishment of an Islamic republic (as in Iran), won and carried a majority even in the big cities. The platform on which it ran was "Islam Is the Solution"! Many Muslim fundamentalist religious practices are returning, and the Salvation Front may win the legislative election. Echoes were felt in Tunisia and Morocco, and powerful Islamic fundamentalist groups are to be found in Jordan, Egypt, Syria, and among the Palestinians. Indonesia, the fifth most populous state with 155 million, has the largest Muslim population of any country. Muslim fundamentalists are in control in Mauritania; some are flexing their spiritual muscles in Albania and Yugoslavia and far into China. Muslim workers throughout Western Europe are beginning, too, to form enclaves. There are five Muslim republics in the Soviet Union on the southeastern rim of Russia. They are in revolt against the secular Marxist orthodoxy, imposed upon them for so long.

Muslim fundamentalism has been felt as far as Trinidad. A militant group rose in the summer of 1990 and took over the government, occupied the prime minister's office, and captured him. The coup failed, but it showed that Islamic fundamentalism was spreading far and wide.

Fundamentalism and Nationalism A major source of strength for religious fundamentalism, not only Islamic, lies in its linkage with nationalisms or

Far into China the Muslim fundamentalists are active. In the provinces of Xinjiang and Ningxia, new mosques are being built and Islamic study centers are well attended. Many Muslims are branded as separatists.

ethnonationalisms, which we discussed in Chapter 9. Nationalism is a secular ideology inconsistent, on its face, with the religious and transcendental aspirations of fundamentalism. Yet in a number of countries, and notably where there are strong fundamentalists, they have supported nationalist and separatist aspirations. Afghan fundamentalists represent the backbone of the resistance movement against a Soviet-imposed regime. The case was much clearer in Iran, where the fundamentalists claimed liberation and national independence from the Shah *and* American and Western influence. Secular nationalist regimes like those of Iraq, Egypt, or Syria have come increasingly under the influence of fundamentalists and may align themselves on common themes. Throughout the Middle East, the ideology of Muslim fundamentalism—rigid, demanding, mobilizing, anti-Western—is seeking a reconciliation with the secular Arab states as the two most powerful forces in the Middle East—nationalism and fundamentalism—seek an answer to the search for a common identity among Muslims.

Yet while there is every indication that muslim fundamentalism is spreading and that it affects directly the lives and thoughts of hundreds of millions throughout the world, there are also some signs that its political weight may have peaked. Iran, for instance, has begun to reconsider its relations with the West and even the United States in an effort to improve its domestic economy. The grip of the clergy over the government and the people has been loosened. Despite the rhetoric, the muslim masses failed to rise during the Gulf War against the United States and the West. The mosques and the bazaars throughout the moslem world remained remarkably quiet and acts of terrorism were few. The religious zealots are as many and as active as before, but immediate problems of political power and economic survival and even more so, the prospect of military confrontations may have quieted their ardor. For the time being, the Prophet may have to wait until the faithful satisfy their urgent material needs.

The Evangelicals

American Evangelicals—as the fundamentalists are generally referred to in the United States—display the same traits that all fundamentalists do: emphasis on the word of God and the inerrancy of the Bible.[7] They show the same attachment to traditional values and religious practices and the same aversion to modernity. Besieged by a "modern" and liberal society, Evangelicals stand on a solid fortress, occasionally undertaking powerful thrusts at those that besiege them. They revolt against changing mores and societal trends —crime and violence, pornography, drugs, homosexuality, prostitution, teen pregnancies, premarital sex—and the dangers they seem to pose to the fabric of the society, to the family and stable family relations, to the school, and to the church.

In the last two decades, the Evangelicals have been gaining. In the United States, the most dynamic and mobile society in the world, where the only truth accepted is the freedom to question it, fundamentalists attempt to find a permanent shelter—an anchor that will hold us back from critical inquiry and ex-

---

[7]They also are referred to as the Christian right, the religious right, or the Moral Majority.

perimentation. And the greater and faster the changes in a society, the greater becomes the longing for stability and certainty. As a result, both the depth and pace of change have forced many fundamentalists to come out and fight in order to protect what they feel is being threatened. They have become activists not only to preserve the values they cherish, but also to restore them. They have entered politics and their theology has been transformed into a political movement designed to enact or change legislation to promote their conservative views. They have moved "from the Pew to the Precinct," in the words of Jerry Falwell, one of their leaders.

It is not easy to clearly distinguish the theology of the various sects that comprise the religious conservative movement; Baptists and Southern Baptist, Pentecostals, and Southern Lutherans are among the most prominent. The greatest number of believers are situated in the so-called Bible Belt and beyond: Tennessee, Virginia, Georgia, Florida, Arkansas, Louisiana, Mississippi, Texas, North and South Carolina, and Alabama. (A Gallup Poll indicated that 50 percent of all evangelicals are from the South.) But they are also strong in Michigan, Missouri, Ohio, and in a number of western states. Tens of millions throughout the country have been mobilized by fundamentalists. In fact, one-third of the American population proclaims itself as "Born-Again Christians," according to a Gallup Poll.

While religious themes continue to prevail, it is the way they have been shaped into a political program and the way believers have been organized into political action that count. A common political philosophy emerges even when there are theological disputes among sects, as there are, particularly between fundamentalists and evangelicals. This common political ideology has been shaped by a number of prominent religious leaders—Rousas J. Rashdoony, Tim Lattaye, Gary North, Jerry Falwell, George Marsden, Pat Robertson, and others. Through newly established theological seminaries, foundations and universities, newspapers and journals, radio and television, the themes that organize the political battle lines, often in close cooperation with conservative organizations like the Conservative Caucus, the National Conservative Political Action Committee, and others, have become clear.

The shortest distance between the pew and the precinct, one might add, is radio and television. Through the Christian Broadcasting Network (CBN), the third largest cable network in the country, more than 30 million people are reached daily. If one were to add various affiliated stations, the figure is close to 50 million. The evangelicals have become increasingly "tele-evangelicals."

Both general and specific themes have been developed by ministers and theologians and espoused by others for political purposes. The "political ministers" have tried to create a mass movement that cuts across religious lines to include Protestants, Catholics, Jews, blacks, whites, farmers, businessmen, and housewives. This is the Moral Majority, which was formed "to combat the legalization of immorality." The movement directly confronts some of the critical issues that concern Americans, but it lumps together abortion, pornography, the use of drugs, the breakdown of the family, homosexuality, and other "moral cancers" to which AIDS has most recently been added.

Political Action and Organization   The fundamentalists who spearheaded the Moral Majority movement pride themselves on their strong organization, which is defined and described in terms appropriate to a paramilitary organization: commitment of the individual and readiness to sacrifice "even life itself" for the sake of the "company of the faithful"; absolute discipline in the willingness of all to obey the commands of the leadership; evangelical zeal—to spread the gospel and convert people; absolutism—the acceptance of God's word as the absolute truth; and, finally, fanaticism.

Fundamentalists have little patience with dialogue, argument, and self-criticism. But in building the Moral Majority, efforts have been made to allow for internal debate and pluralism, and present a common political front on those basic moral and political positions that unite the greatest number possible. The battle against pornography, drugs, and abortion are likely to receive the most widespread support. So is national defense, though there are differences as to how much defense is needed. A blanket anti-Communist stance (often anti-Soviet) is also widely supported by nationalists and those who fear atheism. School prayer is also overwhelmingly endorsed.

The scope of the movement's political activities has been comprehensive and multifaceted. Voters have been so well mobilized to register that millions of previously indifferent citizens have now joined the voting public. Large amounts of money have been raised to support candidates, but each candidate is carefully screened to determine his or her stand on the critical moral issues. Pamphlets, letters, and radio and television messages have been used to support or reject candidates. Lobbyists have also approached members of Congress in Washington and in state legislatures as well as federal and state officials. Above all, a constant stream of educational and political materials keep coming out of religious study and research centers to reach out to the believers.

In the 1988 presidential race, the Reverend Marion "Pat" Robertson surprised political experts, pollsters, members of the media, and the American electorate. Robertson, a television Evangelist and founder of the Christian Broadcasting Network and the daily "700 Club" program, finished third for the Republican nomination, placing ahead of political veterans, including former Congressman Jack Kemp, former Delaware Governor Pierre DuPont, and General Alexander Haig. Robertson's successes were not only in the deep South, the base of Evangelicalism and fundamentalism; they were spread throughout the country. While he lost the nomination to George Bush, his campaign may have long-standing effects on the American political system.

The Convention of Southern Baptists   The strongest and most numerous group among the Evangelicals are the Southern Baptists—stretching from Georgia to California through Texas, Virginia, Oklahoma, Alabama, Florida, Mississippi, and South Carolina, with offshoots in Michigan, southern Illinois, Ohio, and Nebraska. There are over 15 million Southern Baptists, and a number of Evangelical churches have close links with them. In July 1990, their delegates—"messengers," as they are called—held their convention in New Orleans to select their president, and Mr. Morris H. Chapin was reelected with

58 percent of the votes. The president represented the conservative hard core of the fundamentalist doctrine. He stressed the inerrancy of the Bible. "The Bible," he pointed out, "is not negotiable." It represents the "inspired, infallible, inerrant word of God." The moderate candidate for the election, who lost, agreed. In addition to the inerrancy of the Bible, the platform included, among other things:

1. A demand for laws against pornography.
2. Strong laws against abortion. Abortion was the subject of two resolutions, and the Evangelicals seemed to agree with the Catholic church. They stressed the sanctity of human life and opposed abortion, except to save the life of the mother. They opposed the use of abortion drugs and also proposed a boycott against all businesses that contribute to pro-abortion organizations.
3. Renewed demands for religious education in schools.
4. The need to convert and evangelize; in fact, Evangelicals have been particularly successful in converting Hispanics from Catholicism—both in the United States and in Latin America.

In contrast to other fundamentalist movements, women attended the conference and voted. But they seemed to accept their special role in the society: "Father, let us be the mothers you want us to be" was one of their prayers.[8]

How lasting will the influence of the Evangelicals be? It is difficult to answer, but one thing is clear: the embattled ministers of God have entered politics in earnest. In their emphasis on traditionalism, their rejection of critical inquiry, and their goal of propounding their own moral and religious values, they are beginning to weigh heavily on the political agenda of the country. " Moral–social" issues dominate the political debate and increasingly affect the position of candidates. In other words, the fundamentalists and evangelicals are reshaping the political horizon.

The Soldiers of God

Everywhere religious beliefs are translated into political militancy. In Ulster, Catholics are virtually at war with the Protestants; in Belgium, they hold each other at arm's length; in Jerusalem, Muslims, Greek Orthodox and Jews are fighting about their holy temples; the Hindus and the Muslims are at war over a mosque near Nepal, reputed to be on the burial site of the Hindu God Raman; in Yugoslavia, Roman Catholics, Greek Orthodox Catholics, and Muslims are ready to confront each other. Religious fundamentalist movements are spreading as an increasing number of people join their ranks. They all claim their truth to be superior to that held by all others, and they are ready to defend it by force

---

[8]Quotes from press releases on the 1990 Southern Baptist Convention, June 12–14, 1990.

and to impose it by force. At a time when communism and socialism are waning and democracy remains uncertain, religious fundamentalism (often linked with nationalist movements) marshals the hearts and souls of hundreds of millions seeking their own way of life against all others. "Will religion become the main force that sets one group of mankind against another,"[9] It may!

BIBLIOGRAPHY

Liberation Theology

Abbot, Walter M. *The Documents of Vatican II*. New York: Herder & Herder, 1966.

Arias, Ester and Mortimer. *The Cry of My People: Out of Captivity in Latin America*. New York: Friendship Press, 1980.

Berryman, Philip. *Liberation Theology*. New York: Pantheon, 1987.

Boff, Leonardo. *Liberating Grace*. Maryknoll, N.Y.: Orbis Books, 1981.

————. "Theological Characteristics of a Grassroots Church," in Sergio Torres and John Eagleson (eds.), *Theology in the Americas*. Maryknoll, N.Y.: Orbis Books, 1976, pp. 124–144.

————. *Jesus Christ Liberator*. Maryknoll, N.Y.: Orbis Books, 1978. (Originally published as *Jesus Christo liberador: Ensaio de Cristologia critica para o nosso tempo*. Petropolis: Vozes, 1972.)

————. "Christ's Liberation via Oppression: An Attempt at Theological Construction from the Standpoint of Latin America," in Rosino Gibellini (ed.), *Frontiers in Theology in Latin America*. Maryknoll, N.Y.: Orbis Books, 1979a, pp. 100–132.

————. *The Church: Charisma and Power*. New York: Crossroads, 1985.

Cardoso, F. H.,and E. Faletto. *Dependency and Development in Latin America*. Berkeley: University of California Press, 1975.

Dussel, Enrique. *History and the Theology of Liberation: A Latin American Perspective*. Translated by John Drury. Maryknoll, N.Y.: Orbis Books, 1976.

Gibellini, Rosino (ed.). *Frontiers of Theology in Latin America*. Translated by John Drury. Maryknoll, N.Y.: Orbis Books, 1975.

Goulet, Denis. *A New Moral Order: Studies in Development Ethics and Liberation Theology*. Maryknoll, N.Y.: Orbis Books, 1979.

Gutierrez, Gustavo. *A History of Liberation: History, Politics and Salvation*. Maryknoll, N.Y.: Orbis Books, 1971.

————*A Theology of Liberation: History, Politics and Salvation*. Maryknoll, N.Y.: Orbis Books, 1973. (Originally published as *Teología de la liberacion*. Lima: Perspectives by CEP, 1971.)

————. *The Power of the Poor in History*. Maryknoll, N.Y.: Orbis Books, 1983.

Hanson, Eric. *The Catholic Church in World Politics*. Princeton, N.J.: Princeton University Press, 1987.

Hennelly, Alfred T. *Theologies in Conflict: The Challenge of Juan Luis Segundo*. Maryknoll, N.Y.: Orbis Books, 1979.

---

[9]*The Economist*, "Soldiers of God," November 17, 1990, pp. 15–16.

Medellin Conference Final Documents. *The Church in the Present-day Transformation of Latin America in the Light of the Council*, vol. II. Bogota, Colombia: CELAM, 1968.

————. *Freedom with Justice: Catholic Social Thought and Liberal Institutions*. New York: Harper & Row, 1984.

O'Brien, David J. *The Renewal of American Catholicism*. New York: Oxford University Press, 1972.

Rynne, Xavier. *Vatican Council II*. New York: Farrar, Straus and Giroux, 1964.

Sacred Congregation for the Doctrine of the Faith. "Instruction on Certain Aspects of the 'Theology of Liberation.' " Boston: Daughters of St. Paul, 1984 and 1986.

————. "Instruction on Christian Freedom and Liberation." Boston: Daughters of St. Paul, 1986.

Sigmund, Paul E. *Liberation Theology at the Crossroads*. New York: Oxford University Press, 1990.

Segundo, Juan Luis. *The Hidden Motives of Pastoral Action: Latin American Reflections*. Maryknoll, N.Y.: Orbis Books, 1972.

Smith, Donald E. *Religion, Politics and Social Change in the Third World*. New York: Free Press, 1971.

Islamic Fundamentalism

Chehabi, Houchang E. *Iranian Politics and Religious Modernism: The Liberation Movement of Iran under the Shah and Khomeini*. London: Cornell University Press & I. B. Tauris, 1990.

Esposito, John. *Islam: The Straight Path*, expanded ed. New York: Oxford University Press, 1991.

Hiro Dilip. *Iran under the Ayatollahs*. New York: Routledge, 1987.

———— . *Holy Wars: The Rise of Islamic Fundamentalism*, New York: Routledge, 1989.

Landau, Jacob M. *The Politics of Pan-Islam: Ideology and Organization*. New York: Oxford University Press, 1990.

Lazarus–Yafeh, Hava. "Contemporary Fundamentalism." *The Jerusalem Quarterly*, No. 47, Summer 1988, pp. 27–39.

Sivan, Emmanuel. *Radical Islam*. New Haven, Conn.: Yale University Press, 1985.

Watt, W. Montgomery. *Islamic Fundamentalism and Modernity*. New York: Routledge, 1988.

Evangelicals

Cole, Steward Grant. *History of Fundamentalism*. Hamden, Conn.: Archon Books, 1963.

Conway, Flo, and Jim Siegelman. *Holy Terror*. Garden City, N.Y.: Doubleday, 1982.

Fackre, Gabriel. *The Religious Right and Christian Faith*. Grand Rapids, Mich.: William B. Eerdmans, 1982.

Falwell, Jerry. *The Fundamentalist Phenomenon*. Garden City, N.Y.: Doubleday, 1981.

Gasper, Louis. *The Fundamentalist Movement*. Paris: Tenn. Mouton & Co., 1963.

Hadden, Jeffrey, and Anson Shupe. *Televangelism, Power and Politics*. Boston: Beacon Press, 1988.

Jorsted Erlig. *Politics of Doomsday.* Nashville, Tenn.: Abington Press, 1970.

Kater, John. *Christians on the Right: The Moral Majority in Perspective.* New York: Seabury Press, 1982.

Marsden, George M. *Fundamentalism and American Culture.* New York: Oxford University Press, 1980.

Wills, Garry. *Under God: Religion and American Politics.* New York: Simon and Schuster, 1990.

Chapter
11

Feminism

To gain the supreme victory, it is necessary . . . that by and through their natural differentiation men and women unequivocally affirm their brotherhood.

Simone de Beauvoir
The Second Sex

*A*ll liberation and revolutionary ideologies, including liberalism, promise to free individuals from oppression and subjection. Their major theme is to restore to individuals what they have lost: the autonomy of their wills, the freedom of their consciences, and equality for all. Feminism shares these same overall goals—to establish equality between women and men and to liberate women from submission to men.

We may consider feminism, then, as a set of ideas espoused by a number of people—women and men—to form a movement whose goal is to attain the full equality of women. It began in the middle of the nineteenth century with demands for the right to vote and has continued since with efforts by women to secure in the workplace, the professions, and the household full equality with men not only in terms of opportunities but in the material condition of their lives. In certain respects, this movement (and the ideology that spawns it) may not differ substantively from other liberating ideologies: for blacks, minority groups, workers, or farmers. Thus it may be more of a movement than an ideology.

According to a more comprehensive view of feminism, however, the liberation of women will bring about radical changes in our society and its values. It assumes that throughout history the roles women have played and the images held about women have been shaped by men. In the process, women became alienated, viewing themselves in a mirror made for them by men. They accepted a false set of images—a false ideology—and they identified with it. They lost their individuality, a loss that adversely affects all of us, since it deprives women of their true selves, their spontaneity, and their potentiality. This broader view of feminism postulates, therefore, that "feminine values" and their realization will build a better world for all. The feminine ingredient, fully liberated, will become the leaven that will radically transform our values and our world.

In this chapter, we explore feminism as an ideology and a political movement. Before we begin, however, let us take an overview of the condition of women over the centuries. Actually, it is more of a predicament than a condition.

THE SUBJECTION OF WOMEN[1]

Aside from some rare circumstances where under special socioeconomic conditions "matriarchical" societies (societies in which women rule) existed, the common lot of women has been subjection to men. Their roles and positions, their physical living conditions, including the disposition of their bodies, were determined by men—fathers, grandfathers, husbands, or sons. Subjection did not necessarily manifest itself in the actual use of force, though force was ever-present; it resulted from the dominant ideology. Women, even if exalted as mothers or wives or as talented courtesans, and even if often relied upon by men because of their talents, were considered inferior to men and were held in inferior positions. In most societies women had no rights until the middle of the nineteenth century. They could not participate in the economy or the political life of the society; they had no property and were not allowed to manage property bequeathed to them; they could not choose their own husbands; they had no access to education and the professions, and if they did, education was specially arranged or specially tailored for them.

Despite notable shifts and changes in ideology, the subjection of women was constant, and still remains in many parts of the world today, especially among the less developed countries of the Third World. In many of these countries women are simply not valued; they work hard for little pay and receive little protection from the public authorities. Medical care is noticeably of lower quality (if any at all) than what is available to males; less food is available to them whether through the market, the family, or the distribution agencies that attempt to cope with famine in many Third World countries. They have less access to the educational facilities that are available. Although international agencies, the United Nations, and also religious organizations have noted women's tragic conditions and the compelling need to improve them, poverty and subjection continue to afflict women more than men in the underdeveloped world. It is important that we constantly keep their predicament in mind as we outline the significant changes that have taken place in the position of women elsewhere.

---

[1]This is the title of John Stuart Mill's essay first published in 1869. For the essay and an introduction by Susan Moller Okin: John Stuart Mill, *The Subjection of Women*, Cambridge: Hackett Publishing Co., Inc., 1989.

The reasons given for women's subjection have been many. Some societies deemed women as "weak" and "irrational." Roman law referred to the "imbecility" of the sex and put women under the tutelage of men. The Christian fathers, despite their professed compassion for all, considered women "sinful" and inferior; man was "complete," woman was a "part of" man; she came from Adam's rib.

The reality of subjection written into the law was reinforced by the writings of philosophers, intellectuals, and theologians. Few came out to plead for women's equality, freedom, and inherent rationality. Only Plato allowed them within the "guardian" class and provided them with the same education given to men, but their ultimate function, some have argued, was to provide male children of high quality for the ruling elite. For Aristotle, subjection was "natural": like slaves, women were by nature "defective." Christian theologians, even though they admired chastity and the "obedient wife," saw women as the embodiment of Satan—vile creatures of the flesh. The liberal philosophers did not consider them capable of facing the responsibilities of a citizen and coping with the cruel but necessary world of the capitalist market. Their paramount obligations to produce and rear children and maintain the conjugal family were emphasized to the point where women were excluded from political participation and the management of property.

It is true that John Stuart Mill pleaded their cause by asking that education be provided to them, but then education was for John Stuart Mill the cure for all inequities for all people. Even Karl Marx paid little attention to the special situation of women, assuming that the collectivization of the means of production—communism—would provide liberation for them, as it would for all the exploited and underprivileged groups. Engels, following Marx, attributed their enslavement to the property relationships established under capitalism, especially that of the conjugal family in which the husband owned everything and reigned supreme, but Engels did not explain why subjection was also prevalent in noncapitalist societies. In general, Marxism paid no attention to the specifics of women's subjugation and provided no programmatic cures under communism.[2]

EGALITARIANISM AND LIBERALISM

Liberalism provided the first impetus toward the emancipation of women. But as Simone de Beauvoir wrote, "It might have been expected that the [French] Revolution would change the lot of women. It did nothing of the sort."[3] Throughout the nineteenth century, women remained in an inferior position to

---

[2]See Susan Okin, *Women in Western Political Thought* and Allison Jaggar, *Feminist Politics and Human Nature*.

[3]Simone de Beauvoir, *The Second Sex*, p. 100.

men. The French Civil Code and the jurisprudence that followed consecrated the supremacy of the husband in the household. No civil or property rights were provided to married women as well as no political rights. Divorce remained outlawed in many countries in Europe and difficult for women elsewhere. As for the women who entered the labor force in factories of the rapidly industrializing societies or who did piecework at home, primarily in the booming textile manufacturing industry, no legislation protected them, despite the "frailty" of their sex. In fact, until almost the end of the century, women had worked longer hours and for less pay than men. On the farm (more than half the population of most European countries, the United States, and England were farmers until the beginning of the twentieth century) women labored hard in the fields, while taking care of the household, giving birth, and raising children.

Protests were mounted throughout the nineteenth century by intellectuals, political leaders, and women's organizations. They all advocated the improvement of women's position and opportunities in the marketplace, the factory, at home, and in politics. There were demands to grant women the right to vote, the right to own and dispose of a business, equal civil rights, the right to an equal education, and access to the professions.

Demands for the right to vote raised passionate debates and conflicts. It was not until the turn of the nineteenth century that women were granted the right to vote, first in Australia, New Zealand, and the Scandinavian countries, and in some of the western states in America. Woman suffrage became law for all states in the United States with the passage of the Nineteenth Amendment in 1920; in England it became law in 1928. It was only after the end of World War II that universal suffrage became the norm. Legislation was enacted as late as 1945 in France and even later in Greece, Spain, and Portugal. Switzerland has the distinction of being the last democracy to grant it—in 1971.[4]

The "Suffragette" Movement in England

The women's movement to gain the right to vote (the "suffragette" movement as it became known) began in 1857 with the establishment of the Sheffield Female Political Association that demanded voting rights for women, as well as full civil and property rights.[5] It was followed with the establishment of the Kensington Society under the leadership of Miss Helen Taylor, stepdaughter of John Stuart Mill. In 1870, the *Women's Suffrage Journal* appeared. Local committees sprang up all over the country and, in 1867, Parliament was petitioned for the first time to enact legislation granting women the right to vote. Petitions were regularly submitted to Parliament and they were regularly ignored or re-

---

[4] Two Swiss cantons, however, do not allow women to vote in local elections!

[5] "Suffragette," the term used at the time, had and continues to have a condescending ring; hence the quotes.

The majesty and panoply of "the law" were brought to bear upon the "suffragette" leaders in England, who asked for nothing more than the right to vote (c. 1910).

jected. Between 1876 and 1880, demonstrations and meetings were organized throughout the country and, in 1883, the Liberal Party Conference voted a resolution in favor of women's suffrage. Yet the Reform Act of 1884 extended voting rights only to males.

It was during the first decade of the twentieth century, under the leadership of Christian Pankhurst, that the movement grew both in scope and militancy. In 1903, the Women's Social and Political Union, a large umbrella organization, was formed. It gradually grew into a force that included millions of women and men, and it received the support of labor and liberal political leaders, trade unionists, and intellectuals. At first the movement used educational tactics: sermons, lectures, meetings, pamphlets and other publications, as well as peaceful demonstrations, marches, and lobbying. But eventually it took violent forms. Women broke up public meetings and stopped traffic; they were arrested and jailed; in jail they went on hunger strikes and were force-fed. Increasingly, the "weaker" sex showed its fortitude and became confrontational, throwing stones at the police, burning public and private buildings, physically assaulting political leaders. More women were arrested; more of them went on hunger strikes. The movement was briefly interrupted with the coming of World War I in 1914 when women (despite many pacifists in their ranks) began to work in munitions factories and in paramilitary services. Only a limited franchise was granted in 1920, but the battle had been won. Full voting rights were granted in 1928.

The Suffragette Movement in the United States

Ever since the drafting of the U.S. Constitution, women's rights and especially the right to vote, remained a salient issue until it was finally granted, first by some states and then for the country as a whole, in 1920. Intermingled with demands for the right to vote were powerful moral and religious issues: the antislavery movement, in which some women began to play an important role; and later the temperance movement against the sale and distribution of liquor, spearheaded by the Women's Christian Temperance Association, which was founded in 1874. Demands for opportunities in securing employment, the right to divorce, equal rights with men in education, access to professions and commerce, and the right to own and dispose of property also played an important role.

The women's movement began in earnest with the Seneca Falls Convention in 1848. It was a convention "to discuss . . . social, civil, and religious rights." Although the first day of the meeting was supposed to be exclusively for women, the gathering of several hundred people also included many men, and after two days a Declaration of Principles was drafted which, in the spirit of the Declaration of Independence, called for the complete enfranchisement of women. In addition, other civil rights were addressed. Most important of all was a change in the law to give women rights over their property and income, which at that time remained under the control of their husbands; women also demanded the freedom to engage in business and commerce. The convention ended with a ringing affirmation of the need for women's emancipation: "The history of mankind is a history of repeated injuries and usurpations on the part of man toward woman, having for direct object the establishment of tyranny over her."[6]

Conventions were again called in 1849 and 1851. The movement gained momentum. Susan Anthony, brought up in an abolitionist family, assumed the leadership shortly after the Seneca Falls Convention, together with E. C. Stanton. Black women and men—most of them freed slaves—also joined. One of them, Sojourner Truth, spoke at the convention of 1851 on race and liberation. Countering the arguments that women should not be given the right to vote because they were "weak" and "helpless," she spoke with the same passion we find in some of Martin Luther King's speeches:

> Look at my arm! I have ploughed and planted and gathered into barns and no man could head me—and ain't I a woman? I could work as much and eat as much as a man—when I could get it—and bear the lash as well—And ain't I a woman? I have born thirteen children and seen most of them sold into slavery . . . and when I cried with my mother's grief none but Jesus hear me—and ain't I a woman?[7]

---

[6]For the full account, see Eleanor Flexner, *Century of Struggle.* I am indebted to the author for much of the account I give here.

[7]Cited in Eleanor Flexner, *Century of Struggle,* p. 91.

The Fourteenth (1868) and Fifteenth (1870) Amendments, which abolished slavery and gave blacks extended civil and citizenship rights, including the right to vote, also gave the "suffragette" movement renewed determination and militancy. It was triggered by the fact that the citizenship rights were given only to *males*.

In their struggle to gain the right to vote, American women used tactics similar to those used in England: pamphlets and other writings, meetings, lectures, and lobbying. And as in England, women were arrested and kept the jails crowded; they went on hunger strikes and were force-fed. They abandoned peaceful tactics and took to civil disobedience. Women activists picketed the White House, refused to participate in war work (there were a significant number of pacifists among them), and some activists promised to "punish" President Woodrow Wilson. By 1917, the leading women's organization, the National Women's Suffrage Association, had a membership of 2 million. Women's organizations singled out congressmen and senators, both Democrats and Republicans, promising support and help to friends and threatening to bring the enemies down in defeat. Friends and enemies were defined in terms of where they stood on the issue of the women's franchise.

With the enactment of the Nineteenth Amendment on August 18, 1920[8] (after it was ratified by the thirty-third state, Tennessee), women entered the mainstream of political life as voters. In concrete terms, they could now make the weight of their numbers and organization felt on both national and state elections and legislation.

THE STRUGGLE FOR EQUALITY

Equality has many facets. For women, being able to influence the public authorities through their vote was only one, but an important, first step in their struggle for equality. Beyond lay many other disabilities that had to be confronted and eliminated before genuine equality could be attained. Economic rights loomed large: training for employment, the right to be employed, full access to all jobs, upward mobility within the job, nondiscrimination in hiring and firing by employers, and equal pay and benefits. The social position and roles of women also had to be reconsidered. Their virtually exclusive role as mother and housekeeper, while their husbands worked, had to be modified. This would involve a restructuring of family values to allow for greater, indeed equal, sharing by the husband. Another important issue involved what we could call personal freedoms: the right to have or not have children within or outside marriage, the unfettered right of divorce, protection against abuse to which women continue to be subjected, and ultimately the right to terminate pregnancy. It was not only a long list—and many of these aspirations remain as yet

---

[8]When the amendment was passed in 1920, twenty-two states did not allow women to vote.

Susan B. Anthony (1820–1906)

Susan B. Anthony was born in South Adams, Massachusetts, on February 15, 1820, the second oldest of eight children. Her mother was a devout Baptist and her father a Quaker. As with the rest of her sisters and brothers, she received fairly extensive early education and was trained for the only profession then deemed suitable for a woman—teaching—to which she devoted fifteen years of her life.

Along with her early interest in abolitionism (many of the most prominent abolitionists, including William Lloyd Garrison, visited her family), she was committed to the temperance movement. In 1847 she joined the Daughters of Temperance, and in 1852 she organized the New York State Women's Temperance Association. From about 1850 on, she and Elizabeth Cody Stanton devoted themselves in earnest to the cause of women's suffrage. Between 1868 and 1870, she produced in collaboration with Stanton a feminist magazine entitled *The Revolution.* In 1872 she was arrested along with several other women for voting in the presidential election and was brought to trial. When asked by the judge after she had pleaded not guilty, "You voted as a woman, did you not?" She replied, "No, sir, I voted as a citizen of the United States." In response to the $100 fine that was imposed, Anthony stated, "Resistance to tyranny is obedience to God, and I shall never pay a penny of this unjust claim." She never did. Anthony doggedly wore the "Bloomer" outfit throughout her life, and by the time of her death, she had come to symbolize women's rights and determination.

unfulfilled—but one whose goals were difficult to realize without a drastic political action and without a change in the values and ideas that even modern societies hold about women.

However, there were some steps taken to improve the position of women. Maternity and pediatric clinics were established by states with matching grants from the federal government; some legislation for improved working conditions and limiting working hours for children and women was also enacted but, in most cases (unless health hazards were particularly obnoxious), they were not implemented. The courts found legislative regulations to be contrary to the Fourteenth Amendment, which guaranteed employers and employees their freedom to contract.

The New Deal

It was in terms of its overall reforms rather than specifics that the New Deal had a positive impact on the status of women. Inasmuch as women constituted almost one-fourth of the labor force, they benefited from legislative measures such as the National Industrial Recovery Act of 1933 and the National Recovery Administration, measures designed to expand employment opportunities and safeguard jobs. Employed women also benefited from wage raises, shorter working hours, and a broader range of employment opportunities.[9] Since maximum hour and minimum wage provisions applied to *all* workers, women in low-paying jobs under "sweatshop" conditions saw their status upgraded. But all these provisions applied only to industry and trade, and women engaged in domestic service, clerical work, and on the farm were not helped. The establishment of the National Labor Relations Board, however, gave women workers, especially in the textile industries, the right to bargain collectively for better wages and working conditions.

Thus one may say that the benefits women received during the New Deal legislation were derivative: they came from legislation and programs addressed to overall social and economic predicaments, especially unemployment. There was no specific effort to advance the position of women materially or otherwise. It was only World War II that gave women new and unprecedented opportunities in the labor market, at least while it lasted.

Even if the New Deal did not address itself to particular women-related problems, however, a number of women in the Roosevelt administration kept women's issues alive—most notably the president's wife, Eleanor Roosevelt, and the Secretary of Labor, Frances Perkins, as well as many women who worked in the federal relief programs. There was a growing sensitivity to these issues within the political elites and especially within the Democratic party. With the formation of the Women's Joint Congressional Committee in 1930,

---

[9]Susan Ware, *Holding Their Own: American Women in the 1930s.*

women began to lobby in earnest. For the first time, birth control issues were debated by the House Judiciary Committee, and gradually birth control measures were legalized. In 1945, federal agencies provided funds for the establishment of some day care centers. In 1960, under strong pressure from many women's organizations, President John F. Kennedy appointed a Committee on the Status of Women, chaired by Eleanor Roosevelt. The report issued in 1963 was fairly tame and disappointing to many women activists. It avoided a number of pending demands and urged only greater educational and training facilities for women.

A major landmark was the Equal Pay Act (1963), which prescribed equal pay for men and women for the same job and prohibited discriminatory practices against women. This was broadened by the Civil Rights Act of 1964, expressly prohibiting all discrimination on the base of race *and* sex,[10] and an Equal Opportunity Employment Commission was established to oversee its implementation and enforcement. With the formation of the National Organization for Women (NOW) in 1966 and the Women's Bipartisan Caucus in 1971, feminist demands for equality grew. These groups disseminated information, mobilized the voters, and lobbied Congress. In 1972, the Education Act prohibited sex discrimination. Finally, the courts, reticent if not outright hostile at first, became increasingly well-disposed to women's issues and demands and began to strike down discriminatory legislation and practices. In the famous *Roe* v. *Wade* case (1973), a state's antiabortion law was deemed unconstitutional, and in the same year the Equal Rights Amendment (ERA) was overwhelmingly endorsed by Congress. The franchise that was won and the subsequent expansion of civil rights, affirmative action for women, no-fault divorce laws, solid educational opportunities, the availability of birth control measures, and the freedom to exercise choice in having or not having children, all seem to have brought to a realization many of the earlier feminists' demands for equality. Figure 11.1 and Table 11.1 show the gains made by women between 1970 and 1986.

Women have been gaining everywhere. Table 11.1 indicates the gains in employment between 1970 and 1988 in the twelve member countries of the European community. Women have been inching closer to securing equal pay with men—but the gap still remains. Women *on the average* receive about 20 percent less pay than men.

In most of the advanced industrialized democracies—but not so as yet in the United States—the state also provides comprehensive aid for child care and supports for all working mothers. In Sweden, public day care centers cater to 90 percent of the children between one and a half and six; in Denmark, the figure is 50 percent; in France, "nurseries," partially supported by the state, provide care to about 25 percent of children under three and to about 90 percent of those between three and five. Furthermore, generous family allowances

---

[10]Ironically enough, the word "sex" had been inserted by conservative Southern senators in their hope that this would defeat the proposal!

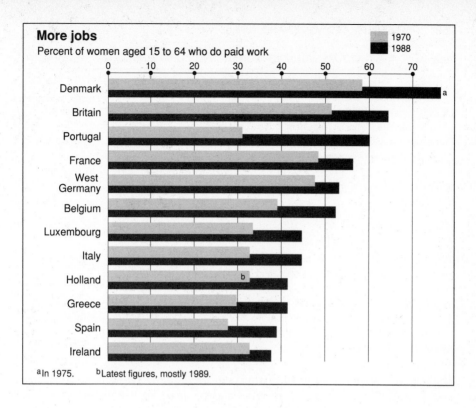

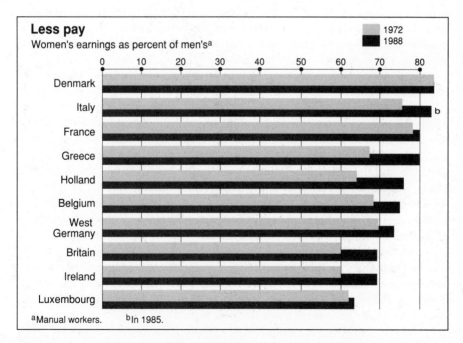

Figure 11.1. An increase in jobs but a decrease in pay among European women. Copyright © 1990 The Economist Newspaper Limited. Reprinted by permission.

Table 11.1   THE GAINS OF WORKING WOMEN IN OCCUPATIONS

	1970	1986
Managerial and professional speciality (administrators, financial managers, buyers, etc.)	33.9%	43.4%
Professional specialty (lawyers, teachers, writers, etc.)	44.3	49.4
Sales occupations	41.3	48.2
Administrative support, including clerical	73.2	80.4
Service occupations	60.4	62.6
Precision, production, craft, and repair (mechanics, etc.)	7.3	8.6
Operators, fabricators, and laborers	25.9	25.4
Transportation and material moving occupations	4.1	8.9
Handlers, equipment cleaners, helpers, and laborers	17.4	16.3
Farming, forestry, and fishing	9.1	15.9

Source: "The Gains of Working Women," from *The New York Times,* July 17, 1987. Copyright © 1987 by the New York Times Company. Reprinted by permission.

tax benefits are provided to all mothers. In the Federal Republic of Germany and in Holland, tax relief and subsidies and generous leave policies encourage working mothers to stay at home. In most of the European community, leave policies (with the obligation on the part of the employer to rehire) are available to all mothers. Only the United States remains behind with regard to both the establishment of publicly supported day care centers and the provision of an adequate leave policy for working mothers.

Curiously enough, while women have been making significant strides in the workplace, the professions, the universities, and the managerial positions in private corporations, they have shown less and only incremental progress in what they originally sought most—political involvement and leadership. The record is, at best, spotty. There is a negative tally in a number of countries—particularly so in the Soviet Union, Eastern Europe, Japan, China, the whole of Africa, and throughout the Middle East. In the United States, there are only thirty women in the House of Representatives—and only three in the Senate. In state legislatures, the number of women in 1989 had risen to about 20 percent as compared to 8 percent in 1975. On the other hand, the nomination of Geraldine Ferraro as vice-presidential candidate in the election of 1984 and the prospect that Pat Schroeder, congresswoman from Colorado, was ready to run for the presidency in 1988 indicated that the public was prepared to consider women candidates for election to the highest post—as it has been the case in England, Pakistan, India, Israel, the Philippines and Nicaragua. The Scandinavian countries have maintained the best record.

Women, on the other hand, in the United States have been far more successful in organizing to lobby for their causes and in mobilizing the voters. They have learned how to put pressure on members of Congress to defend par-

---

NOW

The organization that best expresses women's demands within the context of American democratic liberalism and continues to push for the full realization of equal rights is the National Organization for Women (NOW). Founded in 1966, it currently has a membership of about 250,000. In lobbying for women's causes it has been an active political force, supporting or opposing candidates for Congress, the Senate, and the White House. It challenges legislative measures that adversely affect women and promotes legislation favorable to them. It is without doubt the major feminist organization, advocating full participation and equality of women, as well as special provisions for women who are both mothers and workers. NOW insists on child care arrangements for working women, liberal policies for maternity and parental leave, affirmative action in hiring, free choice for and subsidizing of abortion, and of course equal pay. Like so many other groups, NOW is asking for full integration of women into the society but not a change in the liberal society as we know it.

---

ticular women's interests, to promote legislation favorable to women's issues, and to scrutinize and monitor their implementation. One such organization has been particularly active in the United States—the National Organization for Women (NOW).

RADICAL FEMINISM

Radical feminists address squarely and confront directly the values that a male society has propagated about women. Radical feminists make a distinction between sex, on the one hand, and gender, on the other. The first is strictly biological and relates to pregnancy and motherhood. Women can do something that men cannot do—bring forth children. The second, gender, comprises all the sex-related institutional arrangements, notably the role of women in the family and their obligations for childrearing.

Are there any special characteristics that are directly attributable to sex *other* than the biological reality of pregnancy and motherhood? Simone de Beauvoir refers to a woman's state of immanence. Women are immersed in motherhood and childrearing; conversely, men are portrayed as "transcendent," in part because they are free from the burden of motherhood. Men strive to conquer and transform their environment through an active interplay with it. This is another way of repeating the stereotypes: women are "passive" and men are "active." Women submit to what is given; men strive to change it. How fixed, if true, are these traits? Where did they arise from, if not from the difference in sex? Can they be modified?

Another distinction between men and women stems, according to some, not only from sex but also from the assigned gender role in the family and childrearing. Women have particularistic attachments and concerns, mainly the children and the family. Men, on the other hand, direct their attention to broader interests—public life, for instance. In contrast to women's particularistic concerns, they display more universalistic ones. These distinctions correspond once more to the stereotypes of women's traditional attachment to the family and the household, while men soar over and beyond them. Again, how fixed, if true, are these traits? Are they sex-determined or gender-related? How can they be changed?

While sex accounts for some specific and unalterable traits, such as motherhood, it is doubtful that it accounts for the gender—that is, the sex-related—arrangements in our society, especially the responsibility for raising children. As mothers, women have assumed the primary role in childrearing in accordance with the existing norms of the society. However, it seems equally true that men can raise children and that significant changes can occur within the present conjugal family. Some new arrangements are already in evidence. In some households, for example, fathers have taken on a partnership role in childrearing, and day care centers for preschoolers have further freed mothers to pursue careers outside the home.

Many, therefore, argue that women's equality can be attained only when the bringing up of children from the earliest age is shared by others—the father, child care centers, communal programs, or even public agencies. Such changes may go a long way in doing away with what Betty Friedan called the "feminine mystique"—the exaltation by a male-dominated society of women's role in the household and in childrearing duties during a good part of their lives. In reality, this mystique is a drudgery that prevents women from developing their own talents outside of the home. When the "mystique" is lifted and the drudgery gone, women will be freer to share the same roles within the society that men play and become truly equal. Men's roles will change correspondingly when the present division of labor in the family gives place to a genuine cooperative sharing.

Many of the claims of radical feminists to do away with the socially determined "gender" distinctions have, by and large, entered the mainstream feminist movement. But radical feminism—particularly that of the 1960s and 1970s—went beyond these claims by calling for the total revolutionary overhaul of the society and the elimination of the family.

In its extreme formulation, radical feminists, in line with some of the implications that one can draw from Simon de Beauvoir's writings, argue for the complete assimilation of women into men's roles. Shulamith Firestone and some others pushed this to the extremes by calling for the full and complete abolition of all social distinctions derived from sex, including the abolition of the conjugal family; the full liberation of women from the burdens of pregnancy to be achieved with the development of medical techniques for in vitro fertilization; the upbringing of children in communal arrangements—not the household as we know it; the full emancipation of women from a subordinate relationship that property entails in a society where men control property, to be accomplished through the socialization of the means of production and, if necessary, revolution. According to Shulamith Firestone, history is not a record of class oppression, but rather of oppression of women by a "sex class system." Natural differences between the sexes associated with childbearing enabled the invention of cultural differences associated with childrearing, and are wrongly perceived as natural and inescapable. Firestone regards such ideas as femininity, motherliness, and romantic love as cultural inventions which, throughout history, have rendered women a distinct oppressed class. Only a feminist revolution can and must liberate women.[11]

THE RISE AND FALL OF THE EQUAL RIGHTS AMENDMENT (ERA)

Immediately after women gained the right to vote in 1920, a movement for a constitutional amendment to provide "equality of rights" between the two sexes was initiated. It was not until 1970 that the amendment—"Equality of rights under the law shall not be denied or abridged by the United States or any state on account of sex"—passed the House of Representatives by a vote of 350 to 15, well beyond the requisite two-thirds. In 1972 it passed the Senate by 84 to 8. By 1977, thirty-five state legislatures had ratified the amendment and only three more states were needed for the amendment to become part of the Constitution. It did not come to pass. The deadline for ratification by the requisite three-fourths of the states, after being extended, expired in 1982.[12]

The purpose of the amendment was to formally guarantee women equal rights with men across the board by prohibiting any differential treatment. But many activists envisioned radical changes. They saw the ERA not only as the formal recognition of equality but also as the symbol of the elimination of all gender distinctions. It was at this juncture that support for the ERA weakened. To many, it had become a symbol of radical feminism, away from the mainstream of the liberal feminist movement. It also became increasingly linked to the proabortion forces and those who demanded radical changes in the institutions of marriage and the family.

The perception that the ERA had become the mantle of radical feminists was strengthened by the fact that in the 1970s many of the women's claims began, as we have seen, to be realized. Through legislation or court decisions, women were granted equal protection before the law, equal educational opportunities, affirmative action for securing jobs and against being dismissed from them, and, finally, the right to have an abortion when in the *Roe* v. *Wade* case (1973) the Supreme Court struck down a state law forbidding abortion. The court ruled that the law was an intrusion on privacy. At a time when women's rights were being supported and strengthened, many advocates thought that the ERA embodied only a symbolic affirmation of liberation with no tangible

---

[11]Shulamith Firestone. *The Dialectic of Sex*. (1970).

[12]For a full account of the history of the ERA, see Jane Mansbridge, *Why We Lost the ERA*.

benefits. Others began to fear, rightly or wrongly, that its enactment might actually *deprive* women of many of the gains they had realized. For widows, divorcées, older women, and in many instances for young women too, the ERA could impose burdens: for example, serving in the army, being deprived of a husband's pension, being denied custody of a child, or losing the preferential treatment obtained through affirmative action in the workplace.

Conservative groups and religious activists were the first to seize on these issues and distort them in an effort to preserve the traditional status of women. The political parties began to divide, with the Republicans taking an increasingly anti-ERA stance[13] and the Democrats paying only lip service to it. While it is true that the amendment to the federal constitution lost because it failed in two Southern states (but also in Illinois), it is equally true that the ERA amendments to state constitutions failed in "progressive" states. In 1975, ERA amendments to the New York and New Jersey constitutions failed with 57 percent voting against it in New York and 51 percent voting against it in New Jersey. Subsequently, it failed in Iowa (1980) and in Maine (1984).

THE STRUGGLE GOES ON

Women's issues have regained both urgency and saliency in the United States in the last few years. For one thing, protection of women's rights in their search for equality in the United States has been a judicial, not an outright political or legislative, matter. Issues pertaining to job discrimination, the implementation of affirmative action, and abortion rights were in the hands of the courts whose decisions have been constantly revised and qualified—leaving a "no-woman's land" of uncertainty. In almost all countries, for instance, the specific conditions allowing for abortion have been decided in one way or another through legislative enactments; the same has been the case with matters related to hiring, wages, working conditions, and protection in hazardous occupations. Judicial interpretation, indeed protection through judicial enactment in the United States, demobilized women by depoliticizing certain issues. Courts and judges are not subject to election or political pressure through lobbying.

Pro-Choice and Pro-Life

What has mobilized women over the last years has been the issue of abortion—their right to decide. At first and for some time, the issue seemed to have been settled by the Supreme Court in the *Roe* v. *Wade* decision of 1973. In this landmark decision, Justice Blackman, who wrote for the 5–4 majority,

---

[13]There were women and some women's organizations that opposed the ERA. They became known derisively as "Auntie Toms."

grounded the right of women to choose an abortion on the "right to privacy," presumed to be guaranteed through the Fourth and Fifth Amendments of the Constitution, even though it is a right that is nowhere explicitly mentioned.

It was a decision that incensed many conservative organizations and was rejected by most of the influential religious denominations—notably the Catholic church and the Evangelicals, including the Southern Baptists. It became a hotly debated issue among political parties and candidates running for state and federal offices. How could the elected leadership influence change and, if need be, call for constitutional amendment? Antiabortion organizations—the Pro-Life movement (as they call themselves)—mobilized rapidly throughout the country, and the issue became part of the nation's political agenda, affecting all elections at all levels as well as the appointment of federal judges and Supreme Court justices.

Roe v. *Wade* held until 1989 when the Supreme Court handed down a new decision: *Webster* v. *Reproductive Health Services*. The Webster decision gave to the states the right to formulate their own standards by legislation. In forty-one out of the fifty state legislatures, proposals to enact abortion laws have been introduced since 1989, and the debate and action have ranged far and wide. Pro-Choicers and Pro-Lifers organized themselves (see Table 11.2) and took to the streets. Pro-Lifers attempted to close abortion clinics by force; Pro-Choicers, for their part, closed ranks to prevent any interference with the operation of these clinics.

Restrictive statutes were enacted in a number of states. There were other states, however, that simply refused to restrict "free choice." The gubernatorial election in Virginia in November 1989 pitted Douglas Wilder, a pro-choice advocate, against a pro-life advocate, and Wilder was elected the first black governor of Virginia. In the gubernatorial election in California in November 1990, both Republican and Democratic candidates were strongly Pro-Choice. The political battle was on and it will continue to mobilize women and the public in general.

The Need for Feminist Politics

Most feminist scholars and political leaders agree that there is a continuing need for feminist politics. So does the American public. A recent *New York Times* poll revealed that 59 percent of all American adults agreed that "the U.S. continues to need a strong women's movement to push for changes that benefit women." A full 71 percent of women between eighteen and forty-four agreed, compared with 55 percent of the men in the same age range; 60 percent of the women over forty-five agreed compared with 45 percent of men over forty-five.[14]

---

[14]*New York Times*, August 20, 1990.

Table 11.2　PRO-CHOICERS VERSUS PRO-LIFERS

Pro-Choice
  National Abortion Rights League (NARAL)
  Planned Parenthood
  National Organization for Women (NOW)
  Feminist Health Networks
  Abortion Rights Mobilization
  National Women's Political Caucus
  American Association of University Women (AAUW)
  Religious Coalition for Abortion Rights
  National Women's Health Network
  Black Women's Health Network
  American Civil Liberties Union
  Catholics for a Free Choice
Pro-Life
  Human Life Center
  Pro-Family Forum
  Catholics United for Life
  Christian Action Council
  Americans for Life
  American Citizens Concerned for Life
  Alliance for Life
  Crusade for Life
  Pro-Life Council
  Pro-Life League
  Right-to-Life League
  Life Amendment Political Action Committee
  U.S. Coalition for Life
  Birthright
  Operation Rescue
  National Conference of Catholic Bishops (and the Committee for Pro-Life Activities therein)

Several recent political developments and social issues associated help to explain the continuing need for feminist politics. They include:

1. Most central, perhaps, is the question of abortion rights.
2. Child care provisions, both with regard to state support for facilities and state-granted compensations (e.g., tax credits) for private child care options, will be fundamental in allowing women full equality of opportunity.
3. Parental leave, increasingly seen as "family leave," in which care for the sick and the elderly would also qualify as legitimate grounds for leaves of absence from the workplace, must be addressed, as women continue to work *and* carry the social burden of raising and caring for a family.

4. Pay equity issues are key and require attention since many women are heads of households and carry a heavy financial burden.
5. Welfare "rights," particularly as the trend toward female-headed families (predominantly black) at or below the poverty line continues. Given that the most mobilized and vocal of the national women's groups tend to be dominated by white women of rather stable financial backgrounds, it is perhaps not surprising that the needs of the "feminized poor" are more directly addressed by groups gathering under the banner of "welfare rights activists" or racially attuned groups led by blacks.
6. Finally, attention has been drawn recently to the role of women in the military. About 11 percent of all military personnel are women. Congress does not allow them to engage in combat. Yet in the Gulf War women served on the front, and flew helicopters; some were taken prisoners and one was killed. For all practical purposes they were engaged in combat. But will they be granted the right to do so?

CONCLUSION

Feminism—in all its various phases and manifestations—may be viewed in the last analysis as the consecration of the moral and universal values of equality held at bay for so long by the supremacy of males and the ideologies developed to legitimize their supremacy. Even though the feminist movement does not advocate a revolution, it is nonetheless what revolutions are all about: to undermine the power of some (men) and enhance the power of others (women). It proposes cooperation instead of subjection and equality instead of discrimination. In this sense, feminism is one of the many protest movements for the liberation of the powerless against the powerholders.

But is feminism anything else or anything other than a movement advocating change in social (and power) relations and in socially defined roles? All revolutionary ideologies attempt not only to change the position and roles of those in power in a given society but also to transform the values of the society as well. Granting that feminism as a movement aspires to restore women to the full equality and power to which they are entitled as human beings, how will this change the society's norms within which men and women interact? What will the new norms be? In what way will children be reared to espouse new norms and values? Will there be a radical change in property relations? In matters of war and peace? In working conditions? In education? In the production and distribution of goods and services? Will there be new outlets for individual self-realization? Will the "feminine ingredient," fully liberated, become the leaven of a new society, or will it simply assimilate itself, once liberated, to the values that have been developed by a male-dominated society?

The answer is not at all clear because the theory underlining feminism is not yet clear. Most feminists (but not all) argue that there are no *innate* differences between women and men other than the biology of pregnancy and motherhood. All other differences, they claim, are socially determined. If that is true, how will their full and equal participation in the society transform the society? Unless special qualities—other than biological—are attributed to women, how and why can we expect the society to be changed? In what sense will women's liberation lead to a social transformation? In other words, will women become fully part of our society *as we know it*, or will they, in becoming fully part of it, *change it*? And if so, how?

It still remains for feminist theory to identify what new values and new characteristics will transform our society. Otherwise, feminism as an ideology is but another movement toward freedom and equality for all—very much in line with the egalitarian liberal ethos. It is another building block in the development of the comprehensive values of equality and freedom—in the fulfillment of the universal ethic of liberalism.

BIBLIOGRAPHY

Benhabib, Seyla, and Drucilla Cornell (eds.). *Feminism as Critique: On the Politics of Gender.* Minneapolis: University of Minnesota Press, 1987.

Bradshaw, Jan (ed.). *The Women's Liberation Movement: Europe and North America.* Elmsford, N.Y.: Pergamon Press, 1982.

Brownmiller, Susan. *Against Our Will: Men, Women, and Rape.* New York: Simon and Schuster, 1975.

Bunch, Charlotte, and Nancy Myron (eds.). *Class and Feminism.* Baltimore: Diana Press, 1974.

Chodorow, Nancy. *The Reproduction of Mothering: Psychoanalysis and the Sociology of Gender.* Berkeley: University of California Press, 1978.

Cocks, Joan Elizabeth. *The Oppositional Imagination: Feminism, Critique and Political Theory.* New York: Routledge, 1989.

de Beauvoir, Simone. *The Second Sex.* New York: Bantam Books, 1961. (First published in 1952.)

Dinnerstein, Dorothy. *The Mermaid and the Minotaur: Sexual Arrangements and Human Malaise.* New York: Harper & Row, 1976.

Eisenstein, Zillah. *The Radical Future of Liberation Feminism.* New York: Longman, 1980.

Elshtain, Jean Bethke. *Public Man, Private Woman: Women in Social and Political Thought.* Princeton, N.J.: Princeton University Press, 1981.

———. *Women and War.* New York: Basic Books, 1984.

Firestone, Shulamith. *The Dialectic of Sex: The Case for Feminist Revolution.* New York: Morrow, 1970.

Flexner, Eleanor. *Century of Struggle: The Women's Rights Movement in the USA,* rev. ed. Cambridge, Mass.: Harvard Paperbacks, 1975.

Forster, Margaret. *Significant Sisters: The Grassroots of Activist Feminism, 1839–1939.* New York: Knopf, 1984.

Friedan, Betty. *The Feminine Mystique.* New York: Norton, 1963.

———. *The Second Stage.* New York: Summit Books, 1986.

Gay, Virginia. *Feminism and the New Right.* New York: Praeger, 1983.

Gilman, Charlotte Perkins. *Women and Economics, 1898.* New York: Harper & Row, 1966.

Gurko, Miriam. *The Ladies of Seneca Falls.* New York: Schocken Books, 1974.

Hole, Judith, and Ellen Levine. *Rebirth of Feminism.* New York: Quadrangle Books, 1971.

Jaggar, Allison. *Feminist Politics and Human Nature.* Totowa, N.J.: Rowman and Allanheld, 1983.

Jenner, Leslie. *Voices for Women's Liberation.* New York: American Library, 1970.

Kaminer, Wendy. *A Fearful Freedom: Women's Flight from Equality.* Addison-Wesley, Reading, Mass., 1990.

Klein, Ethel. *Gender Politics.* Cambridge, Mass.: Harvard University Press, 1987.

Mackinnon, Catharine. *Feminism Unmodified: Discourses on Life and Law.* Cambridge, Mass.: Harvard University Press, 1987.

Mansbridge, Jane. *Why We Lost the ERA.* Chicago: University of Chicago Press, 1986.

Mill, John Stuart. *The Subjection of Women.* Revised edition with Introduction by Susan Moller Okin. Cambridge, Mass.: Hackett Publishing, 1989. (Originally published in 1869.)

Millett, Kate. *Sexual Politics.* Garden City, N.Y.: Doubleday, 1970.

Mitchell, Juliet. *Women's Estate.* New York: Vintage Books, 1971.

Morgan, Robin (ed). *Sisterhood Is Global: The International Women's Movement Anthology.* New York: Anchor-Doubleday, 1984.

Okin, Susan. *Women in Western Political Thought.* Princeton, N.J.: Princeton University Press, 1979.

———. *Justice, Gender and the Family.* New York: Basic Books, 1989.

O'Neill, William. *Everyone Was Brave.* Chicago: Quadrangle Books, 1969.

Rich, Adrienne. *Of Women Born: Motherhood as Experience and Institution.* New York: Norton, 1976.

Ruddick, Sara. *Maternal Thinking: Towards a Politics on Peace.* Boston: Beacon Press, 1989.

Sidel, Ruth. *Women and Children Last: The Plight of Poor Women in Affluent America.* New York: Penguin, 1987.

Spender, Dale. *Feminist Theorists: Three Centuries of Key Women Thinkers.* New York: Pantheon, 1984.

Tinker, Irene (ed.). *Persistent Inequalities: Women and World Development.* New York: Oxford University Press, 1990.

Ware, Susan. *Beyond Suffrage: Women in the New Deal.* Cambridge, Mass.: Harvard University Press, 1981.

———. *Holding Their Own: American Women in the 1930s.* Boston: Twayne, 1982.

Chapter
12

Environmentalism

An Ideology in the Making?

Where will the old Duke live?
They say he is already in the
Forest of Arden. . . . They say
many young gentlemen flock to
him everyday and fleet the time carelessly
as they did in the Golden World

Shakespeare
As You Like It

There was a time when meadow, grove and stream
The earth and every common sight,
To me did seem
Apparelled in celestial light
. . .

It is not now as it hath been of yore;—
Turn whereso'er I may
By night and day
The things which I have seen
I can now see no more.

William Wordsworth
Ode to Immortality

We have seen in the previous chapters that ideologies are responses to predicaments. For instance, socialist ideology was, for many, a response to the perceived drawbacks—both economic and moral—of capitalism, and feminism to the unequal status of women in our society. Similarly, *environmentalism*, in its broadest sense, is the set of ideas and prescriptions men and women develop and organize and act upon in order to put an end to the degradation and spoiliation of our environment. It is an ideology committed to the survival of the human species on this planet. Our forests have been spoiled, lakes and rivers polluted, neighborhoods uprooted in the name of urban renewal, and millions of people in Europe and the USA (even larger numbers in Eastern Europe, in the Soviet Union, in Asia and Africa) live in areas where the air is fast becoming unbreathable and the water undrinkable. As population growth continues unchecked, urban agglomerations without any consideration to minimal health standards are sprawling—by 2000 there will be twenty "cities" with populations of over 10 million each.

Environmentalism is not a utopian movement, though the writings and actions of some environmentalists take on some aspects of utopian thinkers. In the last analysis, it is a movement born and sustained by the oldest and most selfish of interests—our survival and that of our children. There are, of course, other considerations: a romantic view of nature; a realization that quantitative considerations related to economic growth distort the quality of our lives; a search for a new social order that will stress human happiness and development; and to many the compelling need to preserve the species on our planet.[1]

In contrast to other ideologies addressed to social predicaments, environmentalism faces special difficulties.

1. The environmental predicaments are many, diverse, and complex; for example, the linkage between hairspray and the ozone layer is difficult to make.
2. They are diffuse—some environmental problems affect directly our lives; most do not.
3. They vary in intensity—from what is immediate to what is remote.
4. Except in extreme cases, they lack saliency. They appear less important and urgent than security in jobs or inflation. They do not arouse the needed emotional responses—an ingredient of all ideologies. Public opinion polls, however, show everywhere a rapidly growing concern with environmental issues, such as air and water pollution, acid rain, deforestation, soil erosion, and toxic waste. But they are overshadowed by more pressing concerns.
5. There is no "school" of thought as yet—no comprehensive theory—that represents environmentalism; the political movements that represent it are scattered and diverse and motivated by different economic, ideological, and moral concerns, ranging from pure self-interest (what to do with my well?) to the loftiest ones—to make sure that not a single one of the many millions of living species that live with us, and not only the bald eagle, disappears from our planet!

THE IDEOLOGICAL BLOCS

While there is no theory yet, environmentalists draw their inspiration from many sources.

---

[1]The degradation of the environment is detailed in all its aspects in the excellent *The Global Ecology Handbook*, edited by Walter H. Corson.

Romanticism

For a long time "nature" was considered a threat to men and women. Nature was full of hazards, just as great perhaps as the ones we have inflicted upon it (and indirectly upon ourselves) in the last century or so. For the ancient Greeks the city–state was a haven of safety, order, and law. Nature, on the other hand, was unpredictable, dangerous, and exacting—a constant struggle was needed to make it yield its fruits. Lightning, fire, floods, earthquakes, pestilence, and wild beasts were a constant threat to humans. This picture was virtually turned upside down with Christianity and the notion of paradise, where tranquility, purity, and abundance reigned. Thus, there was sometime, somewhere, in the past a "Golden Age" (for Shakespeare it was the Forest of Arden), and it became the source of a romantic vision clearly articulated by in the middle of the eighteenth century by Jean-Jacques Rosseau. For Rousseau, the state of nature was a state of purity, even nobility. The "noble savage," or the "infant man," was endowed with sociability and rationality. This state of nature contrasted sharply with the evils, ambitions, wars, and selfishness of political society. We had to return to nature, so to speak, to recapture moral virtues that had been destroyed. An additional argument that indirectly glorified "nature" was offered in the early twentieth century by Sigmund Freud, for whom civilized life and civilization produced serious "discontents"—all of them the result of repressive social mechanisms that stunted our desires. Nature, in contrast, embodied the pleasures of a free and communal life.

It is this imagery of nature that continues to be evoked today by some environmentalists—nature is a safe haven to which we should return. Hence we must maintain it as pure as possible. This imagery is very noticeable among some Utopians and proponents of the New Left, whom we address in the next chapter. Their vision conjures up a simple life in the village, near the farm, and in small communities or associations where goods are held in common. Men and women have been alienated by being separated from nature; to return to it would provide fulfillment.[2]

Socialism and Marxism

The spoilation of the environment, according to Marx, is inextricably linked to capitalism. The profit motive becomes the spur for production (and industrialization) and knows no bounds. Production is not geared to the satisfaction of wants, especially basic wants, but to profit. In the process, the primary modes of production—for example, agriculture, forestry, fishing—become subordinated to extractive industries that provide the raw materials to produce capital

---

[2]See, for example, Erich F. Schumacher, *Small Is Beautiful: Economics As If people mattered.*

goods, which include factories, ships, railways, steel mills, coal mines, and so forth, which in turn account for industrial production. Capitalists use and abuse the "free goods" we have—the oceans, rivers and streams, the soil, the forests, the animal world—without any consideration to the "ultimate cost" for the community. Nor will the "capitalist ethic" change because of the societal havoc it brings about. Consumerism relegates all concerns to that of the production of a variety of goods that whet our appetite for more, while basic needs of health, education, housing, decent living standards, transportation, and leisure are neglected.

It was, as we discussed, part and parcel of Marxism to do away with this state of things and to impose a new "collective ethic" that would provide, in abundance, the satisfaction of common needs. The degradation of nature would be addressed through economic planning and regulation that took into account long-range needs. This is the simplified version of Marxism endorsed by environmentalists. For many, clearly so in the sixties and early seventies, the "environmentalist ethic" was a "socialist ethic." It remains so for some.

Pacifism

A part of today's environmentalist movement derives from an earlier movement that began after 1945 and was directed against nuclear energy as well as nuclear weapons. Its rhetoric was couched, as it still is, in pacifist terms, especially as voiced by the German "Greens." It was a movement addressed particularly against U.S. nuclear military installations in Germany, England, and elsewhere and was widely supported by Communist parties.[3] It was not addressed against the Soviet nuclear military installations, and there was, at the time, no environmental movements in Eastern Europe or in the Soviet Union.

The antinuclear posture of these environmentalists has been echoed recently in the present-day movement where it is directed against just as critical an issue: nuclear plants as a source of energy. And now even more crucial is the problem of the disposal of nuclear waste, to which no solution has been found, as many nuclear plants and submarines are aging and go out of commission throughout the world. The accident at Three Mile Island, Pennsylvania, in 1979 and the Chernobyl disaster in the Soviet Union in 1986, as well as other "incidents," have spurred this movement against nuclear energy. Environmentalists advocate the dismantling of nuclear weapons and the cessation of all underground nuclear testing, as it has been the case for the last twenty years in the air. Their position is not always the same, however, with regard to the use of

---

[3]A good and short comparative overview has been published by Raymond Dominick, "The Roots of the Green Movement in the United States and West Germany," in *Environmental Review*, pp. 1–30.

nuclear power as a source of energy. For some of the French environmentalists, nuclear energy, in times of oil scarcity, is acceptable.

A Development Model

To clarify the position of environmentalists, it might be best to start with the distinction often made between growth and development. *Growth* is simply geared to quantitative consideration and is measured in terms of per capita product—that is, the total national product divided by the number of people in the nation. The goal of industrialization is to increase the total output. The greater the output, the wealthier the society and, hence, the better off we all are—so runs the argument. Industrialization, as it occurred in the West, was also the model originally suggested for the Third World: to create the conditions for higher production and productivity, after which the societies would "take off" to eventually land in our familiar industrialized world. Capital investment, factories, and the production of consumer goods would lift the Third World from the mire of poverty.

The notion of *development*, as opposed to growth, reverses the priorities and questions the "industrialization model." The emphasis is put on the provision of basic needs—health, housing, education, and employment—consistent with cultural and societal imperatives. Industrialization and growth are, of course, needed, but they are subordinate to the production of basic needs and the qualitative improvement of our lives. An Index of Development is established—to measure health, longevity (health care), education, and social services, and it is supposed to be more indicative of human happiness than the per capita product index. To quote from the Human Development Report, issued by the United Nations Development Program:

> The central message is that while growth in gross domestic product is absolutely necessary to meet all essential human objectives, what is important is to study how this growth translates—or fails to translate—into human development. Some societies have achieved high levels of human development at modest levels of per capita income. Others have failed to translate their comparatively high income levels and rapid economic growth into commensurate levels of human development.[4]

Environmentalists endorse this model of human development. It leads to a rearrangement of economic priorities and to the harnessing of natural resources, where economic activity is redirected to the satisfaction of basic needs. Industrialization should be accordingly circumscribed. In short, qualitative considerations and considerations of public service should become the foremost priorities.

---

[4]Cited in *Development Journal*, No. 2, June 1990, p. 43

Malthusianism

Robert Malthus, a British economist (1766–1834), was the first to develop the notion of limited growth, or finite growth. There is a clear correlation, Malthus argued in his *Essay on the Principles of Population*, between population growth and the availability of resources—notably food. "Population when unchecked," he wrote, "increases in a geometric fashion. Subsistence increases only in an arithmetic ratio." Thus a rise in population puts pressure on food supplies and is reflected in higher food prices until they reach a level that many cannot afford. Then the population drops. When it does so, workers become scarce; they get better wages and have more children. Hence, there is a self-regulating mechanism to keep population down—or at least manageable.

Malthus had been ridiculed until recently, and to be a "Malthusian" was equivalent to being a pessimist—a person who did not believe that industrialization could find the resources to cope with an ever-growing number of people and to produce an ever-growing number of goods for them. The whole of the nineteenth century until the 1960s, but even more especially the years after World War II, proved him wrong. The population increased and there was food for all—at least virtually for all. Pesticides and chemicals increased agricultural production even faster than the population increased, even as fewer people worked on the farm. With genetic engineering and the alteration of plants, this may indeed continue. But for how long?

For some environmentalists, population growth is sustainable if the economy is geared to providing food and shelter and if appropriate changes are made to direct more people back to agriculture. On balance, however, a majority of environmentalists have adopted what appears to be a Malthusian position. They consider the continuing population growth to be one of the most important reasons for poverty and environmental degradation. This theme was developed in the first Club of Rome Report of 1970, characteristically entitled "The Limits of Growth." Most environmentalists favor population-control measures just as they favor clear air and clean water.

Pragmatism

Over the years environmentalists have shed some of their ideological fervor—romantic, Marxist, socialist, pacifist—in favor of pragmatic considerations. One of them is the outright acceptance that growth is necessary on condition that growth is "sustainable."

Sustainable growth was succinctly defined in a U.N. report of 1987, entitled "Our Common Future," prepared under the chairmanship of Mrs. Gro Harlem Brundtland, prime minister of Norway. It was defined as the "development that meets the needs of the present without compromising the ability of future generations to meet their needs." It helped differentiate sharply between "renewable" resources and "nonrenewable" ones—those that once used are gone for our children and grandchildren forever. Thus special care will have to be taken to maintain our "resource patrimony" or "resource bank" for future generations. If we draw a check on it, we must pay it back.[5]

Unless spectacular breakthroughs in technology are made, and until they are made, resources are viewed by virtually all environmentalists as finite. There will be an end to the oil supply, to coal deposits, to the water we drink, to forests and cultivable land, to the fish in the oceans—they are all our common patrimony. This is a view that invites, therefore, both government and business to gear production, industrialization, and growth in a way that will preserve our resources. It calls for a wholesale transfer to alternate sources of energy—solar, biothermal, and tidal, even including the use of windmills. It means also a careful regimentation, for instance, of water use for any other than drinking purposes. It suggests the most stringent use of agricultural chemicals in irrigation and farming that pollute the water supply. Control of toxic waste is a battle cry of most environmentalists. But how expensive will such programs be?

Once the question "how expensive" is asked, the notion of sustainable growth has gained ground to become part of the political debate. It amounts to a victory for conservationists and environmentalists. It becomes a concept that will have to be considered by industries and the government, debated, and implemented in terms that call for feasible solutions acceptable to industry, the government, and the public.

To the notion of sustainable growth, other pragmatic considerations have been added as well. One is that of "social cost." According to it, industries must assume the cost for what they have destroyed in the process of production. For instance, take the obvious case of a nuclear plant that has allowed radioactive leakage to despoil a river. As a result, fishing must be given up; the water becomes undrinkable; thousands must abandon their homes. Or take a factory that has been pouring toxic fumes into the air—making the adjoining area progressively uninhabitable. Or take farms irrigated by water in an area where water becomes increasingly scarce and therefore expensive to have for those who drink it. Each of these and so many other cases amount to damages inflicted on a neighborhood, a community, a region, sometimes to the whole country, and even to the planet. They are not paid for by private industry but by the public—ultimately, by the taxpayers. Common sense—a pragmatic consideration—would suggest that costs, past, present, and estimated for the future, must be paid by those who incur them. "Make the Polluters Pay!" It is a policy that will deter firms from using and abusing environmental resources. It will introduce restraint.

An analogous proposition is to consider environmental resources as public assets and their depletion as losses. Public account statements should be pre-

---

[5]Some economists, it should be noted, reject the notion of "finite" resources. Some argue that population growth, economic growth, and growth in resources go hand in hand partly because of the rapid development of new technologies to meet growing demand.

pared in a manner that shows the assets lost in the course of production. How much oil, how much coal, how much deforestation, how much natural gas, how many rivers and streams were polluted and "lost" in one year? Such a formula would have a salutary effect simply because it would show that, if environmental losses are taken into account, growth is much lower than indicated. It would put a price tag on natural resources.

The very fact that environmentalists and policymakers have begun to raise and discuss the notions of sustainable growth, social costs, and a new "Public accounts" formula, in which resources used or depleted are deducted from the Gross National Product, indicates the growing maturity of environmentalism as a political movement. It indicates a gradual shift from the original solely ideological positions to new pragmatic considerations. Some have begun to think that there is the possibility that "enlightened" capitalist policies and practices may become compatible with environmentalism, and vice versa.

ENVIRONMENTALISTS IN ACTION

The variety and the complexity of the environmental problems, and the different outlooks and ideological backgrounds from which environmental movements stem, account for a great disparity in the programs that environmental organizations, parties, and activists espouse. Many target a specific issue—"Save the whales"; "Save the spotted owl"; "Save the dolphins." Others address themselves to more general themes: wild life, wetlands, clear air, nuclear energy, clean water, toxic waste, the preservation of the species. Others link their appeals to specific programmatic formulations about the economy and the society—that is, human development as opposed to growth. Some are local and highly intensive in their action—for example, how to prevent a waste dump in their town; others are committed to global issues—deforestation, the warming trend, or the ozone layer. Tactics also vary; they cover the spectrum from confrontationalism and violence, on the one hand, to compromise solutions, on the other, in which government, industry, scientists, and representative groups among those concerned deliberate and decide to provide coherent suggestions and articulate common concerns.

There are, however, a growing consensus and a growing involvement. *First,* a priority listing of environmental issues is emerging. *Second,* the number of concerned policymakers is increasing rapidly. *Third,* the public's awareness and concern with environmental issues are also rapidly increasing. *Fourth,* environmental political parties have emerged and have gained respectability and momentum, almost everywhere except in the United States, where, however, environmentalist lobbies have become very active and begin to weigh just as heavily on the electoral and legislative process. *Fifth,* basic environmental concerns have become part of the political agenda just about everywhere. *Sixth,* environmental issues and how to deal with them have moved beyond the boundaries of nation–states—they have become, as many are by their very nature, regionalized and internationalized. They are increasingly

The northern spotted owl lives in the national forests of Oregon, Washington, northern California, and southern British Columbia. There are an estimated 3000 pairs left, and if the ancient forests where they live continue to be cut down, they will disappear. So will the jobs of about 28,000 people in the timber industry.

being dealt with, therefore, by regional organizations, international organizations, and treaties.

A Growing Consensus

An agreement on the major priorities is emerging among environmentalists: reduction of population growth in the direction, if possible, of zero growth, clean water, clean air, the prevention of toxic waste, and the protection of the ozone layer, which is eroding due to chlorofluorocarbons (CFCs). Other issues are deforestation, the preservation of tropical forests, conservation of our resources, and the preservation of the various species. We are unable, however, to discuss these issues in any detail here, except for some highlights.

Population Growth and Poverty. Of particular interest is the stand taken by environmentalists on population growth and its side effect. It is expected that in about one hundred years the population of the planet will have grown to about ten billion from around four billion in 1975. Can the planet and its resources sustain it? Most environmentalists doubt it. If so, it will result in misery and poverty which, according to environmentalists, work as a driving force for desperate people to overexploit their resource bases, sacrificing the future to salvage the present. The landless poor people often have no choice, for instance, but to expand into and ruthlessly log forests in order to grow some crops for themselves.

In summing up the challenges and problems related to the growth of the world population and its impact on global food production, Lester Brown and John Young state:

> Barring any dramatic technological breakthroughs on the food front, the widening of the gap between population growth and food production of the last several years will continue . . . Feeding people adequately in the nineties will depend on quickly slowing world population growth to bring it in line with the likely increase in food output.[6]

Noticeable—indeed tragically so—is the predicament of the Third World's children, especially those below the age of five. Most are born in poverty, and if they survive, are very likely to remain in it. Some 15 million children die each year before their fifth birthday. Tens of millions suffer of malnutrition; hundreds of millions receive no education.

Air Pollution, Global Warming, and Toxic Waste   Besides the population growth and poverty, the current patterns of energy consumption pose a severe danger to the environment. During the last 200 years, the consumption of fossil fuel for energy production has increased slowly but steadily and, since the middle of this century, dramatically. A by-product of fossil fuel, carbon dioxide, is alleged to contribute to the greenhouse effect in the atmosphere, which is producing a global warming with far-reaching effects. How to arrest toxic waste in the soil, streams, rivers, and oceans is also a top priority. The toxicity is caused by chemicals that are allowed into the soil and the air. All environmentalists advocate, with growing urgency, the imposition of strict controls upon industrial firms and the adoption of new techniques of production and farming that do not rely upon noxious chemical substances.

To sum up: Most environmentalists agree on the major problems confronting us—one can say their minimum platform is: control of population growth and, related to this, poverty; adoption of strict measures to prevent toxic waste; the rapid transfer in industry to the use of nonpollutants; an emphasis on qualitative rather than quantitative measurement of economic growth. Most environmentalists agree too that nuclear energy should be abandoned both because of the dangers it poses but also because of unresolved questions of how to deal with nuclear waste.

---

[6]Lester Brown and John Young, "Feeding the World in the Nineties," in Lester Brown, et al., *State of the World*, p. 77.

Table 12.1   MEMBERSHIP OF ENVIRONMENTAL ORGANIZATIONS

	1970	1980	1985	1990
National Wildlife Federation	2.6 m	4.6 m	4.5 m	5.8 m
Sierra Club	114,000	182,000	363,000	566,000
National Audubon Society	105,000	310,000	425,000	515,000
Wilderness Society	66,000	63,000	97,000	363,000
Environmental Defence Fund	10,000	45,000	50,000	150,000
Greenpeace (1971)	—	80,000	450,000	2 m
Natural Resources Defence Council	—	35,000	65,000	140,000

Source: From The Economist, April 21, 1990. Used by permission.

Public Awareness

In the last twenty years, public awareness of environmental issues and dangers has grown rapidly. Americans were asked in 1981 and again in 1990 to agree or disagree with the following statement:

> Probably the environment is so important that . . . environmental improvements must be made regardless of cost.

In 1981, 45 percent agreed; in 1990, 74 percent.

In many opinion polls carried by the official polling center of the European community—Eurobarometre—the same high levels of awareness are found among the twelve members of the community. In many, the "environment" was mentioned as one of the three major problems by about half of the public in all of Western Europe. In a public survey conducted for the German news-magazine *Der Spiegel*, the survey institute EMNID found that 74 percent of the Germans (West and East) considered the political goal of achieving effective environmental protection as particularly important.[7] The degradation of the environment in the Soviet Union and Eastern Europe after almost half a century of neglect is becoming similarly a major concern that is widely debated in the public.

Organizations and Lobbies   In his *Global Ecology Handbook,* Walter Corson lists about 320 environmentalist organizations in the United States and points out the growing number of environmentalist "think-tanks"—on university campuses and among private groups, industries, and scientists. Many of them are linked with foreign organizations, so that international links are being established in a common pursuit. Since 1970, the membership in these organizations has been growing as well—among students, housewives, consumers, and scientists. Their overall membership (no complete figures are available) may well exceed 15 million (see Table 12.1).

---

[7]*Der Speigel,* No. 47, November 19, 1990, p. 48

Members of the environmental group "Earth First" use militant tactics. Their purpose is to stop deforestation and save the spotted owl.

All these groups engage in what is generally known as lobbying—the pressuring of government officials. But, even more important, they educate and mobilize the public. There have been environmental sit-ins in schools and universities. Demonstrations in which tens of millions throughout the world took part were organized on the twentieth anniversary of Earth Day on April 23, 1990. These environmental organizations have gained respectability and they increasingly participate in governmental deliberations to formulate policy. They are constantly on the alert to prevent legislation prejudicial to the environment and to advance the kind of legislation and regulation they espouse. Members of Congress and public officials in the various department or ministries and within specially designed government agencies set up to protect the environment are being constantly approached by environmentalist groups, and at election time the "environment" record of candidates is carefully checked and disseminated to the voters. But there is also what may be called direct action—this is notably the case with the militant "Earth First" movement that has mounted pickets and in the Northwest tried to prevent the cutting of redwood trees and the disappearance of the spotted owl. For almost three years, demonstrators blocked the opening of the Seabrook nuclear plant in New Hampshire, and they remain vigilant and active. Even consumers themselves have been organized, and their message is that they will not buy products from companies that pollute. There is a Consumer Action for the Protection of the Environment (C.A.R.E.), which monitors the activities of industry. Oil companies, chemical companies, chain-food restaurants like McDonalds, and many others are particularly sensitive to consumers. Indeed, after the *Exxon Valdez* oil spill in Alaska that Mobil gas sales fell. As a result, many corporations are beginning to advertise themselves, truly or falsely, as "environmental companies."

Environmentalist movements have also surfaced in the Soviet Union and Eastern Europe. They did so with a vengeance that pent-up resentments often cause. A rapidly growing rate of mortality among adults, widespread water contamination, fear and anguish among those living near nuclear plants after the catastrophe of Chernobyl in 1986—all under the vigilant eye of Communist parties that supposedly represented best the interests and needs of the society.

Environmentalism emerged in the Soviet Union with the coming of *glasnost* and *perestroika* and has been gaining since. Today we can count tens of environmentalist organizations and candidates at election time. The movement is also spreading into Eastern Europe where emphasis on coal and widespread use of toxins and fertilizers has led to serious environmental degradation—far more serious than that in Western Europe, the United States, or Canada. Many people in the erstwhile Soviet Bloc consider environmental issues among the most critical. Twenty-five percent of the delegates of the Twenty-Eighth Congress of the Communist party of the Soviet Union held in June–July 1990 considered the "environment" as one of the eight most important problems facing the country.

THE GOVERNMENT RESPONSE

Special governmental agencies to deal with the environment have been established virtually everywhere. In the United States, the Environmental Protection Agency was set up in 1970.[8] In England, Germany, France and the whole of the European Community, a minister oversees the environment. In the Scandinavian countries environmental governmental agencies have been active for much longer than those of other countries. Major legislative enactments have imposed clear standards for ridding the atmosphere of air pollution, soil pollution, and water pollution and for preserving species. Similarly, in the United States, there have been a number of major legislative enactments: the Clean Water Act (1972), the Clear Air Act (1970), and the so-called "Super Fund" (the Comprehensive Environmental Responses, Compensations and Liability Act 1980) to fight and eliminate toxic waste. In October 1990, Congress enacted an omnibus air pollution act dealing with the ozone layer, motor vehicles and their emissions, urban smog, acid rain, and toxic air pollutants.

---

[8]For a critical assessment, see Marc Landy, Steven Thomas, and Mark Roberts, *The Environmental Protection Agency: Asking the Wrong Questions.*

SOME MAJOR "ENVIRONMENTAL" LANDMARKS, 1970–1990

1970 Club of Rome Report
1970 The first Earth Day
1978 Oil spill of tanker *Amoco Cadiz* at Bretagne, France
1978 Dioxin contamination of the town of Seveso, Italy
1979 Near-explosion of a nuclear plant, Three Mile Island, Pennsylvania
1984 Union Carbide factory blew up, killing about 3000 people in Bhopal, India
1986 The Chernobyl disaster—Meltdown of a nuclear plant in the Ukraine
1986 Poisoning of the river Rhine with chemicals after a great fire in the Sandoz factory, Basel, Switzerland
1987 U.N. report: "Our Common Future"
1989 *Exxon Valdez* accident—the Alaskan oil spill
1990 Twentieth anniversary of Earth Day

ENVIRONMENTALIST PARTIES

The "Greens"

National environmental parties, as opposed to local citizens, groups, and lobbies, appeared throughout Europe in the 1970s, but only after *Glasnost* in 1985 in the Soviet Union and Eastern Europe. They began to contest elections at the national level in the late seventies in France, the Federal Republic of Germany, Austria, Sweden, and Belgium and seen their strength rise throughout Europe. In national elections held for the legislature, the German "Greens" moved from 1.5 percent in 1980 to 8.3 percent in 1987. It was only in the last all-German election, held after the unification of Germany on December 2, 1990, that they slipped to about 5 percent. In France they languished to no more than 5 percent in the various legislative elections held in the 1980s, but gained a record vote of 10.59% in the elections held for the European parliament in 1989. In Sweden they moved from 1.7 percent in the legislative election of 1982 to 5.6 percent in 1988. In Austria they saw their strength pass the 5 percent mark in the presidential election held on May 1986. In England, where environmentalists had shown hardly any strength in previous elections, they won an astounding 14.5 percent in the European election of June 1989. In Belgium, Holland, Norway, Italy, Greece, Spain, Portugal and Denmark, the strength of the Greens has been on the rise. And environmentalist groups have been mushrooming throughout Eastern Europe and in the Soviet Union.

The formation of environmentalist parties reflected at first many ideological strands: pacifists, antinuclearists, Marxists, Radicals, anarchists and proponents of direct action. Almost everywhere environmentalism began as a radical movement to overhaul drastically the capitalist industrial order, to inject moral imperatives, and to overthrow the political agencies of central control—the state. At their inception, they all shared the same vision of a pure and simple society without hierarchies and without inequalities.

The German Greens

Only gradually did environmentalists in the Federal Republic of Germany[10] become interested in exploring a political option within the framework of liberal democracy. The first Green Party Manifesto (1980) called for a "complete restructuring of our current near-sighted planning." It said, in part:

> Our ecology policy represents an unconditional rejection of an exploitative economy and the unscrupulous plundering of natural resources and raw materials, as well as the destructive attacks on nature's ability to renew itself.[11]

In the eighties, however, a split developed between leftists and moderates—the first endorsed "ecological, self-managed and emancipated socialism"; while the moderates advocated reforms and were inclined to cooperate with Social Democrats. The first became known as the fundamentalists (or "Fundis") and the second as the realists (or "Realos"). Fundamentalists call for a drastic "qualitative change in society" that can be accomplished only by the overthrow of capitalism by force. Reformist tactics, in order to change the system from within, are rejected. Realists, on the other hand, choose reformist tactics, political cooperation, and coalition-building with other political forces in Germany, primarily the Social Democrats. One of the leaders of the Realos outlined their strategy in 1985 as follows:

> I am no longer motivated by utopias but by the description of existing conditions. The ecological crisis, the arms race, the crisis in criminality—those are more than enough for me. I am no missionary with a promise of a new tomorrow. . . . If we can take one step in the right direction, one step which moves us away from the abyss, then this is sufficient justification for the existence of the party.[12]

A stable political compromise between these two political currents of the Green party has not been achieved thus far.

The French Environmentalists

French environmentalists organized into a movement at about the same time as the German Greens. As in Germany, we find the same ideological origins in

---

[10]Major sources for this part are: Werner Hülsberg, "The Greens at the Crossroads," in *New Left Review*, pp. 5–29; Werner Hülsberg, *The German Greens: A Social and Political Profile*; Sara Perkins, *Green Parties: An International Guide*; Gerd Langguth, *The Green Factor in German Politics: From Protest Movement to Political Party*.

[11]Quoted in Werner Hülsberg, *The German Greens*, p. 62

[12]Joschka Fischer, as quoted in Werner Hüslberg, *The German Greens*, p. 128.

the revolutionary movements among students and intellectuals of the late sixties and early seventies—the New Left—which we discuss briefly in our next chapter. Finally, as in Germany, there was a split between early revolutionaries and a growing body of moderates, with the emergence of a "realistic" platform.

A number of assorted "ecologists" formed a National Council in 1984, with delegates from all over France. But in contrast to the German Greens, their electoral successes were very limited and their organization weak. They elected one candidate to the National Assembly in the election of May 1988—thanks to socialist support—and they had some modest successes in municipal elections. In the presidential election of the same year, they had their "best" score with not more than 3.4 percent of the vote, but their candidate for the presidential election, Antoine Waechter, became Minister of Ecology. It was only in the European election of 1989 that they received over 10 percent.

What is their platform? By and large, after shedding the revolutionary and romantic stance of the 1970s, they have become "realists." They accept the U.N. report of 1987, "Our Common Future," and emphasize sustainable growth. They are particularly vocal in their criticism of "productivism"—that is, unqualified industrial growth—and stress the need for societal changes to reduce the disparities between rich and poor nations (and peoples) to do away with poverty and unemployment. In so doing, they stress feminist and Third World issues and project a society that comes even closer to a socialist model than the one espoused by the French Socialist party.

What the French ecologists managed to do is raise the consciousness of the French public. Forty-five percent of students polled in 1989 considered the environment to be the most important issue of the coming decades. As happened elsewhere, they have forced the Socialists and Conservatives to take up environmentalist themes and pledges. The environment has become a part of the French political agenda and will continue to weigh on all political parties, especially the Socialists, with whom the environmentalists may ally themselves. It will increasingly attract the vote of feminists and all those for whom communism as an ideology has lost its appeal.

CONCLUSION

In response to a series of crises and the rapid degradation of the environment, environmentalism as an ideology and as a movement has been gaining momentum and is becoming increasingly global. If war afflicts us all, so does deforestation or the loss of the ozone layer. Cooperation and solidarity among peoples and nations are essential. The notion of interdependence seems far more credible with matters that affect the environment than with matters of the economy and trade. Environmentalism may yet emerge as a cosmopolitan ideology, subordinating national and state requirements and needs to its global imperatives.

But before this happens, the road the environmentalists will have to travel is long. The poor in the underdeveloped countries, and with them what we have called the "global underclass," will need aid to reach the level of education and political consciousness that people in industrialized nations are just beginning to attain. Population pressures and, concomitantly, poverty and ignorance remain the critical issues. Another central issue is the depletion of national resources unless it is offset by the development of new technologies and alternate resources. A new understanding of development, as opposed to industrial growth and production, will have to evolve. Environmentalism will have to overcome nationalisms and nationalist rivalries and will have to confront, when it comes to population control, powerful Pro-Life movements. On the other hand, the environmentalist movement may become, at least in Europe, the basis for a broad coalition of forces—among the poor, women, students, intellectuals, many Socialists, ex-Communists, and "welfare liberals." As such, it may become a party committed to broad societal programs engineered to change the structures and goals of our industrial society and to emphasize human development and social services. Lobbying in the United States and widespread public involvement may infuse the U.S. political parties with similar environmental objectives.

As environmentalism matures and gains supporters, it is not impossible to envisage a series of crises, nuclear or environmental, that may bring about a moral indignation to infuse the movement with fervor. But environmentalists will have to wait for their Adam Smith or their Marx—someone who will develop a coherent theory to analyze the environmental predicaments we humans have wrought upon ourselves and to suggest a comprehensive economic and social platform to arrest the degradation and improve our lives. Only then can we talk of an environmentalist ideology that deeply involves the people and propels them into political action. Environmentalism and environmentalists have yet to develop a theory that will "grip the masses"!

BIBLIOGRAPHY

Brown, Lester R. *In the Human Interest: A Strategy to Stabilize World Population.* New York: Norton, 1974.

——— . *Building a Sustainable Society.* New York: Norton, 1981.

———, et al. *State of the World, 1990.* New York: Norton, 1990.

Corson, Walter H. (ed.). *The Global Ecology Handbook.* Boston: Beacon Press, 1990.

Council on Environmental Quality, Department of State. *The Global 2000 Report to the President: Entering the Twenty-First Century, Volume One.* Washington, D.C.: U.S. Government Printing Office, 1980.

Dominick, Raymond. "The Roots of the Green Movement in the United States and West Germany." *Environmental Review,* Vol. 12, No. 3, Fall 1988, pp. 1–30.

Ehrlich, Paul. *The Population Bomb.* New York: Ballantine Books, 1968.

Hülsberg, Werner. "The Greens at the Crossroads." *New Left Review,* No. 152, July–August 1985, pp. 5–29.

——— . *The German Greens: A Social and Political Profile.* Translated by Gus Fagan, New York: Routledge, 1987.

Langguth, Gerd. *The Green Factor in German Politics: From Protest Movement to Political Party.* Boulder, Colo: Westview, 1984.

Leggett, Jeremy (ed.). *Global Warming: The Greenpeace Report*. New York: Oxford University Press, 1991.

McDonagh, Sean. *The Greening of the Church*. New York: Orbis Books, 1990.

Meadows, Donella H., Dennis L. Meadows, Jorgen Randers, and William W. Behrens. *The Limits to Growth: A Report for the Club of Rome's Project on the Predicament of Mankind*, 2nd ed. New York: Universe Books, 1974.

Parkin, Sara. *Green Parties: An International Guide*. London: Heretic Books, 1988.

Schumacher, Erich. *Small Is Beautiful: Economics As If People Mattered*. New York: Harper & Row, 1973.

Tinbergen, Jan (coordinator), Antony J. Dolman (editor), and Jan Van Ettinger (director). *Reshaping the International Order: A Report to the Club of Rome*. New York: Dutton, 1976.

United Nations Development Porgramme. *Human Development Report 1990*. New York: Oxford University Press, 1990.

World Commission on Environment and Development. *Our Common Future (Brundtland Report)*. New York: Oxford University Press, 1987.

Chapter
13

Ideologies of Revolution
Hints and Fragments

I am nothing and I should be everything.

Karl Marx
Critique of Hegel's Philosophy

Until they have become conscious they will never rebel, and until after they have rebelled they cannot become conscious.

George Orwell,
1984

Most people have romantic notions about revolutions—the mob storming the Bastille, the tea thrown into the Boston Harbor, the Bolsheviks storming the Winter Palace, Gandhi and his followers lying on the railroad tracks in a movement of civil disobedience that paralyzed the British rule in India. Heroic statements come to our minds: "Give me liberty, or give me death"; "the despotism of liberty against tyranny"; "workers of the world arise: you have nothing to lose but your chains." Muslim fundamentalists mount a *jihad*—a holy war—promising heaven to those who die fighting it.

The conventional wisdom suggests that the poor and the downtrodden will rebel, that poverty will beget revolutionary movements. But it is hardly so. As Leon Trotsky, a foremost practitioner of the art of revolution observed, if poverty was the cause of revolutions, we would all be sitting on an exploding powder keg! Similarly, George Orwell, in his book *1984*, raises the possibility of revolution against the established powerholders, Big Brother, the Inner Brotherhood, and the Party, who have a tight grip over the "proles"—the poor, wretched, and disregarded masses that account for the vast majority of the population in his imaginary state. They could destroy those who have enslaved them. If they could become conscious of their own strength, they would rise up "and shake them like a horse shaking off flies." But Orwell quickly stifles all hope: "Until [the proles] become conscious, they will never rebel, and until after they have rebelled, they cannot become conscious." The poor, the underprivileged, the slaves, and the wretched of the earth are in a box! There is much more than rhetoric and romantic imagery to a revolution and it takes much more than poverty or moral indignation to make it. A *revolution* is an act of organized violence to bring about radical changes in the economic, social, and political relations within a given system. It uses force to destroy (sometimes physically) and replace those who hold power. Protests, civil disobedience, turmoil, demonstrations, and acts of violence are not revolutions, as such, though they may precede them. All depends on the degree of mobilization and organization and on the ideas people share when they commit acts of violence.

Gandhi's disobedience in India was aimed at driving out the British and replacing colonial rule with an Indian government—it was a revolutionary movement. Martin Luther King, on the other hand, simply wanted to force concessions that would allow the blacks to participate (as they were entitled to do) in the American system. In the past, periodic peasants' rebellions in Germany, France, Italy, and Eastern Europe aimed to reclaim the land from the nobility. These rebellions did not have broad political goals such as changing the political regime.

Major revolutions have been associated with (1) a national or a colonial independence movement against a foreign occupying power—a phenomenon common in Europe in the nineteenth century and throughout most of the colonial world in the twentieth century; (2) separatist movements mobilizing ethnic or religious groups to secede from the state in which they live; (3) a movement organized by some social groups or classes against those that hold power within a given regime. The French Revolution, the Bolshevik Revolution in 1917, and the Chinese Communist Revolution in 1949 are the archetypal cases. But the national independence movements in the nineteenth century, and the guerrilla warfare in Vietnam, Algeria, and elsewhere only a decade or so ago, and in some of the Latin American countries, in the Middle East, Africa, and Asia today, are also revolutions. Revolutions and revolutionary movements continue to stud the political landscape of the world, especially where guerrilla fighters mount civil war as in the Philippines, Peru, Ethiopia, Angola, El Salvador, Afghanistan, and so many others. The list is long. The post-Cold War era that appears to have put an end to the rivalry between the Soviet Union and the United States has not brought about an end to revolutionary warfare. It remains an everyday fare—more plentiful than wheat and medicine.

THEORIES OF REVOLUTION

People do not revolt unless they first get the idea that the use of organized force is a remedy for their situation. Some philosophers have suggested that conflict and revolutions lie in the interstices of the historical process—and we have noted that both Hegel and Marx assumed that a dialectic process (involving conflict between opposing forces) was historically inevitable. According to this notion, history itself is what counts—the actors, individuals, and groups act in accord with "its laws." Conflict and revolutions are, in a sense, predetermined; and so are the ideologies related to them.

Marx developed the most complete ideology *of* a revolution and *for* a revolution. It is the material conditions that by and large shape ideology. The ruling class—the bourgeoisie—tries to impose its ideology upon all others. But the workers, though not immune to it, ultimately reject it in order to develop a revolutionary ideology—a "counterideology." We saw that Lenin claimed that only a small elite could act for the workers in leading them against their masters.

If circumstances (the material conditions) shape ideologies, what role do ideologies play in shaping circumstances? It is an endless argument. Determinists tend to look primarily at the circumstances and claim that ideologies cannot arise or function independently. Marxists, as we have seen, perform a balancing act between the two—there is interplay between *both* the circumstances *and* the ideology. Other revolutionaries tend to emphasize *will* and *ideas*—so much as to attribute to them an independent role. For these revolutionaries ideology is primary. It is what Marx called the "theory that becomes a material force when it grips the masses."

As for the substance of a revolutionary ideology, a number of elements shape it. A distinction is often made by some between an "inherent" and a "derived" ideology. The first is another name for the culture of a people—the sum total of their experiences and customs, their oral traditions, their habits, and their common memories of past rights, privileges, and claims. The inherent ideology usually provides the context for the development of a revolutionary consciousness, but this is not enough. What is needed is a theory—a derived ideology—that will spell out, in a structured and organized manner, the reasons why force is necessary and will outline the goals that force will realize.

"Derived ideologies" come from political theorists such as Marx, Rousseau, Hegel, Bergson, Tom Paine, and many others. The transmission belts between "derived" and "inherent" are the intellectuals. They blend theory, popular culture, and traditions in order to shape a revolutionary ideology and a revolutionary movement. Theory will provide the vocabulary of the revolution, leaving it to the intellectuals and organizers to do the spelling. Ideology that blends theory and popular culture is developed and propagated by the intellectuals—the "organic" intellectuals as the Italian Communist intellectual Antonio Gramsci called them—. They mobilize and organize people. The intellectuals distill the new ideology drop by drop to convince the masses slowly; they build ideological pockets and bastions that become immune to the prevailing ideology. It is not an exaggeration to say that the revolution was, for Gramsci, primarily a vast educational and organizational effort that did not necessarily require the use of force (though never excluding it) against the ruling class. Force would come in handy, but only to enhance the ideological awareness and preparedness of the masses.

The Circumstances: Structural Factors

When does the "theory . . . grip the masses" to become a revolutionary move-ment? Crane Brinton, after a survey of the major revolutions (the Puritan Revolution, the French Revolution, the Bolshevik Revolution, and the American Revolution), found some common structural characteristics.[1] They are the following:

1. The political societies in which revolutions occurred were "on the whole on the upgrade economically before the revolution." In most cases they were revolutions of hope and not despair; the actors were not downtrodden, starving, poor, or slaves. The ideology they shared was one of optimism. There was an expectation of better opportunities.

2. In all cases, although perhaps less so with the American Revolution, there were strong class antagonisms. But revolutions cannot be explained in terms of one class fighting against another. In fact, revolutions occur when social classes come closer together, so that the privileges and power of some appear intolerable. As de Tocqueville had noted, people resent inequalities only when they become a little more equal! Untouchables and slaves rarely revolt. The idea of revolution comes in the minds of men and women who become relatively better-off, whose wants and expectations are on the rise.

3. Another phenomenon associated with revolution is the "desertion of the intellectuals"—of those who write and preach, of the "clerks" and the teachers. They shift their allegiance from the regime in search of alternatives. By doing so, they sap its strength. Revolution, then, "begins" in the minds of the intellectuals, those we called "ideologues" in our first chapter. They think and ger-minate the thoughts of revolution long before these thoughts trickle down to the hovel of the peasant or the artisan's basement or the slums or the workshops.

4. Before a revolution there is a breakdown in the efficiency and perfor-mance of the government. This is due to the fact that economic changes occur, such as industrialization with new technological innovations. The government is unable to take these economic changes into account, to respond to new needs and demands, and to adjust to them. The government officials lose faith in their ability to control events and to govern. Relatedly, the finances and the admin-istration of the government suffer. The "organized discontented groups" press their demands at this juncture and the governmental apparatus is unable to re-act. In almost all cases, the government and the regime are in a state of virtual collapse *before* the revolution succeeds. A crucial factor in a revolution is the weakness shown at the top of the existing structure and not only the strength mustered at the bottom.

It is possible, then, to say that a revolution as a process seems to start at the top? That there are structural societal factors that can best explain it? All one

---

[1]Crane Brinton, *The Anatomy of Revolution.*

can say is that they play a very important role. Marx was clearly aware of it because the timing of the workers' revolution was related to major structural changes in the capitalistic economy and the political regime that reflected it. This was not so for Lenin and many of his followers, who emphasized will and leadership.

The Individual: Subjective Factors

Even if revolution is a mass organized movement, it is the individual who must be mobilized. Nobody will leave home and family, job, or farm unless prompted by powerful reasons to do so. Only a handful of individuals are "born radicals"; personality propels them to radical action to change things. Most people venture into the unknown world of revolution and violence only because they feel, or are made to feel, that their lives are at stake.

The feeling of threat, particularly the threat of deprivation, is the most common psychological motivation for a revolution. The most common threat is to one's livelihood, one's expectations, and one's position in society—his or her status. Rising material opportunities provide for the hope of more, and when for one reason or another opportunities do not materialize, people become apprehensive. Even more, *they feel deprived* in two ways: (1) their expectations of what they believe they are worth—of what they should be getting—do not materialize; (2) their standard of living falls behind others. This is often referred to as "relative deprivation." The threat to status is generally shared more or less among well-established groups that find their position, income, and importance in the society threatened by other groups. Revolutions motivated by a threat to status have been common among middle-class and lower middle-class groups and are considered, as we have seen, the major reasons for fascism and nazism. Direct deprivation of one's livelihood and expectations is commonly associated with revolutions by peasantry, working classes, and often lower middle-class groups.

Will and Revolution: The Meaning of Praxis

Historical, economic, psychological, and structural conditions and circumstances prepare men and women for a revolution; they do not make it! Will, leadership, organization, mass involvement and support, or even acquiescence are needed. Revolutionaries emphasize will; they stress the voluntaristic, organizational, and elitist nature of a revolution. They want "praxis"—they want action! Action mobilizes groups such as students and the intelligentsia into a revolutionary formation that propagates its own ideology—a counterideology; second, revolutionary action appeals to all the discontents and the claims inherited by the culture, the history, and the traditions of a society, what is referred to as the "inherent ideology." Through praxis, the discontent of the farmers may blend with the frustration of the unemployed and the resentment of ethnic or racial minority groups. In this manner, the counterideology gradually gains momentum and the official ideology along with the state and its various institutions are rendered impotent. The important thing is to begin—to move into action. "We engage the enemy and then we shall see." Both Napoleon, a great general, and Lenin, a great revolutionary, were fond of this expression.

Praxis, then, is the starting point of a revolution to reshape society. But it is also a vast effort consisting of a series of multiple acts of violence and defiance that may stretch over a long period, to create the conditions for a revolution—to shape the counterideology. Praxis, gradually and cumulatively, prepares the society for a new way of life with new institutions in accord with the counterideology that is gaining roots. However, both as a frontal revolutionary act and as a gradual process to develop a new revolutionary consciousness, praxis displays the same characteristics: emphasis on political will and leadership and the importance it gives to ideology. Praxis gives a lot of room to "subjective" as opposed to "objective" factors.

In contrast to liberalism and Marxism—both of them powerful revolutionary ideologies—the revolutionary ideologies to be discussed in this chapter and many nationalist ideologies, old and new, have been intensive and unstructured ideological movements. Not only do they appeal to powerful ethical imperatives but they pay little attention to history and circumstances in order to develop a coherent body of theory and to suggest tactics. They seem to have these things in common: to change by an effort of will and organization what has been deeply traced over many centuries, to reshape social, economic, and political life, and to refashion even human nature. Like the Commissar in Orwell's *1984*, many of the contemporary revolutionaries would say: "Forget all these notions about human nature; WE make human nature." All of them are committed to action—revolutionary action—even when the theory behind it is uncertain and the goals unclear. Action by itself and in itself will provide the experience that will guide the revolutionary leaders to reform and change. The revolutionary is expected to learn from the revolution. Contemporary revolutionaries put the accent on will and action, relying in part upon the rich background of anarchism.

ANARCHISM

As with terrorists today, anarchists stalked the earth in the latter part of the nineteenth century and continued their work until the 1930s. Of all revolutionaries, they have been and are the most committed to direct action—to praxis. Anarchism as a doctrine was inspired by some of the greatest philosophers and was steeped profoundly in moral idealism. A number of powerful intellectual forces shaped the doctrine of anarchism: Christianity, liberalism, socialism, and idealism were among the most important.

Christianity   Christianity (despite the fact that most anarchists are against religion and the church) provided a strong ingredient for the development of anarchist thought. The individual as God's creature, endowed with rationality, should be free to live his or her temporal life. He or she should not be subject to any secular powers. Christianity pitted moral individual consciousness against temporal authority and, in so doing, promoted an attitude of defiance and insubordination.

Liberalism Anarchism also followed the "moral core" of liberalism and the first priority was to maintain the moral autonomy of the individual. To do so, the anarchists proposed to eliminate the state, democratic or not, and to do away with all the coercive traits of political authority and to replace them with free and spontaneously formed associations. This was only a step beyond classic liberalism according to which, as we saw earlier, the state is formed by a voluntary contract among the citizens. Since any contract involves some degree of alienation of one's freedom, anarchists wish, in effect, to revoke the contract and put an end to all obligations undertaken by the citizen. But the same was true for society and societal relations; they, too, must be purged of everything that allows some people to dominate others—everything and anything that allows for subordination and inequalities. The major institution that makes for inequalities is property, and some anarchists, notably Michael Bakunin (1814–1876), favored communism as a solution. Others, however, especially P. J. Proudhon (1809–1864), would allow for some individual property but favored economic democracy with the control and organization of production and productive forces lodged in voluntary "associations."

Socialism Most anarchists shared the attitudes of the Utopian Socialists, which we discussed briefly in Chapter 3. They favored the elimination of private property—or at least of large-scale private holdings in land, industry, or finances. They also favored collectivism and socialism in various forms. The extent to which private property was to be allowed by some anarchists related only to small holdings and to property held by voluntary associations. For all of them the destruction of the propertied classes was necessary for the liberation of the individual.

Idealism Anarchism in the nineteenth century received a powerful infusion of intellectual life from German idealist philosophy, notably that of Hegel. His scheme of history embodied the gradual unfolding of the Spirit in our world. Anarchists concluded that the spirit manifested itself through individuals who, after all, *are* the agents of history. It was the individual as an individual that embodied truth, and it was up to the individual to assert it even against the prevailing circumstances. The individual is unique as a rational and sentient being. To remain so it was imperative, first of all, to destroy all coercive institutions, including the state, and put an end to everything that the individual had given up (alienated) to others. Only then would he or she recover what Max Stirner (1806–1856) called full "personal gratification"—the reaffirmation of one's ego—the "Unique I." The only appropriate institutions for such a reaffirmation were the spontaneous associations into which people would gather voluntarily.

Anarchism as a Movement

The many intellectual roots of anarchism also account for the fragmentation of the movement as it appeared within the First International in 1864. Some anarchists became fully committed to socialism—to the collective ownership of the means of production—while others insisted that some degree of private property should be permitted. Those who argued for collectivization, however, were opposed to state ownership. Indeed, Bakunin and his followers were in favor of the destruction of the state. They had no patience with bureaucracy even if it were to be controlled by the workers as the Marxists favored. The collective property would be handled by associations formed on a voluntary basis. Those who favored some degree of private property were also opposed to the state. But in contrast to the Marxists, they favored workers' direct action; they became known as *anarchosyndicalists*. The workers by their own efforts, not through political and party action, would undertake to destroy the dominant position of the capitalists and emancipate themselves. Finally, some anarchists became committed to personal direct action, including assassination, against all agents of authority. In the reaffirmation of their moral autonomy they became known as *nihilists*—accepting nothing and committed to the rejection of everything.

Unable to organize a movement, fragmented into many sects, and often propelled by sheer individual determination, the anarchists began to rely more and more on what we might call individual praxis—individual acts of violence to undermine authority, to disrupt order, and even to physically exterminate the "enemy." Assassinations and bombings became widespread. Terrorism was often directed against persons in authority irrespective of any consideration of responsibility or guilt. The more innocent and the more respected the victim and the more senseless the crime, the greater was the damage to the legal order. Random acts of terror such as theft, fire, bombings, and assassination became ennobling in themselves. Destruction wrought for its own sake—the rejection of anything and everything—became the political credo and practice of anarchists according to the *Catechism of an Anarchist*, attributed to Bakunin. The czar of Russia and some of his ministers, the emperor of Germany, the president of the French Republic, and the king of Italy received special attention, which often resulted in their assassination. In 1893, a bomb, containing hundreds of nails, exploded in the French Parliament. In 1901, President McKinley was assassinated by an anarchist who had moved to the United States. The "Unique I" seemed to be on the rampage. As with terrorism today, the anarchist impulse was not without appeal. To the romantics and the discontented, many of the anarchists became heroes before they were sentenced to death and after they were executed. In some cases, their burial places became places of pilgrimages. "What a magnificent gesture," said a French poet in commenting on the explosion of the bomb in the French Parliament. "Who cares about the victims!"

THE NEW LEFT

The term *New Left,* or *radical left,* is used to describe the general movement of agitation, protest, and revolt organized and led, in great part, by young people and university students in the 1960s. The system under attack was, and continues to be, that of the modern industrialized societies—democratic or not. As seen by its opponents, the system's major characteristics are repressiveness and comprehensiveness; it is bureaucratic, impersonal, and authoritarian. Everything is subordinated to management, thanks to the advances of technology; production is geared to material gain and profit; and standards of measurement and evaluation become exclusively quantitative. The state, hand in hand with the huge industrial organizations, socializes people to accept the values the system manufactures—the ideology of consumerism, wasteful production, and the inculcation of work discipline. The individual becomes an empty shell, losing all capacity for pleasure, joy, and fulfillment. He or she becomes "dehumanized." This is the system the New Left painted in order to call for its destruction.

One of the high points of the New Left movement was the uprising of May and June 1968 in Paris and many other French cities. The students led the way by striking, occupying the universities, throwing out their professors, deriding the meaning and validity of what they were being taught, and asking for a new university—the "antiuniversity." The revolt spread to workers, public servants, and salaried personnel. Public buildings were occupied, TV and radio stations taken over, barricades built, battles with the "forces of order" fought, and the students seemed on the verge of taking power. In an unprecedented show of spontaneity, and against the instructions of their trade unions and political leaders, the French workers began to join. They went on strike, occupied factories, and brought the whole economy to a standstill. One firm after another, one organization after another, one administration after another, and one service after another were taken over by those who worked in them. Theaters, newspapers, the opera, the ballet, and even soccer teams were taken over by actors, reporters, singers, dancers, and players. The only organization not taken over was the Paris Stock Exchange—it was set on fire!

Another high point in the political and revolutionary activity of the New Left took place in the United States at the Democratic party convention held in Chicago at the end of August 1968. Demonstrations against the war in Vietnam had already reached a peak, forcing Lyndon Johnson to announce that he would not seek renomination. A number of students and leftist organizations decided to demonstrate at the Chicago convention and to force a peace candidate upon the Democratic party. But their demands were broader, and the participants ranged from those who favored peace and were against the military draft to gen-

"Under the cobblestones, the beach!" This a street scene from the 1968 student uprising in Paris.

uine revolutionaries who were driven by the vision of a new society. The National Mobilization Committee to End the War in Vietnam (a loose organization which appealed to all people who were against the war) played an important role. In addition, there were the Committee for an Open Convention, seeking the nomination of Eugene McCarthy; the Students for Democratic Society; and the Youth International Party (Yippies), advocates of the "counterculture."

The New Left and the student uprisings should be put in their proper historical and intellectual context. Like anarchism, the New Left represented the long-standing grievances against industrialization and the impersonality and coerciveness of modern society with its complexity—all of which were seen to distort human nature and account for "alienation." Even though the movement subsided in the 1980s—especially among the young who spearheaded it—its message of protest and rejection is by no means forgotten. It flares up constantly among environmentalists, ethnonationalist movements, and, of course, anarchists.

The demand for efficiency and profit develops its own logic, which leads to the production of goods as an end in itself without reference to social goals. Herbert Marcuse, philosopher of the New Left, claims that in advanced industrialized societies

> the technical apparatus of production and distribution (with an increased sector of automation) functions not as the sum total of mere instruments which can be isolated from their social and political effects, but rather as a system that determines . . . the product of the apparatus as well as the operations of servicing and extending it. . . . The productive apparatus tends *to become totalitarian to the extent to which it determines not only the socially needed occupations and skills and attitudes but also individual needs and aspirations.*[2]

The Role of Ideology

The absorption of the individual into the system of the advanced industrialized societies is a gradual process, and ideology plays the crucial role. It rationalizes and legitimizes production and efficiency; socializes the young people in the school and the university to accept them; and sets the tone for their preparation to play special roles within the system. It is primarily in the ideology of production that consumerism and material satisfactions predominate. Modernization and growth are viewed exclusively in quantitative terms. It is a materialist ethic that gradually invades our lives until we can no longer refute or avoid it. It affects our moral judgments, our tastes, our pleasures, and our leisure time. Political and ethical considerations are subordinated to it. Education, performance, and lifestyles are reduced to pure material considerations that can be checked, double-checked, and tabulated.

The student will notice here the sharp departure from the classic Marxist critique. The argument against capitalism is not that it fails to produce enough but that it produces a great deal! The indictment made is that capitalism has created abundance and continues to be capable of producing an ever-growing variety of material goods.

---

[2]Herbert Marcuse, *One Dimensional Man*, p. xv.

The Explosion

The uprising against the industrial society of our times can come only in the form of a moral outburst. It will stem from moral indignation, and its objective will be moral rehabilitation. It will not spring from deprivation, nor will it come from the workers. It will come from all those who have maintained their inner self intact from the ideological contamination the advanced industrial societies spread. It will come from the intellectuals who have somehow managed to maintain their true consciousness and who will defy the society that tries to mold and shape them.

Revolutions follow careful guidelines, which revolutionaries provide. They spell out organization, discipline, leadership, and specific procedures. The New Left produced no such guidelines. By appealing directly to the individual conscience, they neglected the requirements of common organized effort. In fact, they seemed to rely to a great degree on anarchy as the only creative response to organization and totalitarian control. For them, the three essential elements for revolution are *imagination, action,* and *rejection.* All three are linked together in terms of a deeply moral disavowal, almost religious in its fervor, of the ways of life of our contemporary industrialized societies.

Imagination   The French sociologist Alain Touraine points out that the revolution of the students and the New Left in general was "the revolution of the imagination" and that, perhaps, because of it, it turned out to be "an imaginary revolution."[3] "Be realistic; think of the impossible"; "Under the cobblestones, the beach"—these were two recurring slogans of the French students during their uprising in 1968. Imagination is clearly seen as the outlet for the enslaved self. It is the vision of a new world, without police officers, coercion, rules, roles, and duties; where time will not be measured by minutes and hours; material needs will no longer weigh on our minds; desires will be fulfilled almost instantly; where intuition will provide for truth that can be "understood" and not measured and verified; where there will be no masters, no bosses, no hierarchies; where struggle, domestic and international, will give place to peace; where, finally, everything that separates us from each other—walls, rooms, offices, blocks, and national boundaries—will be erased. There will be no "No Trespass" signs anywhere: this will be the world of the "real self," of the natural self—spontaneous, creative, intuitive, and almost instinctual. It is the exact opposite of the alienated self. It is the real "I," not the fabricated and collective "we."

Action   Imagination must be coupled with action. To be "engaged" is essential not only to promote one's ends but to understand them better. "Being" should not be, and cannot be, separated from "doing." Theory must lead to action and

---

[3] Alain Touraine, *The May Movement.*

action will refine theory. For it is only in action, and only by acting, that an individual can "enter into the essence of things" and understand them fully. To think of something in a detached way is meaningless, but to think of something and to do it is the essence of comprehension. We learn while we act, and we act in order to learn! Praxis becomes all-important.

Rejection   Imagination and action, however, must both be inspired by a powerful personal and moral rejection of the existing order of things. In the philosophy of the new left, there was a nihilist streak—a disavowal not only of the established order of things but an outright rejection of many aspects of societal life—organization, structured work, hierarchy and discipline, political order and civic obligation, the family, and of course industrial organization. Rejection amounts to the assertion of the individual and of individual spontaneity free from all constraints.

The Vision   What will the world be like after the explosion? The revolution of the imagination will result in a utopia. Even if there is no comprehensive blueprint, and even if the New Left assumes that once the revolution started it would gain momentum and shape as the people gain knowledge from the revolutionary experience, there are enough bits and pieces that we can put together. What emerges from them, as Theodore Roszak points out, is a "vision."[4]

In the vision of the future new society, three elements predominate: *anarchism, participation,* and the *quality of life*.

Anarchism   The proponents of the New Left echo some of the same anarchist themes: rejection of bigness, destruction of authority and political and economic organizational hierarchies, and, of course, elimination of the state. They emphasize working and living in small groups—communes and associations through which individuals control their environment, organize their work, and take charge of their own affairs. The New Left shares with the anarchists the same quest for individualization, for spontaneity and creativity, and for free play. They, too, reject private property in favor of communal or associational collectivism. They also believe in the use of force and direct action and share the anarchists' outright moral rejections of existing society. A small number of activists among the New Left joined conspiratorial and terrorist organizations bent upon destruction and political assassination.

Participation   For the New Left, participation of all in the management of common affairs is one of the most potent instruments for putting an end to alienation. Limited forms of participation, especially of the workers in industrial firms, have been practiced in many countries. They involve consultations, profit-sharing, and the autonomy of the workers to determine their working

---

[4]Theodore Roszak, *The Making of a Counter-Culture*, p. 246.

conditions. They do not question, however, the basic rules of the capitalistic economy with regard to property ownership and the managerial and hierarchical organization of the firms.

The demands of the New Left are far more comprehensive. First, they apply not only to industrial firms and economic activities, but to all others, political, social, and cultural; all those involved in a given activity and in any organization that makes decisions that affect them should participate in making decisions. Second, the New Left has specific notions about organizational structures, advocating their reduction in size and complexity. Finally, it proposes the socialization of all economic units that are privately owned. Participation is, in effect, equivalent to socialism plus internal democracy.

The Quality of Life   One of the recurrent themes of the New Left and the many environmentalist groups it has spawned (see Chapter 12) is the degradation (past, present, and future) of the quality of our lives in the industrially advanced societies. Our environment has been used and abused for the sake of immediate benefits and profits. Even more important, men and women have lost their "personality." They have become cogwheels in a huge machine that endlessly produces material goods and services devoid of qualitative content. Moral values, such as self-expression and individuality, have been squashed.

This, then, is the new world the New Left painted in the sixties and seventies. For collectivity, read individualism; for bigness, smallness; for complexity, simplicity, for imposition, self-government; for coercion, freedom; for hierarchy, equality; for private property, socialism; for profit, social need; for materialism, spirituality; for war, peace; for competition, cooperation; for science and technology, intuition and spontaneity; for knowledge, experience; for reason, feeling. It is a different, new, and shiny world. One of its advocates stated that the first step of the revolution will be "to proclaim a new heaven and a new earth so vast, so marvelous that the inordinate claims of technical expertise must of necessity withdraw in the presence of such a splendor to a subordinate and marginal status in the lives of men."[5] It was and it remains a call for religious and moral reawakening.

Revolutionary Guerrillas

Guerrilla warfare has been one of the major instruments of revolutions in much of the colonial world. These revolutions have been directed against a colonial power and against the native rulers, landowners, or a bourgeoisie that act on behalf of the interests, or in a manner congruent with the interests, of a colonial power (in the case of Latin America, The United States is a dominant power). The themes invariably are ethnic assertiveness, national independence, and the radical overhaul of social and economic relations. In El Salvador, Guatemala,

---

[5]Roszak, p. 240.

Nicaragua, Peru (the Tupamaros), Ethiopia, the Philippines, Angola, Mozambique (the Frelinos), Afghanistan, Sri Lanka (the Tamils), and in many parts of Africa, guerrillas are active.

Guerrilla revolutionary warfare depends, above all, on the organization of a small avant-garde that will lead the masses, mostly the peasantry, into an insurrectional struggle. It is synonymous with praxis. There is a great deal of discussion about the existing conditions—are they "ripe" for a revolution or not? But many believe that, even if they are not, the proper action—military and political—will create these conditions. Ché Guevara, considered one of the foremost theoreticians of guerrilla warfare for Latin America, wrote the catechism, or at least what has been taken as such in Latin America, for guerrilla revolutionary warfare.[6] There are three basic precepts and three phases to a successful guerrilla revolution.

The three precepts are:

1. Popular forces can win a war against an army.
2. It is not always necessary to wait until the conditions for making revolution exist; the "insurrectional focus" can create them.
3. In underdeveloped America, the countryside is the basic area for the armed fighting.

The three phases correspond to:

1. The establishment and the consolidation of the "insurrectional focus."
2. Guerrilla warfare against the armed forces of the enemy and the gradual conquest of the hearts and minds of the people, particularly the peasantry.
3. The weakening of the governmental forces and, with it, the final assault on them and the takeover of political and economic power by the leadership of guerrilla forces.

In guerrilla warfare there are many ups and downs. What counts above all is the development of an awareness on the part of the people that their deliverance is possible. A guerrilla war may fail, but the awareness will remain to spark future guerrilla-war-like efforts. Praxis shapes the revolutionary even if the revolution fails.

According to Ché Guevara, the starting point in the guerrilla revolutionary war is the establishment of what has been called an "insurrectional focus" ("*foco*" in Spanish means a hearth, a home, a base in broad terms). It is where the guerrillas find shelter, rest, food, and ammunitions, and where they plan their moves. The "home," in order to be secure, must be located in a hospitable environment—among friendly peasants—and ideally should be immune from enemy detection and direct threats. The establishment of such an insurrectional base is the first step in a long political and military struggle, but it is an irreversible step as it commits the leadership to the revolution.

---

[6]Ché Guevara, *Guerrilla Warfare.*

In many parts of Central America, guerrilla warfare and insurrectional up-risings are ever-present. A committed avant-garde continues to seek the sup-port of the peasantry, the poor, and the underprivileged in order to oust from power the political and economic elites that have dominated them for so long. What accounts for the revolutionary efforts and their successes, against govern-ments supported by the United States, is that the people continue to be mo-bilized by the will and the organization of a few, in terms of an ideology that promises so much to the many. Guerrillas, in the words of Ché Guevara, are "the Jesuits of the revolution," committed to spreading the revolutionary faith far and wide. Until about 1990, "the Jesuits of the Revolution" almost every-where had one faith—Marxism. In Latin America, they received inspiration from the Cuban revolutionary experience of the 1950s and Cuban military fi-nancial and technical support. Cuba became a model. And despite the world-wide waning of Marxism as an ideology and of the Soviet system as a model of governance, communism remains their faith. This is the case in the Philippines. A reformed and national Communist party in South Africa is also resurfacing. Eritrean rebels continue to call themselves Marxist.

But Marxism has lost the monopoly of faith. Nationalist and ethnonation-alist ideologies, Islamic fundamentalism, but also Catholic liberationists ac-count for and support many guerrilla movements as well. Guerrillas continue, in almost every part of our globe, to defy the political order they do not accept or one that has been imposed upon them and the society in which they live by force. Guerrilla warfare remains the most extreme form of political protest, the most desperate form of rejection.

THE WRETCHED OF THE EARTH

After World War II, African intellectuals, and some American blacks, began to move restlessly toward a redefinition of their own identity. Frantz Fanon (1925–1961)[7] merits special mention. An Algerian psychiatrist (trained in France), he reconciled elements of Marxism with Freudian psychology to develop a theory of colonial and racial revolutions. He put all the emphasis on praxis—on the act of rebelling and on the use of violence by the black "subjects" against their white colonial "masters."

He rejected the "liberal" model of revolution in which the more developed and middle-class native groups using Western institutions such as political par-ties, representative government, lobbying, trade unions, and the like, would put pressure upon the colonial governments to gain reforms leading to national independence. Fanon believed that the native middle classes were parasitic and lived off their colonial masters. They could not be relied upon, nor could they be expected to gain independence for their peoples. They have "black skins but

---

[7]Frantz Fanon's *The Wretched of the Earth*—was, in his own words, "the handbook for the Black Revolution that is changing the shape of the world."

wear white masks!" Many from among them had come in contact with Western civilization, studied in Western universities, and had become "assimilated" in Western culture.

Fanon, though paying lip service to it, also rejected Marxism. As we noted, Marxism called for some degree of industrial development and the existence even of a small working class, such as dock workers, transport workers, and workers in manufacturing. As late as 1960, more than 90 percent of the Africans were peasants. In Algeria—the most developed African "colony"—the figure was 85 percent. They were peasants in almost the feudal sense of the term, with the land often owned by the white colonizers or otherwise cultivated in communal arrangements. Without a working class, how could one fit the Marxist scheme into Africa?

Fanon chose a third way. This was to use the mass of the peasantry and their abject poverty to bring about an "explosion"—in Marcuse's terms—or, a violent confrontation, much like a "general strike." Action—praxis—was of utmost importance, even when the theory behind it was uncertain. Violence against the whites, in fact, pitting race against race, should take every possible form— political, military, guerrilla war, cultural rejection, individual violence, and assassination. To kill a white man was deemed a liberating act—a revenge for centuries of deprivation, oppression, and rejection, a reaffirmation of black individual worth and identity, a badge of honor and equality. The whites were the enemies. They had lived by the sword and now it was time for them to die by the sword.

Fanon appealed to the poor and the peasants. Organizers and intellectuals, he felt, should reach out to the masses of the peasantry and adapt their slogans and strategy to their "inherent ideology"—their traditional ways and folklore. With the first acts of violence, revolutionary praxis would become a collective effort that would lead to national liberation. Freed from the West, politically and psychologically independent, the African nations would then put their revolution in some kind of order.

Franz Fanon's gospel for a revolution was not followed; in fact, it was sharply criticized by many Marxists, but it left a deep imprint and infused many anticolonial and national liberation movements "with passion." In Kenya, in Zaire, in Algeria, in the Portuguese colonies of Mozambique, and in Angola, violence often became an end in itself. It had a powerful organizing effect. Emphasis on praxis led to the exaltation of individual action—the liberation and the reaffirmation of one's ego. Fanon gave a powerful impulse to colonial uprisings and to the mobilization of the poor and the "wretched."

But whatever the justification of violence and murder, they do not represent standards on the basis of which a new society can be built. If Fanon was justifying acts of violence against the white colonizers because they had perpetrated them first against the native blacks, he was building a philosophy of revolt on what was just as uncertain, unjust, and morally as reprehensible as the rule of violence by the whites that he rejected. Fanon represents more a philosophy of revenge than a praxis of revolution. He sought in individual and mass violence the psychic liberation of those who commit it. He ignored, like so many other revolutionaries, Goethe's words: "The evil which you fear becomes a certainty by what you do!"

TERRORISM AND TERRORISTS

The ideologies of terrorism spring from the works and actions of many revolutionary thinkers and practitioners—Bakunin, Marx, Stirner, Netchaev, Kropotokin, Sorel, Marcuse, among many others. But it is also a direct—almost visceral—reaction to long years of pain, misery, and deprivation. Terrorism is a child with many fathers and mothers. The vision of a better and brighter world, the individualism of the anarchists, the discontent with the big impersonal, bureaucratized society, the appeal to the moral conscience of many for the blatant injustices that divide humanity into a small comfortable minority and into a vast majority that lives in wretched conditions—all fueled the recrudescence of terrorism in the sixties and seventies as it continues in many parts of the world today. Special circumstances trigger it: the prospects of nuclear war, the hatred of the Muslims for Israel and for "the West," the rage of the dispossessed farmers against the landlords, the arrogance of privilege among the wealthy and powerful.

The target of all terrorist organizations and individual terrorists is the established order—whatever it may be. The apocalyptic vision is that of a just social order ending the oppression of the many by the few. Terrorists attack indiscriminantly "innocent" persons who have no official position with the established order that the terrorists wish to bring down. They attack indiscriminantly children and shoppers in the marketplace and planes with tourists. They take hostages and destroy university buildings. All these acts are expected to undermine the confidence of the people in the ability of governments to maintain order and protect them. But they also attack directly officials and institutions that are linked with the establishment: police stations, courts, the military officers, diplomats, legislators, and cabinet officers. The ultimate goal is, of course, to involve the masses in a general movement of rejection of the established order.

Destruction in itself and by itself, like murder for Fanon, is purifying and constructive. The father of all terrorists, Bakunin, in his *Catechism of a Revolutionary* made the point:

> A revolutionary, continues to live in our world in order to level it down. . . . He must despise any doctrine, renounce science, culture and knowledge. . . . His only science is destruction. For this and only this purpose he should study practical sciences, physics, chemistry and even medicine in order to be able to destroy better . . . the established order.[8]

---

[8]M. A. Bakunin's *Catechism of a Revolutionary* has also been attributed to another great anarchist—Netchaev.

It is a frightening catechism! It is a message that accounts for the hundreds of terrorist bands that have blossomed forth—the Weathermen, the Minutemen, the Symbionese Liberation Army in the United States, as well as the Black Panthers and the Black Liberation Army—all minuscule organizations. These bands would attack police stations, banks, and military recruitment centers, while student groups such as the Students for Democratic Action Society (SDS) often focused their attention on university buildings, administrators, and professors. The "Red Army" became menacing in Japan, as did the Group of Direct Action in France. It is an international array—the Baader–Hoff band and other terrorist groups in West Germany, which claimed Frankfurt as its headquarters; the Red Brigades in Italy; and their counterparts in Greece and Spain. The Irish Revolutionary Army continues its armed combat against British soldiers and officials through bombings and assassinations. In the Middle East, Palestinians and other organizations, some inspired by Muslim fundamentalism, wage terrorist attacks against Israelis and Westerners, particularly Americans. There are "El Fatal" and the "Abou Nidhal" group—reputedly responsible for destroying a Pan American flight with over 250 innocent passengers over Lockerbie, Scotland, on December 21, 1988—and many, many others.

More recently, terrorism and some related terrorist acts appear to have lost their political meaning. Many are no longer linked with any political ideology—revolutionary or nationalist. They have become organized forms of violence for personal gain and profit. Hostages are taken for ransom; assassinations and bombings are conducted by cocaine producers in Colombia and elsewhere; violence and murder are carried out by members of drug cartels; even downright gangsterism is responsible for some of this random violence. But even in such cases, the acts of violence undermine societal order and its values and, above all, cast doubts upon the legitimacy and effectiveness of the political order. Only an ideology that creates order and harnesses the lives of men and women to a commonly shared purpose can ultimately combat terrorism in its various forms.

BIBLIOGRAPHY

Albright, David E. (ed.). *Communism in Africa*. Bloomington: Indiana University Press, 1980.

Aron, Raymond. *The Elusive Revolution*. London: Pall Mall, 1969.

Bakunin, M. A. *The Political Philosophy of Bakunin*. Edited and compiled by G. P. Maximoff. New York: Free Press, 1953.

Bouchier, David. *Ideal and Revolution: New Ideologies of Liberation in Britain and the United States*. London: Edward Arnold, 1978.

Brinton, Crane. *The Anatomy of Revolution*. Englewood Cliffs, N.J.: Prentice-Hall, 1939.

Brown, Bernard E. *Protest in Paris: Anatomy of a Revolt*. Morristown, N.J.: General Learning Press, 1974.

Carmichael, Stokely, and Charles V. Hamilton. *Black Power: The Politics of Liberation in America*. New York: Vintage Books, 1967.

Carr, E. H. *Michael Bakunin*. New York: Vintage, 1937.

Carter, A. *The Political Theory of Anarchism*. New York: Harper & Row, 1971.

Chaliand, Gerard. *Revolution in the Third World*. Harmondsworth, England: Penguin, 1978.

Cleaver, Eldridge. *Soul on Ice*. New York: Dell, 1965.

Clutterbuck, Richard. *Terrorism and Guerrilla Warfare: Forecasts and Remedies*. New York: Routledge, 1990.

Cohn–Bendit, Daniel and Gabriel. *Obsolete Communism: The Left-Wing Alternative*. London: André Deutsch, 1968.

Davies, James C. (ed.). *When Men Revolt and Why*. New York: Free Press, 1971.

Draper, Hal. *Berkeley: The New Student Revolt*. New York: Grove Press, 1965.

Ellis, John. *A Short History of Guerrilla Warfare*. London: Ian Allan, 1975.

Erikson, Erik H. (ed.). *The Challenge of Youth*. New York: Anchor-Doubleday, 1965.

Fanon, Frantz. *The Wretched of the Earth*. Translated by Constance Farrington. New York: Grove Press, 1963.

————. *Black Skin, White Masks*. New York: Grove, 1967.

Gerassi, John (ed.). *Venceremos! The Speeches and Writings of Ernesto Ché Guevara*. New York: Simon and Schuster, 1968.

Giap, Vo Nguyen. *The Military Art of People's War: Selected Writings*. New York: Monthly Review Press, 1970.

Goldstone, Jack A. *Revolutions: Theoretical, Comparative, and Historical*. San Diego, Calif.: Harcourt Brace Jovanovich, 1990.

Goldthorpe, J. E. *The Sociology of the Third World: Disparity and Involvement*. Cambridge, England: Cambridge University Press, 1975.

Greene, Thomas H. *Comparative Revolutionary Movements*, 2nd ed. Englewood Cliffs, N.J.: Prentice-Hall, 1984.

Guevara, Ché. *Guerrilla Warfare*. New York: MR Press, 1961.

Gurr, Ted Robert. *Why Men Rebel*. Princeton, N.J.: Princeton University Press, 1970.

Gusfield, Joseph R. *Protest, Reform and Revolt: A Reader in Social Movements*. New York: Wiley, 1970.

Hayden, C. *Rebellion and Repression*. New York: World Publishers, 1969.

Hoffman, Abbie. *Revolution for the Hell of It*. New York: Dial Press, 1968.

Jacobs, Paul, and Saul Landau. *The New Radicals*. New York: Vintage, 1966.

Kanter, Rosabeth Moss. *Commitment and Community: Communes and Utopias in Sociological Perspective*. Cambridge, Mass.: Harvard University Press, 1972.

Kaplan, Lawrence. *Revolutions: A Comparative Study from Cromwell to Castro*. New York: Vintage, 1973.

Kerouac, Jack. *On the Road*. New York: New American Library, 1957.

Lamb, Robert, et al. *Political Alienation*. New York: St. Martin's Press, 1975.

Laqueur, Walter. *A Guerrilla Reader: A Historical Anthology*. New York: Meridian, 1977.

Lipset, Seymour Martin, and Philip G. Altbach, (eds.). *Students in Revolt*. Boston: Houghton Mifflin, 1969.

Long, Priscilla (ed.). *The New Left: A Collection of Essays*. Boston: Porter Sargent, 1970.

Mao Tse-tung. *On Guerrilla Warfare*. New York: Praeger, 1961.

Marcuse, Herbert. *One-Dimensional Man*. Boston: Beacon Press, 1968.

Miles, Michael W. *The Radical Probe: The Logic of Student Rebellion*. New York: Atheneum, 1973.

Nasser, Gamal Abdel. *The Philosophy of the Revolution*. Buffalo, N.Y.: Smith, Keynes & Marshall, 1959.

Olman, B. *Alienation*. New York: Cambridge University Press, 1977.

Reich, Charles. *The Greening of America*. New York: Bantam, 1971.

Roszak, Theodore, *The Making of a Counter-Culture*. New York: Doubleday, 1969.

Rudi, George. *Ideology and Popular Protest*. New York: Pantheon Books, 1980.

Sale, Kirkpatrick, *SDS*. New York: Vintage, 1973.

Sargent, Lyman T. *The Ideology of the New Left*. Homewood, Ill.: Dorsey Press, 1972.

Teodori, Massimo (ed.). *The New Left: A Documentary History*. New York: Bobbs-Merrill, 1969.

Touraine, Alain. *The May Movement*. New York: Random House, 1971.

Trotsky, Leon. *Terrorism and Communism: A Reply to Karl Kautsky*. Ann Arbor: University of Michigan Press, 1965.

Ulam, Adam. *The Unfinished Revolution*, rev. ed. Boulder, Colo.: Westview Press, 1979.

Vickers, George R. *The Formation of the New Left: The Early Years*. Lexington, Mass.: Lexington Books, 1975.

von der Mehden, Fred R. *Comparative Political Violence*. Englewood Cliffs, N.J.: Prentice-Hall, 1973.

Wardlaw, Grant. *Political Terrorism*. New York: Cambridge University Press, 1989.

Wolf, Eric. *Peasant Wars in the Twentieth Century*. New York: Harper & Row, 1965.

Wood, James L. *The New Left Ideology: Its Dimensions and Development*. Beverly Hills, Calif.: Sage, 1975.

Yablonsky, Lewis. *The Hippie Trip*. New York: Pegasus, 1968.

Chapter
14

Ideologies and the Future
Some Concluding Remarks

Yet, Freedom! yet thy banner, torn, but flying
Streams like the thunderstorm against the wind.

Lord Byron,

Childes Harold xcviii

We have surveyed a host of ideologies that have been particularly vibrant
in the twentieth century—even though many of them trace their origin long
before this century. We find liberal democracy, gaining; right-wing authoritarianism, and in particular nazism, still smouldering; communism, everywhere in
retreat; nationalism, experiencing a resurgence; the renewed emergence of religion, especially in liberation theology, Muslim fundamentalism, and the Evangelicals; democratic socialism, having abandoned its commitment to state
ownership and moving increasingly in the direction of welfare and even liberal
economic policies; finally, feminism and environmentalism, both aiming to
transform social relations—the first, by eliminating "gender" distinctions that
subordinated women and tied them to maternity and the family; the second, by
providing a new ethic of social and economic life that preserves our planet and
its resources for posterity. We touched upon anarchism, the New Left, so active
in the sixties and early seventies with a message that continues to echo today;
discussed the prospects of internationalism; and surveyed some ideologies of
violence and revolution.

As we come to the end of the twentieth century, we continue to be bedev-
illed and blessed with many faiths and creeds, with many "ideas" about ourselves and our relationships with each other. It has been a very exciting century.
Some argue, indeed, that with the demise of communism as an ideology and a
system of governance, we may have reached a point of fulfillment that leaves
little room for new ideologies to emerge. Liberal democratic ideologies are
comprehensive and represent universal values. Our cup is full.

THE REAFFIRMATION OF UNIVERSAL VALUES

Beginning with the French Revolution of 1789, intellectuals and philosophers have sought a culminating point in history and ideology—a terminal point for the realization of basic human values and rights. History, according to many, and the ideas developed in the interstices of history, has a purpose—*telos*—to create a universal order of freedom, equality, peace, and brotherhood. The French Revolution and later the American Revolution had ushered these basic human values, asserting individual rights and freedoms—political, moral, religious, and economic. According to this view, despite many distortions, deviations, and "detours," the message of democratic liberalism remains universal and comprehensive. It provides the common core of values in terms of which all of us in the world confront and solve our problems. It represents the final stage in the evolution of ideas, in that it asserts the universality of rights—of human rights. These ideas were and are challenged, of course, but only to gain strength. The ideologues and ideologies that challenged them gradually exhausted themselves, according to Daniel Bell. "For the radical Intelligentsia," he wrote in the early fifties, "the old ideologies have lost their truth and their power to persuade." Referring to conservatives and welfare liberals, he pointed out that their arguments had become obsolete. "Few classic economists insist that the state should not play a role in the economy and few conservatives . . . believe that the welfare state is the 'road to serfdom.' " The acceptance of the welfare state, decentralized political power, a mixed economy, and political pluralism—all indicate a broad consensus. "The ideological age has ended," he declared.[1]

Some forty years later, Francis Fukuyama, in a widely discussed essay,[2] declared triumphantly the end of history—the end of ideology—in what appears to be the definitive acceptance of the universalistic values proclaimed by the French and American revolutions. He asserted, boldly, that the liberal democratic revolutions in France and America represented, in fact, the last word in the formulation of human aspirations and rights. He pointed out that, whatever the deviations, first the collapse of nazism and then of communism, democratic and liberal values triumphantly reassert themselves. They are being shared by an ever-growing number of people in our world. No other ideologies are in sight to challenge them. If Marxism was one, it was only a bumpy detour. We are now back on the highway, whose destination is clear—the full realization of the values of liberal democracy and of a moral order, founded on the acceptance of liberty and equality for all, to work, to worship, to live in decent conditions, to have enough leisure to engage in various forms of self-expression, and to be protected from violence and not to allow it to encroach upon others. In short, the end of ideology (or history) has come about. The three cores of liberalism we discussed in Chapter 2—moral, political, and economic—are coming together.

---

[1]Daniel Bell, *The End of Ideology*, pp. 402–403.

[2]Francis Fukuyama, "The End of History," *The National Interest*, Nos. 16 and 18, Winter 1989/1990.

Violetta Barrios de Chamorro

On April 25, 1990, Violetta Barrios de Chamorro was elected President of Nicaragua after more than ten years of one-party, Communist-style rule by the Sandinistas. As in Chile, Brazil, the Philippines, Argentina, and elsewhere, many saw in her victory in a free election the strengthening of democracy in Latin America and beyond.

In this survey of ideologies, I have shied away from the notion that there is an "inevitability" in history. I have rather tended to subscribe to the notion that we play an important role in making our history and that we fashion ideologies in order to do so. We constantly look for new ideas to respond to new challenges. We are a little bit like Sisyphus, cursed by the ancient gods to carry a heavy rock to the top of a mountain, only to fall as he reaches it, then to start again and again and again. The moment we have reached the end of history, as some claim, we may have to begin again. The moment people deliver an obituary to ideology, new ideologies are born.

Many ideological movements have striving to gain hold, and we have discussed them without passing judgment or predicting the course they will take. We must be always prepared for the unanticipated. All we can do is to try to discern the predicaments that may undermine some ideologies, strengthen others, and give rise to new ones.

The Challenge to Democracy

Even if one were to accept the view that the universal values embedded in liberal democracy are in the process of being realized, a number of questions, many raised in the individual chapters of this book, will have to be answered. Foremost is the manner in which the universal values of liberal democracy will be implemented. They require a peaceful universe and the right policies to implement them. Political order, national and international; the implementation of human rights, and especially economic rights; and equality and the legitimization of democratic values are needed—for otherwise the Great Myth of Democracy may appear to be a Big Lie.

Table 14.1 TOWARDS DEMOCRACY?

Greece (1973)	Philippines (1986)
Portugal (1976)	Pakistan (1988)?
Spain (1977)	South Korea (1988)
Peru (1980)	Chile (1989)
Thailand (1980)	Paraguay (1989)
Bolivia (1982)	Poland (1989)
Honduras (1982)	Bulgaria (1990)?
Argentina (1983)	Czechoslovakia (1990)
Senegal (1983)?	East Germany (1990; now part of a
Turkey (1983)	united Germany)
Ecuador (1984)	Hungary (1990)
Nicaragua (1984 and election of 1990)	Mongolia (1990)?
Uruguay (1984)	Namibia (1990)
Brazil (1985)	Romania (1990)?

Note: This listing is only meant to be illustrative and suggestive of the trend that seems to have gathered momentum. The criteria used are: the replacement of militiary by civilian government; the end of a one-party rule; the holding of at least one free and open election. Where the trend remains uncertain, I have put a question mark. The student should not hurry to draw any conclusions about the spread of democracy. China, Indonesia, and the Soviet Union, which account for more than 30 percent of the world's population, are not democracies. Virtually the whole of Africa, the Middle East, and most of Southeast Asia are still ruled by authoritarian regimes. And free elections and the downfall of military rule in no way presage the future course in many of the countries we list. It takes time for democracy to gain legitimacy.

There are many critical problems associated with democracy, especially when linked with capitalism, to which there are no easy answers. To begin with, democracy lacks a transcendental ideology. There are no absolutes associated with it, except the moral autonomy of the individual. Democracy consists of a set of procedures to preserve and to promote this profoundly individualist ethic. But otherwise as an ideology—to use Marx's phrase—democracy does not "grip the masses." It offers no easy solution to many of our predicaments and it promises no blue horizons except the ones that we open up through our own exertions. It is not geared to a scheme of history which tells us that a democratic development is inevitable and just. On the contrary, it tells us that we make our history and that in the process we may make mistakes. It sets no unifying themes. It tells us that we are all different from each other and that we rightfully should follow our own drummer; we are not meant to "march in step." In short, there is no vision to guide us. There are no "true believers" among real democrats—only skeptics! Democracy provides the means, the instruments, and the processes of political life; it does not, like so many ideologies, tell us what life is all about. We are free to find out—or to give up and have somebody tell us!

Democratic representative institutions, either in parliamentary or presidential systems, face a double crisis in performance and legitimacy. Gone are the days when the radical democrats believed that universal manhood suffrage and representative government would solve all social and economic evils. Only a small number now believe that representative assemblies really represent the people. Few think that, out of the welter of interests represented in the representative assemblies, a common purpose and common policies for society as a whole can evolve.

If the representative assemblies are no longer viewed as being truly representative, new institutions must be sought to safeguard the interests of the people at large. One such proposal is direct participation. This is the demand for a direct say in decision making by all those who are affected. The corollary is decentralization of the decision-making mechanism; the virtual dismantling of the bureaucratic apparatus of the states into small and manageable units such as the city, the locality, the particular administrative services, the neighborhood. Thus the citizen can participate, and the recipients or beneficiaries of services may have a direct say and direct supervision of them. Questions about urban renewal or new housing construction should be decided by those living in the particular areas concerned, and welfare service should be decentralized in a manner to allow for the recipients' direct control and management. The accent is put on "community control," on "neighborhood city halls," and "direct democracy" in the economy. Small towns, localities, and neighborhoods are beginning to claim precedence over national representative organs.

Institutional weakness, real or imaginary, seems to parallel a profound moral crisis—a crisis of the authority in many democratic states. Many of the traditional authority structures have weakened—for instance, the church, the family, the social elites, and more recently the trade unions. Similarly, highly valued organizations like the army or the university have declined in importance. None of them play the role they played in the past, serving to structure demands, to slow down the urge for immediate fulfillment, and to inculcate respect for existing institutions. These agencies no longer play the role of intermediary between the state and the public at large to sustain its authority and to secure agreement on its decisions. On the contrary, particularisms have begun to assert their primacy—special interests, particular ethnic groups, special localities, different religious bodies. They all assert their virtual autonomy. This further undermines consensus for a democratic policy and makes compliance with the decisions of the democratic state uncertain.

Finally, there is a crisis of legitimacy in all modern democracies. These are the words of a noted sociologist:

> Democracy, as the sorry history of Europe has shown, is a fragile system . . . [it may collapse] when political parties or social movements can successfully establish "private armies" whose resort to violence—street fighting, bombings, the breakup of their opponent's meetings or simply intimidation—cannot be controlled by the elected authorities . . .[3]

Daniel Bell is, of course, referring here to the Nazi and Fascist movements and their counterparts in Central Europe, which we discussed in Chapter 8.

---

[3]Daniel Bell, (ed.), *The Radical Right*, p. 503.

But a pressing danger is that democratic societies faced again with dissent and acts of violence may seek counterrevolutionary policies that will force them to jettison democratic principles and practices. Repressive measures, serious qualifications of political and individual freedoms, special forms of control and police surveillance may be introduced, indeed *have* been introduced, in the name of counterterrorism. Democracy remains fragile indeed—at the very moment when many consider its resurgence to signify the vindication and fulfillment of universal and ultimate human values.

NEW IDEOLOGIES?

There are many difficulties and challenges ahead that are very likely to spawn new ideologies and movements and provide additional challenges to democracy.

1. Under the double pressure of international forces from above and ethnonationalisms from below, the political order as we have known it in the last 300 years—embodied in a national sovereign state—is weakening. Internationalist ideologies may develop to fill the vacuum. But, unavoidably, there will be a period of stress and strain and violence everywhere before they do so.

2. Private violence and civil wars are rampant everywhere.

3. The hugh global underclass remains apathetic, mired in its misery and ignorance. If history has "come to an end" for the wealthy countries of the world in the form of liberal democracy, it has yet to begin for them! The "underclass" waits for its intellectual prophet to shape an ideology that will help the "wretched of the earth" to assert their human heritage. Will it be a Fanon preaching sheer violence? Will it be a modified version of Leninism in which a ruling political party sheds the economics of Marxism but maintains authoritarian political controls? Will uprisings lead to the formation of small communitarian ethnic, religious, and linguistic groups that seek their identity, proclaiming their desire to live together independently of others, espousing, in effect, some of the prescriptions of utopian socialism and the New Left?

4. Faced with the abstractness and impersonality of the principles and values of liberal democratic universalism, will there be a reversion to the emotional warmth that religious sects provide? Some such movements are already gaining, as we saw in discussing religious fundamentalism, and challenge the norms of democracy.

5. As the population grows and the environment becomes degraded to the point where we may not be able to support the projected 10 billion inhabitants on our globe by the end of 2100, what will the impact be? How will it affect existing ideologies or lead to the formulation of new ones? Environmentalism is emerging, but, as we noted, it has not yet managed to formulate a comprehensive theory and a comprehensive program of action. What is most relevant politically is whether population growth and environmental degradation will lead to regimentation and the imposition of tight controls that may seriously affect individual rights.

6. Regarding poverty, one should keep in mind the so-called economic refugees. Millions from the Third World have gained or are seeking asylum in relatively wealthy states. They seek food and shelter. What will the impact of this momentous immigration be if it continues? Reactions in Western Europe and elsewhere have spawned racist and nationalist political movements. Xenophobia, racism, and nationalism have been the mainsprings of authoritarian movements to subvert the democratic liberal order, as they did after the end of World War I. Communist parties may join extreme nationalist movements to reassert, even under a different label, their claims of political monopoly and control and to defy constitutional and democratic governments.

7. There is, finally, the haunting question: Will the resurgence of capitalism—of free enterprise or free-market economy and free trade, which we discussed in Chapter 3—succeed in producing what Communist regimes had promised to deliver—namely, a modicum of abundance and well-being. Despite remarkable economic growth since World War II came to an end in 1945, capitalism has failed to reduce inequalities, except in some of the most prosperous and welfarist states—for instance, in the Scandinavian countries. It has failed dismally to reduce global poverty. The Great Depression in the early 1930s seemed to vindicate Marx and triggered, as we noted in Chapter 8, extremist right-wing movements. Another depression may trigger any of the protest movements we have surveyed—nationalism, ethnonationalism, religious fundamentalism, anarchism, environmentalism, feminism, or an extremist revolutionary movement. Much of the universalism of democratic liberalism depends on its ability to sustain its values through an economic system that provides and guarantees minimal conditions of well-being. A serious breakdown in the economy, as it was with the Great Depression of 1929 will open a Pandora's box from which militant ideologies will emerge.

There is, of course, one remaining object in Pandora's box: the optimistic view—Hope! Democratic liberalism with a flourishing economy will extend its universal values and the frontiers of equality and freedom to all—to a world in which free and equal peoples will resolve differences and find solutions to problems on the basis of free and open deliberation, tolerance, and mutual respect. If it is so, then again we should not conclude that ideology has died and history is dead. On the contrary, we should recall what Engels had prophesized to come after the advent of communism. With liberal democracy—not communism—history will truly begin! For the first time, men and women will be free to decide about their common future—and make their own history. But to do so, ideologies that trace new pursuits and common endeavors with passion and commitment will be necessary.

The new millenium may be just as exciting, as new ideologies trace new endeavors—and cause new conflicts—for the generations to come.

Index